CHURCH AND STATE UNDER GOD

CHURCH AND STATE
UNDER GOD

EDITED BY ALBERT G. HUEGLI

CONCORDIA PUBLISHING HOUSE

Saint Louis, Missouri

Concordia Publishing House, St. Louis, Missouri
Concordia Publishing House Ltd., London, W. C. 1.
© 1964 Concordia Publishing House

Library of Congress Catalog Card No. 64-18881

MANUFACTURED IN THE UNITED STATES OF AMERICA

Acknowledgments

The editor and the authors are deeply indebted to the following publishers and copyright owners for permission to quote as indicated.

The Christian Century Foundation for an excerpt from the editorial "Navy to Educate Chaplains," in *The Christian Century,* March 10, 1943. Copyright 1943 Christian Century Foundation.

Harper & Row, Publishers, Incorporated, for quotations from *Creeds in Competition,* by Leo Pfeffer, and from *Church and State in the United States,* III, by Anson Phelps Stokes.

Charles Scribner's Sons for a quotation from *Christians and the State,* by John Bennett. Copyright 1958.

University of Florida Press for quotations from *The American Theory of Church and State,* by Loren P. Beth. Copyright 1958.

The Westminster Press for the quotation from *Calvin: Theological Treatises,* trans. J. K. S. Reid, Vol. XXII, LCC. Published 1954.

FOREWORD

HOW CAN CHURCH AND STATE exist together without getting in each other's way? That the question is not academic has been amply demonstrated by public furore over now familiar Supreme Court decisions attempting to define proper church-state relations under terms of the Constitution of the United States.

This study directs its attention mainly to church-state relations in the United States, where a certain freedom of religion has developed under a distinctively American policy, often misunderstood and ill defined, of "separation of church and state."

Enjoying the able editorial direction of Albert G. Huegli, educator and political scientist, Lutheran authorities in various disciplines have contributed their insights to the understanding of problems involved in modern church-state relations and have succeeded in pointing the way to some creative solutions of church-state problems as they exist, particularly on the American scene.

The process of putting together this symposium has produced what might be fairly described as "a Lutheran view" on at least some of the complications created by the interacting forces of church and state. It is not *the only* Lutheran view (a claim that would immediately establish it as un-Lutheran!). This work does present Lutheran judgments firmly grounded in history and theology, endeavoring to preserve intellectual integrity — a quality very often lacking in the superheated atmosphere of church-state discussions.

If Dr. Huegli and his associates have succeeded in fashioning a standard reference work which cannot be ignored in future assessments of church-state relations within the United States, this will probably be because the whole study proceeds from a definite theological position, explicitly stated (a rarity in this field), informed by a wide and thoroughgoing historical perspective (almost completely wanting among those interested merely in a propaganda of slogans).

This Lutheran view on proper relations between church and state will give as little comfort to the absolute separationist as it does to the advocate of the modern corporate state or to the complete secularist. In the Lutheran view, absolute separationism, like its 20th-century cousin, secular pragmatism, which is perfectly prepared to accept state supremacy and state control of almost all aspects of human life, can be justified neither theologically nor historically.

Comparing Calvinist, Puritan, Anglican, and Roman Catholic positions on church and state with the classic Lutheran tradition, this study considers subjects like religion in public schools, in military life, and in family life, along with Sunday legislation and governmental aid to denominationally controlled education. Not content with the repetition of half-understood slogans, its authors have produced a solid piece of scholarship based on a sound theology that is not static but creative, not pragmatic but thoroughly and sometimes disconcertingly practical when coming to grips with church-state questions presently in controversy.

If theology is divine truth put to work amid the practical realities of ordinary life, this study deserves to be called theological. If understanding his own history gives a man the right to speak to his fellow citizens about their national destiny, these observers of history — legal, political, and socio-cultural — deserve the right to speak.

Oswald C. J. Hoffmann

CONTENTS

Introduction   3
    ALBERT G. HUEGLI

PART I   THE CHURCH IN ITS RELATION TO THE STATE
  1. *Scriptural Concepts of the Church and the State*   13
    MARTIN H. SCHARLEMANN
  2. *Impact of the Reformation on Church-State Issues*   59
    LEWIS W. SPITZ, JR.
  3. *Church and State in Theological Expression Since the*
    Reformation   113
    H. RICHARD KLANN AND WILLIAM H. LEHMANN, JR.

PART II   THE STATE IN ITS RELATION TO THE CHURCH
  4. *European Experience in Church-State Relations*   151
    NEELAK S. TJERNAGEL
  5. *Development of the American Pattern in Church-State Relations* 195
    CARL S. MEYER
  6. *Religious Liberty in the Constitution*   257
    ROY C. FRANK

PART III   TENSIONS IN THE INTERACTION OF CHURCH AND STATE
  7. *Church, State, and Education*   299
    JOHN H. STRIETELMEIER, *editor*
    I. *Religion in the Public Schools*   300
      ARNOLD C. MUELLER
    II. *Church Schools and the Church-State Issue*   322
      ARTHUR L. MILLER
  8. *Custom and Law in Church-State Practices*   363
    I. *The Chaplaincy in American Public Life*   365
      EUGENE F. KLUG
    II. *Legal Contacts of Church and State*   393
      JAMES S. SAVAGE

PART IV   APPLICATION OF PRINCIPLES IN CHURCH-STATE RELATIONS
  9. *Alternative Approaches in Church-State Relations*   411
    MARTIN E. MARTY
  10. *New Dimensions in Church-State Relations*   433
    ALBERT G. HUEGLI

Notes   457
Index   509

CHURCH AND STATE UNDER GOD

INTRODUCTION

Albert G. Huegli

THE RELATIONSHIPS of church and state have become one of the most widely discussed subjects of our time. Once regarded as a field of discussion so remote from daily living that it could safely be left to lawyers and theologians, it is today acknowledged to be of concern to almost everyone.

Problems of church-state relations are as old as the most ancient records of human history and as modern as this morning's newspaper. Israel wrestled with them in the days of the judges and the kings. The new nations born since World War II are confronted with them. In France the church schools seek more substantial aid, and in England the established church resists the jurisdiction of Parliament over its affairs. The churches of Russia struggle to maintain their existence against the pressures of the state. In Italy, Spain, and some South American countries the governments are besieged with Protestant complaints about restrictions imposed on them; Roman Catholics, however, have official blessing. Christians are unhappy over the cold reception given them in the new state of Israel, and Jews are dissatisfied with the discrimination against them in Scandinavian countries.

In the United States the issues of church-state relations, almost dormant for a century and a half, have suddenly received new attention. More cases involving these questions were brought before the Supreme Court in 1961–63 than in all the years of the Court's previous existence. The most hotly debated issues center in the schools; but there are other conflicts which have important implications for the total pattern of adjustment between church and state in our country.

Some issues seem small. A girl in an Ohio high school is threatened with suspension because the religious scruples of her family prevent her from wearing shorts as required in her gym class. The religious convictions of several Pennsylvania farmers conflict with the idea of Social Security, and the government threatens to take their horses in lieu of taxes. The child of a couple who belongs to Jehovah's Witnesses and does not believe in blood tranfusion is ordered by the courts into the custody of the head of a hospital medical staff so that transfusion can be given.

Other issues affect many more people. Connecticut keeps an 1879 anti-birth-control law on its books as a result of the pressure of certain church groups, despite the protests of other citizens. State laws requiring business houses to close on Sunday are upheld by the Supreme Court, but Seventh-day Adventists, Jews, and others who keep Saturdays holy are placed at an economic disadvantage. The public observance of the birth of Christ is resented by non-Christians and atheists but deeply appreciated by vast numbers who call themselves Christians.

Whatever the nature of the issue and whether it affects many or a few people, the problem of determining the proper spheres for church and state is exceedingly complicated in modern society. It is even more difficult for our country because we have a deliberate policy which makes room for all religions and for non-religion at the same time. We have majority rule but minority rights. We have time-honored traditions which clash with contemporary developments having no precedent.

These problems of church-state relations could be solved by legislative action and judicial decisions. But such solutions might not be the most salutary either for the churches or for the national well-being. It is the nature of governmental decision to draw restrictions, and in these circumstances the churches, which have helped to build our country, might well have their contribution to its destiny sharply curtailed in the future. It is essential therefore that the churches, having much at stake, participate vigorously in searching for solutions.

The Lutheran Church — Missouri Synod through its Board of Parish Education has long kept a watchful eye on developments in church-state relations. The board, which has a natural interest in the subject because of the extensive Christian day school system maintained by the congregations of the Synod, assigned the specific responsibility for this area to a Committee on Church-State Relations.

In 1955 the committee agreed that a thorough study of the problems in church-state relations from a Lutheran point of view needed to be made. An application for funds to conduct such a study was submitted to the Synod's Committee for Research, which recommended that the Board of Directors of the church body appropriate the necessary money. The Board of Directors approved the project and its purpose, defined as "a reevaluation of the Lutheran position on church-state relations, based on Scripture and the Lutheran Confessions, with special reference to contemporary problem areas and emerging trends in political and social life." The editor of this volume was designated to lead the project, with the assistance of the Committee on Church-State Relations and a group of research associates.

On Nov. 16–17, 1956, a conference was called at River Forest, Illinois, by the editor, together with the Committee on Church-State Relations. A number of research associates were invited to attend and discuss tentative writing assignments. The details of a projected book were worked out. Because most of the contributors were busy men, the chapters were slow in development. Under the direction of the editor the chapters were reworked, some of them several times. Finally, in the closing weeks of 1962, all materials were available for editing. Meanwhile events of considerable significance in church-state relations had transpired, and further revisions of the manuscript were required.

The approach which this project has taken to church-state

relations has been essentially theological and historical. Christians begin their evaluation of social issues with a study of the Scriptures to see what God may have said about them. Lutheran Christians naturally turn to the writings of Martin Luther and the Lutheran Confessions for insights into these problems. But there are other Christian points of view which must be considered as well. The writers of Part I were assigned all of these fields of investigation. As the chapters in Part I were developed, it became clear that there could be no single or simple statement of relationships between church and state which all Christians or even all Lutherans would necessarily accept. The God-given principles for the social order are clear enough. It is in the practical application of them to varying types of societal structures that a wide range of opinions is discernible.

Christians in America are of course especially concerned about church-state relations in this country. Thus it was necessary for the investigation to review the development of the American solution to critical relationships in the area and to define its present status. The contributors to Part II were given this aspect of the study. European counterparts in church-state relations were evaluated for clues to a better understanding of the American experiment. From such experience the American fathers and founders had to draw for the new concepts which they devised. But the nature of the American pattern in adjusting church and state to each other needed to be analyzed in detail, both in its legal aspects and in its historical and cultural development. The writers of this section were therefore asked to contribute to an understanding of the manner in which American Christians try to solve their own problems with the political environment.

Probably no church-state pattern is more beset by friction and conflict than that of the United States. In a country where the state dominates the church completely, or where the church rules the state, there are problems, to be sure. But at least there is a ready-made, though perhaps not universally acceptable, solution to those problems. The same might be said of a situation where the separation of church and state is so complete that not even friendly cooperation is permitted. It may not be an ideal pattern, but it has the advantage of simplicity. The American people chose to try their own approach. As will be seen, it is one of separation with cordiality and mutual goodwill. Here the borderline becomes blurred more easily, and here the pattern of accommodation becomes more complicated. As the social setting within which our pattern of adjustment emerged became battered by the winds of change, the need for new definitions of the relationships of the two institutions was pointed up.

In Part III an effort was made to look at selected problem areas in the relations of church and state in our country. Education was chosen for special treatment for two reasons. It is probably the most sensitive focus of conflict, and Lutherans, with extensive school systems of their own, have the most at stake here among Protestant groups. Some attention is also given to the chaplaincy, on which not all Lutherans are agreed; to Sunday laws; and to several other areas of tension.

Although the writers in this symposium had hoped to arrive at a distinctively Lutheran position for many of the current church-state problems, this expectation was bound to meet with disappointment. In the Lutheran tradition the right of the individual Christian to exercise his own judgment in the light of Scripture is respected. Lutherans therefore hold a variety of opinions about specific instances where church and state have overlapping or conflicting interests. The clear-cut cases, such as governmental interference with religious worship, generally find a high degree of unanimity among all Christians. But in the modern day there are fewer and fewer black-versus-white situations to make the choice easy. Instead, as the church adapts itself to a changing environment and as the state broadens its concerns to include areas formerly left to the churches, the difficulty of arriving at a universally acceptable position on individual cases has increased.

The application of basic principles to contemporary social and political life can be a baffling experience. For example, it is important to the state that the teachers of its future citizens be properly qualified for their jobs. If a religious group maintains its own schools, must its teachers meet certification standards of the state, or is this solely the decision of the sponsoring body to make? A reasonable case could be made for either position. Yet going down one or the other road can lead to widely different concepts of the role of the church and of the state and of their relations to each other. Or, given the nature of our democratic processes, may the church bring pressure to bear on government for the outlawing of gambling, or is this exceeding the bounds of propriety? Again, if the church accepts government funds for sorely needed hospitals or for social services in crowded cities, is there any danger that the church will lose some of its prophetic function in society? If the majority favors prayers on public occasions, must the practice be stopped because the minority objects? The answers to such questions are not easy, nor do they command undivided support when they are given.

The writers of Part IV of this book therefore do not pretend to provide a convenient catalog of solutions to problems in church-state relations. Rather the attempt is made to point out alternative approaches which might be considered and then to outline some of the developments which are bound to give new shape and meaning to these old and familiar issues. Moving within this framework and aware of the Lutheran emphasis on the judgment of the enlightened individual conscience, reasonably well-informed people should find it possible to reach decisions on church-state problems that confront them day by day. In other words the project goes back to fundamentals, shows their relationships to contemporary conditions, and encourages sound action at the direction of the Christian's own insights.

Much credit for valuable services toward the culmination of this long-protracted project must go to many people. The unflagging interest of men like Arthur L. Miller and A. C. Mueller in the subject of church-state relations antedates this venture by several decades and was largely responsible for its finally materializing. John Strietelmeier and William Lehmann have read the manuscript in various stages of its preparation and have given invaluable advice. Elmer Foelber went over each chapter with authoritative skill. The routine chores connected with the preparation of the manuscript were ably and patiently performed in some aspects of the project by Mrs. Mabel Eccles and Miss Ruth Glick, and for all of its development from birth pangs to maturity by Mrs. A. G. Huegli.

The author or authors of each chapter must be responsible for their own ideas and do not presume to speak for the church body that sponsored the project, nor necessarily for each other. The editor, however, is to be held accountable for the general structure, style, and tone of the entire volume.

The pledge of allegiance to the American flag speaks of "one nation under God." This is a reminder of the overarching providence of God, who uses the two institutions, the church and the state, as His Right and Left Hands. "Church and state under God" — it is toward the deepening of the understanding of this relationship that our book is intended.

PART I

*The Church
in Its Relation to the State*

MARTIN H. SCHARLEMANN

LEWIS W. SPITZ, JR.

H. RICHARD KLANN AND
WILLIAM H. LEHMANN, JR.

WE BEGIN WITH THE CHURCH. What does it have to say about relations with the state? Part I seeks to answer this question. For Christians the place to start is the Bible. Chapter 1 explores Biblical attitudes and concepts on the institutions of the church and of government. For modern Christians especially the Reformation had a significant impact on thought and practice in church-state relations extending down to our own time. This is the burden of chapter 2. Theological statements since the Reformation will help illuminate existing trends and patterns. The section therefore closes with chapter 3 describing Lutheran, Catholic, and Reformed expressions on the relations of church and state.

The author of the first chapter, on Scriptural concepts, is *Martin H. Scharlemann*, Ph. D., professor of New Testament exegesis, Concordia Seminary, St. Louis. His approach differs from the customary treatment of the subject. He does not simply bring together and interpret pertinent Scripture passages. Rather he evaluates the whole divine plan of human existence as revealed in the Word of God and describes the cosmic background which provides the setting for the functions of the church and of government. Existing side by side, these two institutions are God's instruments for different purposes. Government is to keep order, using the sword. The church is to bring men back to God, using the Gospel. Both are God's agencies. Each calls for a response. Tension arises because the Christian is a member of two kingdoms. Conflict comes when government overreaches itself or when the church forgets its proper sphere. The two have mutual responsibilities over against each other, and the Christian citizen has obligations toward them both.

Although the nation-state as we know it today did not exist in Biblical times, the basic concepts of relationships between God and Caesar are as applicable now as they were when the writers of Scripture first described them.

Chapter 1

SCRIPTURAL CONCEPTS OF THE CHURCH AND THE STATE

Martin H. Scharlemann

WE INHERIT A WORLD that is politically divided into over a hundred sovereign nations. Modern systems of communication and transportation have reduced dimensions of space and time to such a degree that we often feel we are living in a large city run by a hundred mayors, each with his own interests and instruments of power. Moreover, as a consequence of the incredible technological progress of the 20th century, our life has become infinitely complex. Interdependence has become an inescapable necessity not only for the various segments of society but even for modern nations. Again, the 20th century has produced the instruments of mass communication and psychological manipulation that make totalitarianism possible and practicable for the first time in history.

In a sense, therefore, the problem of church and state in our society confronts us with situations that were unknown to the authors of Holy Scripture. They lived in simpler days and under political conditions quite different from our own.

It would be a mistake in method to expect to find everywhere a one-to-one correspondence between a Biblical passage and our present situation. Here, as in many other instances, we must reckon with a wide sociological distance between ourselves and the sacred writers. Otherwise we shall prove unequal to our task of discovering the Biblical perspective on the matter of church-state relations in terms that are relevant for our day. When, for example, St. Paul wrote to the Philippians (3:20) that their "citizenship" was in heaven, he used a word that can be understood only in terms of Rome's relationship to individual cities that had become her colonies and enjoyed all the privileges and rights of those of her citizens that lived in Rome itself.

Yet, despite the fact that there is a great distance between us and the way of life prevailing in the centuries during which the documents of the Scriptures were written, the essence of the question as to how church and state must live and work together is very clearly set forth in the Word of God. In point of fact the whole matter of church-and-state relations lies near the center of our theology. Our very mention of Pontius Pilate in the Apostles' Creed is a continuing reminder of this fact. For, if we were to translate the superscription on the cross into legal parlance, it would say that our Lord was hanged as a rebel against Rome. At the moment when Jesus was sentenced to be crucified, the relationship between Christ and Caesar was moved to the very heart of the Christian faith. Moreover, the problem of church and state, with its many ramifications, is posed for the church of all times by the circumstance that we stand in the succession of those disciples to whom Jesus once said: "You will be dragged before governors and kings for My sake, to bear testimony before them and the Gentiles." (Matt. 10:18)[1]

The present study is not intended to be an exhaustive treatment of either the church or the state. It is limited to an inquiry into the question of the relationship prevailing between these two entities as they exist in our society. In our discussion, therefore, we shall avoid the statistical method of gathering together at one place every passage of Scripture that says anything about either the state or the church and then discussing each one on the basis of what the words say. For this would represent a tour de force, which would leave us entirely unaware of the most significant dimensions of our basic concern. Rather our method will consist in subjecting our entire discussion to the total thrust of the Scriptures. As we proceed, the most significant passages and portions of the Bible will of course need to come under scrutiny. If most of these sections are from the New Testament, this is not accidental. It is there that we confront the demands of the new aeon which, with the coming of Jesus Christ, has also affected church-state relations.

In the church of this new era the powers of God's kingdom of grace are at work. Its members are not of this world, yet they live in it. Their real citizenship is in heaven, yet they belong to a body politic here on earth. In the words of the second-century Epistle to Diognetus: "Christians are not distinguished from the rest of mankind by locality or speech or custom. They dwell in their own countries, but only as sojourners; they take their share in everything as citizens, and they endure all hardships as strangers. Every foreign country is a fatherland to them and every fatherland is foreign. . . . Their existence is on earth, but their citizenship is in heaven." [2]

In short, Christians are members of the church, and yet they live under the authority of some form of government. What does this mean in terms of understanding the mutual responsibilities of church and state in modern society? That is the basic question to which we must address ourselves after we have considered the total dimensions of the problem.

THE COSMIC BACKGROUND

The subject of church-state relations cannot be understood in its many ramifications without an appreciation of the metaphysical background of our life here on earth. No facet of our existence can be understood fully without a discussion of that transcendental rift which runs through the whole universe and right through the heart of each one of us. Our Scriptures describe in most vivid terms the source and the nature of this cosmic split. The universe is, in the Biblical occount, the scene of a widespread revolt against God Himself. There exist two distinct realms, known as the heavenly and the terrestrial spheres, and a rift runs through both, cleaving each asunder.

God Himself is the Creator. He made the world in order

that everything in it might glorify Him and serve Him. In this purpose, however, He is opposed by him who in the words of Milton took as his slogan:

> Evil, be thou my Good: by thee at least
> Divided empire with Heaven's King I hold.[3]

The war that ensued is described in part in Rev. 12:7-9:

> Now war arose in heaven, Michael and his angels fighting against the dragon; and the dragon and his angels fought, but they were defeated and there was no longer any place for them in heaven. And the great dragon was thrown down, that ancient serpent, who is called the Devil and Satan, the deceiver of the whole world — he was thrown down to the earth, and his angels were thrown down with him.

Man joined in this revolt and among God's visible creatures became the front and center of a rebellion against the sovereign will of the Creator. This is man's tragedy: he was made to be the very crown of creation, but, tempted by the prospect of becoming like God, he chose to enter the ranks of those who had determined to usurp God's rule; and now apart from Christ "the whole world is in the power of the evil one" (1 John 5:19). In this way the heavenly rift has become of decisive importance, for it has projected itself into the sphere of human life in all its relationships, including that of church and state.

No one has given us a more graphic description of our rent universe than St. Paul in his Epistle to the Ephesians. He gathers up the main body of the opposition against God in the expression "spiritual hosts of wickedness in the heavenly places" (6:12). Behind man's unwillingness to serve his Maker are demonic beings of such great strength that in this same verse they are called "world rulers of this darkness," whose activities are carried on in heavenly places. These "heavenlies," as they are called, constitute that immaterial region which lies behind the world of the senses.

> In it great forces are at work: forces which are conceived of as having an order and constitution of their own; as having in part transgressed against that order, and so having become

disordered; forces which in part are opposed to us and wrestle against us; forces again which take an intelligent interest in the purpose of God with this world.[4]

These principalities and powers are led by one whom the apostle calls the "prince of the power of the air" (2:2). He is the master strategist of this gigantic revolt. He has in fact become the "god of this world" (2 Cor. 4:4), who "through pride and worse ambition" once sought to equal the Most High. Here is his own account as given by Milton:

> Lifted up so high,
> I 'dained subjection, and thought one step higher
> Would set me highest, and in a moment quit
> The debt immense of endless gratitude,
> So burthensome, still paying, still to owe.[5]

Satan's weapons are deceit and destruction. God creates and preserves; His adversary is determined to pervert and to uproot. His cleverest wile is to convince men that he does not exist. God says: "I AM WHO I AM" (Ex. 3:14). The Devil, however, envious of God and bent on imitating Him wherever necessary and desirable, says, "My name is Nobody; there is Nobody: whom should you be afraid of? Are you going to shudder before the non-existent?"[6] He does things in reverse; for he looks at everything from below. With this device he has been able to transvalue all of life as God intended it to be and to bring upon all creation that groaning and travailing to which the apostle refers in Rom. 8:22.

To extricate man from his plight God Himself chose to become our Redeemer in Christ. He entered our historical context to show us a new way of obedience. Since the day that Jesus came proclaiming, "The time is fulfilled; the kingdom of God is at hand" (Mark 1:14), we have become part of that final conflict of kingdoms whose ultimate outcome has been assured by Christ's rising from the dead. This is a contest so fierce that St. Paul feels constrained to warn his readers that nothing less than the whole armor of God is adequate to its demands. (Eph. 6:11)

What this cosmic contest means in terms of church-state relations may be gathered in part from the record of our Lord's temptations. At one point Satan proposed that Jesus seize the instruments of political power in order to impose God's will on man by decree. Luke's account is most explicit on this point: "And the devil took Him up and showed Him all the kingdoms of the world in a moment of time and said to Him, 'To You I will give all this authority and their glory; for it has been delivered to me, and I give it to whom I will'" (4:5, 6). In essence this temptation consisted in the prospect of using the power of the state to establish and maintain the church. This promised to be an easier method of gathering people than by death on a cross. However, Jesus rejected Satan's suggestion on the grounds that His people were to serve Him in glad obedience rather than by political compulsion. If our Lord had yielded to this temptation, the church would have been reduced to the method of the state and, like it, would have become just one more instrument of the old aeon. In fact, church and state would have been combined to create the conditions of absolute totalitarian control and direction. Men would have been reduced to being digits in one vast political machine, "the quotient of one billion divided by one billion," to borrow a phrase from Arthur Koestler's *Darkness at Noon.*

Jesus, however, had come to bring an age of life. Small wonder that the devil resisted the proclamation of the new day with every weapon in his arsenal. In the person of Jesus the kingdom of heaven had irrupted among men. In this way God opened wide the vistas of His own rule. But Satan set out to challenge the words and works of Jesus at every turn, as witness the opening chapter of St. Mark, where literally "all hell breaks loose" to keep the powers of the new age out of man's reach. In time Jesus Himself was haled before the authorities of this age and nailed to a tree. A battle seemed to have been lost; yet this very defeat, reversed by the resurrection, became the means of winning the war. D day became the assurance of an eventual V day.

This outcome Satan could not and did not anticipate, for it was God's secret. "None of the rulers of this age understood this; for if they had, they would not have crucified the Lord of glory"

(1 Cor. 2:8). With these words the great apostle succinctly described the front on which the first great battle raged in all its fury. On the one side was the Lord of glory; arrayed against Him were the powers of the old aeon as embodied in the political personages of His day.

The passage just quoted from 1 Corinthians may serve as a wholesome reminder of the cosmic dimensions of Calvary. On the one hand "the rulers of this world" can mean "earthly political powers." To the profane author and reader of the apostolic age the words would mean no more than that. However, to Paul, coming from a Jewish background, this phrase included the thought of those "demonic, invisible powers which stand behind all earthly happenings and use human beings as their effective agents." [7] He applies to political rulers the term used in John 16:11 of the devil, who is there called "the ruler [KJV: prince] of this world."

The transcendental dimension of the apostle's statement will become more evident later, when we take up Rom. 13:1-7. [8] Paul had in mind the same invisible powers he later spoke of in Ephesians. At the same time, of course, he was thinking of the earthly rulers, the political administrators of Palestine. This follows clearly from a consideration of the apostle's sermon at Antioch in Pisidia: "For those who live in Jerusalem and their rulers, because they did not recognize Him nor understand the utterances of the prophets which are read every Sabbath, fulfilled these by condemning Him" (Acts 13:27). This thought Peter had already expressed when shortly after Pentecost he told a crowd in the temple court: "I know that you acted in ignorance, as did also your rulers." (Acts 3:17)

We must not, however, fail to see the language of Paul in the light of the cosmic conflict between the powers of the new aeon and those of the old. For since the crucifixion and the resurrection of our Lord the existence and exercise of political authority lie in the twilight zone between the old and the new. In fact the state itself is exposed in a very special way to the perverting intent of Satan; for, wielding its power, the state is often tempted to manifest the same kind of pride for which the devil with his legions was expelled from God's presence. To a very high degree political power is tempted to become demonic. Speaking in modern terms, the state is constantly exposed to an inherent inclination toward becoming totalitarian, as the late Russian philosopher-theologian Nikolai Berdyaev observed when he wrote:

> Caesar always and irresistibly tends toward demanding for himself not only that which is Caesar's but that which is God's — Caesar wishes to subject to himself the whole of man. This is the main tragedy of history, the tragedy of freedom and necessity, of man's fate and historic destiny.[9]

Despite the evils that are often let loose among men in this way, the demonic exercise of power by the state can and frequently does serve to further God's cause, even as Jesus' death became the means of a great redemptive victory. For Satan is a creature and cannot pass beyond the limits which God Himself has set for him. The devil knows this and in his fury constantly overreaches himself, only to be struck down as he outruns the Creator's permissive will. Each such experience makes him more "devilish" than before. For "he knows that his time is short" (Rev. 12:12). In the meantime he is determined to destroy men and to turn the ordinance of government into the monstrous perversion of Daniel's vision: "terrible and dreadful and exceedingly strong; and it had great iron teeth; it devoured and broke in pieces and stamped the residue with its feet" (Dan. 7:7). Yet the rule, even of this beast, lasts but "for a time, two times, and half a time" (7:25), that is, for a definite but limited period. After that the kingdom and the dominion shall be given to the saints of the Most High. For evil, too, has been overcome by Him who came to heal the great rift running from heavenly places through all the affairs of men.

CHURCH AND STATE IN COEXISTENCE

In any understanding of the proper relationship between church and state we must begin with the empirical situation

The Church

The church of today is the new Israel. That is how the New Testament speaks of it and describes it. This very expression contains the story of the long centuries of God's revelation and action in history as He set about gathering a people for Himself.

In the days of the Old Covenant, Israel as a nation was chosen to be God's "own possession among all peoples" (Ex. 19:5). Other nations might have their kings, but Israel was to be a theocracy. It had been chosen from among the nations of the earth to show how a people would be blessed by serving God directly and with a whole heart.

In time Israel despised its heritage and demanded to be like other nations, with a king of its own. God expressed deep disappointment with this request; yet He honored it. He gave His people a king despite the remonstrances of Samuel. Its kings in time led the people into idolatry. Again and again Israel proved unfaithful to its destiny. God therefore chose a remnant to be His own.

In the fullness of time a new people, gathered out of all nations and tongues, came into being. The connection between the old Israel, the remnant, and the New Testament church is nowhere described more succinctly than in the salutation of Peter's First Epistle (1:1, 2):

> Peter, an apostle of Jesus Christ, to the exiles of the dispersion . . . chosen and destined by God the Father and sanctified by the Spirit for obedience to Jesus Christ and for sprinkling with His blood.

It will help us in our understanding of church-state relations to analyze this description of the church somewhat in detail. The apostle first of all applies the term "exiles" to his readers. That is to say, they are people who are not fully at home here in this life. They are pilgrims, a people on their way. They go through this world, to be sure; while they are here, they live at a certain place and under a certain form of government. Yet, like Israel of old in all its wanderings, the church never loses

sight of the fact that it is headed for a promised land. In the
words of Bishop Newbigin of South India:

> The church is the pilgrim people of God. It is on the move —
> hastening to the end of the earth to beseech all men to be recon-
> ciled to God, and hastening to the end of time to meet its
> Lord, Who will gather all into one. Therefore the nature of
> the church is never to be finally defined in static terms, but
> only in terms of that to which it is going.[14]

The members of the church are in dispersion, we are told
by the apostle. They are a scattered people, outside of and most
frequently in opposition to the current social stream. They are
in the minority, sprinkled thinly among the peoples of the world.
Even after 19 centuries professed Christians number less than
one fourth of the population of the world, and that proportion is
decreasing in the face of the tremendous increase in the population of the earth.

Despite this fact, Christians are assured of being "chosen."
At this point the apostle uses a term employed in the Old Testament to describe God's act of reaching into history and selecting
His people. Fundamentally this was and is a work of grace.
In choosing a people to be His very own God did not, does not
now look to human achievement. "You did not choose Me,
but I chose you," is the way Jesus put this thought to His disciples. (John 15:16)

Now, all this has taken place because God has so destined it.
Behind this simple expression in Peter's salutation is the awe-
some awareness that the church antedates all human institutions;
its creation resulted from the Father's foreknowledge. Before
time began, the Father drew up the blueprint of our redemption,
and His design included the church. Our redemption, then, is
no afterthought on God's part; it is part of His eternal will.
True, the church of the New Testament was not historically
realized until Easter and Pentecost. Yet its conception reaches
back to the creation of time itself.

Before any state came into being, even before man himself
was created, God had already determined to choose a people
"sanctified by the Spirit for obedience to Jesus Christ and for

sprinkling with His blood." For this last phrase the apostle reaches back into the Old Testament, to that moment when Moses read the terms of God's covenant to Israel and it in turn accepted Jehovah's commands and conditions. At that point Moses took half the blood of sacrificial animals and sprinkled it against the altar. The other half of this blood he threw on the people with the words: "Behold the blood of the covenant which the Lord has made with you in accordance with all these words" (Ex. 24:8). Now, the new covenant, under which we live, has been sealed by the blood of none less than Jesus Christ, as the apostle reminds us. In this way we have become God's new covenant people.

We must keep this description of the church constantly in mind as we consider its relationship to the state. The church owes its existence to a divine decision reached in eternity; the state is an arrangement in time. The state is of this world, limited in its existence and functions to what we call history; the church has its roots in that eternity which transcends time, and its destiny lies in the eternal ages beyond this world. The coexistence of these two entities can be understood only within this Biblical framework.

CHURCH AND STATE IN JUXTAPOSITION

The problems arising from the coexistence of church and state could be greatly reduced, even completely eliminated, if these two were completely separate entities in human society. Monastic orders have frequently used this way of escape from a great burden. To Protestants they seem to have surrendered the world to destruction as if the state were not worth saving. However, this solution hardly does justice to the Biblical view that church and state must live not only next to each other but even one within the other. Both the church and the state are comprised to some extent of the same persons.

Christians are at one and the same time members of the church and citizens of a particular nation. Luther would say that they are subjects of both the kingdom on God's left hand and that on His right. They live in both the old and the new aeons, and they would be unfaithful to their trust were they to ignore or attempt to escape a situation described by our Lord in His high-priestly prayer when He said: "I do not pray that Thou shouldst take them out of the world but that Thou shouldst keep them from the evil one." (John 17:15)

At this juncture the incident of the tribute money, as recorded in St. Mark, can be instructive. We must understand, of course, that Jesus answered the question "Is it lawful to pay taxes to Caesar, or not?" in a given situation and under particular circumstances. Yet His reply was of such a nature as to provide general guidance in this difficult area. "Render to Caesar," He said, "the things that are Caesar's and to God the things that are God's." (12:17)

It should be noted in passing that these words cannot be used as an explicit statement in support of the principle of separation of church and state as that view has been set forth in various decisions by the courts of our land and as it was expressed in Jefferson's famous letter to the Danbury Baptist Association 10 years after the adoption of the First Amendment:

> Believing with you that religion is a matter which lies solely between man and his God, that he owes account to none other for his faith or his worship, that the legislative powers of government reach actions only, and not opinion, I contemplate with sovereign reverence that act of the whole American people which declared that their legislature should "make no law respecting an establishment of religion or prohibiting the free exercise thereof," thus building a wall of separation between church and state.[15]

Jesus was addressing Himself primarily to representatives of a sect which thought of God's people as an isolated community, living by its own God-given law in an unfriendly and doomed world, aflame with the hope of Israel's eventual triumph over all its enemies. There were political opportunists in His audience, to be sure. They were the Herodians. Yet it was the Pharisees for whom the payment of tribute constituted a theological problem. They were at times half inclined to accept, in theory at least, the rallying cry of the Zealots: "No tribute for Rome!"

In this context Jesus asserts the principle that there are two distinct spheres in life's obligations: Caesar's and God's. But He insists on their juxtaposition and on the necessity of not confounding the two.

His enemies, it ought to be added, had not raised the question to receive guidance. They were determined to impale Him on the horns of a dilemma, hoping to discredit the Prophet of Nazareth either with the common folk, who followed Him, or with the Roman authorities, who ignored Him. Their query was put as though there must needs be a conflict between Caesar and God. In His reply the Lord indicated He would not allow such an assumption to stand.

During the course of this discussion, Jesus asked to see a coin known as the denarius, with its image of Caesar. He did so, no doubt, to point out that both the Herodians and the Pharisees had already tacitly recognized the rights of Rome. Strictly speaking, Jewish law forbade the use of images of any kind. Yet neither the Herodians nor the Pharisees had hesitated to use the coin of the realm. They had availed themselves of their privileges under Roman law, as, for instance, when they claimed exemption from military service and from the rite of burning incense to the image of Caesar. The denarius represented the right of government to exact its dues in turn.

In responding to a question designed to trap Him, our Lord went beyond the point of extricating Himself from a different situation. He took the occasion to assert the validity of the state's claims on the individual citizen. We must add that He Himself in every way became subject and remained obedient to governmental authority, both Jewish and Roman, even though He might well have set Himself above the law as the Son of Him from whom all such power is derived.

This prerogative of exemption He referred to quite directly in the story of the coin found in the mouth of a fish, as given in Matt. 17. This incident involved the collectors of the temple tax, who came to Peter one day to inquire whether Jesus would pay this tax. In this circumstance Jesus stressed the right of royal sons to be excused from paying taxes. However, to avoid misunderstanding and offense, He ordered Peter to catch a fish that would provide the necessary funds for both Himself and His apostle.

Jesus came to "fulfill all righteousness," as He told John the Baptist (Matt. 3:15). Obedience to civil authorities was included in that task. His subjection to the state was particularly pronounced during the time of His trials. For that reason the apostle Peter could properly point to our Lord's example in suggesting a motivation for the subjection he expected of his readers (1 Peter 2:13). There is nowhere in the words and works of Jesus even the shadow of a suggestion that the state and its authority were institutions He proposed to ignore or to escape. On the contrary, before Pilate He recognized the claims of political authority over Him as a subject of Rome, although He had to remind the Roman procurator that he exercised a power that did not basically derive from his position as a Roman official but from God's will. (John 19:11)

In Paul's life we see the same attitude toward government. He was a Roman citizen and insisted on his rights whenever the occasion required it. He did not hesitate to let himself be taken into the protective custody of Claudius Lysius, the Roman commander in Jerusalem, when the mob threatened to lynch him, or, again, when a band of fanatics resolved to ambush him on the way to Caesarea. Most interesting was his demand that the magistrates of Philippi accord him the respect due to a Roman citizen (Acts 16:38). Again, before Festus the apostle took advantage of his status in appealing his case directly to Caesar (Acts 25:11). He understood the contribution that Rome had made by way of creating and maintaining conditions of peace. These made possible his own extensive missionary journeys. On this basis he at various times in his epistles touched on the necessity of subjection to the state.

To be sure, there was then no institutionally organized church as yet. Christianity was still treated by the Roman authorities as a sect in Judaism. It did not acquire legal status until the days of Constantine. Only then could it acquire and own property as a church, a prerogative which it employed at once in the purchase of the catacombs under the city of Rome. With this change in its relation to the state another dimension was added to the problem of church and state.

Today the church in its manifold divisions is a political entity. It is an association before the law. As such it owns property, employs people under conditions laid down by government, carries on its work under articles of incorporation. In fact, in addition to enjoying the right of assembly, the church in our country is in most areas protected by special laws, such as local ordinances prohibiting disturbances during the hours of worship. Its property is almost universally exempt from state and federal taxation.

In this way, too, government is a minister for good. Luther therefore quite properly listed good government among the blessings we pray for in saying, "Give us this day our daily bread." To revert to the words of the apostle Peter (1 Peter 2:13), the state is an institution ordained for the benefit of men. It exists for the good of men, and the church, too, benefits from its concern for law and order. Its members find in its existence a large measure of protection not only as citizens but as members of the church, whose primary loyalty is to a city beyond time and place.

The church on its part renders certain services to the state. These will be taken up in some detail later on. All this is embraced in the concept of juxtaposition.

However, this alignment is not without its end. The existence of the state is purely provisional; it is limited to the old age. The church represents the powers of the new aeon; its destiny is eternal. This of necessity creates at times a situation of tension between these two entities as they live in juxtaposition within a given social order. To this circumstance of potential conflict we must now turn our attention.

CHURCH AND STATE IN TENSION

The tension under which the Christian lives in being at one and the same time the citizen of a state and a member of the church has its source, for one thing, in the difference of functions ascribed by the Scriptures to these two entities in society. The state exists primarily to establish justice and maintain order among men; its job is of this world. The church, on the other hand, has the task of calling men away from the evils of the world and preparing them for eternal life with God.

That government has the task of preserving civic order is clearly suggested, in the first instance, by St. Paul's insistence that persons vested with political authority are "servant[s] of God to execute His wrath on the wrongdoer" (Rom. 13:4). In this context the apostle contends that resistance to governing authorities is opposition to God's arrangements. Twice, in the opening verses of this chapter of Romans, St. Paul describes the state as an arrangement created in the interest of order. Our Lord is a God of order; consequently His divine providence includes His desire that there be orderliness among His creatures. Peter supplements Paul's observation by adding that government also has the responsibility "to praise those who do right." (1 Peter 2:14)

The state therefore is sometimes referred to in theology as an order of preservation. This expression is used to point up that in His relationship to men as creatures it is God's intent that there be such governing authorities. The structure of our existence here on earth is determined in large part by what St. Paul calls "the powers that be." This is part of the framework of the old aeon. Jesus Himself recognized such authority as being a normal part of life here on earth. "If My kingship were of this world, My servants would fight that I might not be handed over to the Jews," He told Pilate (John 18:36). In another place He observed: "You know that the rulers of the Gentiles lord it over them, and their great men exercise authority over them" (Matt. 20:25). He said this, it would seem, only to draw a contrast between the old aeon and the new and in no way for the purpose of criticizing earthly rulers.

The State

In 1 Peter 2:14 the apostle speaks of the emperor in Rome and of his provincial governors as persons who have the task of punishing those who do wrong and praising those who are interested in doing what is right and good. To the state has been given the assignment from God Himself to fight against the chaos that would ensue if there were no instruments of power to restrain the self-assertion and aggression of men. As a matter of fact, wherever and whenever governments have been too weak to carry out this mission of preserving order in society, anarchy has engulfed the citizens of that land, as witness the trying times in the establishment of an independent republic of the Congo.

The early church was practically unanimous in its belief that the words of St. Paul in 2 Thess. 2:3-7 contained a description of the Roman *imperium* as a power restraining that man who, in the apostle's way of speaking, embodied the mystery of lawlessness. These are his words:

> Let no one deceive you in any way; for that day will not come unless the rebellion comes first and the man of lawlessness is revealed, the son of perdition, who opposes and exalts himself against every so-called god or object of worship, so that he takes his seat in the temple of God, proclaiming himself to be God. Do you not remember that when I was still with you I told you this? And you know what is restraining him now so that he may be revealed in his time. For the mystery of lawlessness is already at work; only he who now restrains it will do so until he is out of the way.

This passage has been much discussed and hotly debated through the centuries. Yet the view that St. Paul used the term "the restrainer" with reference to the political power of Rome has pretty well won out in modern theology.[16] According to this interpretation the Roman empire, with the *imperator* at its head, was at that time the defense which God had set up to keep the forces of chaos and anarchy at bay.

In modern parlance we would speak of this as the police power of the state. Modern governments, however, have gone beyond the mere exercise of this restraining influence. Today the state is formally described as "a body politic, or society of men, united together for the purpose of promoting their mutual safety and advantage, by the joint efforts of their combined strength."[17] In most instances the states of the 20th century include in their

scope of activities what we call "the general welfare," which has
been at times and continues to be a source of temptation on the
part of government to substitute the welfare state for God Himself. Bishop Eivind Berggrav, a former primate of the Church
of Norway, made a point of this before the Assembly of the
Lutheran World Federation in 1952, when he said:

> The specific characteristic of the welfare state is this: on the
> one hand, it is totally secular, and does not in any way what-
> ever acknowledge God as the Lord of life; on the other hand,
> it acts as though it were Providence itself and assumes the
> right of entering into all the spheres of human life. . . . This
> state wishes to become, as we have seen, a kind of "All-Father,"
> it wants to be omnipotent. There will be no actual demands
> to worship the state, in the traditional sense; rather, it will be
> said that the state is sufficient; that the *state is all we need;*
> that we need no Providence beyond the STATE.[18]

However, even apart from the concerns which are often
bracketed under the term "welfare," the state helps to restrain
the disruptive and chaotic tendencies of men's self-assertion by
providing for society a calculable future. In fact, this is what
the framers of the Constitution had in mind when they wrote
of securing the blessings of liberty "to ourselves and to our
posterity." Government in a very real sense promotes the continuous creation of society.

It is necessary to emphasize all this particularly at this time;
for since the days of Lenin's *The State and Revolution* (1917),
we have to reckon with a philosophy which holds that it is possible to create a stateless society, where laws and rules become
no more than daily habits. Of course, the chief thing Lenin had
in mind was the police power of the state, which he and his
movement feared greatly; yet his disciples of today keep insisting
that at the next "leap" in history the state will wither for lack
of any specific function in society.

The primary purpose of the state in the tradition of the
United States is to secure and safeguard the "inherent, unalienable, God-given rights" of its citizens and to arrange for the
orderly employment of these rights by all. In this way the state

becomes an institution of justice. This is the moral basis of the state.

Government, of course, has other tasks to perform. These are concerned with the advancement of the welfare of its citizens. Since it is impossible for individuals to live to themselves, especially in a complex life like ours, it becomes the duty of the state to encourage the development of its various resources in means and men, thus promoting the general welfare of its citizens.

Then, too, the state must devote much effort to maintaining relations with other nations in the interest of peace and order. Here, too, it must at times wield the sword through its military establishment, which in modern society has come to embrace almost every facet of a people's capacity. In passing it might be noted that it is the purpose of the profession of arms to stand on the side of order against the destructive forces of life on this planet.

The Church

The church, on the other hand, consisting as it does of the company of the redeemed, has functions quite different from those of the state. Its primary task is to proclaim the good news of God's grace. As it goes about its work, it calls men out of this world to serve the God of promise, and so it develops in the individual Christian a loyalty that is focused on the heavenly city. By proclaiming the Word and administering its sacraments, the church gathers a people destined to live with God eternally under conditions that will not require the restraining hand of government; for then His children will serve God and their fellow citizens in complete and perfect love.

As the herald of God's Word the church must at times become critical of society and of the state. In this respect it has fallen heir to the spirit and message of the ancient prophets of God. The church must stand like a watchman, condemning injustice wherever it occurs. In this capacity it must often show the prince how to wear the sword, to borrow a phrase from Luther. It is especially bound to alert the state to its temptations to become demonic, constantly reminding governing authorities of their functions and destiny under God.

Twenty years before the Roman armies broke down the walls of Jerusalem and burned down the city, St. Paul wrote to the Galatians (4:22-26):

> Abraham had two sons, one by a slave and one by a free woman. But the son of the slave was born according to the flesh, the son of the free woman through promise. Now this is an allegory: these women are two covenants. One is from Mount Sinai, bearing children for slavery; she is Hagar. Now Hagar is Mount Sinai in Arabia; she corresponds to the present Jerusalem, for she is in slavery with her children. But the Jerusalem above is free, and she is our mother.

Rightly or wrongly this passage suggested the theory of two cities, which was fully developed by St. Augustine in his *De civitate Dei* in a form that has deeply influenced Christian politics ever since. There are two cities. Christians live in both of them. In the city of this world, of which Rome was the symbol in Augustine's day, men must keep the law, which God has ordained to hold in check the destructive impulses of men. Human government exists because men are sinners. It is a child of necessity. Christians have their true citizenship, however, in the city of God, which is governed in the freedom of love. It is the child of promise.

Now, even redeemed men are sinners, and so they, too, come under the control of the state. This creates serious tensions at times, especially in those instances where the state fails to recognize its own limitations and neglects its understanding of that prophetic criticism which is part of the church's work.

The early Christians came into conflict with the state on the issue of emperor worship. Many a member of the church suffered martyrdom because he refused to recognize the divine claims of Caesar, who wanted to be known not only as *dominus* (lord) but as *deus* (god). The member of the church could not in good conscience render to the state what properly belongs only to God. His faith, expressed most briefly in the formula "Jesus is Lord," ran head on into the pagan insistence that "Caesar is Lord."

The Source of Conflict

In a very real way this is still the heart of the conflict between church and state in totalitarian countries; for totalitarianism is a philosophy of government and an exercise of political authority that proposes to direct and regulate the whole man. This kind of state refuses to recognize the independence of religion, culture, education, and the family, each in its own sphere. It seeks to impose on all its subjects a particular philosophy of life and sets out, with all the techniques of psychology and all the instruments of mass communication that have become available to it in this century, to create a particular type of man in accordance with its own understanding of the meaning and end of man's existence.

The life of the church under totalitarian regimes is probably the most crucial issue in Christendom today, if for no other reason than that all states face the temptation to become omnicompetent and all-embracing. The very complexity of life today and the size of our social problems tend to heighten this inclination. It may be instructive, therefore, at this point to consider a passage in the Revelation of St. John the Divine to gain some understanding of the Biblical perspective in this matter. Here is part of the passage:

> And I saw a beast rising out of the sea, with ten horns and seven heads, with ten diadems upon its horns and a blasphemous name upon its heads. And the beast that I saw was like a leopard, its feet were like a bear's, and its mouth was like a lion's mouth. And to it the dragon gave his power and his throne and his great authority. (Rev. 13:1, 2)

It is more than likely that the beast from the abyss was intended to represent the Roman empire in its demands that Caesar be worshiped as god. In this respect it serves as an example of every state insofar as it becomes demonic. For a government that exceeds its proper bounds can be regarded as the most tangible embodiment of the Dragon's — Satan's — power.

In his description of the beast, St. John leans heavily on the language of Dan. 7. There the four beasts represent four kingdoms. In Revelation the features of all these kingdoms are concentrated in the one beast. It is a cunning panther, a strong bear, and a devouring lion all at the same time.

This beast is described as being eminently successful (Rev. 13:4) by acting like God. It belongs to the devil's cleverest wile that he imitates God, and so the state, represented by the beast, demands what is God's. It does so by applying to itself the very attributes of God. In consequence the worshiping masses acclaim the beast in the very words of Ex. 15:11, applied there to God Himself: "Who is like Thee?" The speciality of this beast is to wage war against God's saints. For this battle, according to Rev. 17, he finds allies among the kings of the earth. And he almost succeeds in getting all the inhabitants of the earth to accept him as God. There are some, however, who do not bow down before him. These are the people whose names are written in the book of life.

At this point in the chapter we are introduced to the second beast. This one rises out of the earth. Here are St. John's words:

> Then I saw another beast, which rose out of the earth; it had two horns like a lamb, and it spoke like a dragon. It exercises all the authority of the first beast in its presence. (Rev. 13:11, 12)

In Rev. 16:13; 19:20; and 20:10 this monster is identified with the false prophet. Oscar Cullmann suggests that this second creature represents "the religio-idealogical propaganda authority of the totalitarian state," which makes propaganda for his chief, the devil.[19] Here, too, Satan imitates God, even as every totalitarian state needs an ideology which is a parody of the Christian faith. The beast orders the people of the world to put up an image of the first beast and to worship it. That is precisely what Caesar had done. For this we have evidence from correspondence between Pliny, the governor of Pontus, and Emperor Trajan.[20] Christians were ordered to sacrifice before an image of Caesar and to say, "Caesar is Lord; let Christ be accursed." If they did this, they were free to go on living as citizens of the empire; if they refused, they were put to death.

At the end of Rev. 13 the number 666, or 616, is given this

second beast. This account has puzzled all interpreters of the Apocalypse. Many suggestions have been made as to the significance of this number. The early Christians probably understood it very well. Most commentators today agree that it is a veiled reference to Caesar. Various ways have been suggested for deciphering the numeral. None of them is conclusive; and yet they all lead to the conviction that St. John here referred to the emperor.

The burden of this chapter in the Apocalypse is that a government which exceeds its proper limits must be resisted at that point. It does not intend to set aside the principles expressed by St. Paul in Rom. 13, but it does call attention to the demonic possibilities of a state and describes such tendencies in terms of that gigantic conflict between God and His chief adversary.

That no contradiction of Rom. 13 is intended can be seen especially from verse 10: "If anyone slays with the sword, with the sword must he be slain." These are words that echo a statement of the Lord Himself and serve as a strong reminder of the limitations placed on resistance even to the totalitarian state. Except for the most unusual instances, Christians have no business taking up the sword and waging war against a state in order to destroy it. Otherwise they would fall into the error of the Zealots of Jesus' day, who raised the sword against Rome in order to destroy it. This is an approach to the problem of conflict which Jesus decisively repudiated in Gethsemane when He said to Peter: "Put your sword back into its place; for all who take the sword will perish by the sword" (Matt. 26:52). And yet we must resist those demands of the state which invade the sphere that properly belongs only to God and His church.

Differences in Functions, Means, and Destiny

The difference in functions between the state and the church that was discussed above is supported by a difference in the means used by each of these entities to carry on its own work. The state properly wields the sword. The church on the other hand has been entrusted with Word and sacrament. In it the swords are turned into plowshares and spears into pruning hooks

(Is. 2:4; Micah 4:3). The state can compel its citizens to do what is demanded; the church can only persuade, not coerce.

There is also a difference in destiny between church and state. Government is a divine but provisional arrangement, designed to see men through the period of time from the Fall to the return of Christ on Judgment Day. The church transcends history in its destiny; its lot is to be with God forever.

In a way the finite limits of the state are marked by its use of the sword; for, carrying out its assigned task, civil power cannot but fight with the bloodstained instruments of this world. In due course it must succumb to these same weapons. Our Scriptures recognize the peculiar greatness but also the hidden tragedy of political life. Government is a bulwark against the powers of chaos, but it can only keep these powers in check, never really subdue them. As soon as it believes it can completely remove "the man of lawlessness," it falls prey to the temptation of wanting to be more than God has in mind. It becomes demonic.

The state carries within itself the tendency to reach beyond itself. An earthly ruler may forget that he holds office under an authority that comes, in the last analysis, only from above, regardless of the political machinery devised in a particular country to bring certain individuals to power. He may even begin to accept acclaim like that accorded to Herod, when the people shouted, "The voice of a god and not of man" (Acts 12:22). He is tempted to forget the glory of God and to strive for his own honor, and so he becomes a "desolating sacrilege" (Mark 13:14), like Antiochus Epiphanes and Caligula, both of whom proposed to set up images of themselves in the temple at Jerusalem.

By this glorification of itself an individual state may reach that particular boundary in time which God sets for each nation (Acts 17:26). One thought, however, has to be added to this Biblical assertion: the state as such, the institution of government, is limited in its existence to this present aeon. This characteristic of political authority can be understood only in the light of what the New Testament tells us of the distinction between the old and the new eras as well as their interpenetration of each other.

That, in turn, can best be done by a rather detailed discussion of what is without question the most significant section of the New Testament on the nature and the functions of the state:

> Let every person be subject to the governing authorities. For there is no authority except from God, and those that exist have been instituted by God. Therefore he who resists the authorities resists what God has appointed, and those who resist will incur judgment. For rulers are not a terror to good conduct but to bad. Would you have no fear of him who is in authority? Then do what is good, and you will receive his approval, for he is God's servant for your good. But if you do wrong, be afraid, for he does not bear the sword in vain; he is the servant of God to execute His wrath on the wrongdoer. Therefore one must be subject, not only to avoid God's wrath but also for the sake of conscience. For the same reason you also pay taxes, for the authorities are ministers of God, attending to this very thing. Pay all of them their dues, taxes to whom taxes are due, revenue to whom revenue is due, respect to whom respect is due, honor to whom honor is due. (Rom. 13:1-7)

We must observe at once that these verses depend for their full impact on a consideration of both the preceding and the subsequent contexts. Each of these has to be taken into account to bring St. Paul's directive into focus.

The preceding chapter in Romans is devoted to a description of the new life in Christ. Love is central to the changed situation in which Christians find themselves. This love never avenges itself but loves even an enemy. Members of the church in Rome are to walk in that kind of love. They live in the new aeon, and so they are not to pattern their lives according to this world. Yet they live here, in this age. Someone might suggest that they ought to separate themselves completely from the institutions of this world, since Christians had been set free from all the powers that reign in the old aeon. Because their citizenship is in heaven, it might be argued, members of the church are no longer under any obligation toward earthly rulers.

This kind of logic could be heard in parts of the early church, as we see from 1 Peter. In the very context of his discussion on civil authority, the apostle felt constrained to add the caution, "Live as free men, yet without using your freedom as a pretext for evil" (1 Peter 2:16). The message of freedom in Christ was a heady drink for these early converts, especially for those who came from the ranks of slavery. The new liberty was at times misunderstood and misapplied as if it were an unlimited quantity that permitted the Christian to go his own way without regard for the social order. For that reason Peter took the occasion to warn his readers precisely against the false notion that they could now shun such earthly obligations.

In point of fact, God has put the Christian into this world and subjected him to the ruling powers. Hence St. Paul takes vigorous exception also to that other fanatical view which would make the Gospel into a law for society. The two aeons coexist, but they must not be confused. It is not proper to take what belongs to the new age and apply it simply as a law for the old.

Moreover, despite its belonging to the old order of things, the state is a valid and even a necessary institution also for Christians. As members of the new community in Christ they may not avenge themselves. The Lord has entrusted to government the task of executing wrath. That is its function under God.

This does not mean that all persons in political positions always act according to God's will. There are good and bad authorities. There are some that use their power in harmony with God's will and others that abuse their authority. Paul is not talking about such distinctions. He is speaking of that which all authorities have in common: they are God's institutions. That there are governments at all is not the result of man's invention but of God's ordination. Even the offenses of government do not undo the fact that it is God who has given this power.

If a Christian thinks he is absolved from all obedience to government, he must remember that he is in fact resisting not only the authorities but an institution which God has ordained. He thereby calls down upon himself not only punishment from the civil powers but also the judgment of God. The member of the church must never pretend that he is already living in the glorified state of the new aeon. His destiny in glory is still heavily veiled by the circumstances in which he lives here. It is not God's intention that he anticipate his future condition by setting himself above the orders of this present existence. When at last the new age reaches its consummation, the power of earthly rulers will come to an end. However, as long as the world endures, government, too, will continue; for God has so willed it.

To be sure, governing authorities belong to an order of existence that is judged and must pass away. Yet here, in this life, such rulers are servants of God. The state is an instrument of God's wrath, and as such it bears the sword, with which it is to combat evil. The man that does what is good will not bring the sword down on himself. In his case the ruler is God's servant for good.

"Good" and "evil" are not, of course, used in their absolute sense here. Nor is the former to be understood as synonymous with that good which can flow only from a regenerate heart. The social order, which government is ordained to maintain, is a blessing; in that sense the state is a minister for good. Rebellion, resistance, and disobedience run counter to God's intent for society; hence they are evil. "Therefore," says St. Paul, "one must be subject, not only to avoid God's wrath but also for the sake of conscience."

St. Paul therefore concurs with his Lord that Christians are to pay taxes and revenue. He adds the details of respect and honor that are to be given to whom they are due. Members of the church are actually the only ones able to give the esteem and honor that is due the state. Others must look upon governing authorities as necessary and useful for human society; their view is limited to this observation. The Christian, however, knows that "there is no authority except from God." He sees in the earthly ruler a servant of God, who carries out the work assigned to him. According to Luther's distinction this may be an "alien" work, but it is still God's.

Paul accentuates the provisional nature of the state in the context that follows his discourse on government. There, in verse 11, he reminds his readers that they are living in the end-

time. The very fact that St. Paul relates his statement on governing authorities to this basic consideration is of paramount importance for an understanding of church-state relations; for it
bears out the observation that the state is limited in its existence
and function to that interval of time which will terminate with
our Lord's return.

St. Paul strongly suggests this fact by the language he uses
at the very beginning of his discourse on political authority; for
there he chooses to apply the Hellenistic word ἐξουσίαι to political
rulers. Now, this term has a twofold significance. On the one
hand it means governmental authorities as such; this is how the
Greeks understood it. But we must remember that St. Paul writes
less from a Greek background than from a thorough acquaintance
with the Biblical world of thought. According to this view,
mighty invisible beings are behind the phenomena of creation.
In every other instance where St. Paul uses the word ἐξουσίαι
(in the plural) it designates angelic powers, created cosmic
beings, to whom God has entrusted certain tasks in His government of the world. Behind the empirical state, in the view
of St. Paul, there are these supramundane "authorities."

Exception has been taken from time to time to this interpretation of Rom. 13, but it has been quite feeble in the face of the
fact that the apostle in every other case uses ἐξουσίαι in the sense
of angelic powers.[21] This in itself would create a strong pre-
sumption for the view here presented. Add to this the use of
the same word in the Greek version of Dan. 7:27, where the
English has: "And all *dominions* shall serve and obey them."
Moreover, the angelic princes of Persia, Greece, and Israel, mentioned later in the book of Daniel, become the rulers of this age.[22]
The prophet Isaiah expresses the view in 24:21 when he says:
"On that day the Lord will punish the host of heaven, in heaven,
and the kings of the earth, on the earth."

If our interpretation is correct, it will help us to understand
another passage from St. Paul. In 1 Cor. 6 the apostle pleads with
his readers not to go to law with their grievances but to settle
their difficulties within the church. In this connection he asks
(v. 3): "Do you not know that we are to judge angels?" This

is certainly a puzzling query unless it be taken in the light of
St. Paul's general view that behind the secular state, as represented in this instance by the courts of Corinth, there are these
mighty created beings whom he calls "angels," "principalities,"
"lordships," or, as in Rom. 13, "authorities."

The apostle requests the Christians in Corinth not to have
their cases adjudicated in pagan courts, on the grounds that they
themselves will one day judge angels.[23] He is reminding his
readers that the state is nothing absolute or final. For this reason
Christians ought to forgo using the instruments of the state whenever that is possible without destroying the existence of government, especially in problems and quarrels that arise from within
the life of the church. That is the apostle's suggestion.

In Colossians St. Paul reminds us that in Christ "all things . . .
whether thrones or dominions or principalities or authorities
. . . hold together" (1:16, 17). To this Peter adds his own insistence that after the crucifixion and resurrection Christ ascended
and took His place at the right hand of the Father, "with angels,
authorities, and powers subject to Him." (1 Peter 3:22)

All this is of immeasurable significance for a full appreciation
of the state in its limitations. Governments do not exist simply
on the basis of natural law. In the new age, too, they serve God's
ultimate purposes. In this respect the state has been affected by
the coming of God's kingdom in Christ. In the Old Testament
government was part of God's pedagogy, by which He was preparing the world for the "fullness of the times" that was yet
to come. Hence, under the theocracy of Israel, church and state
were one; the rule of David was in a real sense the kingdom of
God. In the New Testament the two, church and state, are to
be thought of as working in two different spheres. The state
may therefore in our Christian era be called an institution established and maintained by God's grace for the subsidiary purpose
of making possible the work of the church in society.

All of these considerations recall us to the cosmic dimensions
of the relation between church and state. From the Biblical
point of view this whole problem cannot possibly be understood
when the issue is reduced to the "Mercator map" of an existence

unguided by divine revelation; for church and state constitute
part of the structure of our life "between the ages," a time in
the history of mankind marked by the interpenetration of the
old and the new aeons.

We live in that period of history to which the apostle Paul
applies the words from Psalm 110, where the Father is depicted
as bringing all things, especially the enemies of our Lord, into
subjection under Christ (1 Cor. 15:27). This is his interpretation
of what is now going on in the world. For the apostle the history
of mankind is the story of God's judgment over it. In this age
of judgment, where each crisis is only a rehearsal for the final
day of reckoning, a struggle is going on in the invisible realm
behind the world of sense. In this contest, mighty angelic beings
are engaged in mortal combat. God's hosts stand at His service,
but their power and their position are constantly challenged by
the minions of Satan. As this battle rages through the centuries,
individual governments, exposed as they are in a special way to
the temptation of wanting to be absolute, at times come under
the control of demonic powers. When this happens, the Christian is thrown back with special force on the assurance of ultimate
victory through our Lord Jesus Christ, who has overcome also
these mighty beings that occupy one side of the cosmic rift.
The Christian is persuaded, moreover, that when demonic power
becomes actualized it is only for a particular moment and for
a limited time. This is very succinctly implied by the words of
the Savior in Gethsemane: "But this is your hour and the power
of darkness." (Luke 22:53)

Mutual Responsibilities of Church and State

The very tensions deriving from the differences between
church and state in terms of functions, means, and destiny are
reason enough to consider somewhat in detail the responsibilities
that each has to the other. For the Christian is at times caught
in a cross fire between the claims that each institution makes
for itself. He can try to escape this difficulty by ignoring or
neglecting his obligation to one or the other. However, he does
so only at the risk of being less than a Christian citizen.

There have been times when governments themselves have attempted to resolve the tension between themselves and the church by such executive or legislative action as was designed to reduce the church to impotence. Moreover, in some areas of Christendom churches have acquiesced to this procedure. To this day, for example, the majority of Eastern churches, especially those in Russia and her satellites, suffer from an arrangement to which we apply the label "Caesaropapism." In a very real way, it should be added, this is part of the historical heritage of these particular churches, dating from the days of the Byzantine emperors. In this respect, as in many others, the story of Eastern Christianity differs radically from that of the West. No Byzantine or Russian ruler, for example, ever went to his Canossa. In fact, just at those moments when the church might have served as a check on temporal rulers, it was usually embroiled in internal conflicts that kept it from asserting its claims. As a consequence the church allowed itself at times to become little more than an arm of government, even in the face of injustice and oppression.

A resolution of the tension between church and state has also been attempted from the side of the church by imposing its desires on the state in such a way as to reduce government to being no more than another side of church life. Calvin did this in Geneva; and the Puritans were determined to keep this pattern of life in New England. Their chief error lay in this, that they thought to return church members to the days of the Old Testament, when, for a time at least, church and state were merged in a common national enterprise.

Neither of these approaches is Biblical. According to the Scriptures, both the church and the state are God's creation, and both serve His ultimate purposes of grace. The New Testament insists that the Head of the church is at the same time the Lord of the universe. This can imply only that church and state, in the dialectic of history, must somehow strike a workable balance in their attitudes and actions toward each other. Each has responsibilities toward and for the other.

On the Part of the State

In terms of mutual responsibilities the state must, in the view of the church, attempt above all to understand as much as it can the church's life and functions. It cannot, of course, comprehend fully the nature of the church except where individuals in government accept the revelation given in the Scriptures. The church's glory is still hidden, and a grasp of its place in the counsels of God to a large degree escapes man's natural insights. Yet the state can take seriously the church's claim that it wields the powers of the new age.

This assertion on the part of the church may at times cause embarrassment and even resentment. Its proclamation of the Gospel and its instruction in God's Law may under certain conditions look like an attempt at interference. Governing authorities may find it troublesome to be reminded of their limited place in God's plans. Nevertheless they must be reminded by the crucifixion of our Lord that government is capable of exceeding the bounds of justice and is even tempted to do so. At the same time this once-for-all event in history can serve to alert political rulers to the fact that the angelic powers behind their activities must also acknowledge the lordship of Christ. Nor is this some far-off event, to take place at the sound of the last trumpet. It is God's intent that even now "through the church the manifold wisdom of God might now be made known to the principalities and powers in the heavenly places." (Eph. 3:10)

As a corollary to all this the state also has the task of curbing inordinate ambition on the part of any segment of the church. It has a right and a duty to reject, as a violation of the principle of the two spheres, any arrogant claims to domination on the part of the church. It can and must at times keep the authority exercised by officials in the church from becoming demonic. Obviously this calls for the greatest possible competence in understanding the role of the church in modern society.

Moreover, the state has the primary responsibility of providing protection for its citizens, including members of the church, from physical violence, injustice, delinquency, and general disorder.

It has been endowed with police powers because it is the only instrument that is capable of enforcing a minimal order of justice in the face of the innumerable selfish drives in individuals and groups of society.

Under conditions as they prevail in the 20th century we must at this point include among the obligations of the state a concern for what is called the general welfare of its people, involving, as it does, peaceful relations with other governments. The various nations of today's world have become so interdependent in their needs that foreign relations are not a matter of indifference or even of secondary interest, because they have a very direct bearing on such items as employment as well as the personal safety of individuals and the security of whole communities. Internal order can hardly be maintained today without an intense absorption in and a concern for worldwide issues. The church is directly affected by all this. Conditions of peace and order enable Christians to lead that "quiet and peaceable life" for which they pray (1 Tim. 2:2). However, for the church peace is not an end in itself but a means by which such circumstances are made to prevail as make it possible for Christians to go about their assignment of proclaiming the Gospel to all the world. St. Paul's appeal to the authority of Caesar for protection against violence and injustice serves as a good illustration of how government as "the servant of God" made possible his later mission activities.

To the degree that government recognizes the independent character and functions of the state, it encourages conditions of freedom not only for the church but also for other groups within the social order. The organized church, as an association before the law, can be and ought to be one of the primary checks on political power. At this point we encounter one of the essential differences between democratic and totalitarian practices. In an omnicompetent state every individual is surrounded on all sides by the naked power of government. It is part of the nature of such a political structure that nothing is permitted to stand guard between the exercise of political power and the citizenry. In an open society, on the contrary, the family and numerous associations, each of them permitted to pursue its own special interests within the broad framework of such devices as articles of incorporation, provide room for the individual to be and remain fully a person rather than a statistical quantity. These several areas of free activity serve as cushions against the exercise of arbitrary power. Normally the degree of freedom which the church enjoys is the measure of liberty in general within a nation; hence the church is often one of the first organizations to be attacked where totalitarian tendencies begin to develop. When other institutions have been suppressed or rendered innocuous, the church continues to speak out against oppression and injustice. It remains the last bulwark against tyranny, which always turns "justice to wormwood." (Amos 5:7)

On the Part of the Church

The church and its members on their part have the responsibility of honoring and respecting government for what God intends it to be: a bulwark against anarchy. This is why the church includes governing authorities in its public intercessions. For instance: "Bestow Thy grace upon all the nations of the earth. Especially do we entreat Thee to bless our land and all its inhabitants *and all who are in authority.*" [24] Or in another prayer: "Grant also health and prosperity to *all that are in authority,* especially to the President and Congress of the United States, the Governor and Legislature of this Commonwealth, and to all our Judges and Magistrates, and endue them with grace to rule after Thy good pleasure, to the maintenance of righteousness and to the hindrance and punishment of wickedness, that we may lead a quiet and peaceable life in all godliness and honesty." [25]

All this is part of the priestly function of the church, to which the apostle Peter refers when he describes Christians as being "a sacred craft of priests that offers up spiritual sacrifices which are well-pleasing to God through Jesus Christ" (1 Peter 2:5; our own translation). For this expression the apostle must have had in mind the relationship of the priests at the temple in Jerusalem to God's people as a whole. Each morning and evening the smoke of incense rose above the walls of the temple as a symbol of the intercessory function of the priests. The church as the new Israel has inherited this task, praying through all the centuries also for governing authorities.

Within society the church also renders an educational service which is of direct benefit to government. It helps train good citizens. This it does in two ways: by proclaiming the Gospel and by teaching the Law. Both of these activities lie within its province.

As it sounds out the Good News, the church provides the proper motivation for citizenship. Peter did just this when he exhorted his readers to be subject "for the Lord's sake" (1 Peter 2:13). The lordship of Christ lies at the heart of the Gospel. Hence the earliest formulation of the church's creed consisted of the brief statement "Jesus is Lord." Acknowledging Him as our Lord means that the honor of His name is involved in our every attitude and action. Moreover, Jesus Christ is our Example. He Himself, even though He might have insisted on His equality with the Father (Phil. 2:6), became subject first of all to His mother and foster father and then also to civil ordinances, both Jewish and Roman.

With this statement we come to the chief responsibility of the Christian: to be subject. This in fact is the keynote of all Scriptural directions on the matter of the Christian's responsibility toward the state. It is possible to misunderstand the English word "subjection." There is no real equivalent for the term used by the apostles. As they understood the relationship of the Christian to governing authorities, they called for that attitude of faith which recognizes the institutions and purposes of God. Hence the verb in the original is in the passive voice; behind the attitude expressed by it lies the prior action of God. Being subject implies the extension of the general principle that Christians are to think more of others than of themselves.[26] Subjection is the opposite of that spirit of aggression and exploitation of which man becomes guilty when he goes about "doing what comes naturally." In their attitude of self-effacement Christians live out the strange paradox that man can gain inner freedom only by subjecting himself to that which is above him.

As the members of the church go about their business of honoring and respecting government as God's institution, they may be confronted by a situation in which they are requested and even commanded by those in authority to do something contrary to their faith. Whenever such circumstances develop, Christians can only refuse to obey. In this they will be following the example of Peter and the apostles; for when the latter were ordered to cease speaking in the name of Jesus, they replied, "We must obey God rather than men" (Acts 5:29). Such disobedience, however, must be limited to the point at issue.

From the Biblical point of view revolution and rebellion are rarely justified. The Scriptures in fact suggest that a Christian suffer rather than rebel, even as the Lord preferred to endure the cross rather than call upon 12 legions of angels to rescue Him from the powers of the Roman procurator. For the Christian is aware that oppression is often the means God uses to punish a particular society. The Christian also realizes that such judgment often begins "with the household of God" (1 Peter 4:17); that is to say, the church may be subjected to prior and to greater suffering than other groups just because its sins may be greater than those of others in view of the fact that its members live in the full light of God's Word and have possibly become lukewarm and even ungrateful for their privileges. On this very basis Jesus could say to Pilate of Caiaphas: "He who delivered Me to you has the greater sin" (John 19:11). The judgment that later overtook Jerusalem, in which Caiaphas served for many years as high priest, has scarcely ever been matched, not to say surpassed, in the annals of mankind.

When they are true to their faith, Christians serve as a kind of mortar in society. To borrow a sentence from an ancient church father, they hold the world together. Their relation to the community at large is quite parallel to that of the righteous in Sodom and Gomorrah that might have lived there in sufficient number to save that city from destruction. At Abraham's request the Lord was quite willing to stay His wrath provided 10 upright people could be found in those godless cities (Gen. 18:32). But there were not that many; judgment was swift and total. In much the same way the church serves as a kind of preservative. In fact, governments exist mostly as a demonstration of God's patience with mankind while His people are being gathered from the four corners of the earth. The state is part of the scaffolding for the kingdom of heaven.

The Responsibilities of the Church Vary

There is no clear list of the detailed obligations which devolve on all Christians in every generation, for the details of such a prescription vary somewhat from age to age and from place to place. Much depends on the polity adopted by a particular church and also on the system of government prevailing in a given state. We must now give some thought to this facet of our theme.

The obligations of the church and its members vary somewhat in proportion to the strength of the Christian religion in a particular social order. Before the Edict of Milan (A. D. 313), just as a case in point, the magistrates of the Roman empire were required by law to treat Christianity as a forbidden cult. Under these conditions the church could do little more than strengthen its own inner life. This it did with great effect, for example in its approach to the problem of slavery.

Since the church had no legal right to exist, it could not agitate for the abolition of slavery in society at large. Nevertheless it vigorously attacked the problem within its own sphere. For one thing, it treated slaves as persons. This was unheard of in a day when slaves and even women were generally considered to be chattel. Second, the church admitted both master and slave to the same Lord's Table. Furthermore, it insisted that Christian masters in their homes treat their slaves as children of God. And finally, the church eliminated all distinctions of social status in the selection of its various officials, so that, for instance, in the third century Callistus I, an ex-slave, became the bishop of Rome.

With the conversion of Constantine the church's position in society and before the law became radically different. It became a recognized form of worship. In fact, the new Christian emperor rather looked to the Christian religion as the one force that might

be able to hold the empire together. At once bishops like Euse-
bius of Caesarea and Hosius of Cordova began to insist on
changing the laws that dealt with such items as slavery, the
exposure of children, and prison conditions. In other words,
the church almost immediately began to make use of the instruments of authority to which it now had access, and it did so
in the interest of justice and charity. The direct influence of
the Christian religion can be seen, for instance, in the abolition
of the practice of branding the face of a criminal; such mutilation
was now forbidden by law on the principle that "the face is
fashioned after the likeness of heavenly beauty." [27] Moreover,
the exclusion of divorce for light reasons and the heavy penalties
inflicted for sexual offenses were certainly also due to the
church's influence, first as a legal cult and then, under Theodosius,
as the religion of the state.

To relate this point to our contemporary situation we might
cite the case of the Christian churches in India as occupying
a position in society somewhat similar to that of the early
Christians. Church members number only about 9,000,000 in
that ancient land. In a small way, of course, they can and do
agitate for certain Christian principles in the areas of welfare
and education. However, their effectiveness is limited almost
entirely to the church's own life. Because of its small size the
responsibilities of the church in India are less than those of
American Christianity.

If a church is organized along episcopal lines, to take up
another side of the issue, the individual member is likely to
have smaller obligations in certain areas of church-state relations
than in a congregational or presbyterial system. The church of
Norway in the days of Nazi occupation might serve as a good
illustration for this point. When Hitler's agents proposed to
that church an arrangement which was bound to compromise
the integrity of ecclesiastical authority, the bishops and especially
the primate of Norway, Bishop Eivind Berggrav, became the
symbols of resistance to enemy oppression and intrigue. The
leaders of the church of course were sure that the majority of
the members stood with them in their attitude of opposition.

Yet it was the bishops who assumed the responsibility. These distinctions are reduced and even eliminated where the life of the church is organized along more democratic lines.

Again, the church's responsibilities are determined somewhat by the form of government found in a given nation. Under the monarchies of the past century the obligations devolving upon individual Christians were surely less in scope and number than in countries that had accepted a democratic way of life, if for no other reason than that in the former most of the issues of life were decided from above.

In a totalitarian state of today the church's responsibilities, moreover, are greatly reduced. Under such a government it has hardly enough room to nurture its own inner life. This very fact sometimes gives rise to doubts that the church can do so much as survive in Communist countries, to say nothing of leavening the social order.

In a free way of society, on the other hand, the church and the individual Christian have maximum responsibilities also for the social order. To cover some of the more significant aspects of this thought, we must begin to make a distinction between the obligations of the church as an organization and of the individual Christian as a citizen. We shall discuss the latter instance first.

In a democracy every Christian shares in the responsibility for government, for he is part of that people which is the direct source of political authority. As such he must help to shape the content and direction of public opinion. A distinguished authority on our form of government, Robert M. MacIver, has said: "Democracy is not a way of governing, whether by majority or otherwise, but primarily a way of determining who shall govern and, broadly, to what ends." [28]

The basic instrument of freedom is known as the marketplace, where ideas are expressed, discussed, and modified. Out of this exchange and conflict of thought public opinion is developed. The Christian citizen has as great an obligation as anyone — in fact a great deal more than others — to get out into the marketplace to articulate his own convictions and beliefs so that government may indeed stay on course or return to its proper sphere.

Moreover, the individual Christian must be just as concerned as his unchurched neighbor with civic affairs, beginning with those of the local community and reaching to the national level. At the hand of God's revelation he has in fact a better understanding of the nature of political authority. This, if nothing else, should persuade him to seek public office wherever possible and necessary. On this point Luther remarked: "You are under obligation to serve and further the sword by whatever means you can, with body, soul, honor or goods. For it is nothing that you need, but something quite useful and profitable for the whole world and for your neighbor. Therefore, should you see that there is a lack of hangmen, beadles, judges, lords, or princes, and find that you are qualified, you should offer your services and seek the place." [29] For all this we have ample Scriptural warrant in the words of Jeremiah to his captive people. According to the instructions he received from the Lord they were to build houses, plant gardens, marry, and raise families, but they were also to "seek the welfare of the city where I have sent you into exile, and pray to the Lord on its behalf, for in its welfare you will find your welfare." (Jer. 29:7)

One of the most significant contributions that an individual Christian can make to his country is his prayers. These can and should include the welfare of the nation. Luther therefore properly included good government in his interpretation of the Fourth Petition. No Christian ought to say, "Give us this day our daily bread," without thinking of the governing authorities that God has put over him. In a very real sense such praying amounts to political action.

We must now proceed to a discussion of the responsibilities of the church as an association of people. It, too, has certain obligations over against the state. These do not normally include engaging in partisan politics, or imposing its own particular requirements on society by making the Gospel a new form of law, or lobbying on national issues, competing with secular organizations for a place in the political sun.[30] But the church does have a right to be heard on controversial issues. Moreover, it has certain definite general obligations prescribed for it in the Scriptures.

First and foremost, it must engage in intercessory prayer, as we have already indicated. This is in keeping with the apostolic directive:

> First of all, then, I urge that supplications, prayers, intercessions, and thanksgivings be made for all men, for kings and all who are in high positions, that we may lead a quiet and peaceable life, godly and respectful in every way. This is good, and it is acceptable in the sight of God our Savior, who desires all men to be saved and to come to the knowledge of the truth. (1 Tim. 2:1-3)

Of course, such prayers should not be so worded as to suggest that the church underwrites every action of government, for the church must always stand above civic administration and apart from injustice. Above all else the church must refuse to let itself be made the instrument of any political movement that may assume a messianic character,[31] for righteousness will take up permanent residence only in the new heavens and the new earth for which we wait (2 Peter 3:13). At times it must even take its position with Ambrose of old in his condemnation of both emperor and empress for the wrongs they had done. The intercessions of the church therefore are normally of the kind that implore God's guidance in the maintenance of righteousness for the welfare of all men.

Then, too, the church, especially under conditions of freedom, must be aware of the basic assumptions that make possible the preservation of liberty. It is directly involved, for example, in an appreciation and understanding of that moral law of the universe to which a free way of life appeals against injustice and oppression. Even unaided by divine revelation the general content of that Law is derived from men's conscience [32] as it reflects the Law of God written in man's heart (Rom. 2:15). The church, however, has the privilege of filling in the specifics of this Law that rules above the laws, for it knows and teaches the revealed Moral Law with its specific injunctions and prohibitions.

We cannot possibly stress too strongly that the church also teaches the Law as a curb on unrighteousness. It must be vitally interested, therefore, in what our Confessions call civic righteousness. It is not true to its full task if it fails to support and insist on this quality of life in society at large. It cannot therefore ignore or remain indifferent to groups and forces that encourage upright living, for to this virtue the Confessions ascribe the words of Aristotle: "Neither the evening star nor the morning star is more beautiful than righteousness." [33]

In addition to teaching the specific requirements of the Moral Law, the church has the task of sharpening the conscience of its individual members to develop a greater respect and a higher degree of obedience on the part of each Christian. For this reason St. Paul appealed to the Christians in Rome that they be subject "for the sake of conscience" (Rom. 13:5). Their consciences were much better informed and directed than those of their pagan contemporaries, and so he could appeal to them on this basis too.

Finally, the church must constantly insist on the essential distinction between the church and the state. This may not include everything that Jefferson's metaphor of the "wall of separation" was intended to imply, and yet the church may never fail to be alert to the tendency of power to feed on itself. No institution can be more sensitive to this issue than that people to whom God has revealed the full dimensions of the cosmic conflict being waged behind and above the realm of events as we see them and as we live them.

At the same time the church must be conscious of the importance of having governments acknowledge their dependence on the blessing of God. To that end the church will lend all its energies to the task of keeping states from being purely secular institutions in the sense that they ignore the existence of God. And the church will most certainly never grow weary in the task of preventing government from becoming demonic, that is, displacing God by its own claims on the total life of man. For it is as true now as it has always been: "Righteousness exalts a nation, but sin is a reproach to any people." (Prov. 14:34)

LEWIS W. SPITZ, JR., PH. D., associate professor of history at Stanford University, in this chapter evaluates the significance of the Reformation for our thinking about church-state relations. With a brief glance at the medieval framework in which the reformers began their task, he directs attention to the expressions of Martin Luther which bear on our subject. Luther's concepts of the church and the state, while unique in their time, were Pauline in their origin. Few writers have been as clear as Luther in their definitions of authority and the proper understanding of the Two Kingdoms. When it came to organizing his followers for their task in the world, Luther had to settle for something less than he wanted. But his vision was broader and his proposals more complex and hazardous than those of other reformers.

A subsection on the Lutheran confessional writings, prepared by *Arthur Carl Piepkorn*, Ph. D., professor of systematic theology at Concordia Seminary, St. Louis, tells us that the Symbols on this issue "reflect the anticlerical, antipapalist attitude of the empire, specifically of the particularistically more self-conscious evangelical jurisdictions." The Confessions restate the New Testament understanding of the role of political institutions and differentiate sharply between the spheres of the church and the state.

Dr. Spitz continues his analysis of the Reformation with an assessment of the attitudes of Zwingli and Calvin in church-state relations. Calvin's assertion of the obligation of government "to cherish and support the external worship of God, to preserve the pure doctrine of religion, to defend the constitution of the church" led him far beyond Luther in his respect for governmental functions. The intermingling of church and state was frequently in evidence wherever Calvinism took hold.

Chapter 2

IMPACT OF THE REFORMATION
ON CHURCH-STATE ISSUES

Lewis W. Spitz, Jr.

THE REFORMATION LAY midway between the present-day problem of church-state relations and the medieval struggle of the spiritual and temporal powers within Christendom. A man cannot understand the present unless he appreciates fully the impact of the Reformation on today's concepts of church and state. It is equally impossible to understand the Reformation merely in terms of its era without reference to its medieval inheritance. Such is the nature of man in history and history in man, as Goethe so nicely expressed it in *Faust:*

> What you the spirit of the ages call
> Is nothing but the spirit of you all
> Wherein the ages are reflected.

A millennium and a half had rolled by since Christ suffered under Pontius Pilate when Luther made his great stand before the emperor at Worms in what J. A. Froude has described as one of the most magnificent scenes in human history. Between the New Testament epoch and the century of the resurgence of the Gospel lay a long and tortuous struggle of ecclesiastical and temporal rulers for the realization of that relationship most congenial to their own interests and definitions. That story, even briefly told, is highly instructive.

The Medieval Background

During the fourth century the Christian church, persecuted by the state since the days of the apostles, was not only granted toleration by Emperor Galerius in A. D. 311 but in A. D. 381 was even given official status by Emperor Theodosius I, who proscribed paganism.[1] The resulting popular identification of the Christian church with the "Christian" state was a factor of momentous historical importance. It brought with it new prestige for the outward ecclesiastical institution but at tremendous cost to the spiritual integrity of the church.[2]

The reversed historical situation inverted the prevailing theories on the relationship between church and state. St. Augustine justified the state as a check on evil doers and a promoter of relative justice in human society with authority rooted in natural law. The Augustinians of the Carolingian period, however, understood the term justice, *iustitia*, as righteousness in the theological sense and came to the congenial conclusion that the state is duty-bound to support the cause of the church.[3] During the Merovingian and Carolingian periods the rulers exercised virtually complete control over the church in their domain. On the local level, too, the processes of economic and political decentralization led to the feudalization of the church and the general acceptance of the proprietary church as a legal construction.[4]

To a large extent it was the momentum gained by the papacy in the effort to counteract secular control over the church on all levels which carried it to the height of its power in the 13th century. The papal reform movement of the 10th and 11th centuries represented an effort to establish the "right order of things in the world," as Pope Gregory VII put it, by which he meant establishing the dominance of the spiritual over the secular sword.[5] The high tide of papal power was reached with the reign of Innocent III (d. A. D. 1216), who considered himself the true emperor of Christendom. By the time of Boniface VIII, who made extravagant claims for the supremacy of the spiritual over the temporal power in his bull *Unam Sanctam*, A. D. 1302, papal power was largely spent. The so-called Babylonian captivity, when the papal see was transferred from Rome to Avignon, was followed by an even greater catastrophe, the papal schism, which divided the allegiance of Europe among the various claimants. The conciliar movement, while healing the schism, failed to check the power within the church of the Roman monarchical episcopate.[6] During the Renaissance the papacy reached the nadir of its moral prestige and influence.

Particularism and the Proprietary Church

Neither in their external boundaries nor in the scope of their political power were the states of the 15th and 16th centuries what the modern sovereign national states have come to be. The old ecumenical institutions, however, the empire and the papacy, had lost status and were being pushed aside in western Europe by the drive toward dynastic consolidation. In Italy and in the Holy Roman Empire there developed on the city-state and territorial level increased cohesiveness and transcendence over feudal limitations parallel to that of the larger kingdoms.

During the 15th century the territorial princes achieved maximum control over the church, a domination which was particularly thorough and effective in the larger states such as Austria, Bavaria, the Palatinate, Brandenburg, and ducal and electoral Saxony.[7] In the imperial cities detailed direction of church affairs by the council paralleled that of the princes in the territories. The current of ill will against the Roman curia ran deep and emerged in the grievances *(gravamina)* of the German nation against the church.[8] If the predominant papal theory of the relationship of ecclesiastical and secular powers had never precisely corresponded to political realities, the discrepancy was never more apparent than on the eve of the Reformation.

LUTHER'S CONCEPTS OF CHURCH AND STATE

The Reformation, one of the most dynamic and revolutionary movements in western history, was basically theological. In its purest essence it represented a resurgence of evangelical Christianity which perforce burst the bonds of the old theology and ecclesiastical institutions. But as an event of first magnitude and great complexity it immediately involved also social, economic, and political forces, effecting fundamental changes in almost all areas of life, including the concepts of church and state.

Luther himself approached the problem of church and state with his usual direct concreteness, not as a theoretician or political philosopher. He was passionately political in his concern for the welfare of the people and the prospering of the cause, but he left behind no treatise on statecraft or commentary on the medieval-Aristotelian ideals of civic life. His own last journey was undertaken through icy storms in the dead of winter to restore amity between two territorial princes, the counts of Mansfeld, who were brothers. His final sermons outspokenly criticize the vices of rulers and the necessity for their obedience to the laws of God. He wrote against "the foolish princes," not a treatise *On the Governance of Princes*.[9] He began with political realities involving specific persons, not with abstractions such as the social contract theory or subjective rights idea. In fact Luther did not use the concept "state" as representing a juridical, political, or social entity above the individual in the modern sense. The term "state" seems to have come into common usage only in the last half of the 16th century via French jurists drawing on Italian sources.[10] Luther as a rule spoke of *Obrigkeit*, or secular authority.

Luther thought of church and state, symbolized for him by Peter and Nero, not as passive associations of men or externally structured institutions but as dynamic, positive, active realms in which the immanent God works through people for good in the world in two ways. In the regime of the church the revealed God *(Deus revelatus)* is at work through the Gospel, converting and redeeming men. "For this reason," he explains, "the church is and is called the kingdom of God, because in it God alone rules, commands, speaks, acts, and is glorified." [11] In the regime of the state the immanent God is at work in the natural order, also through men, establishing peace and prosperity on earth. "For there is no power," he asserts, "which is not ordained, since, as he says here [Romans 13:1], there is no power which is not

of God. . . ." [12] Luther's views of church and state have been
so all-important for the development of the modern world that
they merit special examination.

The Church

"Thank God, a child seven years old knows what the church
is, namely, the holy believers and lambs who hear the voice of
their Shepherd," wrote Luther.[13] Luther restored the apostolic
understanding of the church as the communion of saints *(communio sanctorum, die Gemeinde der Gläubigen).*[14] "The creed
clearly indicates what the church is: a communion of saints, that
is, a company, or assembly, of such people as are Christians and
holy, which is called a Christian, holy company or church. But
this word church *(Kirche)* is too un-German for us now and
does not give the sense or thought one must get from the article,"
he explained.[15] This one Christian church is made up of all true
believers in Christ as Lord and Redeemer. "I believe," he wrote
in 1520, "that there is on earth, through the whole wide world,
no more than one holy, common, Christian Church, which is
nothing else than the congregation, or assembly of the saints, i. e.,
the pious, believing men on earth, which is gathered, preserved,
and ruled by the Holy Ghost, and daily increased by means of
the sacraments and the Word of God." [16] The spiritual kingdom
is a realm of listening *(audire).* To hear the Word in the right
sense means to be governed by God.

Luther asserted that the true church is spiritual in nature
and is to be found wherever men accept the Gospel of Christ:
"Where you hear this Word or see it preached, believed, confessed, and acted upon, do not doubt that there most certainly
is and must be the true, holy, universal church, a holy Christian
people." [17] Since only God knows who has saving faith, the
church is hidden from human eyes, for "no one sees who is sanctified or believes." [18]

Luther gave a precise dogmatic formulation to this episte-
mology of faith in his *Commentary on the Psalms:*

> "The understanding" or "the instruction" *('intellectus' vel 'eru-
> ditio'),* placed in the superscription of psalms, always points to

invisible, spiritual things, things that cannot be seen but can be arrived at only by the intellect and faith. . . . Therefore to understand is not to be taken in the same way in Scripture as in philosophy, whether it be particular or universal, because philosophy always speaks of visible, apparent things or at least of deductions from apparent things. Faith, however, does not have to do with apparent things, nor is it deduced from apparent things; indeed, it is from heaven, since from apparent things rather the opposite of faith is always deduced, as is evident.[19]

Again he explained:

Understanding is from the Lord alone. . . . For this reason such understanding is not that of the philosophers or a natural one, with which we also observe visible things, but it is a theological and freely given one, with which by faith we contemplate things that are not apparent.[20]

The church, Luther made a special point of emphasizing, is not invisible in a platonic sense but in the sense of being abscondite. In 1521 he answered his critics plainly: "When I called the Christian church spiritual congregation, you ridiculed me as if I wished to build a church as Plato a city which nowhere exists. . . ."[21] There could be no church outside of specific persons as Peter, John, Amsdorf, and the like, and yet in the church there is neither Greek nor Jew but Christ alone.[22] Moreover, Luther read St. Paul correctly and did not by his construction separate the soul as spiritual from the body as corporeal. In believing Christians the whole person is active, although absolute ethical perfection is never achieved in this life.[23]

The presence of the true visible church may be known by three signs *(notae):* the preaching of the Word and administration of the sacraments of Baptism and the Eucharist, the very means of grace by which faith is created in men and the church as God's kingdom of grace comes into being. The holy catholic church, no matter how small numerically, exists wherever the Word and sacraments are present as the marks and cause of church life, for "where God's Word is, there the church must exist, and also where Baptism and the Sacrament [of the Eu-

charist] are, there God's people must be and vice versa." [24]
Where a number of Christians are assembled by and around
the Word, they possess the rights of the church.[25]

Every congregation of Christians, Luther taught, in line with
his proclamation of the priesthood of all believers — a phrase
which he first used in 1520 — has the right of church government, control of the preaching office including the administration of the sacraments, ordination, the orders of worship, and
the office of the keys. The congregation even has the right to
depose a minister hostile to the Gospel and install a new one.[26]
"Throughout Christendom things should be so ordered that
every town chooses from amongst its congregation a learned
and pious burgher, commits to him the office of pastor, and sees
that he is given enough for his upkeep," Luther urged.

In 1520 he showed the relationship of the office of the ministry to the priesthood of all believers:

> If they [the clergy] were forced to admit that as many of us
> as have been baptized are all equally priests, as we truly are,
> and that only the ministry was committed to them, but with
> our consent, they would soon know that they have no right to
> rule over us except insofar as we freely agree to it.[27]

In 1523 Luther penned a publication entitled *That a Christian
Assembly or Congregation Has the Right and Power to Judge
All Teaching, to Call All Teachers, Install and Depose Them,
the Basis and Grounds Taken from Holy Scripture.*[28] In his *German Mass and Order of Worship* of 1526 he went the farthest
in expressing the ideal of the church as a congregation of committed Christians which assembles voluntarily.

Deeply impressed with the New Testament pattern of church
life, Luther often used the word bishop *(episcopus)* to designate
the local minister. The minister differs from the layman only in
his office with its powers derived from the congregation, not in
being of a different station *(Amt, not Stand).* One cannot by
putting all the papists together find a single bishop.[29] He held
that the episcopal office grew out of the practice of visitation
in the early church, which was concerned with the purity of
word and life.[30] He wrote:

A pastor exercises the office of the keys, baptizes, preaches, administers the sacrament, and performs other functions not for his own sake but for the sake of the congregation. For he is a servant of the whole congregation, to whom the keys have been given, even though he himself is a knave. For if he does it in place of the congregation, the church does it. If the church does it, God does it.[31]

The congregation, each having its own pastor or bishop, is supreme in deciding on the order of service, and the order of one congregation, such as that of Wittenberg, should in no way be mandatory for any other.[32] When a fellow reformer urged that a Lutheran council should be formed to enforce the common church orders, Luther replied that one congregation should follow the example of the other voluntarily and should not be forced by a council to conform to rules and regulations laid down by it.[33] The church does not therefore derive legal powers from the universal priesthood of believers in the Roman manner of externalized institutionalism but operates with love in the spiritual sphere.

The State

When Luther wrote: ". . . since the time of the apostles the secular sword and authority has never been so clearly described and grandly lauded as by me, which even my enemies must acknowledge," he showed an awareness of the far-reaching implications of his reassertion of the apostolic view of the state, lost from sight during the course of the Middle Ages.[34] Luther, in restoring to the best of his ability the Scriptural definitions of the origin, nature, and goal of the state, came naturally to a reassessment of the relationship of church and state which proved to be of momentous historical importance.

God works in the spiritual realm through the Gospel. Though only faith can perceive, it is also God working in the temporal realm through the secular authority, both originating and dynamically directing the external rule and setting forth its goals (*causa efficiens; causa finalis*).[35] Neither the New Testament nor the *Corpus juris* conceived of the state as a community of citizens

but as authority and power. "Let every soul be subject to the
higher powers," St. Paul admonished.[36] It is therefore not surprising that Luther identified the state as rule and authority
rather than as a people's state *(Volksstaat).*[37] The state has a divinely appointed task, for God did not withdraw after creation
or lapse into indifference *(deus otiosus)*, turning the direction of
affairs over to the autonomous sovereignty of man. Rather, the
rulers in authority are the instruments of God's governance
though He is hidden and disguised in them as in all His creatures, as behind a mask *(larva)*. Every legal order and regime
is therefore under God a passing and historically conditioned
event.

Because the God of creation and redemption works through
persons in authority, good governing is a service to God. In the
Large Catechism Luther speaks of authority under the Fourth
Commandment, which, he observes, as the foundation of the
secular orders, follows directly upon those devoted to God's own
honor.[38] For that reason, in line with a patriarchal family concept, Luther frequently referred to the ruler as a "father and
helper," "gardener and caretaker," "God's official." [39] Service to
the state is the highest calling after service to the Word. Although in the spiritual realm Christ alone rules, in the secular
man cooperates with God, so that Luther can refer to secular
government as "the kingdom of God's left hand." [40] Both realms
have, then, essentially a religious orientation directed toward
a divinely established sanctity.

Reflecting the negative aspect of Augustine's view of the
state, Luther in his early years referred to the state as a great
robbery *(magna latrocinia)*, but from 1520 on at the latest he
consistently considered service to the state a good work.[41] The
earlier line of thought, the "no, but" idea, was derived from the
notion that the state has no real legitimacy except for the fact
that sin and evil make the restraint of the law and the power of
government necessary. But as Luther transcended theologically
the medieval prejudice against creatures *(creaturas)* as carnal
things *(carnalia)* and saw also government as an instrument of

God in the combat with evil, he saw the protective function of the state in a more positive light. In 1526 Luther wrote:

> The other is a secular government through the sword, so that those who do not wish to be made pious and righteous to eternal life through the Word, nevertheless are forced through such secular government to be pious and righteous for the world. And such righteousness He manages through the sword, and although He does not wish to reward such righteousness with eternal life, nevertheless He wants to have it so that peace among men be maintained, and He rewards it with temporal good. . . . Thus God Himself is the Founder, Lord, Master, Promoter, and Rewarder of both kinds of righteousness [i. e., *iustitia civilis* and *iustitia actualis*]. It is not a matter of human order or power but a purely divine thing.[42]

Luther could therefore praise the state as a good thing:

> It [worldly government] is a glorious divine ordinance and an excellent gift of God, who has established and instituted it and wants to have it maintained as something that men can certainly not do without. If there were none, no one could live because of other men: one would devour the other as the brute beasts do one another. . . . Do you not think that if birds and beasts could speak and would see secular government among humans, they would say, "O you dear people, you are not men but gods compared with us. How safe you sit, live, and have everything, while we are never safe from one another for an hour as to life, shelter, or food. Woe to your unthankfulness!" [43]

Satan is behind the evil which good government must combat, and he it is also who corrupts men in government so that as members of the kingdom of Satan *(regnum diaboli)* they misuse the sword and inflict suffering and injustice on their subjects.[44] Dishonest or ineffective rule is therefore a serious sin against God. Every subject should strive for good citizenship in following valid laws. If, however, the regime sets up laws contrary to the love of neighbor, he is bound, according to the apostle, to obey God rather than man (Acts 5:29), and withholding of obedience to the government is demanded. On the basis of his conception of natural reason, his Christological understanding, and specific Scriptural references (especially the classic reference, Rom. 13:1), Luther rejected the idea of active resistance of Christians toward constituted authority except for such "wonder men" or "heroes" as have a special divine vocation and commission to undertake a revolution against injustice, as Samson in his day.[45] It is better for a Christian to endure evil than to resist it. One of his favorite texts was: "Put not your trust in princes" (Ps. 146:3). At the same time he frequently observed that "changing a government was one thing, improving it another." Luther himself from May 1529 to late in 1530 refused to sanction the resistance of Elector John to the emperor, and in the end he yielded only when the jurists convinced him it was permissible for the estates to resist authority on the basis of positive imperial law. He had himself in his most critical hour at Worms withstood the temptation to head a popular national resistance to Rome. "I did nothing; the Word did and achieved everything," he reflected later. "If I had wanted to start trouble, I could have brought all Germany into a great bloodbath. Yes, I could have begun such a game at Worms that the emperor himself would not have been safe. But what would that have been? A fool's game! I did nothing but left it all up to the Word." [46]

Nevertheless, if the government overreaches itself and tyrannically interferes in matters of faith, the Christian is conscience-bound to disobey. "You should not approve of your adversary's sin but warn and rebuke him. . . . For thus you save your conscience," Luther admonished. Whoever remains silent makes himself an accomplice.[47] Ministers bear a special responsibility as public spokesmen in the Christian assembly. "There are lazy and useless preachers who do not denounce the evils of the princes and lords, some because they do not even notice them. . . . Some even fear for their skins and worry that they will lose body and goods for it. They do not stand up and be true to Christ." [48] Luther himself constantly urged rulers to moderation and equity, for whoever cannot "look between his fingers" cannot rule well.[49] He named names.

The Christian and Authority

If the secular rule, then, is an instrument of power and restraint, what is its relevance for the Christian? Laws are necessary, for the "mason must have a law, so that he does not take an ell for a half; a shoemaker has a law, so that he does not make a child a man's shoe. . . . But how do such laws affect spirit and conscience? Also the secular authority has law, so that one does not harm the other in property, honor, and body; but this does not say that the conscience is thereby well governed for God." [50] Luther explained: "All who are not Christians belong to the kingdom of this world, or under the law. For since few believe and a minority lives in Christian manner, therefore, that they may not resist the evil, yes, not themselves do evil, God provided for them besides the Christian estate and God's kingdom also another kingdom and made them subject to the sword." [51] In one of his finest passages Luther spelled this idea out in clearest terms:

> If all the world were composed of real Christians, that is, true believers, no prince, king, lord, sword, or law would be needed. For what were the use of them, since Christians have in their hearts the Holy Spirit, who instructs them and causes them to wrong no one, to love everyone, willingly and cheerfully to suffer injustice and even death from everyone. Where every wrong is suffered and every right is done, no quarrel, strife, trial, judge, penalty, law, or sword is needed. Therefore, it is not possible for the secular sword and law to find any work to do among Christians, since of themselves they do much more than its laws and doctrines can demand. . . . A man would be a fool to make a book of laws and statutes telling an apple tree how to bear apples and not thorns, when it is able by its own nature to do this better than man with all his books can define and direct.[52]

The problem is that there are so few Christians and that Christians themselves in this life do not achieve perfect holiness of life. Luther wrote realistically:

> The world and the great crowd is and remains unchristian, even though they are all baptized and are called Christians.

> For the Christians as the saying goes live far from one another.
> Therefore it is impossible to have a common Christian govern-
> ment over the whole world, indeed, even over a single country
> or a large number of people. For the wicked are always more
> numerous than the pious. Therefore, to try to rule a whole
> land or the world with the Gospel would be like a shepherd
> putting into one stall wolves, lions, eagles, and sheep, letting
> them mingle freely, and saying to them, "Now feed and be
> pious and peaceful among yourselves. . . ." [53]

Christians are rare birds, hence there is "scarcely one true Christian among thousands." For this reason law is necessary, and
although for the Christian as Christian the law is a thing of indifference, yet for the sake of the neighbor the Christian submits
to the government, even as he visits a sick person, not to become
sick himself but to help him to become well again.[54] The government is useful to the church indirectly by maintaining the
external conditions for peaceful existence, just as the church
serves the temporal rule indirectly in producing subjects of goodwill and character.[55]

The Christian, Luther felt strongly, should be politically active, serving, helping, furthering the government wherever possible. In so acting he is doing the Lord's work.

> For all our work — in the field, garden, city, house, in war,
> in governing — what else is it to God but such child's play
> through which God wishes to give His gifts in the field, in the
> home, and everywhere? They are our Lord God's masks
> through which He wishes to remain hidden and yet do all. . . .
> God bestows all good things, but you must take hold and seize
> the bull by the horns; that is, you must do the work and thereby
> give God the opportunity and a disguise.[56]

Luther's social ethics demanded as a matter of conscience the
maximum necessary and possible contribution of the individual
to the affairs of good government.

The individual owes military service for the defense of the
homeland and the just cause, Luther believed, but never in the
case of aggressive or even preventive wars, which could never
be considered just. He chided the Renaissance popes who not

only stirred up hatred for the Turks but also undertook to organize armies and gather fleets which they planned to lead —
all in the name of Christ. Luther said the Christian must avoid
joining a crusading army as he would the devil. When the Christian cannot decide whether a cause is just or if he lacks information, he should give his own government the benefit of the
doubt. In no circumstances, cost what it may, can the Christian
serve against conscience in an unjust war.[57] The individual conscience must bear the burden of decision where the divine will
is known, for "neither the pope nor parents nor the emperor has
this title: I AM THE LORD THY GOD."[58] The law of love
must therefore be the guiding principle for the individual Christian citizen.

The law of love is not restricted to private citizens, however,
but should be the rule also for men in authority. The judge and
the soldier alike act in love by protecting the neighbor's life and
body. He is the best judge who fears a higher judge, Luther
believed. Love of neighbor, then, must be the motivation also
for public service:

> Here you ask further whether the policemen, hangmen, jurists,
> counselors, and lesser officials can also be Christians and have
> a blessed estate. I answer: If the government and its sword
> are a divine service . . . then also that must also be divine
> service which the government needs to wield the sword. . . .
> Therefore, when [the authorities] do this, not with the in-
> tention of seeking their own ends but only of helping to main-
> tain the law and power with which the wicked are restrained,
> there is no peril in it for them, and they may follow it like any
> other pursuit and use it as a means of support. . . . For . . .
> love of neighbor seeks not its own, considers not how great
> or small but how profitable and how needful for the neighbor
> or the community the actions are.[59]

Even though the law of love should be the guiding principle
for men in authority, the state is for Luther not in itself a Christian authority. The legitimate rule of non-Christian governments
is as surely God's ordinance as that of any government within
Christendom with at least nominally Christian rulers, for God

as the Lord of history can use also virtuous rational pagans to combat evil in the world. "For we surely see," wrote Luther, "that God scatters the most glorious knowledge and worldly rule and kingdoms among the heathen, just as He does the dear sun and rain to serve over and among the godless. . . . So He calls such worldly government among the heathen His own ordinance and creation." [60] Such non-Christian rulers may in their way, in fact, be wiser than the children of light:

> For God is a mild, rich Lord who scatters much gold, silver, riches, principalities, and kingdoms among the heathen as if they were chaff or sand. So He also scatters among them lofty reason, wisdom, languages, rhetoric, so that His dear Christians look like plain children, fools, and beggars next to them.[61]

Thus, in contrast to the high theory of medieval papalism which had to view non-Christian governments as illegitimate in not being subservient to the spiritual sword, Luther saw them as sanctioned by God to serve temporal ends.

Since, however, the rulers should govern in accord with the law of love, ideally a true Christian should make the best ruler. Even though secular authority rests on reason and not on faith as such, unbelief and superstition are damaging to the state in the long run. Luther exclaimed: "Would to God they [the worldly rulers] would all be Christians or that there would have to be no prince who is not a Christian!" [62] The ideal ruler, whose regime is based on an intelligent application of the law of love, would look to Christ as his "mirror of the prince" *(speculum principis):*

> He must be concerned about his subjects and thoroughly devote himself to this. . . . He should picture Christ to himself and say, "Behold, Christ, the highest Prince, came and served me. . . . Therefore I will do the same, not seek my own advantage at my subjects' expense but their advantage. . . ." And so a prince should in his heart empty himself of his power and authority and be concerned about the need of his subjects, dealing with it as if it were his own need. For this is what Christ did for us, and these are the proper works of Christian love.[63]

On specific state problems the minister should not try to dictate the solution to the ruler any more than he should try to teach a tailor how to make a suit, but he should constantly admonish him to act like a Christian. Thus he will influence the quality of the decisions made.[64] In his famous treatise *On Secular Authority (Von weltlicher Oberkeit . . .)*, 1523, Luther gives a good example of this type of admonition. The ruler should (1) fear God; (2) show love to his subjects, keeping his eye on Christ as an example of love, and help widows and orphans; (3) be cautious about human counselors; and (4) practice equity (the Aristotelian ἐπιείκεια, *Billigkeit*, fairness) and moderation toward evildoers.[65]

Divine Right, Natural Law, and Human Reason

Just as Luther opposed every description of the state as an instrument of naked power devoid of morality, love of fellowman, and responsibility to God, so he rejected all purely naturalistic accounts of the origin of government and its legal foundation. In his commentary on Ps. 82, Luther discussed this problem:

> Now, because this is not a matter of human will or devising, but God Himself appoints and preserves all authority, and if He no longer held it up, it would all fall down, even though all the world held it fast — therefore it is rightly called a divine thing, a divine ordinance. And such persons are rightly called divine, godlike, or gods. . . . He calls Nineveh "a city of God." For He has made, and makes, all communities. He still brings them together, feeds them, lets them grow, blesses and preserves them. . . . For what have we, and what has all the world, that does not come unceasingly from Him? But even though experience ought to teach us this, He has to say it in plain words, and openly confess and boast that the communities are His. . . . All the worldly-wise do not know at all that a community is God's creature and His ordinance. They have no other thought about it than that it has come into being by accident, through people holding together and living side by side in the same way murderers and robbers and other wicked bands gather to disturb the peace and the ordinance of God; these are the devil's congregations.[66]

If communities are of divine ordinance, then also the good positive laws of the community are rooted in law inherent in human nature, having a theonomic, divinely obligating character, that is, natural law.

From the time of the Stoic philosophers to the end of the 18th century the concept of natural law in political theory was generally understood to mean a body of principles which, resting on a divinely implanted endowment of human nature, underlie all acceptable ethical precepts, just laws, and sound political institutions.[67] In accordance with this long tradition Luther, too, thought of natural law as unwritten law whose requirements lay imbedded in reality itself. There is apart from revelation a moral order of nature, special moral sense *(synteresis)* in man, for God has placed into the human conscience a knowledge of natural law and has established a hidden inner law in the historical forms of human society. The imprint of God's eternal rightness *(ius divinum)* finds expression in natural law *(lex naturae)*, by which men everywhere can judge right and wrong according to their measure of understanding. St. Paul's discussion of the Gentiles' knowledge of moral law, Rom. 2:15, was the key passage for this conception also for Luther, fixing the moral responsibility of all mankind. Natural law and natural reason form the heart and source of all written law.[68]

The natural-law theory of Luther has a strongly religious tone. He was not so concerned, in spite of his connection with the historical natural-law tradition, with natural law *(lex naturalis)* or the law of the nations *(ius gentium)* as with that basic law of God, the law of love. Thus one should always act in such a way, he admonished, "that love and natural law always prevail. For when you judge according to love, you will easily decide and judge all things without any lawbooks. But when you ignore love and natural law, you will never manage to please God, even though you have devoured all the lawbooks and jurists." [69]

The epitome of natural law, Luther held, is purely and simply: "Thou shalt love thy neighbor as thyself." [70] This golden rule is central in the Sermon on the Mount (Matt. 7:12). Luther insisted, moreover, that the precepts of the Sermon were valid

demands of the law on all men and not merely evangelical counsels for the spiritually more advanced, as the medieval church
had come to interpret them. Love is the fulfilling of the natural
and moral law: "Therefore also Paul (Rom. 13) comprehends
all the commandments of Moses in love, which natural law naturally teaches: 'Thou shalt love thy neighbor as thyself.' " [71] All
the orders of society are to work harmoniously together in love
to the glory of God, for power itself is an instrument of love.

For Luther natural law was not itself a codex of laws but
rather the source rooted in reality from which all positive laws
(leges) and civil rights *(iura civilia)* are derived.[72] Luther considered the Decalog to be the best formulation of the general
precepts of natural law related to and derived from the law of
love.[73] The Mosaic ceremonial law, on the other hand, he held
to be the positive law of the Jews, as the Saxon law *(Sachsen-
spiegel)* was for the Germans; a better positive law, as a matter
of fact, than Roman law, which catered too much to selfish interests, placing property rights over human rights. Though individuals generally know and obey the law under which they live,
positive law is a condition law which only in a very relative way
reflects unchanging natural law and should be publicly criticized
and constantly improved upon.[74]

In the realm of civil affairs the highest rational gifts of man
are essential in the formulation of laws and their administration.
Reason is the "empress of worldly rule." "It is necessary," wrote
Luther, "for men to rule also with reason and not with power
alone, as is already now the case, for sheer power without reason
cannot last long and keeps the subjects in a state of everlasting
hatred against authority, as all history loudly testifies." [75]

Only especially gifted rulers and judges, "wonder men," are
equipped by God with the lofty endowments necessary for the
difficult task of legislating and executing laws. Luther saw the
problem:

> The great error is that everyone imagines that natural law exists
> inside his own head. . . . For if natural law and reason were
> to be found in all heads that resemble human heads, then fools,
> children, and women could rule and wage war as well as David,

Augustus, or Hannibal. . . . Indeed, all men would have to
be alike and none rule over the others. What a turmoil and
wild state of affairs would result! [76]

Luther did not hold the natural orders of society to be immutable, but he believed that with reason effectively employed,
positive law and social relationships can be constantly improved.
Without reason and morality, on the other hand, where men
rule without regard for natural law, there ruin can overtake the
state and, as history shows, has often done so. Luther himself
was quick to chide the folly, false pride, and unreasonableness
of the rulers of his day and their legal advisers. A good prince
is "a rare bird," and it takes the virtue of a Hercules or a David
inspired by God to resist the corrupting influence of power. [77]
Princes are prone to forget God and despise their subjects. In
a typical passage Luther thundered:

> But if a lord or prince does not take this his office and duty
> to heart and thinks he is prince, not for the sake of his subjects
> but because of his beautiful, blond hair, as if God had made
> him a prince so that he should rejoice in his power, property,
> and honor, take pleasure and pride in these things and rely on
> them — such a one belongs among the heathen, indeed, he is
> a fool. For such a prince would start a war over an empty
> nut and think of nothing how to satisfy his wantonness. God
> keeps such a prince in check by the fact that others have fists
> too and that other people live on the other side of the hill too. [78]

A ruler in name may become a monster in deed. Luther found
it necessary to remind the emperor himself that he was a mere
"mortal bag of worms." [79] That it is God who sits in judgment
also on the wicked rulers of men Luther makes plain in a characteristically colorful passage:

> For such godless people are so sure and secure in their own
> wisdom as if our Lord God must sit idle and not come into
> their clever counsels. And so He has to chat for a while with
> His angel Gabriel and says, "Friend, what are the clever ones
> planning in that council chamber that they won't take us into
> their counsel? Perhaps they're planning to build another Tower
> of Babel. . . . Dear Gabriel, go down, and take Isaiah with

you and give them a little reading in through the window and say, 'With seeing eyes shall ye not see, with hearing ears shall ye not hear, with understanding hearts shall ye not understand. Make your Plan and nothing will come . . . for mine is not only the Plan but the deed.' " [80]

The Relationship of Church and State

In modern America the constitutional provision for the separation of church and state has the almost unanimous support of those who are concerned about preserving the independence of the church from political domination and of the state from ecclesiastical interference. Though indirectly and belatedly, this liberal conception owes much to Luther's insistence on the essential dissimilarity of the spiritual and temporal authorities and the need to distinguish them and their areas of activity carefully in practice. The difference between them was one of the most basic in his theology. He made his first clear reference to this distinction in his *Sermon on the Virtue of Excommunication* in 1518.[81] He expressed the need for the clear distinction of the two realms in his writing of 1523, *On Secular Authority, to What Extent It Should Be Obeyed*, his closest approximation to a political treatise:

> Unbearable loss follows where it [the state] is given too much room, and it is likewise not without loss where it is too restricted. Here it punishes too little, there it punishes too much. It is more bearable, however, that it offend on the side of punishing too little, since it is always better to permit a knave to live than to put a good man to death, inasmuch as the world still has and must have knaves but has few good men.
>
> In the first place, it is to be noted that the two classes of Adam's children, the one in the kingdom of God under Christ, the other in the kingdom of the world under civil authority . . . have two kinds of laws. For every kingdom must have its laws and statutes, and no kingdom or regime can stand without law, as daily experience shows. Temporal government has laws which extend no farther than to person and property and what is external on earth; for God cannot and will not permit anyone to rule over the soul of man but Himself. Therefore where

temporal power presumes to give laws to the soul, it meddles in God's rule and only misleads and destroys the souls. We wish to make this so clear that men may comprehend it, in order that our noblemen, the princes and bishops, may see what fools they are when with their laws and commands they want to force people to believe thus and so. When someone imposes a human law on the soul, that it must believe this or that as he prescribes, there is assuredly no word of God for it. . . . Therefore it is utter folly to command a man to believe the church, the fathers, the councils even though there be no word of God for it. . . . And finally, this is the meaning, as St. Peter says: "We ought to obey God rather than men" [Acts 5:29]. Thereby he also clearly sets a limit to temporal authority.[82]

In his *Commentary on the Gospel of St. John* (1529) Luther reiterated this distinction:

The secular kingdom extends over the rascals and bad boys; the spiritual kingdom extends over the Christians and children of God. The emperor is a rascally landlord, for in his kingdom and house he has only rascals and mischievous boys. Christ, however, is a King of the pious, for in His kingdom He has only Christians.[83]

The two treatises *On Secular Authority* and *Whether Soldiers Can Be Saved* could give the erroneous impression that the secular authority is for the "bad men" and the spiritual for the "good." In reality, however, a Christian never achieves perfection in this life but remains at the same time a righteous man and a sinner (*simul iustus et peccator*). As sinner the Christian, too, is under the enforced restrictions of secular law, and Luther often emphasizes the contemporaneity of both authorities over one and the same man.[84] Insofar as a man acts under the compulsion of Christian love, the restraints of the power of the sword (*potestas gladii*) are not necessary for him.

In his distinction between the secular and spiritual power, Luther was much influenced by Occam, who held that the power of the pope related only to spiritual things, and so far as influence over secular affairs was concerned, he had only the right to support himself and maintain the means for carrying out his official acts in the church.[85] The apostles themselves had made no presumptuous claims to secular authority but had rather stressed obedience to the secular powers. Luther frequently asserted emphatically how pernicious the confusion of the two rules was. In 1534, for example, he wrote:

> I must always drum in and rub in, drive in and hammer home such a distinction between these two kingdoms, even though it is written and spoken so often that it is annoying. For the cursed devil himself does not cease to cook and brew these two kingdoms into each other. In the devil's name the secular lords always want to teach and instruct Christ how He should run His church and the spiritual government. So also the false persons and factious spirits, not in God's name, always want to teach and instruct how one should order the secular government. . . . But it is a confusing and mingling of secular and spiritual government when those sublime spirits, or wiseacres, in a dictatorial and domineering fashion want to change and correct the civil law, though they have no directive or authority to do so, either from God or from men. The same is true when spiritual and secular princes and lords in a dictatorial and domineering fashion want to change and correct God's Word, that they themselves say what is to be preached and taught, though this is as much forbidden for them as for the lowest beggar.[86]

This passage neatly summarizes the charge against the three chief offenders: the papists, the enthusiasts, and the secular lords.

"Under the papacy," chided Luther, "there was such a marvelous confusion that a man did not know what was corporal and what spiritual." [87] The papacy with its pretensions to power as a "more perfect state" had during the Middle Ages perverted the spiritual vocation of the church by entanglements in economic, political, and juridical affairs not properly its sphere, even in Christ's name humbling emperors and making war on the Turks. The priests and bishops had made themselves intermediaries between God and man instead of serving as messengers of Christ. The result was to darken the light of the Gospel and destroy men's souls and conversely to rob the secular authority

of the honor and respect due it under God. The papal pretensions were rationalized and justified by the canonists and scholastics in the later Middle Ages. For Thomas Aquinas the spiritual
rule was as much of a governance *(gubernatio)* as the temporal
and had indirect power in temporal things *(potestas indirecta in
temporalia)* and even a divine right *(ius divinum)* to interfere.

The enthusiasts, that is, the spiritualists and sectaries, the
"new jurists and sophists," seemed to Luther to have fallen into
the same error in their own way. By withdrawing from society
they injured secular authority in not participating in government
or serving society as a Christian should. They insisted on common property, forbade oaths, government, law courts, protection and defense, sometimes even abandoned wife and children
and thus set up false good works and holiness. What they began
as a misuse of evangelical freedom ended up as unmitigated
legalism. The revolutionaries exploited the Gospel as a slogan
for material gain for themselves. Münzer, Zwingli, and others
seized the sword and shed blood in God's name. The antinomians
by eliminating the Law destroyed the basis of social life in the
world. The enthusiasts, then, seemed to Luther to err on two
accounts: demanding sheer mercy in the worldly kingdom while
fanatically introducing wrath into the spiritual kingdom.[88] The
temporal lords, for their part, did great wrong in striving to become masters over the Word of God, deciding what should be
preached and believed, which should not be their province. Like
Lucifer, these tyrants and hypocrites, as Luther called them,
sought to replace God Himself.[89]

Christendom, or God's Two Kingdoms

In defining the relationship of church and state, one leading
medieval theory conceived of the spiritual and secular authorities
as two powers encompassed within a large religious-metaphysical
entity, Christendom *(corpus christianum)*, basically intact, teaching that the body of Christ *(soma Christou* or *corpus mysticum)*
was the church *(ekklesia)*, which belonged as the spiritual
authority to Christendom *(corpus christianum)*, as did the empire *(imperium)* as the chief political authority. This implies

that the Christian people are organized in a Christian state, that is, under Christian authority.[90] The problem is whether such a conception of the relationship of church and state would really have been compatible with Luther's transformed conceptions of the church and of the state.

The representatives of the view that Luther held to the Christendom *(corpus christianum)* idea point mainly to his programmatic *Address to the Christian Nobility*, 1520, and particularly to two statements:

> Christ has not two bodies or two kinds of body, one secular, the other spiritual. He is one Head and has one body. . . . Secular authority has become a member of the Christian body and, although it has a bodily work, nevertheless belongs to the clergy. Therefore its work should proceed unhindered in all parts of the whole body, punishing and carrying on wherever guilt deserves or necessity demands, regardless of pope, bishop, priest, they may threaten or excommunicate as they will.[91]

In the same year in *On the Papacy in Rome* he wrote of Christendom as if it were a body whose soul is the invisible church and whose frame is the external Christendom.[92] It is possible, therefore, to interpret the *Address* as being directed to the secular authority over Christendom. The princes as Christian authority, in their totality as the Christian nobility of the nation, should care for the improvement of the Christian estates. According to this interpretation the spiritual as well as the secular authority must be seen as a function of the Christian commonwealth.

An easy escape from the problem would be to assume that in his writings of 1520 Luther had not yet freed himself from the Christendom concept, just as he still retained a third sacrament. The suggestion has in fact been made that Luther naively at first thought in terms of a Christian authority, but after the great disillusionment in 1521 began to think of secular authority in less complimentary terms. His definitive position would in this context have to be formed in later years. A close examination of the *Address* itself, however, reveals that Luther is using the term Christendom for the spiritual body of which

Christ is the Head, the communion of saints, the church with its priesthood of all believers. The authorities are addressed as members of this body and are being reminded of the general priesthood (*sacerdotium*) of their baptism and are being urged to exercise their ministry (*ministerium*) by summoning a council and preventing the financial exploitation by the pope. The nobility is to act, not as a secular sword but as fellow Christians in behalf of all believers.[93] Luther, of course, thought of Christendom as opposed to the lands of the Turks, for example, but there he had in mind the unity of people with a common religious and cultural heritage, not a union of two organisms within a higher one.

That some of Luther's terminology was borrowed from the scholastics or was Biblical and patristic, common also to them (e. g., *pax mundi, pax aeterna, regnum corporale, civile*, etc.) has contributed to the misconception that he repristinated the medieval pattern or merely "spiritualized" it somewhat. But the intention of the canonists and scholastics had naturally been to fit the secular authority into a church-dominated unity. Unlike the Thomistic principle of unity, Luther's concern was to differentiate the areas of competence of the two rules. The unity of all life which Luther saw transcended a mere concept of a spiritual-secular, religious-metaphysical entity, Christendom. The bond of unity was to be found in God's own direct sovereign rule in power and grace. Luther's dynamic view of creation and redemption, of God's immanence in both realms, though in the one He is concealed behind a mask and in the other revealed in Christ, in contrast to the scholastic transcendent ontological emphasis, meant that the same divinity was present in both rules, preventing them from becoming two antagonistic spheres. "Their order and power are good things and are from God," Luther declared also of earthly rulers.[94] Luther restored a theonomous view of the world order. Let God be God!

THE ORGANIZATION OF LUTHERANISM

Though the church is not of the world, it is in the world (*ecclesia est in civitate*, sighed Melanchthon). The historical developments in church-state relationships arrived at during the first two thirds of the 16th century proved to be basic for all later times. The bishops of the old church had failed in their duty toward the church, as the *gravamina* of the Diet of Augsburg in 1518 amply showed. In his treatise *Of the Papacy at Rome* and his *Sermon on Good Works* Luther sharply depicted the plight of the church. During the necessary disturbance of the first turbulent years of the Reformation nothing could be gained by way of peace and order in the church.

It was to be expected on the basis of the growth in power of the territorial princes and of the councils, particularly in the south German and Swiss cities, that the temporal rulers would be immediately concerned with establishing suitable conditions within the church. Interestingly enough, it was the Catholic princes of southern Germany who came to this conclusion first under the leadership of the Bavarian councilor Leonhard von Eck. As early as 1522 the dukes of Bavaria received power for the extensive supervision of the clergy, to retain a part of the church's income, to uphold the purity of faith and to defend it against heretics, and to maintain external order in the church. The Catholic princes at Regensburg and Dessau organized alliances, but soon also the evangelical princes were stirring.

In his *Address to the Christian Nobility* Luther turned to Christian men in authority to act for the good of the church. The nobles should end annates, pallium payments, and other abuses. As secular rulers they were to act in the public interest by ending "Roman greed, the greatest thief and robber." In such material things the secular power was no more subject to the spiritual authority than tailors, shoemakers, or people of other callings were. But as members of the body of Christ and the universal priesthood of all believers the Christian nobility had the duty of calling a council in order to rescue Christendom, just as every baptized Christian has the right to call such a council; for before he can speak to a congregation, which is every Christian's right, he must first summon it together. Regarding a council and reforms of doctrine and church practice the princes should act as "fellow Christians, fellow priests, fellow clergy, fellow lords in all things, and should give free rein to their office and work, which they have received from God above everyone, wherever it is necessary and useful," for no one can act "so well" as they.[95] Similarly Luther later urged the council of Altenburg to act on the basis of "two kinds of duties, namely, for the sake of the civil government and in behalf of brotherly Christian love." [96] Luther never referred to the princes as "the highest bishop" *(summus episcopus),* but rather always only as an "emergency bishop" *(Notbischof)* who should act because of the need of the church and because of the lack of others with initiative and ability. Referring to his ideal of the congregational form of church life, Luther from first to last complained, "But I do not yet have available the persons necessary to accomplish it; nor do I see many who strongly urge it." [97]

There was, then, practically no alternative to the course of organization which the evangelical churches followed. In October 1525 the Prince Elector John Frederick of Saxony and Landgrave Philipp of Hessia reached an agreement for mutual defense, and early the following year the first league of evangelical princes came into being, the League of Gotha and Torgau. The growth of self-conscious leadership vis-a-vis the Catholic estates, evidenced that year at Speyer, found its counterpart in the concern for the church at home. Both the social disturbances of the mid-twenties and the rapid success of the Reformation movement added to the urgency for speedy positive action in the organization of the evangelical church.

With the destruction of the hierarchical power structure and the authority of canon law, a number of alternate solutions to the problem of church organization were possible. One pattern was set by the sectaries who withdrew from the state, organized a church and community of their own, set up legalistic standards of conformity, and maintained a congregational form of government. Another was to create for the church, comprised of elect and enthusiastic members, a new structure of "evangelical" church law and develop an organization on "the New Testament model," the plan attempted in due course by the church in Geneva.

Luther's vision was broader, more complex and hazardous, but not without merit, even though the historical reality tended with time to fall farther and farther behind his ideal. He wished to have a church of "true Christians" which, as a community of like-minded men dwelling in love, needed no hard and fast external "confessional church" *(Bekenntniskirche)*. At the same time he did not wish to abandon society to purely secular amorality but worked for the interpenetration of the whole social order with religious ethics through the activity of an official church for all the people *(Volkskirche)*. This church with its mixture of true believers and hypocrites needed some form of church government. For the establishment of a new order the help of the Christians in authority was needed. If a more radical approach was possible in the Protestant cities of southern Germany, no other plan than the one put into effect suggests itself even in retrospect for the sprawling territories of northern Germany.

Luther's first reference to a plan for an official visitation of the churches was in a letter of October 1525 to Elector John regarding the use of church properties and the support of ministers.[98] In his treatise *The German Mass and Order of Divine Public Service*, 1526, Luther offered a sample of good church order but emphasized that the adoption of the evangelical confession was not to be forced. When Luther was at last convinced that for lack of any other means of self-help the assistance *(Nothilfe)* of the princes was necessary, he acted without considering the far-reaching results, for these he left to God. The visitation undertaken by an electoral commission at Luther's suggestion revealed the wretched condition of the churches in Saxony. Elector John's *Instruction (Instruction und Befelch . . .)* of 1527 showed some regard for Luther's distinction between the spiritual and secular authorities in providing for four visitors: two for secular and two for spiritual purposes. The visitors were instructed not to bind anyone as to what he should hold and believe; nevertheless they should prevent sectarian and separatistic tendencies as well as other disturbances, so that no one dare "teach otherwise, preach or administer the sacrament and ceremonies otherwise than according to God's Word." [99]

Even though the next (1528) *Instruction (Unterricht der Visitatorn an die Pfarhern . . .)* did not assume the character of a legal document drawn up by the Elector's jurists, there was danger that the Elector's role would be misunderstood and abused. So Luther on request provided the Introduction *(Vorrhede)* to the 1528 *Instruction* and attempted to put the office of visitation in the right perspective, relating that he had urged "that His Electoral Grace out of Christian love (for he is not responsible as secular overlord) and for God's sake for the good of the Gospel and for the benefit and welfare of the distressed Christians in His Electoral Grace's land, graciously would order and ordain some competent persons for this office." This thought is reemphasized throughout the Introduction:

> Although we cannot promulgate this as a stringent command, lest we be setting up new papal decretals, but as a historical account as well as a testimony and confession of our faith, yet we hope that all pious, peace-loving pastors . . . will willingly, without compulsion, submit to such visitation in love and together with us peaceably live according to it till God the Holy Ghost originates something better through them or through us. . . . For although His Electoral Grace is not commanded to teach and to rule spiritually, nevertheless he is responsible, as secular ruler, to maintain things so that dissension, factions, and rebellion do not arise among the subjects.[100]

Clearly Luther's intent in the visitation program was entirely consonant with his basic views concerning the relationship of the temporal and spiritual rules. Three basic emphases are discernible in the Introduction: (1) the great need of the church calls for emergency action; (2) the prince is to act as a Christian in brotherly love; (3) the visitation is to be only a temporary measure until an improved situation and a better plan evolved. Luther to his very end referred to the princes as mere emergency bishops, nothing more. He shared Spalatin's misgivings and also opposed the development of the consistories and of the superintendents in the cities, by 1541 conceding to them the right to handle only external matters. Luther very possibly looked to a new form of evangelical bishops in time, *de iure humano,* free from direct dependence on temporal rulers.[101] Possibly but for his foreshortened eschatology Luther might have acted more radically against the princes to realize his ideal.

The Saxon pattern of church organization was adopted to a great extent by Lutheran princes in northern Germany, just as the church organization of the cities usually followed the example of Wittenberg.[102] Melanchthon and Bugenhagen, the Wittenberg city pastor influential in providing constitutions for many north German cities and assisting in the Danish Reformation, had to bear the brunt of the administration. In working out the church orders and the constitutional briefs for various territories, planning the new reformed educational systems, and arranging visitations, Melanchthon consistently referred to the prince as the preeminent member of the church *(praecipuum membrum ecclesiae),* shifting ground gradually to the prince's right not as a fellow Christian acting in love but as the possessor of power with the most prestige in a hierarchy of dignity rooted in natural law. Melanchthon increasingly associated the church with the visible church of the called *(coetus vocatorum).* He conceived of the civil righteousness as righteousness in the political sphere and was far less critical of the secular power than was Luther, dreading nothing so much as the charge of sedition. Central for Melanchthon was the idea of *societas,* related to the Romanists' *societas christiana,* a concept congenial to theocracy and portending evil for Luther's proclamation of the dissimilarity and differences between the two rules.[103] The territorial bureaucracy, abetted by Melanchthon, Bugenhagen, Amsdorf, and lesser men, prepared the way for the princely consistories through their theological-juridical formulas and helped to create an evangelical church law.

This tendency can be most clearly discerned in Martin Bucer of Strasbourg, who was highly influential in giving a Lutheran cast to the Protestantism of south German cities and territories. The Strasbourg church order of 1534, essentially his, practically turned the confession of the church into an official legal document, forbidding any other teaching on threat of expulsion — a threat directed against the radical sectaries — and introducing the power of the state into the church. That Protestant state and Protestant church were growing closer together is evident from Bucer's lines: "The blessed authorities must not merely use religion as a means to outward peace but should let religion itself be their end." By the year of Calvin's conversion Protestantism had already moved far in the direction of the Geneva *Ordinances* which were yet to come. But the institutional order and security of the evangelical church were paid for in precious spiritual coin.

While the German estates struggled to achieve an ecclesiastical order which would provide internal peace and security against the alternate threats from Italy and Spain, vacillating between offensive tactics and defensive bids for toleration, and arrive at a form of church life consonant with the demands of conscience, the lands to the north achieved reformation as a concomitant of national rebirth. There the Reformation came primarily from on top and violated Luther's own principle against conversion except by conviction, but it was aided by a real evangelical resurgence led by heroic Lutheran reformers.

In Denmark under Christian III the Diet of Copenhagen in 1536 introduced Lutheranism as the sole state religion. The king as "highest bishop" *(summus episcopus)* ruled the church directly without an intermediary consistory. With the cooperation of the evangelical bishops and the support of a strong popular movement, he built the church anew. In Norway, as in Iceland, even more political pressure was necessary for the overthrow of the old church, which was not achieved until 1554. The Reformation in Sweden aided the movement for independence from Danish rule. There the secular power of the bishops and political influence of the feudal nobility, from which the upper clergy were often recruited, were sharply curtailed. But there was a greater continuity of episcopal authority in the church and of traditional congregational life. Swedish Lutheranism prospered and made possible a genuine flourishing of the national culture.[104]

THE LUTHERAN SYMBOLS

The Lutheran Symbols[105] on the issue of relations between church and state reflect the anticlerical, antipapalist attitude of the empire, specifically of the particularistically more self-conscious evangelical jurisdictions. The basic articles are: Augsburg Confession XVI; Apology XVI; Small Catechism, "Concerning Civil Government"; Large Catechism, Fourth Commandment, 141, 142, 150. Except for the two catechisms, the Lutheran particular creeds are in their origin formally the confessions of political entities (lords temporal and spiritual; city administrations). This explains the somewhat Erastian accent of these Symbols. The church in the Symbols is empirical as well as spiritual, but the church existed nowhere in the evangelical jurisdictions as an independent entity. The Symbols do not operate with the modern category of "state." Instead they use such terms as *respublica, magistratus, Obrigkeit,* (authority), *Fürsten* (princes), and related concepts.[106] "State" may be adumbrated in the Apology, XVI.[107] In the Symbols government is part of a larger sphere of external activity which includes man's total corporeal, political, economic, and social life.

The Lutheran Symbols criticize as unbiblical, politically perilous, and legalistic the monastic piety of the Middle Ages as well as the enthusiastic spiritualism of the Anabaptists, both of whom depreciated a career in government as a secular and unspiritual kind of life that militated against the Gospel. They note that even the Middle Ages had on occasion recognized that the vocation of government might transcend the vocation to the monastic life. Against the distortions of medieval monasticism, John Wycliffe, and the Anabaptists, the Symbols sanction the right of private property.[108]

All government in the world and all legitimate political institutions and laws are good works which God has created and instituted and through which He continues to work mediately. Christians are to esteem and respect good civil government — like good ecclesiastical government — as one of God's greatest gifts. Government is part of the Law. The authority of civil government derives from the authority that God conferred on parents.[109] On the analogy of marriage and Baptism, government can even be conceived of as having a quasi-sacramental character.[110] The ultimate enemy of good government is Satan.

Governments must establish courts of law, punish criminals (with death if need be), wage war against invaders, sanction the legality of contracts, encourage marriage, regulate commerce, and support education; they may use such lawful means as these ends require. Governors are to perform their duties faithfully, avoid tyranny, insure the usefulness of their regime to land and people, suppress rebellion, preserve the peace, and protect the poor.[111] The administration of government must be flexible and take cognizance of human frailty.

Political institutions are a Biblically approved datum of human experience to which Christians must submit themselves. Christians are bound for God's sake to respect and obey civil authority — even if it be of pagan origin — as far as they can do so without sin.[112] Flight from civic responsibilities is wrong. Christians may avail themselves of the protection and other benefits of civic administration; the "third stage" of admonition is to hale the offender before the courts of the community.[113]

The respective spheres, ends, and means of spiritual and political authority are so different that the former in no way interferes with the latter. The two areas must be differentiated even though both are of divine origin and even when the same person wields both swords.[114]

The thrust of the Symbols is in general to criticize more severely the usurpation of political authority by the hierarchy of the church than the usurpation of ecclesiastical authority by agencies of secular government. Specific forms of intolerable ecclesiastical interference in political affairs include abrogation of laws, prohibition of legitimate obedience, and interference with the processes of law or the discharge of contractual obligations. The Mosaic laws are not to be imposed on contemporary communities.[115] When the clergy excommunicate notorious evil livers, they are not to add civil penalties or invoke the secular power to secure enforcement of the excommunication.

Christians are to conserve existing political institutions as far as they can without contradicting the Christian revelation. They are to intercede for the civil power. Christians may with a good conscience serve as officers of government and discharge all its duties; this is clear from the examples of the saints of the past. The government can properly depend on the church's schools for the education of its functionaries. Where obedience to political authority involves the Christian in disobedience to God's precepts, he must for conscience' sake disobey the former. Article X of the Formula of Concord enjoins disobedience on clergy and layfolk alike when the government seeks to impose intolerable ceremonial legislation. The pulpit is to instruct government in its obligations, and citizens in the requirements of morality. A general council might well concern itself with political and social abuses as religious matters.

As chief members of the church, princes and kings should concern themselves with the church's welfare and see that errors are abolished and consciences healed. The Preface to the Formula of Concord takes as a matter of course the activity of the princes and estates in the preparation of the Formula and the maintenance of the theological peace afterward. Civil government is to compel the clergy to instruct children, and individuals to receive religious instruction.

The Symbols, then, for the most part reflect Luther's own understanding of the concepts of church and state and the nature of their interrelationship. This correspondence was derived in part from the realities of the historical situation and in part from the direct impact of Luther's own thought and teaching. Like Luther, the Symbols do not operate with the modern term "state" as such. They share his opposition to the monastic and radical spiritualist depreciation of service in the government. They see secular authority as one of the realms in which God Himself is active. They maintain Luther's views on obedience and the right of rebellion. They recapitulate his insistence on the difference of the spheres in which state and church operate. The greater concern of the Symbols over hierarchical interference in political affairs and the somewhat more Erastian accent may reflect in part differences between the point of view of Melanchthon and others and the position taken by Luther, and above all the peculiar political circumstances from which the evangelical church was not to be extricated until recent times.

ZWINGLI'S STATE-CHURCHISM

One sociological fact of major importance gave a unique cast to the relationship of church and state in both German and French Switzerland. In the community organization of the late medieval city the political and ecclesiastical congregations were practically coterminous. Just as in the German territories the proprietary church was of long standing, in the cities of southern Germany and Switzerland it was a good old tradition for the city councils to administer the business of the church without much concern for the distinction between spiritual and temporal affairs. The councils to a large extent preempted control of education and the administration of charities, supervised church properties, and kept under surveillance the lives of clergy and laity alike. There was no differentiation between the acts of the councils as political entities and the acts which they performed as Christians in authority. The council customarily implemented the suggestions and actualized the demands of the pulpit in the moral and religious area, which had the converse effect of making the priests and people's preachers concerned with practical questions, including the moral implications of specific social actions and even the rightness of foreign policy.

In Ulrich Zwingli the city of Zürich possessed a man perfectly molded for the task of directing the reform of both church and public life. Both his family background and his humanist education contributed to his initial concern for public welfare. His native loyalty fused with the pacifist and humane ideas derived from Erasmus to make of him an ardent foe of the traffic in Swiss mercenaries. It was only gradually, especially after the strong influence of Luther's writings began taking effect from 1518 on, that his reform effort took on a more distinctively religious, not to say theological, tone. Even then he was constantly concerned with applying the Gospel directly to immediate economic, political, and social questions. With outstanding personal qualities for leadership and strong popular support (he was skilled at allowing a ground swell of demand for action to develop past ignoring), he virtually ruled the council for over a decade.

Zwingli's reform program rested on two basic principles: (1) all doctrinal and ecclesiastical questions must be settled according to the doctrine or examples of Scripture; and (2) a Christian government has both the right and the duty to see to it that the rulings of Scripture are observed.[116] In line with these principles Zwingli resigned as people's priest and received a commission from the council to preach. Without hesitation he referred to the council purely theological disputed questions such as fasting, clerical celibacy, and veneration of the saints, as well as setting standards of public morality; for he thought the councilors to be true Christians capable of exercising good judgment in ecclesiastical matters which were their concern as men of the highest authority. Moreover, only a Christian authority could demand obedience, and resistance against an unchristian government was permissible. As Christian, however, the magistracy was bound by the Word which the preacher is authorized to expound and proclaim.

Zwingli held the three signs of the true visible church to be the Word, the dominical sacraments, and church discipline. In the area of church discipline the tight cohesion of the political and religious community led under Zwingli's influence to the combination of civil and ecclesiastical juridical action. Zürich even established a special civil court, with state and church representatives, for marital and moral cases. The cantonal government practically assumed the former episcopal functions in the area of both doctrine and church life. Oecolampadius, the Basel reformer and advocate of greater independence for the church, saw the dangers of state-churchism when he wrote to Zwingli on Sept. 17, 1530: "A government that takes over the authority of the church is worse than the antichrist."

In the microcosm of the Swiss city-state Zwingli was perforce and by choice involved in affairs of state, domestic and foreign. As God's prophet Zwingli was naturally carried beyond a concern for his own city, which had become a virtual theocracy under his sway, to bring reform to the whole Confederation. He was prepared to exploit all the political means at hand to achieve this end even though in this arena the final appeal was often to force.

Zwingli was not the most fortunate at playing power politics. His plans for a grand union against the Habsburgs and Catholicism failed. His Christian Civic Alliances with other reformed cities were countered with a pact of five "forest cantons" for the suppression of heresy. He was even prepared to undertake a surprise preventive war against them. In the end he fell, fully armed, by the sword at Kappel on Oct. 11, 1531, during the course of the Swiss civil war which he had done so much to foment.

Luther viewed Zwingli's death as the judgment of the Almighty on his sinful confusion of Christianity with power politics. Vadian, too, even though his own reformation of St. Gall had paralleled Zwingli's work in Zürich in so many ways, thought his bellicosity tragic, and years later he declined an invitation to write a biography of Zwingli for fear of conjuring up the old hostilities.[117] Heinrich Bullinger carried on the tradition in Zürich after Zwingli's death, but he lacked his spark and drive. Leadership passed to Berne and to Geneva.

THE RADICAL PROTEST

While the main course of the Reformation was largely set by the magisterial reformers, the left-wing partisans of the movement emerging out of freedom's ferment posed new critical questions concerning church-state relations. These radicals, often simply named "Anabaptists" by the men of the 16th century, derived many ideas (e. g., opposition to oaths, holding public office, or Infant Baptism) from late-medieval heresies. Moreover, Luther's emphasis on private interpretation of the Scriptures and the priesthood of all believers was an open invitation to exegetical egalitarianism. It was more than coincidence that the chorus of dissonant interpretations grew louder after the publication of Luther's new vernacular translation of the Bible.

Though a larger number of the Anabaptists came from the upper-middle and aristocratic classes than was once supposed, the mass following and the extremist leadership came from the poor, uneducated, disinherited classes. It is impossible to speak of a sect or, with Bullinger, of 13 sects, for there were scores of individuals and groups holding a diversity of opinions and diametrically opposed positions precisely on the basic questions. But they all had one thing in common: they favored a radical reevaluation of the concepts of church and state.

Among the first "enthusiasts" to plague Luther were the Zwickau prophets in 1521, Nicholas Storch and Thomas Münzer, who insisted they were directly inspired by the Holy Ghost (he must have swallowed Him feathers and all, mocked Luther) and proclaimed the approaching reign of Christ and the pending destruction of the ungodly. The first recorded case of adult baptism took place in Zürich in January 1525, when Conrad Grebel rebaptized Georg Blauroch. Grebel, Felix Manz, Balthasar Hubmaier, and other Anabaptists had been assembled at Zürich since 1522 in the wake of Zwingli's reform drive.

From 1525 on a rapid multiplication of peaceful groups of enthusiasts took place. The Hutterites attempted to establish in Moravia a community based on the idea of primitive Christian love. In the Netherlands the followers of Menno Simons, the Mennonites, accepted the duty of suffering obedience to the magistrate in commands not contrary to the divine will but characteristically refused the taking of oaths, holding public office, condoning capital punishment, or doing military service. For the vast majority of Anabaptists pacifism was the normal position.

Certain individuals of the highest type shared certain basic tenets with these Anabaptists. The mystic Hans Denck, the sensitive Sebastian Franck, the philosophical Caspar Schwenckfeld, and others, led by what they believed to be an inner light, sought a highly spiritual form of religion. They awaited the emergence of the true spiritual community which would render the outward ecclesiastical forms unnecessary and the state as an instrument of power superfluous.

It so happened, however, as it often does, that the whole movement became associated with the extremist actions of the lunatic fringe. In the lowlands of the Rhine, that seedbed of mysticism and popular religious heresies in the waning Middle Ages, a new breed of extremists sprang up. There the fierce persecution of all Protestants by Charles V intensified the fears and fervor of the ignorant and the bold. Melchior Hofmann preached patient endurance until the end of the world. Strasbourg was to become the new Jerusalem. Some Melchiorites could not wait for eschatological deliverence in the day of the Lord but rallied around Jan Matthys, who called for the destruction of the godless with earthly arms.

In 1533 this fanaticism, combined with popular revolutionary sentiment, precipitated the overthrow of the bishop and conservative council and guilds in the city of Münster. Jan van Leyden, a common and perverse type, became the tyrant of Münster, proclaimed common property (though merely in the interest of defense) and polygamy (he was personally a lusty fellow), and ruled as "king of the world." The city was captured in June 1535 by the furious bishop and returned to Catholicism. These fanatics brought all "enthusiasts" into disrepute.

For the 16th century, Matthys and Jan van Leyden were the real exemplars of Anabaptism. This was one basic reason why no asylum was given them in Catholic or Protestant lands, but rather expulsion and persecution was their lot, for, as Bullinger expressed it: "God opened the eyes of the governments at Münster so that thereafter nobody would trust even those Anabaptists who claimed to be innocent."

Clearly the most important contribution of the total disparate movement was the conception of the visible church of freely committed believers, practicing holiness of life, if not achieving perfection, though many thought even this was possible. The church is a voluntary association of spiritually reborn and illuminated persons, a community of saints. Baptism as a sign of admission presupposes faith, which is possible only for an adult. State support and protection for the church is a positive evil, and the elect does well to abandon society to its fate and to "come out from among them." Not only is the state hostile to the true church, but it is a positive evil, for it necessarily involves coercion rather than love. Magistrates are agents of the devil, to be obeyed when possible, since one is to endure evil. Oaths, civil office, and military service are not for the saints.

It cannot be said that the Anabaptists conceived of any new form for the state. Rather, they would have preferred to ignore it and all the evil ranks in society. When the perfect theocracy in the rule of Christ and his saints is realized, all government by force, they held, will fall away. Their idealism was clearly out of this world. Yet it was most touching, and for many of them it was crowned with the wreath of saints and heroes — martyrdom.[118]

The radical protest was significant for the concepts of church and state in a number of ways. First of all, as a condemnation of all the time-honored establishments of the century it sounded a caveat against Erastianism, or state supremacy, which was sorely needed then and in the centuries which followed. Second, the immediate negative effect of the frightening extremism and, it was presumed, seditions, and the anarchistic nature of the movement was to drive both Protestant and Catholic Churches closer to their respective states. Third, although the various Anabaptist groups were exclusive and intolerant of nonconformity, their pacifism and their valor as a suffering minority contributed eventually to the growth of toleration in the state. Fourth, the tradition of "remnant" Christian groups and individualism in Christian thought gave encouragement to free Protestantism for years to come. The Baptists, Independents, and Quakers owed something to these spiritual ancestors. Finally, a phenomenon familiar in politics, where the large political parties frequently preempt the platforms of the splinter parties to the left, the major church bodies frequently in subsequent history learned from the radicals.

CALVIN AND CALVINISM

"I felt as though God had laid his mighty hand upon me," confessed John Calvin about his decision to work in Geneva.

This sense of being the instrument of the divine purpose never left him. He remained conscious of his role as the continuator of Luther's labors and the leader of militant Protestantism, little suspecting that no one of equal stature would ever succeed him at the helm.

The two major factors determining the nature of his concepts of church and state were the powerful influence of Luther's evangelical theology and the politico-ecclesiastical circumstances in Geneva. Almost two decades had passed since the posting of the Ninety-five Theses when Calvin appeared on the scene with the publication of the *Institutes* in March 1536. In a typical late-medieval struggle, Geneva had won its independence from the counts of Savoy and the bishop before Calvin's arrival there. The Bernese reformers, the red-haired, choleric Farel, Fromment, and Viret, were struggling to check the radicals and crypto-Romanists. Calvin, shy but orderly, trained in law, and, as it developed, with tremendous genius for organization, was the man of the hour. He possibly appealed to the Genevans precisely because he was different in social outlook from the Zwinglian state-churchists among the Bernese. There was distinct danger of worldly involvement because of the half political, half religious nature of the Genevan revolution. Calvin, whose "quiescent conscience had been rudely awakened from slumber," was by this time steeped in the writings of Luther, the fathers, church history, and the Scriptures. He had the inner resources for a ministry which was to extend beyond his Swiss parish to all countries of western Europe.

Calvin shared Luther's belief that God had established two governments for man: the spiritual and the temporal. In the spiritual realm God ruled through the Word alone preached by His ministers, in the temporal through the sword wielded by His magistrates according to law for the preservation of peace and order in society. The Genevan Catechism of 1545 answered the question "What is the Church?" with the statement: "The body and society of the believers whom God has predestined to eternal life." That was Calvin's answer to the false institutional pretenses of the Romanists. For him, as for Luther, the true church is the mystical body of Christ, the communion of saints known only to God. The true visible church must assume the form which the apostles instituted, as authorized especially in 1 Corinthians and Ephesians 4:11-13 and described in the patristic writers. In his famous reply to Sadoleto, Calvin described the signs of the true church as doctrine, discipline, the sacraments, and ceremonies by which to exercise the people in the duties of piety.[119] This last addition to Luther's signs of the true church suggests the stress on outward piety which was to become a major preoccupation of the reformer in his attempt to turn the whole Genevan community into a practicing confessional church.

The State and the Citizen

Although he did not write a single treatise purely on political theory, Calvin did make more elaborate statements of his views on the state than did the other major reformers. As to systematic writing he was his own Melanchthon. Coming from France with its advanced dynastic consolidation, Calvin had little use for the fiction of the universal imperium of the Hapsburg emperor, who was for him rather a symbol of Catholic reaction than the temporal head of Christendom *(corpus christianum)*. When Calvin spoke of a council, he did not think of it as an organ of the *corpus christianum* but more as a conference of interested world powers. He refers to western civilization more often as "Europe" in the manner of the humanists than did the other reformers. In fact he conceived of the state as a juridical order, not merely as authority in Luther's terminology. Although Beza held that from first to last no change occurred in Calvin, there was a change at least in degree if not in kind. Between the sixth part of the first edition of the *Institutes* (1536), on Christian liberty, ecclesiastical government, and civil administration, to the 20th chapter of the last edition (1559), on civil government, Calvin progressed in the direction of concreteness and certainty in his ideas.

The state, he held, was divinely established by reason of sin, to serve as a check on evil, the provocative cause. Second, the state is an organ of Providence, the efficient cause, for the good ordering of material life. And third, it is an instrument of justice for the preservation of the human race in peace and tranquillity, the final cause.[120] Against those "barbarous men," the Anabaptists, who denied the legality of political power, and against those "flatterers of princes," the Renaissance sycophants and specifically the school of Toulouse, who exalted the sovereignty of rulers, Calvin asserted that government was founded on natural or divine law and that rulers were subject to moral or divine law.[121] Like Luther he associated natural law with the moral law "inborn in the minds of men," expressed in the enduring part of the Mosaic law (*lex Mosaica*) as distinguished from the abrogated ceremonial provisions, and given its clearest expression by Jesus in the law of love. The law of nature (*lex naturae*), then, is the law of God (*lex Dei*), not the Stoics' sum total of rational principles or Aristotle's product of natural reason. Particular laws are to be deduced from right general principles:

> Equity, being natural, is the same to all mankind; and consequently all laws on every subject ought to have the same equity for their end. . . . Now, as it is certain that the law of God, which we call the moral law, is no other than a declaration of natural law and of that conscience which has been engraven by God in the minds of men, the whole rule of this equity, of which we now speak, is prescribed in it. This equity, therefore, must alone be the scope and rule and end of all laws.[122]

Calvin as a lawyer had much more faith in positive laws than did Luther, who put aside legal studies very quickly and trusted the wisdom and equity of judges more than legal statutes. Calvin saw little point to Luther's assertion that for true Christians there is no need for the restraints of law insofar as they are true Christians, for to him this seemed utopian in this present life.

In considering what the best form of government is Calvin became increasingly distrustful of monarchy with its easy transition to despotism and of democracy with its ready perversion into sedition and anarchy, Plato's many-headed beast. "Indeed," he concluded, "I shall by no means deny that either aristocracy, or a mixture of aristocracy and democracy, far excels all others. . . ."[123] He perceived in the history of Israel, especially in the period of the judges, verification for this opinion. Calvin saw the mosaic of governments from city-republics to absolute tyrannies and mused on the wisdom of Providence in permitting a variety of polity suited to various lands and climes. There is no social-contract theory in his thought. Whatever its form, government rests on the divine right *(ius divinum)*.

Christians, Calvin held to the very end, must be absolutely obedient to the government, however tyrannical, unless it commands something contrary to the Word and will of God, in which case they ought to "obey God rather than man." Like Luther, who was at last convinced by the jurists that the princes could constitutionally oppose the emperor, Calvin conceded that lesser magistrates, as in the Estates General, may be obligated, like the Spartan ephors restraining the kings, to protect the people from tyrannous kings.[124] Private persons may never rebel against the ruler unless they have the direct call of God to act as manifest avengers. It is better for all others to suffer until God executes judgment, if not here in time, then in eternity.

The State and the Church

It is symptomatic for the evolution of Calvin's thought that his essay on civil government, which up to 1554 had been a separate chapter of the *Institutes,* in the final edition was incorporated in the fourth book entitled "On the external means or aids by which God calls us into communion with Christ, and retains us in it."[125] Calvin followed Luther in insisting on the fundamental distinction in function between church and state. He proclaimed the autonomy of the church in things spiritual, in doctrine, worship, and discipline, with no power to punish or coerce. Christ alone is Lord and Head of the church. "For I have wished," he wrote, "to distinguish the spiritual power from the civil office, as is reasonable."[126]

But Calvin went far beyond Luther in asserting the obligation of the civil government "to cherish and support the external worship of God, to preserve the pure doctrine of religion, to defend the constitution of the church. . . ."[127] Though distinct, the two regimes are not opposed to each other. Rather, both under God must serve the promotion of Christ's kingdom in their respective ways. The secular authority must provide for the proper honoring of God, prevent all idolatry and false worship, and protect the sacred ministry. In his famous letter to Edward VI, Calvin made clear that princes and kings are lieutenants upholding the kingdom of Jesus Christ. The duty of the government, Calvin stresses, entails upholding both tables of the Law.[128]

The church in Geneva provides a good case study of Calvin's intentions and achievements regarding church-state relations. The pattern there was one of an intricate mixture of the two on the practical level, with Calvin struggling to delimit the medieval proprietary prerogatives of the councils and reserve "purely spiritual" matters for the church officials. Ironically, both his *Articles Concerning the Government of the Church*, 1537, and the definitive constitution, the *Ecclesiastical Ordinances*, 1541, had to be adopted by political bodies, the Little Council and the Council of Two Hundred. The *Ordinances* provided for a fourfold ministry in the church: that of pastors, doctors, elders, and deacons. The ministers of a congregation were to be chosen by the Venerable Company of clergy, presented to the council for approval, and accepted by the common consent of the congregation. The consistory was a new creation consisting of the pastors and 12 lay elders appointed by the council. As guardian of faith and morals, the consistory was charged with decisions on doctrinal matters and with conducting church discipline involving the power of excommunication in the case of gross offenses and impenitence. The city was divided into districts for purposes of supervising the lives of the members. The consistory could invoke the aid of the civil courts in serious cases, and the outcome was seldom doubtful.

The inquisitorial methods, the pettiness, spying, informing, and severe penalties won for Calvin the reputation of tyrant and killjoy, a kind of meddlesome Alpine Savonarola. The moral discipline of the church was intended to enlarge, not replace, that of the city council, which in good medieval tradition already had a sufficiently long catalog of sumptuary laws. There was obviously a large area for jurisdictional disputes between consistory and council with its traditional prerogatives. Here Calvin had to struggle his whole life to preserve for the church its sphere of spiritual competence. In practice within the consistory Calvin and the ministers invariably dominated, though in a numerical minority, and from 1553 on Calvin's prestige became so great that, with no legal hold, he nevertheless influenced also the major political decisions of the council.

Can Calvin's Genevan regime be called a theocracy?[129] A theocracy is a political structure which commits both powers (sacred and secular) to one hand. But Calvin theoretically always distinguished between the two rules and actually held strictly to his own office as a simple preacher of the Word. Historians have often exaggerated his personal influence and not fully assessed the continuing power of the council and his enemies. There was for a long time a kind of cooperative coexistence, and only in the last years did the ecclesiastical authorities actually outweigh the secular in decision making. Under Theodore Beza, Calvin's less forceful successor, the council once more asserted its old authority fully. Although the *Ecclesiastical Ordinances* became a model for Calvinist churches around the world, Calvin's own ideal of an independent church polity was realized, it could be argued, not in Geneva but rather in France, where as a minority church in a hostile state the Huguenots were forced to be independent.

INTERNATIONAL REFORMED PROTESTANTISM

What Calvin's Geneva lost in spiritual richness through its summary treatment of such seeking nonconformists as Acontius, Servetus, Castellio, Gentilis, or Bolsec, it gained in zeal and striking power. In the Academy Calvin's learned and inspired doctors trained a generation of iron-willed theologians, militant Protestantism's shock troops for the struggle against the forces of the Counter-Reformation.[130] From the center in Geneva, ideally located geographically, Calvin carried on a huge correspondence and issued mandates to the daughter congregations and synods of the new truly international reformed Protestantism. In France, the Netherlands, Germany, Eastern Europe, Scotland, England,

and eventually America, Calvin's influence on the concepts of church and state was to play an important role in shaping the course of modern history.

There were to be many deviations from propositions that he considered basic. For example, even in the case of the conspiracy of Amboise in 1560 Calvin stood firm against implicating himself and involving his followers in resistance to the persecuting government. But in Scotland John Knox broke with his dictum of absolute obedience. In his *Franco-Gallia* of 1573 Francois Hotman argued that monarchy is limited by law and tradition and that the Estates General should elect the king and define his authority. In 1576 Beza himself, in the *De iure magistratuum,* argued that the citizen had the duty of keeping the magistrate from exceeding the bounds of his authority. Three years later the Calvinist tract *Vindiciae contra tyrannos* argued that society was based on a series of contracts and if the king exceeds his rights the people may claim breach of contract and revolt. Calvinism, then, had many revolutionary consequences which Calvin could not have foreseen. And yet precisely in the *Form of Oath Prescribed for Ministers,* July 17, 1542, to be made before the Lord Syndic and Council there was a reservation full of promise for later times:

> Finally, I promise and swear to be subject to the polity and constitution of this City, to show a good example of obedience to all others, being for my part subject to the laws and the magistracy, so far as my office allows; that is to say without prejudice to the liberty which we must have to teach according to what God commands us and to do the things which pertain to our office. And in conclusion, I promise to serve the Seigneury and the people in such wise, so long as I be not at all hindered from rendering to God the service which in my vocation I owe Him.[181]

Anglicanism and Commonwealth

The English Reformation followed a pattern in many ways similar to that of the Scandinavian Lutheran lands. The Tudor monarchy, restoring order after protracted civil strife, was immensely popular and rode the crest of aroused national sentiment.

The Protestant leaders, many under direct Lutheran and especially Zwinglian influence, made the most of the genuine dislike of papal interference. Tyndale observed that the pope and bishops had made shadows of kings. Henry VIII was not one to be overshadowed. The humanists contributed many ideas to the complex of Tudor political theory in the drive toward royal supremacy and the realization of a national monarchy in law and in reality.[132] Cranmer taught the divine ordinance of rulers and the necessity for obedience in all secular matters. Latimer insisted on the necessity to suffer for disobedience rather than actively to resist the government.

The Church of England inevitably came to be looked upon as the religious facet of the commonwealth. Like Lutheranism, Anglicanism had the unfortunate good fortune to become the established religion of the realm.[133] Such theorists as Thomas Starkey or Robert Crowley, for all their cerebration, were really rationalizing the *status quo*. Similarly the Elizabethan settlement, more thoroughly Protestant than Henry's reform had been, claimed for the national church the right to determine its own faith, ritual, and organization. Anglicanism of this golden age found its most effective apology in Richard Hooker's *The Laws of Ecclesiastical Polity* (1594 ff.), directed against Puritan criticism of the settlement. The close association of Anglicanism with the fortunes of the monarchy was a major factor in the course of subsequent British history and was important also for Colonial America. The struggle of the Independents and other nonconformists against the establishment proved to be a stimulus to political thought and action of basic importance to the growth of liberalism and representative government. The relationship of the church meeting and the town meeting in New England history has often been described by historians and needs no elaboration at this point.

CONCLUSION

The Reformation forced men to reconsider the old questions of the concepts and relationship of church and state in radically new and different terms. This meant more than a continuation of the medieval struggle and debate between the spiritual and

temporal powers. It forced a recasting of theory to fit new beliefs and altered circumstances. In spite of their differences the
reformers shared a basic community of ideas which were critical
determinants in the development of the modern world.

The reformers, in restoring the New Testament conception
of the church as the communion of saints and a community based
on love rather than power and coercion, returned the reformed
church to its true spiritual tasks and destroyed the claims of the
hierarchy to temporal power. They challenged the religious
propriety and legal validity of canon law and the political use
of the great ban. They thereby removed the church from the
juridical area, where conflict with government was unwarranted
and unfortunate. To be sure, they thereby weakened the papacy
and hierarchy as a political counterpoise to temporal rulers. The
history of the preceding centuries and decades just past made
questionable, however, the effectiveness, to say nothing of the
rightness, of papal political pretensions and maneuvers. The reaction evident during the years of the Reformation indicates that
papal politics had been demoralizing and productive of hostilities
which made the true work of the church in the cause of spiritual
righteousness difficult to the point of being impossible.

The reformers, then, radically altered the concept of the
church, teaching with St. Paul that Christ alone is the Head of
the church and that the true believers are its members, known
only to God. The marks of the true visible church must necessarily be Word and sacraments, through which faith comes,
though Zwingli added discipline and Calvin ceremonies as aids
in distinguishing the true evangelical church. In matters of
church polity, Luther left the question open, suspended midway
between his ideal and the possible. Zwingli, betrayed by his
own patriotism and personal involvement, freely made many
concessions to state-churchism. Calvin, on the other hand, in
attempting to achieve a form of church government based on
the New Testament pattern, developed an organization which,
though closely entwined in Genevan government, in the context
of larger states achieved independence for the church. The Anabaptists turned in a minority report on many of these questions

and deviated also in ecclesiology, insisting that the visible church must be a sanctified body and remain separate from civil society and responsibilities. The nature of England's break with Rome dictated differing views regarding the nature and function of the visible church. The Church of England meant for many clergy the universal church in England, which was one reason why, in spite of the advanced development of nationalism there, the idea of Christendom (*corpus christianum*) as the church coextensive with the Christian world persisted into this century.

The reformers, with their new ethos of Christian vocation, transcended the medieval dualism of the sacred, or religious, and secular callings. Government authority was no longer derived from or dependent on papal sanction. The natural order (*ordo naturalis*) was no longer on a lower plane than the spiritual order (*ordo spiritualis*), as the scholastics, reflecting the general medieval mentality, had taught. God's majesty was revealed in the created world, to which government as a divine ordinance also belonged. The reformers knew nothing of a secular state in the present-day sense, divorced from religious or ethical ties. With a strong sense of God's immanence, they saw the state subject to God's will and judgment. There is no hint in the reformers of the notion held by Jacob Burckhardt and other modern cultural historians that the power of government is evil in itself. Luther comforted the conscience of rulers, calling the state the kingdom of God's left hand, a phrase not to be found in Zwingli and soon dropped by Calvin. All the reformers sought to sharpen the conscience of rulers, none so effectively as Calvin. They enlarged the state's area of competence — in charities and education, for example — a tendency evident already in the proprietary churches of the late Middle Ages. Luther, who had a lively interest in social life and the order of the state, Zwingli, Calvin, and many Anglicans were political activists. They believed it desirable for the rulers to be and act as Christians, though their authority was not diminished if they were not.

The reformers asserted the absolute distinction between the spiritual and secular authorities in line with the words of Jesus: "Render unto Caesar the things which are Caesar's and unto God the things that are God's." According to Leopold von Ranke, this is one of the historically most influential texts in the New Testament. The step from distinction to separation of church and state was taken within the Protestant tradition in later centuries. "Thoughts dwell close together," reflected Goethe, "but things jostle one another in space." It is ironic how often circumstances thwarted the best intentions of the reformers. Protestantism accompanied the development in time of tighter political cohesion on a territorial and national level. After the wars and revolts of the preceding century, the men of the 16th century longed for order. Order required centralization of control and strong rulers.

Many of the effects of the Reformation were indirect and delayed in their realization. The relationship of Protestantism and political progress is a fascinating and much discussed problem. The reformers, by setting aside the papacy and requiring obedience even to tyrants, on the surface appear to have contributed to the growth of absolutism. But for the traditional sanctions they substituted a quickened personal conscience also in matters political, as the Apology to the Augsburg Confession expressed it, "not only because of punishment but on account of conscience." In current parlance, they helped to develop a type of Western man who was inner-directed, not tradition-directed, and also not other-directed like many present-day conformists who are so easily made to fall in line by dictators above or mass pressures below.

The Protestant minorities had the courage to set aside the non-resistance principle and to obey God rather than man, because their conscience was in revolt. With the Scriptures as norm, the individual sought to determine God's will and to act accordingly — an explosive potential. The theocentric orientation of Reformation theology served to put earthly rulers into perspective. They were but mortal men subject to God's laws and to His judgment. Luther's sharp criticism of the rulers found sympathetic and appreciative audiences for centuries to come.[134] Within the Calvinist tradition the stress on predestination served as a leveling device, for the elect subject could feel compassion for the rejected ruler — a sentiment not conducive to a submissive mentality.

Several basic elements derived from the Reformation contributed to the growth of representative government in due course. By easy stages the stress on natural law and the derivation of just positive law from the higher law of divine creation led, together with other forces, to constitutional thinking.[135] The conception of the universal priesthood of all believers was essentially antihierarchical and would tend to corrode the parallel-estate structure of society, where the transfer of ideas could be made. The covenant idea in Calvinism, derived from Calvin's own preoccupation with the history and political experience of Israel, contributed to social-contract thinking, a precondition of constitutionalism. Largely by historical accident and not by virtue of the reformers' initiative, toleration developed as a by-product of the Reformation as minorities struggled for recognition and factions tired of constant strife. The Reformation, by breaking the bonds of uniformity, prepared the way for a liberal state in which minorities could exist and eventually be heard. The evangelical doctrine of vocation contributed to an industrious and self-reliant citizenry, the kind of men useful to any government but absolutely essential to a democracy.

Perhaps the greatest contribution of the Reformation to political thought in this late age may be an element of stability, derived entirely from its purely theological message. In a day when totalitarian forces and total destruction threaten in actual fact, when the minds of men turn from rosy reflections on progress to things eschatological, the faith which the reformers preeminently possessed can still give men courage and a renewed determination to build also this earthly city well and to the glory of God. This was the source of Calvin's strength when he concluded the final edition of his *Institutes* with these last words:

> And that our hearts may not fail us, Paul stimulates us with another consideration — that Christ has redeemed us at the immense price which our redemption cost him, that we may not be submissive to the corrupt desires of men, much less be slaves to their impiety.

Luther's calm reassurance has new meaning in these latter days:

> Our job . . . is to have a large open eye so that we can with
> one glance take in all the kings with all their wisdom and power
> and take them for a burning straw which He who established
> heaven, earth, and all things can extinguish with one breath.
> If you measure by a human standard, the nations, kings, people,
> rulers, are something immense. For this reason we tremble
> when we compare our weakness with their power. . . . It truly
> is like a spark of fire compared with the whole sea, as if He
> wished to say: "Is it not the greatest folly that you, little
> spark, wish to dry up the whole sea?" [136]

IN THE CHRISTIAN WORLD since the Reformation, distinctive theological positions about church-state relations have emerged. The development of these positions is explored in chapter 3 on the basis of the writings of representative theologians.

Authors of the chapter are *H. Richard Klann*, Ph. D., assistant professor of systematic theology at Concordia Seminary, St. Louis, Mo., and *William H. Lehmann, Jr.*, B. D., M. A., associate professor of philosophy at Concordia Teachers College, River Forest, Ill. For the Catholic position the authors cite Cardinal Bellarmine to show how the medieval papal pretensions to the political sword were to be properly understood, and the writings of modern popes to illustrate the frequent reassertions of the traditional Catholic principles. In Jacques Maritain the authors see an American Catholic whose statements represent an approach to accommodation with the American pattern.

The post-Reformation position of the Reformed on church-state relations is voiced on the one hand by the Puritan divines and on the other by two European spokesmen: Karl Barth and Emil Brunner. The New England theories intermingling church and state have long been influential in America. The contemporary Reformed theologians draw a clearer distinction between the two institutions but still allow for the social relevance of the church.

In Lutheranism the authors observe some rethinking after the Reformation. Gerhard went beyond Luther in idealizing the state and accepting the political *status quo*. Walther appreciated and encouraged the separation of church and state in the United States as most wholesome for the work of the church. Berggrav represents the Lutherans of Europe aroused by totalitarian ruthlessness to assert the role of the church as the conscience of the state.

CHURCH AND STATE
IN THEOLOGICAL EXPRESSION
SINCE THE REFORMATION

H. Richard Klann and William H. Lehmann, Jr.

THE PROFOUND EFFECT of the Reformation on church-state problems was felt in the divergent streams of the Christian church. The Roman Catholic, Reformed, and Lutheran theologians in some ways held common positions and in others widely divergent positions. In this chapter an attempt will be made to evaluate each position on the basis of the statements of typical theologians. With the passage of time since the Reformation and with the changing political conditions, interesting modifications have developed which may shed light on the thinking of the church about church-state issues.

In Roman Catholicism the monolithic formal insistence on the primacy of the pope over civil government — one of the striking characteristics of the medieval church — has continued. Two factors, however, have led to various positions within Romanism besides the official one. The first factor is the alteration in the practical situation of the Roman Church since the Reformation. It has become one of many organized religious bodies in Christendom, and it has sometimes found itself in competition with other groups or even banned altogether. Second, in recent centuries it has had to cope with political theories developed by nontheologians and with the realization of those theories in governments which relegated the Roman Church to an inferior position or to none at all. A doctrine of church-state relations which rested on the premise of one church and one empire has come to be a political anomaly in a world of many churches and many nations.

Roman Catholics today are confronted on the one hand with a formal insistence on the unchanged character of the church-state relation and on the other with attempts by Catholic theologians to seek adjustment to the modern realities. This effort at accommodation without sacrificing the dogma of the Roman Church has marked the position of Roman theologians such as Cardinal Bellarmine and Jacques Maritain. On the other hand, efforts to change the political situation to conform to official doctrine have been made by the popes, notably Leo XIII and his successors.

John Calvin's *Institutes of the Christian Religion* closes with a section on the relation of church and state. Since his time Reformed theologians, influenced often by political theories current in the countries where their parishes were flourishing, have sought to develop a political position based either on that section of the *Institutes* or on the central doctrine of the providential care of God for the world. Three times these theologians have had an opportunity to put into practice the principles they espoused: in Geneva, Switzerland, under Calvin; in England under Cromwell; and in America under the Puritan divines. The variety of political expression on these three occasions testifies to the lack of unanimity among the Calvinists. But for all their diversity, there is a core of agreement among them which, when compared with Roman and Lutheran approaches to the same problems, justifies insistence on a distinctively Reformed position on church-state relations. For the sake of brevity only the Puritan position is treated.

In our own day two outstanding Reformed theologians who have written on church-state relations are Karl Barth and Emil Brunner, both of whom have been involved in opposition to antireligious governments. The position taken by these men will be helpful to show how the Reformed attitude has been expressed in relation to contemporary problems; where it has been modified; and in which ways it has remained basically the same.

As is pointed out in the previous chapter, Luther's references to the relationship of church and state were limited. The Scriptures themselves, on which Luther rested his whole theological thinking, speak of church-state relations in only the broadest terms. The Lutheran position has therefore been set off in contrast to the full-blown doctrine of Roman Catholicism and the Reformed churches. It could speak only where Scripture spoke. The statements of such Lutheran theologians as Johann Gerhard and C. F. W. Walther reflect this position. But the political developments of the 20th century, notably the emergence of anticlerical totalitarianism, have distressed Lutherans no less than Reformed and Roman Catholic theologians. Lutherans have therefore been led to a restudy of the Scriptures to find further directives for a position on church-state relations or for assistance in formulating a position which, while not expressed in the Word of God, is not inconsistent with it. Is there such a thing as a government which by its very nature is not sanctioned by God? A government committed to the proposition that there is no God — is it actually still a servant of God? A contemporary Lutheran wrestling with problems of this sort is Eivind Berggrav, and his view is therefore included in this chapter.

CHANGELESS ROMAN CATHOLIC PRINCIPLES ADJUSTED TO THE TIMES

Non-Roman Catholics are often only dimly aware of the massive and far-spreading historical roots of the system of Roman Catholic ideas of church and state and their relation to each other. This theoretic structure has never been dismantled by Rome, and its key ideas have never been repudiated. Rather the change is operational, often expressed with utmost simplicity in the Latin phrase *non possumus* (we are not able) so frequently used by the papacy since the French Revolution. The principles remain, but the historical relativities do not now permit their full application even in the most thoroughly Roman Catholic countries.

Roman Catholic dogma is concerned not merely to express an attitude toward the state but to formulate a theory of the origin, nature, and function of the state itself. During the past century certain of the popes have addressed themselves also to the problem of the relation of the individual and the group to the state as well as to the church itself. The state is viewed as part of the order of creation because man was created to live communally. The state is therefore not merely a "remedy for sin," to use a famous phrase of St. Augustine, nor did man create government as a social necessity after the fall into sin. God intended the state as a part of the order in the first paradise. Only the coercive function of the state necessarily developed after the fall to check the most violent outbursts of sin and to make some sort of social order possible.

The notion of *lex naturalis* (natural law) has always played a prominent role in this political theory. Man by nature has the capability of knowing right from wrong in his dealings with his fellowman. It is in agreement with God's will for human interactivity. Natural law forms the basis for the existence and function of the state, and the criterion for judging its actions. This is the place where church and state come together. The state exists for the general welfare of the community. That welfare is achieved when men live in accordance with natural law. Hence natural law is the judge of the positive laws whereby the actions of citizens are directed.[1]

The Position of Bellarmine

Since the church (Roman) possesses and by divine command interprets the Law of God for all men, of which natural law is only a faint expression, and since the church is concerned and responsible for the eternal welfare of all men, which includes their temporal welfare, the church has the responsibility to judge and to correct the state. Put in its bluntest terms, the church has the authority from God to direct temporal affairs for the welfare of mankind. The political work of the Jesuit Cardinal Robert Bellarmine (died 1621) is particularly noteworthy as representing a tactical retreat from this unworkable position that had been expressed by the medieval popes.[2]

In his *Disputationes de controversiis christianae fidei adversus huius temporis haereticos,* Lib. V: *De potestate summi pontificis in rebus temporalibus,* Bellarmine takes the "middle" position, "common to Catholic theologians, that the pope, as pope, does not possess any kind of direct and immediate secular power but exclusively a spiritual power. But by reason of his spiritual power he does have at least a kind of indirect power — and this in the highest degree — in secular matters." [3]

Bellarmine cites as authority for ultimate *indirect* power in all secular affairs most of the same arguments which the medieval popes had used to urge their claim to supreme *direct* power. The civil magistrate in a Christian state is subject to ecclesiastical power, not merely because he as a Christian is subject to the pope in the church but also because the goals of the state are subordinate to the eternal goal of the church.

> Kings and bishops, the clergy and the laity, do not constitute two states but one, that is, one church. For we are all one body (Rom. 12 and 1 Cor. 12); but in every body the members are joined together and mutually dependent. But it is not a correct statement that spiritual things depend on the secular things; therefore secular things depend on spiritual things and are subjected to them.[4]

It should be noted that Bellarmine was not speaking for the pope in his treatise. His effort to soften the *direct-power* claim of the pope to *indirect power* was intended to reconcile the inconsistency between theological doctrine and the realities of the political situation. To possess a power *(potestas)* but be powerless to exercise it, as in the case of the French Revolution aftermath, when the Catholic hierarchy was driven out of power in France, is a contradiction in terms. If God gives the power, it can and must be exercised. From this it seems to follow that power which cannot be exercised is no power at all. By means of appeal to *indirect power* Bellarmine was able to salvage the authority, the moral right to power, even if he could not preserve the power itself.

The Modern Papal Position

In spite of the popularity of the efforts of Bellarmine to rescue
the papal position on the church-state relation, subsequent popes
continued to claim direct power and sought, generally in vain,
to exercise it. This power was exerted in a variety of directions.
The *Syllabus* of Pius IX (1864), attached to the encyclical *Quanta
cura,* includes a long list of complaints and condemnations including the "insanity" that everyone has the right to liberty of
conscience:

> History shows that states have perished through liberty of
> opinion, freedom of speech, and the craze for reform. The
> liberty of the press is also a horrible thing; errors are spread
> in this way like a curse over all the earth. It is also a wholly
> pernicious assertion that the church's censure of books is ob-
> jectionable and unjustifiable; it is, on the contrary, useful in
> the highest degree.[5]

In his preface to the circular the pope recalls that he has
several times previously condemned the dangerous opinions
which have appeared in his time to the destruction of souls
and damage to the common weal. Now a new condemnation is
needed, especially against those "who transfer the ungodly principle of what is called 'naturalism' to civil society." They wish
either to have society ordered and governed regardless of religion
or at least without distinction between the true religion and the
false. Freedom of conscience, of religion, and of the press are
to be condemned. Those who regard public opinion as the highest
authority in public affairs open every road to the free exercise
of covetousness and moral degeneracy. To think that God must
be pleased also with Protestantism is "latitudinarianism." A program of a free church in a free society is to be condemned. On
the contrary the liberty of the Roman Church must be upheld,
meaning that the pope may intervene in all legislation of the
secular state and require its alteration in order that the various
programs of the church may be executed and family life not be
alienated from the church. Damnable is the error of the separation of church and state. The Roman Church will indeed

support a system of state churches but only in such a way that the state is the obedient handmaiden of Rome. Lastly the various errors of liberalism are condemned, particularly the view "that in our time it is no longer expedient that the Catholic religion should be the religion of the state to the exclusion of all other forms of religion." [5]

The *Syllabus* was issued on the 10th anniversary of the dogma of the Immaculate Conception of Mary. By way of association this document is an important supplement to the Bull of Dec. 8, 1854, and is also a connecting link between it and the subsequent proclamation of the dogma of papal infallibility in 1870. The loss of secular dominion was compensated for by the most insistent claims for the authoritative teaching and directing office of the papacy.

The ensuing German Kulturkampf revealed the far-reaching implications of this *directive power*. The unification of the German states in Bismarck's empire had given German liberalism a strong sense of the omnicompetence of the state. This inevitably collided with the interests of the papacy in Germany. Furthermore, the Roman Catholic clergy, as a result of the Austrian and French wars of 1866 and 1870, were not considered loyal to the new empire. There were good grounds for that judgment. Defeated Austria and France were Roman Catholic countries. As the conflict continued with the suppression of the Jesuit and related orders in 1872, the Roman Catholic press revealed its sentiments without reserve. The influential *Vaterland* editorialized from Munich: "The Jesuits will certainly survive the German Empire with its Freemasons and its Jews. We do not value this German Empire of yours; we have never acknowledged it; it is only a passing storm-cloud." After the passage of the repressive "May Laws," Pope Pius IX wrote the German Emperor William I (Aug. 7, 1873) asserting that everyone who has received Baptism belongs to and is subject to the pope. The old emperor gave the pope no satisfaction at all and indirectly dismissed the pope's claim of authority over him as a baptized Christian: "The evangelical faith which I, like my forefathers and the majority of my subjects, profess, does not permit us in our relation to God to acknowledge any other mediator than our Lord Jesus Christ." [6]

The repressive May Laws were eventually amended or repealed. The German liberals, who particularly supported the Kulturkampf, found that Bismarck, while not willing to "go to Canossa," saw no gain for the interests of the empire by continuing the quarrel with the pope. Negotiations led to acceptable compromises. However, the episode did reveal that the papacy took its claim to *directive power* seriously by zealously mobilizing the Roman Catholic clergy and laity for the defense of this claim.

Pope Leo XIII (1878–1903) represents the adjustment which the modern papacy was compelled to make to the radically changing historical situation. The implication of the *indirect power* claim that the pope may intervene in the internal politics of nations, including the declaration of forfeiture of office of politicians or kings whose policies prove to be injurious to the interest of the Roman Church, is now quietly shelved because it cannot be enforced. Instead we find Leo XIII explicitly assuming a *directive power* in temporal affairs *(potestas directiva papae in temporalibus).* As no pope before him, Leo XIII affirms the autonomy of the state within its limited competence. At the same time he places the heaviest emphasis on the authoritative teaching function of the papacy for princes and nations. This becomes clearly apparent in his encyclical *Diuturnum illud* of June 29, 1881. The traditional arguments concerning the origin of the civil power are here realigned to yield the proposition that the divine authority to govern cannot be well exercised on the basis of fear alone, but that the Roman popes by their creation of the Holy Roman Empire have given the political order a peculiar sanction which is maintained by the church's teaching function. This function extends both to rulers and to ruled, according to the dictum of St. Augustine.[7]

The encyclical *Immortale Dei* (1885), which sets forth Leo's interpretation of the "two powers" theory, affirms that each — the civil and the ecclesiastical power — is supreme in its own limited domain. However, the church has the task of providing for the eternal welfare of mankind. Hence, everything that bears some relation to the ultimate goal: the salvation of souls and the service of God, is properly subject to the claims of the spiritual power. Circumstance may suggest the advisability of a concordat between the Roman pope and the particular civil power concerned. But in any case the secular power has supernatural sanction only within its proper limits, according to the authoritatively interpreted will of God.

In other encyclicals, such as *Libertas* (June 20, 1888), the pope affirms that all positive law of the state must properly have its source in that eternal law of God, the law of nature. In *Rerum novarum* (May 15, 1891) he affirms the duty of the state to intervene for the solution of the social questions (which Bismarck had done in Germany during the previous decade by his social legislation for the purpose of "stealing the Socialist thunder"). These statements continued to implement the asserted power of the pope to give moral and spiritual direction to the state. But *Libertas* deserves particular attention because it sets forth Leo's ideal of the modern state which is governed according to the principles taught by the Roman Church. A godless state, or, what amounts to the same thing, a state which treats all religions impartially and grants them equal rights, places itself in opposition to justice and reason. Responsible statesmen at the head of their governments have the duty to preserve and protect the true religion.

The pope's assertion that he possesses *directive power* which makes Roman Catholic politicians responsible for the welfare and protection of the Roman Church has always aroused the apprehension of non-Roman Catholic citizens in a country such as the United States.

Sapientiae Christianae (Jan. 10, 1890) sets forth in clear terms that the primary obligation of the Roman Catholic citizen is to his church: "Religion should, on the contrary, be accounted by every one as holy and inviolate; nay, in the public order itself of States — which cannot be severed from the laws influencing morals and from religious duties — it is always urgent, and indeed the main preoccupation, to take thought how best to consult the interests of Catholicism. Wherever these appear by reason of the efforts of adversaries to be in danger, all differences of opinion among Catholics should forthwith cease, so that, like thoughts and counsels prevailing, they may hasten to the aid of religion, the general and supreme good, to which all else should be referred." [8]

Pope Pius X (1903–14), Leo's successor, continued the affirmations of papal authority and competence to deal with political and social issues. In his first allocution after his election on Nov. 9, 1903, Pius X emphasized the teaching office of the pope, which extends to both faith and morals and therefore in no wise permits an exclusion of political issues. Likewise the economic problems of labor fall within the authority of the church, because the social question is moral and religious, to be dealt with primarily in terms of the moral law and in accordance with religious judgments.[9]

The difference between Leo XIII and his successors is one of terminological emphasis, not of substance, and with some regard for the momentous changes which the events of the 20th century brought about. The rise of Fascism in Italy benefited the papacy by allowing the establishment of the independent Vatican State. It is therefore not difficult to understand that Pius XI (1922–39) was able to say that a happy beginning for a new social order had been made.[10] "Every social activity in its essence and concept is subsidiary; it should support the members of the social body, but ought never to destroy or absorb them." The "corporate state" was not necessarily uncongenial to the pope, provided the interests of the papacy could be made safe. However, the rise of the Nazi state in Germany presented a real danger to the interests of the Roman Church. In 1937 Pius XI issued his famous encyclical *Mit brennender Sorge (Flagranti cura)* to take direct issue in terms of the natural law with the repressions of the Nazi state. The Roman Church, as the called protector and interpreter of the divine law of nature, must declare the deprivation of the liberties of the Roman Catholic Church in Germany a *Zwangsprodukt* (a product brought about by force) which is devoid of any justification in law.

Pope Pius XII (1939–59) dealt with the shattering con-

ditions of World War II and its aftermath. In his allocution of
Nov. 2, 1954, the pope notes that many men and women consider
the guidance and supervision of the church unworthy of today's
mature person and refuse to accept the practical application of
the church's dogmas and laws for their lives. But the church is
no mere private guide and counselor; it fulfills its function by
the command and authority of the Lord Himself. It has the duty
to govern the souls of men.

The tone of expression has greatly changed since the days
when the Roman pope addressed himself to "Christendom." No
longer is the Roman Church coterminous with the people of
a state. And although the pope is still given a polite hearing in
the world, and the Roman bishops of a country may issue their
doctrinal statements regarding the tasks and limits of the state,
as the German bishops did at Fulda in 1953, the Roman Church
finds, as do other religious groups, that the increasing secularization of life today in nominally Christian countries has greatly
diminished the attention of its audience.[11] Political power in
terms of this present world, as Mao Tse-Tung said, is found at
the end of a gun. Though the nations of the West are much
too polite to say so, they act largely in the context of Stalin's
question to Churchill: "How many divisions has the Pope got?"
If the Roman Church's claim to be a "perfect society" and
a secular power as well is not taken seriously today as it was
during the many centuries of the Middle Ages, this is because
the Christian religion is no longer believed to be relevant to
politics in the same sense as it formerly was.

American Catholic Revisions

The experience of Roman Catholics in the United States under
the conditions of religious liberty for all citizens has had a profound effect on some Catholic theologians. One of the notable
cases is that of Jacques Maritain. In his book *Man and the State*,
for instance, he makes the rather remarkable statement:

> The supreme, immutable principle of the superiority of the
> Kingdom of God over the earthly kingdoms can apply in other
> ways than in making the civil government the secular arm of

the Church, in asking kings to expel heretics, or in using the rights of the spiritual sword to seize upon temporal affairs for the sake of some spiritual necessity (for instance in releasing the subjects of an apostate prince from their oath of allegiance). These things we can admire in the Middle Ages; they are a dead letter in our age.[12]

Maritain, seeking to remove the inconsistency between Catholic dogma and the real situation, makes a distinction between principles and practice. He maintains that the Catholic principles are immutable, but as the political situation changes, their application changes. The principles are to be applied not literally but analogically.[13] This change from literal to analogical attaches the notion of direct power, which the medieval popes had claimed for practice, to principle. It enables Maritain to shift from a normative interpretation to a descriptive interpretation of the church-state relation. Three principles remain immutable: (1) the church is free to teach, preach, and worship; (2) the spiritual is superior to the secular; and (3) church and state are mutually dependent.[14]

The first principle is based on the following reasoning, which has a modern, American flavor. Men by nature have the right of free association and the freedom to believe what they, in conscience, consider to be true. The church is a result of the pursuit of these rights. Therefore the church is free to teach, preach, and worship.

Maritain distinguishes three ages of the relation of the church to the state. The sacral age existed when the unity of faith was prerequisite for political unity. It was destroyed by the emergence of nationalistic states. With the advent of a pluralistic society of men bound in competing states, the secular age came into being. The state has developed full autonomy for itself and ignores the church and its rights. This is particularly apparent in the case of communistic societies. This age, however, cannot last, because it contradicts the third immutable principle, mutual dependence of church and state on one another. Therefore this age must inevitably yield to a future age where this contradiction is removed. The church will function, not by power or legal constraint but through the minds and consciences of the citizenry, from within, to inspire the state to the highest ideals.[15] This will be a period of moral guidance and enlightenment wherein the state will become conscious of the superior goals of the church and lend her support to their attainment.

Maritain uses the expression "the Church" to denote the Roman Catholic Church. He allows a place for other denominations as well as social and fraternal groups in society by the proviso that the state has an obligation to recognize and support all religious and secular organizations, independent of the state itself, which contribute to the common good of the people. Although he holds that the state ought to maintain diplomatic relations with the Vatican if the majority of its citizens are Roman Catholic, at the same time he believes there should be no state religion.[16]

The Roman Church over the long term has demonstrated a realistic sensitivity towards the forces which have historically disputed its unimpeded operation within the claimed domain of the papacy, in particular since the French Revolution,[17] by notable shifts of emphasis [18] or even by a considerable reinterpretation of historic positions.[19] There is a different tone in the presentations of those who favor a greater application of the lessons of the American experience of the Roman Catholic Church.[20] However, it is highly doubtful that we can speak of the emergence of a "liberal" movement among American Roman Catholics.[21] Rather, men like John Courtney Murray, John Cogley, and Thomas O'Dea [22] are to be seen as providing tactical openings which the hierarchy may choose to use when needed. The Roman Catholic distinctions between the permanent and the transitory, between the definite and the relative in church-state relations [23] ought to prevent the easy conclusion that there has been an essential change in the position of the Roman Church regarding the church-state question. But that there have been shifts of emphasis of a significant kind should be noted.[24] Whether the Roman Catholic dynamic view tends to reduce tension between the Roman Church and American society, because it does not contain an objective obligation to alter the existent structure of church-state separation and assumes a minimal correspondence of civil law with natural law, is by no means a practical certainty.[25] Analyses of this kind seem to underestimate the profound and intense religious dynamic which informs the Roman Catholic dogma of the church and therefore determines in the end the temporary conception of a viable church-state relationship.[26]

VARIANTS IN THE REFORMED APPROACH

Puritan Spokesmen

The earliest literature of the American Puritans makes little mention of principles governing church-state relations. The Puritans came to America with the idea of establishing a theocracy. Their earliest literature, journals, and histories record the story of that venture. As they put their ideas into practice, however, problems involving principles of government began to emerge. As the Puritan fathers sought to solve these problems, a new kind of literature also emerged.

Sermons, speeches, pamphlets, and books were prepared to state explicitly what was to be believed concerning church-state relations. Some were written for the benefit of the homeland, which under Cromwell had moved in a direction different from that in the colonies. Some were written by the governmental authorities to defend their actions against the attacks of various clergymen and laymen. Some were prepared by the clergy to defend the rights of the church and the citizenry against their usurpation by government. And the orthodox Puritans and the emergent congregationalists battled over the rights of the individual citizen.

From such literature we can extract the theory of church-state relations held by the Puritans which, in spite of diversity in small matters, retains for the most part a homogeneity. No one writer of the time developed the entire theory in all its ramifications. Each in his concern with particular problems states a part of it. Some of the basic principles bear a marked resemblance to political ideas current in England and on the continent, notably those of Rousseau and Hobbes. Others come from Calvin's

Geneva. Yet the Puritan twist, reflecting the belief that these
people were the New Israel, freed from a modern Egypt and
obedient to the Lord's will, gives their political theory a novelty
and a distinctiveness which justifies ascribing to it an identity
all its own. John Winthrop, John Cotton, John Wise, and Jonathan Mayhew are the primary contributors to this amalgamation
of Puritan ideas.[27]

According to the New England theological thought, man by
nature is in a condition of liberty. He is free to do whatever he
is able to do. This condition of liberty is shared with the beasts
of the field. There are no governments and there are no laws.
There are no rules governing morality. It is a war of all
against all. This condition is not pleasing to God. In His
divine providence He has provided man with a means to protect
himself from the dangers of natural liberty. That means is government. Under government a new kind of freedom comes into
being, the freedom to do what is good, just, and honest. The
function of government is to enable men to live in civil concord.

Government legitimately comes into being when men enter
into a civil compact with one another. The compact expresses
the covenant which is made between the governed and their
governors and spells out their respective rights and duties.

Government has both its human and its divine side. Since
government is an ordinance of God, rulers have their authority from God and are responsible to Him. When they enter
into a compact with men, they enter also into a compact
with God, whether they realize it or not. God expresses His
pleasure or displeasure with their rule by attending it with
success or failure. The ruling authority comes also from the
people with whom rulers enter into compact, and they are
responsible to them. The function of government, on its divine
side, is to seek to carry out the will of God among the citizenry
so that it may constitute a holy community. On its human
side the function of government is to seek the common good
of the people.

Because of the natural depravity of man, government controls
civil conduct by means of laws and sanctions. Natural reason.

which is the vestige of the knowledge of good and evil left in man after the fall into sin, functions as the ground for the formation of law in non-Christian states, where there is no knowledge of the revealed will of God. In Christian states, the revealed law of God is the foundation and criterion of human law.

Three elements enter into the character of a political act, whether it be an act of government or of individuals: God, the compact, and the law. With respect to God, the act is either holy or evil; with respect to the compact, it is either just or unjust; with respect to the law, it is good or bad. The act is holy or unholy because it relates to the will of God, just or unjust because the compact determines what is to be justice in the society, and good or bad because law has a normative character. There is also the possibility of unholy compacts, such as fail to carry out the will of God, and unholy laws. There can also be unjust laws, such as go contrary to the terms of the compact. Thus, in human society there may be a variety of kinds of government and of law.

If government is good, the people will prosper in material affairs, and there will be evidences of divine favor, both spiritual and natural. If government is bad, the people will suffer material losses, and if the cause of God's kingdom is to advance, its progress will come about in spite of the nature of the government. God manifests His displeasure through natural calamities and disasters. It is interesting to note that the Puritans maintained this empirical test for good government. It was purported to apply not only to the human side of government but also to the spiritual. Divine providence oversees the action of government, and God registers His approval or disapproval through natural phenomena.

According to Puritan doctrine, people owe unqualified obedience to good government. They have the right and obligation to disobey government if it commands them to act contrary to the commands of God or if the ordinances of government are contrary to the common good. For if government does not achieve the common good, it has failed its part of the compact, and the people are not required to keep their part.

The form of government most amenable to this theory is a theocracy. Under such a form of government the distinction between church, community, and government becomes hazy. This is particularly the case if it is possible to employ empirical tests to distinguish God's elect from the nonelect, as the early Puritans thought. Under such conditions there are no secular acts or conditions. Everything in the community contributes to or impedes the sanctification of the people. Thus the things men use, their mores and customs, all come under scrutiny of church and state and are licensed or forbidden as they seem to contribute to or detract from the holy living of the people. Those people who can offer no empirical evidence of their election by God are unwelcome in the community and must leave.

This theory of government, however, is also applicable to pagan governments and people, though to a lesser degree. Such governments and people, unaware of God and His will, still are guided by the natural light of reason to seek the common good of the community. While such a state of affairs does not promote the kingdom of God, it does prevent pagan races from overcoming the people of God.

General acceptance of such a political theory is likely to produce the following practical results. Members of the clergy will consider it their right and obligation to criticize and to discuss matters of governmental concern and to urge legislation dealing with moral matters. They will on occasion seek to marshal public opinion against or for measures contemplated for enactment by government. Such matters need not directly concern the church as such but will lie in the area of common good. The clergy will be concerned not simply with a sphere of activities separate from governmental concern but also with questions of political and social justice.

A breach of law will be considered a sin, an act of disobedience to God. Hence church discipline may be instituted, not merely for reasons of heresy or moral turpitude but also for the breach of civil law. The clergy will interest themselves and their parishioners in social and economic problems and will consider it their religious duty to seek proper solution.

They may seek political office or urge their congregational members to seek it on religious grounds. People holding such a theory will attempt to apply religious criteria to their contemplated actions and procedures when they hold political office.

On the other hand, civil authorities in agreement with this theory will want to justify their actions to their church group (or at least to maintain that before God their actions are justified). They will seek the prayers of the church at public functions, perhaps solicit clerical opinion on social and economic problems, and try to support religious activity in civic institutions. They will concern themselves with regulating the customs and mores of the people and with changing the social and economic character of the community through legislation. They may even be concerned with limiting by law the sort of religious worship which is to be practiced.

This sort of theory about church-state relations has been and continues to be influential in the United States of America. In fact it may well be the most influential theory in this country today.

Contemporary European Reformed Theory

It is difficult to classify Karl Barth as Reformed or Lutheran. Part of his career was spent in Germany; more recently he has lived and worked in Switzerland. He has been influenced by both Luther and Calvin and has had an influence on both contemporary Reformed and Lutheran thinking. Barth's thinking on church and state has been conditioned by his experiences with the Nazi state in Germany, one of which was his expulsion from Germany for opposition to the government.

Barth purports to derive his position from a reexamination of Scripture and a close exegesis of it, notably John 18 and 19; Rom. 13; 1 Peter 2; etc. It is important to note that Barth is concerned with developing his theory of the nature and function of the state from New Testament sources; in contrast the Puritans of New England rested heavily on the Old Testament. He, as did they, uses the method of analogy. For the Puritans the state was to be analogized to the Israelite theocracy in the wilderness

of Sinai and in Canaan. For Barth the state is an analog to the
kingdom of God. Having considered various sorts of relations
that the church might consider the state to have to itself, Barth
concludes, "The only possibility that remains — and it suggests
itself compellingly — is to regard the existence of the state as an
allegory, as a correspondence and an analogue to the Kingdom
of God which the Church preaches and believes in." [28] The
Puritans sought to structure their community analogous to the
Israelite community. Barth proposes that the church should
strive for a state which functions in accordance with the principles that underlie the way Christ rules His church.

A second shift from the Puritan position is this: While the
Puritans maintained that government is a divinely ordained tool
of God the Father to carry out the providence of His will, Barth
holds that government is a tool of the Second Person of the
Trinity for the establishment and spread of the kingdom of
Jesus Christ. ". . . the State as such, belongs originally and ultimately to Jesus Christ; that in its comparatively independent
substance, in its dignity, its function and its purpose, it should
serve the Person and Work of Jesus Christ and therefore the
justification of the sinner." [29]

The state, according to Barth, is one of the angelic forces
whereby Christ, as King, rules the universe. This force, like the
angels of old, can fall away from its purpose and become demonic.
It can become indifferent to Christ or oppose His kingdom. The
function of the state is to bring men into order in peace in their
outward relations toward one another. It is contrary to the function of the state to establish or promote a particular philosophy
or attitude toward life or to seek to control man's spirit in any way.

The state is concerned with justice. Justice, for Barth, ultimately is of God. It is derived from the theological conception
of justification. Consequently, in a state where the justification
of God is unknown, justice does not exist. The task of announc-
ing God's justification in Jesus Christ, the Gospel, is committed
to the church. For this purpose it needs freedom. The freedom
of which Barth speaks is not the freedom to speak but rather
the freedom of men living in an orderly society under peaceful

conditions. It is not the church which needs to be free to speak, but rather men free to listen; the church can prosper even under conditions of persecution. For its task the church needs the state that there may be order in the world. This is the reason why the church prays for peace in the state and encourages obedience even to governments which are inimical to the church.

The church is within the state. Men enter the church freely and are bound by love into the kingdom of God. They enter the state by birth and are bound by force into the peace of the earthly community. The state is subordinate to the church because it exists for the sake of the church's work. Yet paradoxically enough, the church subordinates itself to the state to be obedient to its commands, unless the state sets itself in opposition to Christ. But even under these conditions the church is not justified in opposing the state or in seeking to overthrow the government. It may oppose the state only in those particulars where it is in opposition to Christ.

The task of the church with respect to the state is to try by persuasion to reform the state. The church falls between the kingdom of God, which will be perfectly realized in eternity, and the state. It is the church's task to "illuminate the connection between the state and the Kingdom of God" by teaching, instructing, and testifying.

> By its political activity it calls the state from neutrality, ignorance, and paganism into co-responsibility before God, thereby remaining faithful to its own particular mission. It sets in motion the historic process whose aim and content are the moulding of the state into the likeness of the Kingdom of God and hence the fulfillment of the state's own righteous purposes.[30]

The church may illumine also by example. The church manifests itself in an organized polity. For the sake of the state the "real church" must structure itself analogous to the kingdom of God that it may be a sort of prototype of the "real state."

The church, with respect to the state, is not concerned about dealing with issues of a political character or solving problems of the state but rather about forming attitudes and supporting principles. Barth is opposed to the formation of a Christian political party. The church is not to enter politics, to be a state, but to be an example and to build attitudes.

Barth purports to derive the principles for which the church stands by analogy from the way God rules His kingdom. In one place he advocates the following: the inviolable dignity of man, equality of men before the law, social and economic justice, freedom of association, concern for the common good, equality of treatment for all races, creeds, and sexes, public diplomacy, freedom of speech, government for the people, antinationalism, and peaceful solution of problems. He proposes that the church must involve itself politically in the state for the achievement of these goals. It is the continuing task of the church to be in advance of the state, pointing out ways whereby the state may improve itself, and showing the way by the fashion in which it comports itself in its own affairs.

Barth assigns a more conservative function to the church than did the Puritans. It is to show the way, not to sit in judgment on the state. He assigns a noble, exalted position to the church. His approach is intellectually more appealing than that of the Puritans. We cannot imagine Jonathan Edwards haranguing his hearers on behalf of the dignity of man. But it seems as much out of character for Barth to inveigh against the playing of bowls on Boston Common of a Sunday afternoon. Yet there are in practice many similarities. Both positions agree that the church has something to say to the state to improve it while the state has nothing to say to the church. Both the Puritans and Barth agree that the church is justified in involving itself in political affairs, but they differ on the extent and the manner of the involvement.

The position of Emil Brunner of the University of Zurich closely resembles that of Karl Barth. He is perhaps closer than Barth to the Lutheran view on the matter of church and state, but in general he remains in the Reformed tradition.

For Brunner, as for the Puritans and Barth, both church and state are of divine origin. It is the function of the state to be a power which establishes and maintains order among a people.[31] The function of the church is to create a community of believers. The church needs the state because without order the church cannot create such a community, nor can humanity survive. The state needs the church because the church is the witness to and the example of the moral bases on which the state, if it is to function well, must be founded. For purposes of order as an organized institution the church is subject to the rule of the state. And her members are not exempted from the legal system of the state. The church, as kingdom of God, is not subject to the state but is free according to the law of liberty under God.

The church owes the state qualified obedience and is to subject herself to it insofar as the state does not hinder her work and insofar as the state does not poison the thought of the people against the church or jeopardize the balance of their separate orders in life. There is always the danger for the church that the people of the state will be compelled by the state to choose between state and church.[32] But there is also the danger to the state that the church may try to set herself up as a state within a state.

The church has the right to criticize the moral bases of the state and to make moral demands on the state.[33] The state possesses the power of enforcing its will on its people. The church possesses the power of spiritual resistance, marshaling public opinion, and, if these fail, the testimony of martyrdom. She does not have the right to lead a revolution or to form a political opposition party.[34] The church is the "soul" of the secular community, its vital spirit. As such, it is her function, not only to preach the Gospel but also by precept and example to lead the secular community to a social and economic order more commensurate with the will of God.[35]

While the terms of Brunner differ from those of Barth, and their concepts of the status of the church in the state differ, they are not appreciably at variance in substance. Brunner finds an order in "creation and redemption" as a moral foundation for positive law. Barth finds a foundation in the analogy to the kingdom of God. Barth's position is more compatible with a democratic form of government. Brunner is less limited. Both maintain that the function of the church is to preach the Gospel, yet each ultimately goes beyond this point. The Gospel concerns itself, not merely with the relation of man to God but also with his relation to his fellowman. It has also a social character. Hence an entree into the political scene is effected. Both reject the notion of natural law which plays a central role in Roman Catholic doctrine, yet each finds a moral ground which an enlightened state will supposedly recognize as valid. Unlike the American Puritans, both Barth and Brunner consider the notion of an earthly Utopia as self-contradictory. The idea of a state church is also repugnant to them. The church in its organizational manifestation must always submit itself to the order of the state in matters of administration, but it occupies the unique position of moral critic of the state.

LUTHERAN RETHINKING ON CHURCH AND STATE
Johann Gerhard (1582–1637)

The greatest Lutheran dogmatician of the 17th century, Johann Gerhard, illustrates a kind of continuity of the medieval conception of society as "Christendom" *(corpus Christianum)*, an ancient conception which had its roots in Plato's *politeia*. He writes of hierarchies, ranks, and classes in the church — ecclesiastical, political, and business classes, rather like the medieval society divided into priests, lords temporal, and common people. He rejects, however, the Roman Catholic conception of a universal church which has the right to intervene forcibly in all matters of human concern.

We have in Gerhard's thinking the idea of a Christian society within a territorial entity. The secular government acknowledges Christian aims, and the church, broadly speaking, includes all of the population. On the strength of this consensus, the secular government serves the church through its administration, and the church consecrates all acceptable callings in this territorial Christendom, whose purposes and goals remain explicitly religious.

When man fell into sin, God left him with some knowledge

of His Law because social discipline is impossible without it, and man could not thus exist in society.[36] The "first use" of the Law *(usus paedagogicus)* is always to impede the gross excesses of sin, and the natural law fulfills this function by creating a society under law, that is, the state.[37] In this context Gerhard also has a place for the doctrine of the freedom of the will in external things.[38] Believers and infidels share both the external discipline and the liberty in external things.[39]

Natural law and the divine law have the same source — God; and all people, regardless of time, place, and condition, are subject to natural law. Differences between nations, as revealed in their positive laws, express the various characteristics or habits of people which are always historically conditioned.[40] Positive laws are the manifold streams flowing from one unchangeable source, which is the created law of nature.[41] Natural law projects the chief moral imperatives; its detailed or practical applications belong to the function of positive law.

Since the fall man lost the ability to apply the concreated natural law to his individual needs with sure and perfect discernment. Accordingly, the multiplicity of positive law among the nations is another sign of the sin-weakened nature of man.[42] Unlike natural law, positive law has its source in God indirectly or mediately through the action of the community or state whereby God reveals His will.[43] The individual has the unfailing duty to obey the magistrates through whom God rules men.[44] For Gerhard the prince or magistrate is intended to be "vice-regent" of God on earth and consequently ought to exhibit the relevant attributes of God in relation to the ruled. Gerhard seems to envision the possibility of regulating a community of believing Christians to such an extent that the ideal state of affairs may be approached in their recognition of the godly prince or magistrate as the vice-regent of God on earth. The prince or magistrate is in effect placed beyond the criticism of the Christian.

Whereas Luther could recognize the usurpations of Satan as extending also to the political order, so that the prince or magistrate may actually be the servant of Satan and the enemy of the kingdom of God, Gerhard seems interested only in providing a theological sanction for the historically given political order. All actual political orders are of God. The political order is idealized by Gerhard because he fails to observe realistically, as Luther did, that a pious prince is a rather "rare bird" on earth and that a "Christian state" is not a historical possibility.[45]

Gerhard emphasizes out of all proportion the inherited rights and privileges of the princes. To be sure, the prince has many duties, such as the cultivation of his own moral character and that of his subjects, so that he may well perform his chief duty — to mediate God's works. Luther's "rare bird" seems to become in Gerhard's framework the normal picture of the Lutheran prince — studious, pious, fervent in prayer, sober, restrained, a good husband and father, but especially the *Landesvater* of his people. The stability of the state is better protected by a monarch who preserves the historical traditions than by the free expression of the people's will, for they cannot be trusted responsibly to exercise elective rights.[46] The monarchical privileges exacted by the 17th-century Lutheran princes receive their sanction in Gerhard, even to the notorious hunting privileges which allowed the princes to impose the death penalty for poaching. All this seemed a small price to pay for the continuity of the great duty of princes, i. e., that they concern themselves with sacred things. The attitude of Gerhard is most revealing when he advises princes to acquire able advisers devoted to the service of the true religion and sedulously to follow their advice.[47]

St. Paul's picture of the Christian church as a living body is applied by Gerhard to the political community. Members of a community owe their fellow citizens the duty of mutual service and peaceful association, and their prince constant intercessions in prayer as well as the kind of goodwill which is slow to criticize. The citizen has the duty to serve his country with his possessions, his talents, and, if need be, with his very life.

In the event of a conflict between the demands of government and of God, the Christian must obey God rather than the ruler.[48] However, he may not revolt against government but must suffer his martyrdom in patience. If God will not hear the prayers of

Christians to change the heart of the magistrate, they may, if the possibility exists, appeal to another magistrate to intervene, or else flee the country. But if there is no remedy for their oppressive condition, they must resolve to endure their sufferings for the Lord's sake.[49]

Interesting is Gerhard's treatment of resistance to a tyrannical government. If a constitutional government becomes tyrannical, the lesser magistrate has the duty to resist. This follows the Lutheran tradition established at the end of the 1530s, when the Smalcald League was organized to resist the emperor. Other theologians, such as Chemnitz and Nikolaus Hunnius, follow Gerhard. If, however, the prince or government is not constitutional, yet in possession of absolute power, the Christian cannot claim the right to resist.[50]

Gerhard writes as one content in general with the existing order of things. He does not seem disturbed, as Luther was, by the pressure of constantly having to choose the lesser evil. In Gerhard we find an accommodating inclination to accept, approve, or even justify the historically given. By way of comparison, it may be said that the 17th-century orthodoxy lacked Luther's lively sense of the incalculable transforming power of the Gospel by the operation of God's Holy Spirit. There is reasonable argument, wearying persuasion. But the vivifying flashes of the Spirit of Christ, who makes all things new, so overpowering in Luther, seem to have become tamed and controlled by the representatives of Lutheran orthodoxy. Perhaps it is true that Melanchthon and his successors believed the people were not ready for the freedom of the Christian man in Luther's grand sense of the term, but felt that communities must first be educated for freedom by means of widening circles of legalistic elucidations. The consequences were a one-sided emphasis on form and a dangerous neglect of the inner dynamic. The new identification of law and morality results in the kind of legalistic disposition which hopes to usher in the kingdom of God by legislation.[51]

Gerhard sees the purposes of the state fulfilled when it provides the "quiet and peaceable life, godly and respectful in every way" (1 Tim. 2:2). This is achieved in part by application of the Second Table of the Law (Commandments 4 to 10) to the stated purposes of the civil order. However, a "Christian" government also has a responsibility for sacred things. This responsibility is based on the First Table of the Law (Commandments 1 to 3). Old Testament passages are adduced to make this concern really the chief task of the "Christian" government.[52] It fits the state to the divine purpose and gives it a transcendent dignity, because the ultimate destiny of man, eternal life, becomes the final interest of the "Christian" state when it assumes the Christian nurture of its subjects or citizens.[53]

To be sure, Gerhard warns emphatically not to mix the functions of state and church. But the state has the task of providing peace for the development of the life of the church, to foster the piety of its subjects, to care for the training and livelihood of the clergy. The prince functions as the territorial bishop, but not directly, because consistories and superintendents actually govern the church and supervise the pastors. But he alone issues laws for the church, calls synods, and assigns pastors to congregations (theoretically with their consent). It is the task of the prince or state to maintain the true religion and to restore it when and where necessary. The restoration of the true religion in areas where its service has decayed would obligate the prince to admonish and discipline pastors who have become negligent or heretical, and for this task he must not be dependent on his clergy but possess his own theological competence.[54]

Only the state or prince may decree church law.[55] Since the positive laws of the state have their source in natural law,[56] it follows that natural law in effect becomes the standard or norm for the issuance of church laws. The state or prince administers the properties of the church and assumes responsibility for the financial support of the clergy. The state has the right to expel heretics from its territory, but not the right — by way of contrast with Roman Catholic and some Reformed theologians — to punish them with the death penalty.[57] However, if heretics are also revolutionists whose aim is the subversion of the government, the state may deal with them according to its laws.

C. F. W. Walther (1811–87)

The leader of The Lutheran Church — Missouri Synod in its formative stage was Dr. C. F. W. Walther. He emphasized the freedom of the congregation from ecclesiastical control. But the church polity of the Synod in its origins had no connection with secular elements of political theory.[58] On the contray, the early Saxons in Missouri opposed the "self-evident" assumptions of Jefferson's Declaration of Independence because it asserted a status for man which had been lost in the fall, and expressed the hope for indeterminate progress.

Walther's revision of Baier's *Compendium theologiae positivae* reveals emphases different from those of Johann Gerhard.[59] There is a resolute rejection of state interference in the affairs of the church. There is also a clear preference for quotations from the Lutheran fathers which indicate opposition to the traditional German use of consistories, composed of theologians and politicians, to determine social and religious policy.

> Proper government may be abstractly defined as a public office ordained by God wherein certain persons legitimately called and installed in power over civil and sometimes sacred matters in the republic make laws, exercise judgment, and punish criminals, and defend the same against external foes for the sake of public safety.[60]

An excellent illustration of Walther's teaching on the popular level is available in his sermon on Matt. 22:15-22.[61] Christianity, he says, is a religion for all times and for all human beings regardless of country, politics, status, calling, age, or condition. Christ is Lord in both a monarchy and a free republic because His kingdom is not of this world but in the hearts and souls of men. Since He is not subversive to the interests of the secular government, no secular realm can overthrow Him. Christ's word is in force: "Render unto Caesar the things which are Caesar's and unto God the things that are God's." Therefore government of all kinds and on all levels exists by the ordinance of God, to which Christians must be subject for conscience' sake. This obedience extends to the whole range of the social order. But it has a correlative: Give unto God that which is God's — your total self.

It was a principle of Walther's that the liberalism of the day, both theological and political, was subversive of Christian doctrine and morality. But there is relatively little said about it in the official publications of the Missouri Synod. Its polemic is usually in the form of brief comments on current affairs. One of the exceptions is Walther's short exposition on slavery and attendant issues.[62] He and his fellow leaders of the Missouri Synod took a strong position on the principle of the two realms, the secular and the spiritual, against the sectarian preachers who freely pushed their political programs by every means. The kingdom of God, argued the Missourians, cannot and must not be promoted by political action. It is an abuse of the office of the ministry when clergymen enter the political arena.

Walther and many of his contemporaries felt themselves to be alien to the political spirit of their new fatherland. But this did not mean that they had a noticeable affection for the church-state relationship in the German states or in the new German empire. They were loyal to their adopted America. God in His providence had led them to it and allowed them to live and work without interference by the government. They believed that in the polity and life of the newly formed Missouri Synod they had achieved what Luther had intended but was unable to achieve — a church independent of the state and free to accomplish the mission God had assigned to it. The American government was held in very high esteem because of the freedom it provided for the Christian church and for the citizen. At the same time the fathers of the Missouri Synod roundly rejected the moral assumptions of American political philosophy as incongruent with their theology.

They vigorously pressed for the observance of a strict separation of church and state in areas which their descendants no longer think as readily distinguishable. But despite the very considerable accommodation which the Missouri Synod has made to its environment, its basic principles have not changed. In general it shares the basic outlook of contemporary Lutheranism in

America regarding Luther's teaching of the two realms as applicable in principle to modern times. But the Missouri Synod is much more reserved about making public pronouncements on political issues of the day than almost any other major denomination in the land. Granting a few exceptions, its clergy refrains from political activity. Its teaching function extends to the dissemination of the Gospel and the insights of moral law. The specific decisions, however, remain the responsibility of the individual Christian, who confronts his particular task in the place and time where he lives, works, and believes.

Eivind Berggrav (1884–1959)

Continental Lutheran theologians saw no reason to change the traditional Lutheran doctrine of the separation of church and state until the second quarter of the 20th century. The doctrine had survived intact under conditions where Lutheranism was the official state religion and where it was not. No doctrinal modification on the issue was effected at the time of the Prussian Union, when by state order Reformed and Evangelical branches of Christendom were merged in East Prussia. Nor were new provisos adopted to govern or justify the church's action in countries where Roman Catholicism was the only legally permitted religion.

The advent of Naziism in Germany and its spread to Norway during the occupation of World War II, as well as the subsequent spread of communism to eastern Europe after the war, has caused some Lutheran theologians to revise their thinking on church-state relations. One of these was Eivind Berggrav, Lutheran bishop of Oslo and primate of the Lutheran Church in Norway from 1937 to 1950. He led the Lutheran opposition to Naziism in Norway and was first put into a concentration camp by the Germans, then placed under house arrest until the end of the war.

At the beginning of the occupation of Norway, the Lutheran Church cooperated with the occupying powers. As Berggrav put it: "In the beginning it was difficult for us to declare war, as Naziism never showed any hostility toward the Church or Christianity." [63] The two provisos of Lutheranism — "Let every soul be subject to the higher powers," and: "We ought to obey

God rather than men" — seemed compatible with this position. But a number of events occurred in short order in the period from 1940 to 1942 which forced the Norwegian Lutherans to rethink their principles. All pastors in Norway were instructed to offer prayers for the Nazi state. Certain constitutional rights of the Lutheran Church in Norway were abolished. The right of the clergy to preserve the secrecy of the confessional was abrogated. The Nazi government sought to remove and appoint bishops of the state church and began to organize a youth corps for the training of all children in Nazi dogma, ordering the churches to support the program. Unprovoked attacks on Norwegian citizens took place, and there was general unrest and uncertainty in the nation about the stability and justice of the law courts.

Some of the resulting problems involved the legal status of the church in Norway, and as such they fall outside the classical theological concern of the Lutheran church with church-state matters. But the dictation to the church with respect to how it was to be operated, who its leaders were to be, and what it was to teach were issues of grave theological concern. With respect to these Lutheran doctrine was clear. Almost en masse the clergy resigned from the state church and set up a new free church. Their parishes followed the pastors, retaining the properties which they had held but forfeiting the taxes paid for the salaries of the clergy.

Now the clergy began to speak in criticism of government action, for example, in the treatment of the Jews. They sought to find some ground of fundamental human rights on the basis of which the actions and laws of the occupying government could legitimately be criticized. The church in Norway began to take on a new role in the political situation. The theological professors issued a statement which contained the remark: "The Church is not the Lord of the State, nor a state within a state, but the State's conscience." [64] Here is a novel statement for Lutherans to make on the relation of the church to the state. It is the sort of approach which is more characteristically Reformed than Lutheran. As conscience, the church has the right and duty to comment on the moral and religious aspects of events which occur in the nation and to use persuasion and moral force to bring about change. Berggrav states the justification for this position as follows:

> That which decided us was the experience of lawless society —
> something which had never even entered our imagination —
> and we were enlightened by the Word of God and by the
> Confession of our Church, that Right and Justice belong to
> God's own order in the world. Our Lutheran Confession in
> its article 16 thrice repeats the words that all authority shall
> be *de jure* — an authority of Justice and Right. How often
> have we not felt thankful that our Lutheran Confession con-
> tained those clear, strong words! We were to witness how
> innocent people were arbitrarily struck down by the quislings,
> how the latter's uniformed gangs made havoc, how their police
> betrayed their duty towards law and justice, and how their
> leader arbitrarily altered the laws and broke them.[65]

The Lutherans began to look upon themselves as facing a situation analogous to that of Luther at Worms, "the rising of the
Christian conscience against unjust authority, ecclesiastical or
secular." [66] They felt they were defending not only the sacred
autonomy of the church to structure itself and to teach without
outside interference, but also safeguarding the fundamental rights
of man for freedom of belief against the forced support of the
dogma of a totalitarian state.

The argument of Berggrav, supporting this position, seems to
be the following: God is a God of order and not disorder. Therefore the church must support order and oppose disorder in the
state. Disorder in the state is injustice and opposition to the
rights of citizens. Therefore the church must oppose unjust laws
and actions. Article XVI of the Augsburg Confession states that
"just" governments are to be supported by all Christians. Hence
this seems to suggest that "unjust" governments are to be opposed.

With the appearance of modern forms of totalitarianism, it is
understandable that European Lutherans should search anew for
means whereby the church can react in a positive fashion.
Whether the means at the disposal of the church in the Word

of God have been exhausted or contain resources as yet unrecognized is a matter hotly debated by Lutherans in both Europe and America.

CONCLUSION

Roman Catholics, Reformed, and Lutherans are agreed that the state is a divinely sanctioned instrument to be used by mankind for its betterment. The Roman Catholic view is that the state is natural to man, having been built into the nature of things. The Reformed and Lutheran view has generally been that the state is necessary because of man's sinfulness. All three reject the notion that the state is independent of the church, and agree that there is an area of moral concern mutually shared by church and state. The three positions are not in agreement as to the nature of the relations between church and state.

Logically there are four possible relationships which the church and the state may have to each other: independence, identity, interdependence, and subordination of one to the other. The Puritans came close to identifying church with state. Roman Catholics, at least in papal expression, hold the state to be subordinate to the church, i. e., the Roman Catholic Church. The Reformed emphasis is on equal status for church and state, with the church subordinate in the matter of maintenance of order, and the state subordinate in matters of religion and morals. In a conflict, the claim of the church has priority over that of the state. The Lutheran position has tended to subordinate the church to the state in many respects, alloting a larger share of responsibility to the state than either the Reformed or the Roman Catholic views, maintaining at the same time independence of the church over against the state in matters of belief and practice. Where a choice must be made between church and state, the church has priority.

All three groups agree that the church is to preach the Gospel and to serve the needy. Lutherans have tended to stop at this point. The Reformed have maintained that the church is also to influence the morals of the state by testimony, precept, and example, without necessarily using political action. Roman Catholics have held that the church is not only responsible for the morals of the state but has the right of intervention in any matter of state concern. They have not been averse to political action and the formation of religious political parties to implement their view.

There have been changes in all three groups since the days of the Reformation. The Reformed group has probably changed the most in principle, the Roman Catholic the most in practice, and the Lutheran group the least in either respect. During the past 25 years all three groups have been unsettled and forced to reexamine their positions. This has led to a movement toward the middle, Reformed position by both Catholic and Lutheran thought. The shift has occurred most noticeably for Catholics in the United States and for Lutherans in Europe.

The three groups continue a lively discussion of the problems inherent in their positions on church and state and seek new applications of their positions to the changing political situation.

Goto 455

PART II

The State
in Its Relation to the Church

NEELAK S. TJERNAGEL

CARL S. MEYER

ROY C. FRANK

IT IS THE PURPOSE of Part II to provide an overview of the position of the state in church-state relations. The experience of selected European countries supplies a comparison and contrast for American concepts. This is followed by a study of the development of the American pattern. The nature and meaning of the American pattern are then presented in an analysis of the interpretations of the courts.

In chapter 4, which begins Part II, *Neelak S. Tjernagel,* Ph. D., professor of history and religion at Concordia Teachers College, River Forest, Ill., undertakes the task of defining the spirit and intent of various European approaches to church-state relations. From experiences of European countries, the early Americans were influenced to shape their own principles and practices.

Dr. Tjernagel takes up France, Spain, England, and Norway as four specific patterns. In the Roman Catholic countries of France and Spain, papal claims to temporal authority continued to affect the course of church-state relations down to modern times. In Spain, except for the Republican regime of the 1930s, separation of church and state has not been a working principle. The situation turned out differently in France. Although Catholicism had a favored position, it became a "pawn of the state" under the Bourbons and Napoleon I. With the Republic after 1870, separation of church and state was achieved, and the government has been consistently neutral in its attitude toward all religions.

For England the establishment of Anglicanism was vigorously defended on moral grounds. In their characteristic way, however, the English people have managed to arrive at both an established church arrangement and complete freedom of worship. The Lutheran Church of Norway, on the other hand, is regarded as simply the church of the Norwegian people, and the state provides for and administers it.

Chapter 4

EUROPEAN EXPERIENCE
IN CHURCH-STATE RELATIONS

Neelak S. Tjernagel

EUROPEAN PATTERNS of church-state relations should be of more than passing interest to Americans. They developed, in many instances, prior to the adoption of the First Amendment to the Constitution of the United States. Experiences of people under European patterns helped to shape the church-state relationships in this country. Even today the European approach to questions involving church and state presents a contrast to American thinking on these issues. It is well for Americans to realize that there are other methods of arriving at accommodation in church-state relations than those developed in the United States. As we wrestle with the problems that arise in this area, we may find some light shed by the European procedures.

It would be considerably beyond the reach of this chapter to sketch the thought and practice of all modern European countries in their church-state relationships. Instead an effort will be made to illustrate the views of two Roman Catholic countries, France and Spain, and two Protestant countries, England and Norway. Their patterns will be historically treated, for in Europe, even more than in America, so much that is current is a reflection of long tradition and custom.

The four countries chosen are typical of four approaches to church-state problems. Spain is a Roman Catholic country where the position of a national church has been virtually unchallenged.

France, on the other hand, had a national church whose position was effectively altered. Norway and England represent Protestant countries with established churches. The position of the established church in England is conditioned by the presence of numerous independent churches. In Norway no other denomination has a large membership since 98 percent of all Norwegians are Lutherans.

THE APPROACH

IN ROMAN CATHOLIC COUNTRIES

The Catholic view of church-state relations was born of the medieval concept that spirituality is superior to temporality. Practical effect was given to this concept by the acknowledged right of the church to excommunicate any offender against the theology or the morality of the church. Since excommunication broke all contractual obligations to the excommunicated offender, kings and princes could be deprived of the allegiance of their civil subjects by an act of the church. Henry IV at Canossa is a well-known example of the real effect of this procedure.

After the time of the conflict between Gregory VII and Henry IV, however, the national monarchies resisted papal interference in civil affairs with an increasing intensity and success. The captivity of the Avignonese papacy to the French monarchy symbolizes the declining prestige of the ecclesiastical hierarchy and the growing independence of national rulers. But if these national monarchs freed themselves from religious interference, they were also losing the religious sanction that the Middle Ages had given to their authority. The post-Reformation period therefore put them in a position of seeking out a religious basis for their political authority. The result was the growth of the 17th-century European divine-right monarchies. Scriptural quotations were used to support the claim of these monarchies even as they had been employed to support the authoritarian claims of the papacy. James I was more than explicit in claiming divine right in 1610:

> . . . The state of monarchy is the supremest thing upon earth, for kings are not only God's lieutenants upon earth and

sit upon God's throne, but even by God himself are called gods. . . . In the scriptures kings are called gods and so their power after a certain relation compared to fathers of families, for a king is truly *parens patriae,* the politic father of his people. And lastly, kings are compared to the head of this microcosm of the body of man. . . .

I conclude then this point touching the power of kings with this axiom of divinity, that as to dispute what God may do is blasphemy, . . . so is it sedition in subjects to dispute what a king may do in the height of his power. But just kings will ever be willing to declare what they will do, if they will not incur the curse of God. I will not be content that my power be disputed upon; but I shall ever be willing to make the reason appear of all my doings, and rule my actions according to my laws. . . . I would wish you to be careful . . . that you do not meddle with the main points of government; that is my craft. . . . It is an undutiful part in subjects to press their king wherein they know beforehand he will refuse them.[1]

The same view was expressed by the distinguished churchman and scholar Jacques Benigne Bossuet a half century later. He affirmed that royal authority is sacred, paternal, absolute, and subject to reason. Addressing himself to the Dauphin, the son of Louis XIV of France, in 1670, he says:

God is the king of kings; it belongs to Him to instruct and direct them as His ministers. Heed then, Monseigneur, the lessons which He gives them in His Scriptures, and learn from Him the rules and the examples on which they ought to form their conduct.

In addition to the other advantages of the Scriptures, they have also this, that they trace the history of the world from its beginnings and reveal to us by this means, better than all other histories, the basic principles which have formed empires. No history better reveals what is good and what is evil in the human heart, what sustains and what overthrows kingdoms, what religion can do to establish them, what impiety can do toward destroying them.[2]

The unity of church and state under the divine-right monarchy was taken for granted, and Louis XIV found no occasion for being tolerant of either the Jansenists or the Huguenots of 17th-century France. But neither did he suffer a Roman papacy to determine religious, much less political, policy for France.

The problem of church-state relations in Roman Catholic countries ruled by a divine-right monarch was the presence in Rome of a papacy with strongly asserted international authority in matters ecclesiastical. The 18th and 19th centuries were to see a constant tension between rulers and subjects claiming a national religious independence with those looking to and accepting the ultramontane authority of the papacy. Protestant state churches, whatever other problems they had to face, were spared this difficulty which vexed France and Spain for nearly 400 years.

Spain — A National Church Unsuccessfully Challenged

"Spain, evangelizer of half the planet; Spain, hammer of heretics, light of Trent, sword of Rome, cradle of Saint Ignatius. . . ." [3] The 19th-century author of this Spanish claim to fame is scarcely saying too much. The golden century of Spain reached its zenith in the great reigns of Ferdinand and Isabella, Charles V, and Philip II. Schooled in the problem of pushing back the Moorish invaders of Spain, Ferdinand and Isabella soon learned how to deal with the heresies of Jews and Moors. Obtaining papal sanction for a Spanish Inquisition, the rulers of Aragon and Castile found that the auto-da-fé could conveniently be used against political as well as religious nonconformists. The result was the creation of a powerful political absolutism determined to preserve "one faith and one blood" in imperial Spain.

That there was no lack of serious religious purpose in the motives of Ferdinand and Isabella, enriched beyond imagination by the gold and silver of the New World, is apparent from the missionary activity of their reign and that of their two successors. It was indeed during her golden century that Spain, "hammer of heretics," became the "evangelizer of half the planet" under the impetus of St. Francis Xavier and the Society of Jesus.

The dominant political figure of the age of the Reformation was to be the Spanish king, Ferdinand and Isabella's grandson, the Holy Roman Emperor, Charles V. It is completely in the Spanish character of the emperor that he should have made the preservation of peace and religious unity the twin motives of his career. If Charles, and his son Philip II after him, were to provide "the sword of Rome," it was not to be at the expense of subservience to the political pretensions of Rome. The sack of Rome and its aftermath illustrates well how a Spaniard would deal with a pope who ventured to meddle in political affairs.

Charles failed to suppress the Lutheran heresy in Europe, but only because he was faced with the cruel necessity of a war on two fronts, against a Catholic France and the infidel Turks. Yet he had not failed to serve his church. A generation of conflict had forced the papacy to give up its political authority and the church to reform its abuses. While Charles was opposing the Council of Trent, he was unwittingly aiding it in its ultimate achievement.

But not Charles alone. It was another Spaniard, Ignatius Loyola, that saved a crumbling hierarchy and a decaying church. It was the Society of Jesus, the superbly ordered shock troops of the papacy, that breathed a new life and vigor into the church, winning back converts, evangelizing the New World and the Orient, and giving spiritual life and a new piety to a religious organism all but submerged in the excesses of its own wealth and worldliness.

This great achievement, Spanish in origin and character, was the last great flowering of Spanish culture. It was the last great outburst of a Spain that had been preeminent in the 16th century. There remained only the final phase of the Counter-Reformation. It was the effort of Philip II, the emperor's son, to consolidate the gains of Trent and restore to Europe the religious unity that Charles had failed to bring to Germany. But the glory of Spain was gone. The Dutch repulsed Philip, the French would have none of his meddling, and Elizabeth laughed in his face.

Europe became a patchwork of diverse and conflicting religious interests and was plagued by a century of religious conflict. But Spain kept its religious unity. Trained in the harsh discipline of the Inquisition and the Index, Spain was safe in the impoverished security of a political, religious, and intellectual authoritarianism. It had missed the heady stimulus of the Reformation just as it was to miss the provocative stimuli of the Enlightenment.

Well might a modern chronicler write: "Spain, evangelizer of half the planet; Spain, hammer of heretics, light of Trent, sword of Rome, cradle of Saint Ignatius — this is our greatness and our glory: we have no other." [4]

The wealth and resources of Spain and her church have declined since the 16th century. Spanish mysticism and a reverent attitude of worship and individual devotion have continued. Nevertheless ecclesiastical estates once produced an annual income equal to half that of the kingdom, but now the properties owned by the church are returning an income covering only a quarter of her needs. [5]

No less than its rulers in the 16th century, the Spanish kings in the 18th century were concerned about intervention of the papacy in affairs of state and church and about lessening the power and privileges of the Spanish clergy, in particular, that of the Jesuits. Philip IV made an effort to come to terms in these matters in 1737. His successor drew up a concordat in 1753 which, for a heavy financial indemnity, secured the right of patronage for most church offices and the renunciation of several papal taxes in favor of Spain. [6]

Charles III (1759–88), most energetic in his attitude toward papal interference, forbade the publication of papal bulls in Spain and expelled the Jesuits precipitately. That these actions were antipapal and often anticlerical but not anti-Catholic is apparent from the constitution of 1812, which declared: "The religion of the Spanish nation is, and shall be perpetually, Apostolic Roman Catholic, the only true religion. The nation protects it by wise and just laws and prohibits the exercise of any other whatever." [7]

Though, as these words indicate, Spain remained Catholic, the government displayed an increasingly anticlerical disposition as it abolished the Inquisition, seized and confiscated church lands, and imprisoned recalcitrant bishops. The flames of anticlericalism were fanned to a new high by the Carlist wars of the 1830s. After this conflict a new constitution was adopted in 1845 which did not exclude the exercise of other religions. Spain appeared to be on the road toward religious toleration. A law of 1797 had provided that a foreigner in Spain would not be molested because of his religious views. But Spain soon returned to an accommodation with the papacy after the tensions of the Carlist conflict and the minority of Queen Isabel II. In 1851 a new concordat was approved. It provided for the perpetual preservation of the Apostolic Roman Catholic religion to the exclusion of all other cults, for public instruction in accordance with Catholic doctrine in all schools and under the supervision of the church, and for public support of the clergy.[8]

Late in the reign of Isabel II public discontent was increasingly apparent. A rising spirit of liberalism prevailed in a new anticlerical, antiabsolutist ferment. A revolution broke out in 1868, and Isabel II abdicated her throne.

Up to this time there had been little if any demand for religious liberty in Spain. The Inquisition had ruled religious dissent out of Spanish life. Spain was Catholic and no other religious view intruded. However, a long period of anticlerical protests against the power and pretensions of the ecclesiastical order paved the way for the coming of Protestant churchmen to Spain in the latter half of the 19th century. The revolution of 1868 was to open the door to proposals for religious toleration in Spain. It was to give the Spanish evangelical groups that had been supported by Protestant denominations outside Spain a hope for broad religious toleration in the future.

The revolution of 1868 did indeed inaugurate a policy of religious freedom. Religious exiles were invited to return to Spain.[9] Local proclamations of religious freedom were made. The provisional government suppressed some monasteries and convents, expelled the Jesuits, granted freedom to establish private educational institutions, and promised complete religious freedom. An earlier proclamation expelling Jews from Spain was rescinded. In answer to petitions of Catholic associations pleading for suppression of the freedom of religion, the provisional government declared:

> Religious freedom, which is now accepted in all nations of the world and which, far from deadening the faith of the immense number of Catholic people, will help to revive and fortify it, is now truly established.[10]

When a new constitution was formally adopted on June 6, 1869, adequate provisions were made for the maintenance of religious liberty in Spain, and Protestantism enjoyed a period of growth and prosperity. Even broader provisions which went so far as to separate church and state were effected in the short-lived republic of 1873.

When the Bourbon monarchy was restored in the person of Alphonso XII in 1874, the settlement of disputes between liberals and conservatives resulted in a termination of religious freedom in favor of religious toleration. Little by little Protestants lost privileges they had enjoyed before the accession of Alphonso XII.

Just as there had been controversy when the constitution of 1869 was in preparation, so the formulation of a constitution for the regime of the new king stirred up a vociferous debate. Article 11 on religion was eventually adopted as follows:

> The Apostolic Roman Catholic religion is that of the state. The nation binds itself to maintain the cult and its ministers.
>
> No one will be molested in Spanish territory for his religious opinions nor for the observance of his respective cult, provided that he shows due respect to Christian morality.
>
> Public ceremonies and manifestations other than those of the religion of the State, however, will not be permitted.[11]

The constitution of 1878 further provided that while education would be under public scrutiny, the right to maintain private schools would not be questioned. The new constitution provided only for religious toleration, and its provisions were far removed from a concept of equality or liberty for non-Catholic faiths. The policies adopted remained Spanish law until 1931, when the monarchy was abolished. During that time the degree of toleration actually maintained varied from time to time and from place to place.

The religious privileges of Roman Catholicism created problems for Protestants in the matter of burial and marriage as well as in the matter of compulsory attendance at masses for the military. The greatest hardships were in the varying degrees of intensity in enforcement of strictures against assemblies of worshipers in public places.

During the seven years of the dictatorship of Primo de Rivera, from 1923 to 1930, the government tended to tighten restrictions on Protestantism. De Rivera said:

> If in a country of twenty million inhabitants nineteen and a half million are well protected in their rights, it is not of great importance that the other half million want fuller rights.[12]

Shortly after the resignation of General Primo de Rivera in 1930 a growth in socialist and republican sentiment forced the abdication of Alphonso XIII in 1931, and Spain made a relatively quiet transition from monarchy to the establishment of the Second Spanish Republic.

The republican regime was broadly supported by a cross section of Spanish views that included both Protestants and Catholics. The religious motive supporting the republic was mainly an anticlericalism, though there was some Protestant and secular support for religious freedom for its own sake. As might have been expected, one of the first acts of the provisional government was a proclamation of religious liberty. Attendance at Roman Catholic masses was made voluntary for all men in military service as well as for inmates of prisons. Religious education was made voluntary in the schools.

The constitution, adopted in December 1931, provided for separation of church and state, equality for all religions, and a gradual termination of subsidy to the Roman Catholic Church. A later decree abolished the teaching of religion in public schools.

In 1933 extreme Catholic opposition to the republic grew out of a law that nationalized church property and forbade religious orders to engage in commercial activity. Protestantism came under the stricture that all administrators and officials had to be Spaniards.[13]

Unfortunately for the republic, conflict between leftist and rightist factions brought chaos to Spain, and in 1938 the country came under the dictatorship of General Francisco Franco, who soon manifested his determination to favor Roman Catholicism in Spain. Under the Franco government Roman Catholicism was reestablished and the "spoliations" of the Second Republic were restored. In 1945 General Franco wrote into law the Catholic nature of the Spanish school.

In Spain today non-Catholic confessions enjoy liberty and are protected by the article of the charter of the Spanish people, which in theory respects liberty of conscience. Protestant churches now exist as they existed in other regimes. But they are necessarily few, since the religion of almost all the Spanish people is Catholic, and the majority of the few who do not profess it are atheists, thereby reducing Protestantism to foreigners or persons of foreign origin or people who have lived many years outside Spain.[14] By the concordat of 1953 between Spain and the Holy See the establishment of Roman Catholicism was reaffirmed, and compulsory Catholic teaching in public and private schools was assured.

It may be observed that the present official policy of Spain includes the toleration of religious minorities. In practice this toleration is probably carried out as well as can be reasonably expected in a nation that is committed to the preservation and protection of a single communion. Complete religious equality can hardly be expected for minorities so numerically insignificant as non-Catholic groups in Spain.

France — A State Church Successfully Challenged

Unlike Spain, where the foreign influence of Islam long intruded itself, France was the very center of the western progress of Roman Catholicism. Clovis accepted Roman Christianity for his barbarian subjects in the fifth century. In the eighth century the relationship between Rome and the Merovingians was durably fixed. The papal coronation of Charlemagne on Dec. 25,

800, assured the permanence of western Christianity in the Carolingian empire. When the Capetians assumed authority in France in the 10th century, new ties developed between Rome and a dynasty that needed help in consolidating its dynastic and territorial pretensions. However, once France was politically and territorially established, it developed a tradition of ecclesiastical independence from the See of Rome and, during the Babylonian Captivity of the popes at Avignon, 1309—1377, actually controlled the papacy. The independence and freedom of the church in France, usually referred to as Gallicanism, dates back at least as far as the papacy of Boniface VIII and the reign of Philip IV in the 14th century. It is notable that in the previous century Philip Augustus did not sink as low in subservience to Innocent III as did his English counterpart John, and that Saint Louis, with his piety, made rather a better resistance to the political encroachments of the papacy than did most English kings. Likewise in the battle of bulls and pragmatics waged between Philip the Fair of France and Edward III of England, the papacy was marked for its fall and the national monarchies for their ascendancy.

In 1438 an assembly of bishops at Bourges formally declared the Gallican rights of the French church. The Pragmatic Sanction of the same year was the king's affirmation of the position stated by the churchmen of France. It was no break with the church or the papacy like the schism of Henry VIII of England. It was rather a declaration of the prerogatives of the French church and a condemnation of the ecclesiastical abuses and pretensions of the Roman See. The elections of bishops and abbots were restored to their respective religious communities, and the pope was forbidden to circulate bulls or encyclicals in France without the king's permission. In essence the Pragmatic Sanction of 1438 was an expression of the will of France jointly affirmed by the church and the crown. It supported the decrees of the Council of Constance as to the superiority of councils to popes, and looked forward to a continuation of the conciliar principle. Though the papacy never ceased to object to the Pragmatic Sanction of Bourges and the decrees of the Council of Constance, the French church stood firm, independent of both crown and papacy, and governed itself under the prerogatives stated in 1453.

The first serious break in this policy was made by Francis I in the 16th century. The occasion for this change in policy was the Concordat of Bologna of Francis I in 1516, in which Francis reserved for the French monarchy the right to make ecclesiastical appointments and conceded to the pope the right of installation to these offices. The effect of this bargain between king and pope was to remove from the French church the power of electing its own ecclesiastical leaders. Though the Estates General ignored the concordat, and the clergy and the universities opposed it strenuously, it remained an effective instrument for both royal and papal control of the church.

The Reformation made little change in this relationship. However, the generations after the reign of Francis I were to see a weakened monarchy and a struggle for religious control in France. After a series of bloody religious wars, Henry of Navarre, a Huguenot, was crowned Henry IV of France. He submitted to the papacy by renouncing his Huguenot faith in favor of Catholicism and salved his conscience by giving the Huguenots the religious freedom of the Edict of Nantes.

Both the Concordat of Bologna of Francis I and the conversion of Henry of Navarre were concessions to papal authority, and both represent breaches in the liberty of the French church. The Council of Trent, on the other side, represented an effort of the church to reestablish at least the spiritual and administrative supremacy of the religious hierarchy of the church and to maintain an ultramontane control of the national churches.

The unequivocal response of France to the defections of Francis I and Henry of Navarre and the ultramontanism of the Council of Trent was the Gallican Articles of 1662. With other monarchs in the 17th century Louis XIV asserted the divine right of monarchy to counter the papal claims of a spiritual heredity and authority. Under the assumption of his own divine right Louis XIV could no more brook a spiritual supremacy than a temporal authority beyond the Alps. Therefore he made a clear statement of his own personal authority and the freedom of the Gallican church in the Four Articles of 1662.

The first article denied all temporal authority of the pope and rejected the thought that rulers may be deposed by the bishop of Rome. The second affirmed the validity and supremacy of councils and stated that the whole church has the constitutional right to legislate for itself. The principle that the acts of a council are without effect until validated by papal authority was rejected out of hand. The third article limited the authority of the pope to the accepted canons of the church and denied him the right to interfere in the affairs of the national church. The fourth article stated that papal decisions in matters of doctrine were binding only insofar as they were approved by the whole church.[15]

Louis XIV further strengthened Catholicism in France by revoking the Edict of Nantes and upheld the Gallican articles with vigor and consistency during his entire reign. The articles were ordered to be taught in all seminaries, and the Gallican liberties of the French church were fully realized from this time to the French Revolution.

During the 18th century and under the *ancien regime* the tendency developing under the Gallican system was for the church to become an order, or an estate, within the state. It was the highest estate and held vast properties, enjoying the income accruing from these properties as well as the tithes and fees due for religious services.

That the privileged order of the clergy became corrupt and the church largely responsible for the French Revolution at the close of the century was in important measure a result of the corruption of the concept of the Gallican church. Theoretically the Gallican liberties made the church in France a free church. In actuality the Gallican Articles of 1662 left the church no more free under the monarchy after Louis XIV than it had been under the Concordat of Bologna in the 16th-century reign of Francis I. The church in France during the *ancien regime* was as much a pawn of the state as was the Orthodox Church in Czarist Russia. In both cases, deprived of its liberties and maintained in the corrupting influence of enormous wealth, the church became a factor in the revolutionary history of France in 1789 and of Russia in 1917.

The constructive period of the French Revolution was its first two years, in which the relics of feudalism and special privilege were swept away and modern principles of constitutional government established. That a reign of terror followed was due to the *émigrés,* the nobles who left France and invited the interference of other nations in the affairs of France. Not least among those who brought about the conditions which led to the reign of terror were the higher clergy, who rejected the Civil Constitution as a repudiation of Christianity and regarded an oath of civil obedience as a disavowal of the faith. The people and the lower clergy had accepted the Civil Constitution and began to work under it. If the nobility and the clergy had accepted the roles assigned to them by the legislation of the National Assembly, there would have been no occasion for a reign of terror. So far as the clergy were concerned, there was nothing in the Civil Constitution which the principles of Gallicanism had not long since asserted.

In his dreams of empire, Napoleon, at the beginning of the 19th century, recalled that Louis XIV had been the "eldest son of the church" and that the church had traditionally been the strongest support of monarchy. That made him choose for France the Catholic rather than the Constitutional, or Protestant, church. The same Napoleon who had said, "Treat the Pope as if he had 200,000 men," in 1801 proceeded toward an accommodation with the papacy. Former declarations to the contrary, he now declared:

> Persuaded that this religion is the only one which can produce a real happiness to a well-ordered society and strengthen the bases of a government, I assure you that I will apply myself to protect and defend it at all times and by all means. I shall know how to punish whosoever offers the slightest insult to our common religion.[16]

Determined to control France, Napoleon inaugurated his policy of conciliating Catholicism by apologizing for remarks made during his connection with the Directory. Then he moved toward a rapprochement with the nonjuring clergy and toward a concordat with Pope Pius VII. It was necessary for Napoleon to get the same control over the church in France that the Civil Constitution of the Clergy had provided but to accomplish this without the ill will that had been created by that ill-starred document. He knew that for most Franch Catholics no agreement that was not acceptable to the pope would serve the purpose. Months of diplomatic maneuvering followed. In the end his resistance was worn down to the point of acknowledging that Roman Catholicism was the religion of the majority of Frenchmen and that a free exercise of religion would be permitted in France. Beyond these acknowledgements Napoleon had his way in demanding:

1. That all bishops resign their offices;
2. That the church renounce its claims to properties confiscated by the revolution;
3. That the number of sees be reduced;
4. That the choice of bishops be in the hands of the government;
5. That the clergy take an oath of loyalty to the constitution of the year VII [1799].[17]

The pope had called the Civil Constitution an iniquitous thing. The concordat was no different in its provisions except that now the pope had lent his hand to the support of a practice the advantages of which were clearly on Napoleon's side. This was most evident when the pope was compelled to depose bishops who refused to resign their dioceses. Fear of persecution of Catholicism, a threat Napoleon explicitly made, forced the church to give to Napoleon personally every privilege that France had had both under the Concordat of Francis I and under the Gallican Liberties of Louis XIV.

For a time there was apparent goodwill between Napoleon and the pope. The latter was lavishly entertained in Paris when he came there to participate in the coronation of Emperor Napoleon. But the pope failed in all efforts to undo the damage to papal prestige that had resulted from the concessions of the Concordat and the Organic Articles.

In 1805 the emperor followed the pope to Italy to assume the Iron Crown of the Lombard kings with the threat: "God has given it me. Woe to him who touches it." From this point relations went from bad to worse until June 1809, when the pope excommunicated "Napoleon I and all his adherents, fautors, and counsellers." [18] Napoleon countered by arresting and imprisoning the pope after breaking forcibly into His Holiness' chambers in July 1809. He was now strong enough to compel the French church to revise the catechism to include the following question and answer:

> Why are we bound by all these duties towards our Emperor?
>
> First of all because God Who creates Empires and distributes them according to His will, while showering gifts upon our Emperor both in peace and in war, has established him as a sovereign, has made him the minister of His power and His image on earth. To honor and serve our Emperor is therefore to honor and serve God Himself.[19]

Thus Napoleon proceeded from civil supervision to the assumption of the role of a doctrinal arbiter of the church in France. The battle of Waterloo relieved France of personal control of the church by a head of state, and the church awaited the outcome of peacemaking at Vienna.

The primary principle of the Congress of Vienna after the Napoleonic Wars was legitimacy, the demand that the legal hereditary rulers of the prerevolution period be placed back on their thrones. As a result of this policy, there was a general expectation on the part of the *émigrés* of both the first and the second estates that confiscated lands would be restored to both the church and the nobility. But Louis XVIII was too much the realist to envision a return to the conditions that prevailed before 1789. The Concordat of 1801, hated by both the constitutional and the nonjuring clergy, remained the law of the land and a constant reminder of the usurper Napoleon. Soon after the accession of Louis XVIII a new concordat became the subject for discussion. By 1817 a draft acceptable to both pope and king was agreed upon. Eventually a government bill removing some of the objectionable features of the original draft was proposed. These changes the pope was unwilling to accept. The result was that the Concordat of 1817 never became anything more than an interim agreement that was not legally ratified.[20]

In the meantime another issue was developing between the clericals and anticlericals of France. The clergy had held in the greatest abhorrence the national control of education instituted by Napoleon. The church in France had traditionally controlled education and was loath to give up this monopoly. The church decried the educational authority of the university and deplored educational equality, desiring to keep the privileges the schools of the church had traditionally enjoyed. Their demands reached their highest pitch just as a wave of liberal feeling in France was driving Charles X from his throne.

Acknowledging the sovereignty of the people, Louis Philippe assumed office as king of the French. His continuing problem was that he was too liberal for the royalists and too conservative for the liberals. Charles X had been the victim of the liberalism of 1830, but it was the church that most consistently opposed liberal ideals. Yet the restoration church saw a wholesome change in attitudes toward liberal principles, and preachers like the Dominican Lacordaire contributed much toward popularizing preaching and reconciling Catholic theology with contemporary currents of liberal thought.

The provisional government established for France on the fall of Louis Philippe in 1848 was friendly to the church. There was no serious anticlericalism at a time when liberals realized how much the votes of Catholics would mean in republican elections. The charter of the government promised "complete liberty of association, of petition, of the press, of worship; and ministers of all bodies recognized by law were to be paid by the state." [21] The majority of the assembly were Catholics professing liberal principles, and a feeling of goodwill contributed toward the strengthening of the church. However, a dual motive of French Catholicism must be noted for this period. The first involved the strengthening of the papal position in an Italy striving for political unification; the second, the control of the educational system of France.

There were two candidates for the presidency. The first was Cavignat, a liberal, who held no brief for the two Catholic ambitions. The second, Napoleon III, promised both, and "by aid of the church and of the bourgeoisie, the friends of order, and of the Napoleonic tradition, he was elected by a large majority." [22]

A new educational authority was established under Catholic control by a law passed on March 15, 1850. The growing Catholic control of the government symbolized by this act demonstrated that the Catholic liberalism of 1848 was being replaced by reaction that was seen to restrict freedom of the press and other liberties not conducive to the strength of the Catholics' new role in government.

The coup of Napoleon, which resulted in his election as emperor in 1852, was broadly supported by Catholics who were not disturbed by the authoritarianism of a ruler who could be counted on to support and maintain religious privilege in France. Napoleon III's eagerness to please the French clergy continued after his imperial election. Both he and the clergy knew the extent to which he was beholden to them for his election both in 1848 and in 1852. The pope also blessed the empire that had restored and protected the papacy with French troops, while Louis Napoleon remained oblivious to a flagrant violation of both the Concordat and the Organic Articles. Many new ecclesiastical foundations were licensed, and the value of the property of the church in France increased greatly. Public education was absorbed into the educational system of the church.

The fall of the Second Empire of Napoleon III and the Roman pope's loss of the papal states represent a combination of factors that might well have created chaos for Roman Catholicism in France. Though the pope referred to himself as a "prisoner of the Vatican," he was free within his small domain, more free than the papacy had ever been for the fulfillment of its international spiritual functions. So far as France was concerned and despite papal condemnation of liberalism in every form, the government remained respectful of the pope and the church, stating at once that rights of religion and property would be firmly upheld. The right of nomination for ecclesiastical offices asserted in the Concordat was waived, and the custom developed that "the government would give its formal nomination to the ecclesiastic already chosen to receive it by the Holy See." [23]

The government established after the fall of Louis Napoleon had at the outset the support of leading members of the clergy. The first election returned a large number of republicans who were loyal to the church. The majority of delegates to the National Assembly, however, were royalists, who were "reactionary by instinct and ultramontane by profession." [24] But the several factions of royalists, who united might have carried the day, were obliged to stand by and see a moderate republican, Adolphe Thiers, elected to the republican presidency of what was to be the Third Republic. His past record of support of important clerical policies, however, made him not entirely unacceptable to clericals and royalists.

These factors enabled Thiers to establish the republic on the foundation of a successful rout of the Paris Commune and an expeditious settlement of war reparations. The people believed him when he asserted that he was beholden to no party and was determined to serve the best interests of all the people of France.

Thiers was succeeded in the presidency of France by a royalist and anticlerical soldier, Marshall MacMahon. His term of office was torn by constant but futile clashes between the three royalist factions. However, the continuing struggle for control of education concerns us more than the political battles that were waged at this time. His proposal that the church have joint responsibility for education with the state was not acceptable to the church. It wanted full freedom on all levels of education and the authority to give degrees without supervision or restrictions. "Our final end," the ultramontanes said, "is not only to vindicate Catholic teaching but to impose it on the state." The menace to liberalism implicit in this demand becomes clearer when it is realized that this meant the imposition of the reactionary *Syllabus* of Pius IX on the people of France. As Galton indicates, "The papal church and the liberal republic were incompatibles." [25]

It was in the area of education that French liberalism was to triumph. Indeed the victory of liberal educational principles was the sine qua non of French republicanism. "The future of the republic is at stake," it was said.

"We must know whether we are a sovereign people, disposing freely of our destinies, without permission from outside, or whether the decrees of our representatives must be countersigned by the Vatican; whether French law or Roman law is to have precedence. . . . Whoever regulates French schools rules France." [26]

The first notable and visible result of the Dreyfus case was the enactment of effective state control over ecclesiastical orders and organizations in 1902. The records of the next five years show the history of the events inevitably leading to the separation of church and state in 1907.

The Separation Act of 1905 was the outcome of a conflict between the papacy and France rather than of tension between church and state in France. The decisive issue in 1905 was the question of the control of education. The Third Republic, established after the Franco-Prussian War in 1870, had precariously maintained its political control against badly divided royalist factions, which traditionally supported the pretensions of the Roman hierarchy as part of a determination to maintain the status quo in France. Despite royalist and clerical attacks on the Republic during the Dreyfus controversy, the Republic emerged victorious. It now remained for the Republic to get control of education.

The Law of Associations of 1901 provided for the enforcement of the provision in French law that only legally established religious associations or orders could carry out educational programs. The elections of 1902 returned a strong anticlerical chamber. Its leader, Combes, proceeded to close thousands of schools conducted by unauthorized associations.

The Law of Separation of 1905 followed soon after under the leadership of Aristide Briand. The ultramontane ideal had so far deteriorated in France that a majority of churchmen voted for the separation in spite of papal opposition to the bill. French Catholic liberals saw in the bill the possibility of a greater measure of freedom for the church in France in spite of the papal bull *Vehementer nos* (1906), which condemned the idea of a free church in a free state. The papal view was that French Catholicism should continue to enjoy its privileged status in France. It could not tolerate a freedom equal for all religious denominations. However, the Vatican influence had sunk so low in France that by 1907 "only a corporal's guard of diplomats remained in residence there." [27]

The Separation Act of 1905 guaranteed liberty of conscience and public worship. It ended public subsidies for any religion in the budgets on national and local levels of government except in the case of chaplaincies in public secondary schools, hospitals, and prisons. It made provision for the proper use of ecclesiastical properties by authorized religious associations.

With the adoption of the Separation Act of 1905, the Concordat of Napoleon was nullified and the Republic assumed control over education. Clericalism and anticlericalism ceased to be important factors in French politics. A new Gallicanism was created for French Catholicism, and Protestantism, for the first time in French history, occupied a position of equality before the law.

The majority of the French people have remained Catholic. Until 1924 the papacy was sharply critical of the Act of Separation of 1905, but since that time French legislation has shown that the state has no intention of interfering with religious affairs. The papacy has accepted the reality of separation of church and state in France. A Roman Catholic writer has asserted that "by a roundabout route and through much suffering and sacrifice the Church in France at last regained, not indeed the public recognition once given to it by the nation as a whole, but at least an autonomy in its own sphere scarcely known to it since the Middle Ages." [28]

Indeed Roman Catholicism has gone so far in accepting its religious status in France as to have repudiated in 1927 a political movement to restore the monarchy and reestablish the Catholic Church. Protestants and Jews, faring so much better in their religious liberties since the Act of Separation, appear to find little to criticize in the present situation in France.[29]

Since the Act of Separation, France has been completely consistent in an attitude of neutrality to all religions and in giving freedom to all. In the matter of relations between the state and Christian education its attitude is both more severe and more lenient than the American attitude. France does not permit members of religious orders to teach in state schools. It justifies this position on the grounds that "the State cannot maintain in its civil hierarchy functionaries belonging to another hierarchy independent of it, to which they owe absolute obedience in all their actions. It can no more put up with this in education than it could in the army, for example, or in law." [30]

French religious bodies are free to maintain parochial schools on condition that they meet the educational standards of the state. Since 1951 these schools have been eligible for state aid. One legislative act has made scholarships available to students in parochial schools. Another has provided financial allotments to parent's organizations for educational purposes.[31] Since 1955, French legislation has authorized outright grants to parochial schools, with increased government controls.

In summary it may be observed that in comparing France and Spain, both predominantly Roman Catholic, we find that a higher degree of religious liberty and independence has been achieved by the former through separation of church and state. Spain has taken a calloused attitude toward the religious liberty of a small minority on the grounds that the majority is free in its religious observances. But in maintaining a national church Spain has kept it under state control, and Roman Catholicism is much less free and independent in Spain than in France. Therefore in Spain both the faith of the majority and that of minorities is under the shadow of the state.

In separating church and state, France gave a new freedom

and independence to the Roman Catholic Church at the same time that it created an atmosphere of real freedom for those who adhere to the faiths of minority religions. The religious situation in France is quite comparable to that which exists in the United States. In both countries the government is neutral toward all religions and gives special preferences to none. Differences in practice in France and the United States may provide students of American problems in church-state relationships with fruitful lines of investigation and inquiry.

THE APPROACH IN PROTESTANT COUNTRIES

While Protestant reformers in the 16th century attacked the Roman hierarchy in the process of reforming the theology and practice of the medieval church, the separation of church and state was not an issue of the Reformation and was not vigorously asserted by any but the radical Anabaptists of the age. The successful activities of the reformers immediately led to the establishment of Lutheran territorial churches in Germany, Lutheran national churches in the Scandinavian countries, the Anglican Church in England, and Calvinist establishments in Geneva, Scotland, and the Massachusetts Bay Colony. The legal establishment of these churches was normally a matter of specific legislative action in contrast with Catholic countries like Spain and France, where the Roman Catholic Church was taken as a matter of course.

Perhaps the most elaborate and cogent Protestant defense of religious establishment available to the modern student of church-state relations is William Gladstone's *Church and State,* published in London, England, 1841. It was written at a time when numerous voices were being raised in behalf of disestablishment.

In a lengthy discourse on English church history Gladstone recalls that from Henry VIII to Elizabeth I the object of religious supremacy was not to concentrate church power in the crown but to erect on behalf of the church and by means of the crown an effective barrier against foreign force. This was in addition to the conviction that "national religion is the unifying and ennobling principle of all national life." [32] Gladstone did not view church and state as separate entities but rather as the "coalescing of two functions inherent in the first idea of sovereignty." "They represent the two leading processes of Divine government, the one of which works upon what is inward by means of what is outward, the other upon what is outward by means of what is inward and they integrate one another." [33]

Gladstone's first argument for establishment was based on moral grounds. He stated quite frankly his conviction that the state has "a true moral personality and should therefore profess and practice a religion." [34] He believed that Christianity ought to pervade all of human activity from family life to national life. Given this conviction, he was forced to the belief that unity in religion is necessary for the well-being of the state. Though he did not believe that the state ought to use coercion for the propagation of religious truth or for the repression of erroneous opinion, he did believe that the state should aid religion by every appropriate means. "Governments," he said, "are by dutiful necessity cognizant of religious truth and falsehood and bound to the maintenance of the former." [35]

Gladstone accepted John Locke's definition of political power as "the right of making laws with penalties of death, and consequently all less penalties, for the regulating and preserving of property, and of employing the force of the community in the execution of such laws, and in the defense of the commonwealth from foreign injury; and all this for the public good." It was not as full a statement as Gladstone might have made, but, he continued, "even according to this restricted view, I contend that national religion is not only useful, but absolutely requisite in order to the full realisation of the purposes of government." [36]

Therefore he believed that the state, fully qualified for the profession and extension of religion, ought to accept its responsibility by financial as well as by moral means. He believed that the national endowment of the church had a tendency, first, to give the minister of religion a degree of exemption from the arbitrary influence of his congregation, and in the second place, to preserve the purity of doctrine in the church. He said that "when the Christian flock are placed habitually in the position of paymasters, notions of pride and self-sufficiency will infallibly associate themselves with that function, and men will proclaim the right to determine upon the doctrine." [37]

He regarded as completely fallacious all suggestions that religion is secularized by contact with the state. "The law in one case, the crown in the other," he says, "adopts and attests the truths of God, and does them homage." It was his view that the established church supported by government fulfills the highest destiny of religion and that "in containing together the good and the bad, in tolerating the hypocrite while she nourishes the saint, she is fulfilling, for the time of her dispensation, the clear intentions of that Lord whose coming she awaits with joy." [38]

It was his opinion that an established church has greater value than an unestablished religion because it is more highly regarded by the public. He adds: "We might, then, argue for the church on principles of reason as offering, in her oneness and permanency of communion, the only adequate guarantee of that unity which is so important to the state." [39] Later in his discussion he comes to the extreme conclusion that if the church-state relation is broken, "society having lost its principle of unity, the source of all its moral and even physical energy and life, would remain an inorganic mass, capable only of engendering corruption." [40]

This justification for establishment is as applicable to Norway as to England, but in Norway it has always been unnecessary to provide the same theoretical defense of establishment. This is because Norway has never had numerically significant religious minorities. Only an extremely small number of Norwegians are non-Lutherans, and it has therefore not been necessary to offer explicit arguments for the retention of an established church. England, on the contrary, had a substantial number of dissenters even when the Anglican Church was formally established by law during the reign of Elizabeth I. Since that time there have been occasional demands for disestablishment and justifications, like those of Gladstone, for the maintenance of a religious establishment.

Norway — Establishment Unchallenged

In its origins the Reformation in Scandinavia has little of northern Europe's Renaissance humanism to illuminate and explain it. It represents instead a purely political phenomenon. Luther's contemporary, Christian II of Denmark, accepted Luther's theology simply because of the opportunity it gave him to oppose the Scandinavian clergy and nobility. The confiscation of a sizable indulgence collection added incentive to his support of Luther. In 1520 he requested Frederick the Wise of Saxony to send a Lutheran preacher to Denmark.

Frederick I, the successor to the Danish throne, was converted to Luther's teachings, and under the religious leadership of Hans Tausen the Reformation movement spread rapidly through Denmark. The movement was carried further in the reign of Christian III, king of both Denmark and Norway. The overthrow of the medieval church in Denmark was soon followed by the collapse of Roman Catholicism in Norway.

As a result the Lutheran Church was established as the state church in Norway. Johann Bugenhagen, often called the organizer of Lutheranism, wrote a church ordinance and a constitution for the Norwegian Lutheran Church in 1537. Within two years the outward formalities of the Reformation had been carried out.[41] The church came under the direct control of the king. The properties of the church were nationalized, and those which the church retained were under state control.

Religious changes in the church were far from revolutionary. The moral and spiritual level of the Scandinavian church was so low, and religious knowledge was so rudimentary even among the clergy, that few of the Norwegian people realized that a different doctrine was being taught in the church. Since the Reformation was not accompanied by either a political or an economic revolution, the transition from Catholicism was gradual, peaceful, and scarcely noticed by the majority of the people.

Parish priests were left in their parishes, and bishops were replaced by Lutheran superintendents who supervised the reformation of doctrine and the reorganization of the form of worship. By 1555 the secularization of the monasteries was complete.

The last traces of monasticism had disappeared by 1562.[42] Indeed it seems that the spoliation of the medieval church in Norway was a primary interest of the monarchy. A witness of this spoliation writes:

> It is to be regretted, and it is not praiseworthy that at the time of the introduction of the Evangelical faith they did not only take away from the churches and monasteries the articles of gold and silver, and other treasures which were used in the Catholic service, together with vestments and other such things, but they wantonly destroyed things from which they could derive no benefit; they tore down buildings, and needlessly burned valuable books and letters, and destroyed ornaments and decorations of the churches, making God's house cheerless and barren. . . .[43]

An immediate effect of the Reformation in Norway seems to have been a deterioration in morals and a decline in education. Not until late in the century was the church sufficiently oriented in the new faith and organized in its practice to establish an educational system comparable to that which was developing in the territorial churches in Germany.

Late in the 16th century the Jesuits, pursuing the objectives of the Counter-Reformation, infiltrated Norway as merchants attempting to get Norwegian youths to attend Catholic universities. Those who were persuaded to do so often returned to Norway as clergymen. When the king became aware of this activity, he deprived all Jesuits of their offices and inheritances in 1613. This act was the effective end of Catholic activity in Norway.[44] At that time Lutheranism was fully established.

The Reformation was not accompanied by an intellectual revival or a spiritual awakening in Norway, nor was it the product of the spiritual tyranny of an inquisition. The monarchy established Lutheranism in Norway, and the people eventually accepted it and made it a medium of cultural and national as well as spiritual expression.[45]

After the Thirty Years' War, which halted an aggressive continental Catholicism, Roman Catholics were permitted to worship in stipulated places in Norway. Jesuits, however, continued to be banned from the country. However, permission to conduct Catholic services applied only to foreigners. Lutheranism was the only legal religion for the subjects of King Christian IV. Norwegians made no demand for religious liberty, nor did they question the right of the king to establish a religion for them.[46] The fact is that a religious indifference and general moral laxity is characteristic of the 17th-century "age of orthodoxy" in Norway. The church was notably lacking in spiritual depth and evangelical perception. Norwegian Lutheranism lacked the vitality that had been the outcome of continental religious conflict in the 16th and 17th centuries.

Like other Protestant countries, Norway was influenced by 18th-century Pietism with its protest against religious formalism and its effort to raise moral standards and to make religion more personal and evangelical. The result was the promulgation of numerous blue laws and Sabbath ordinances. In 1741 a Conventicle Act was passed to prevent "unauthorized" religious meetings. This law was on the statute books for a hundred years, but it was more ignored than enforced.[47] More praiseworthy was a revived missionary and educational interest growing out of the age of Pietism.

The Pietism of the 18th century eventually gave way to the rationalism of the 19th century. The church in Norway declined to the point of an almost complete loss of evangelical spirituality. From this condition the church was to be revived by the evangelistic preaching of the Norwegian Wesley, Hans Nielsen Hauge. Frequently imprisoned under the provisions of the Conventicle Act of 1741, Hauge had "awakened the conscience" of Norway, and on July 27, 1842, the Conventicle Act of 1741 was repealed and "full freedom in religious matters" was established.[48] Hauge had not only aroused among the people a deep Christian consciousness, but he had "taught them to act and think independently in religious matters, which led to a greater freedom of thought in political matters also. More than any one other influence, Hauge helped to incite the common people and prepare them to take their proper place in the life of the nation." [49]

As a result of the diplomacy of the Napoleonic wars, Norway was ceded to Sweden by the Treaty of Kiel of 1814. The union that had bound Norway to Denmark since 1380 was severed. On May 17, 1814, a constituent assembly adopted a separate constitution for Norway. It established the Lutheran Church in the following words: "The Evangelical Lutheran Church shall be the state church of Norway, but all religious sects shall have the right to worship according to their own faith. Jews shall be excluded from the kingdom." [50]

Traditionally Norway does not regard the church as a separate entity. It has not given it a constitution apart from its constitutional absorption into the fabric of government and national life. It is simply the church of the Norwegian people. As such there is constitutional provision for its maintenance and support.

The state today continues to provide as well as appoint all administrative officials of the church. It leaves some freedom for religious education in the public school system but maintains professional schools for the training of pastors and teachers.

Religious conflict in Norway has always been a matter of an internal Lutheran struggle. An early rejection of Jesuit activity was the most important denial of religious liberty. The Constitution of 1814, as has been seen, legislated against Jews. Apart from these limitations, Norway and the other Scandinavian countries have been tolerant of other faiths. However, the predominance of a Lutheran population is probably much more reason for internal peace than a broad attitude of toleration. In Norway, as in Spain, religious problems arising from lack of religious liberty have been little more than surface conflicts in a large area of peace and tranquillity.

Ninety-eight percent of Norway's population is formally Lutheran. Few Norwegians have ever had contact with any other religious view. Practically all Norwegian children have had a Christian education. In recent times, however, the complacency usually accompanying religious establishment has been apparent in a laxity in church attendance and in general spiritual debility among the Norwegian people.

England — Establishment Unsuccessfully Challenged

By the beginning of the Hanoverian period the English government was permanently committed to the view expressed by Richard Hooker in *The Laws of Ecclesiastical Polity* that "pure and unstained religion ought to be the highest of all cares appertaining to public regiment." [51] England had had its civil war, and it had failed permanently to disestablish the Anglican Church. The Glorious Revolution had resulted in some modification of legislation against nonconformity. The 18th and 19th centuries were to see further adjustments in practical relations with Protestant nonconformity and later also with Catholics, Jews, Unitarians, and atheists.

George I began his reign with the assurance that he would support and defend the Church of England. However, the church was broadly latitudinarian, or tolerant of deviations, in the 18th century, and it was inevitable that numerous controversies should arise.

One of these debates was the Bangorian controversy, in which Benjamin Hoadly of the See of Bangor repudiated the concept of a visible church and called sincerity the test of true religion. Implicit in this was, of course, a questioning of the whole structure of the established church. The result of the controversy was a new impetus to latitudinarianism and the proroguing of convocation of the church, which was not reconvened until 1852.

More characteristic are the views of Henry Sacheverell about the general ideal respecting the relations between church and state in England at this time. His *Discourse Shewing the Dependance of Government on Religion in General: And of The English Monarchy on The Church of England in Particular* spells out the view that Gladstone was to defend so indefatigably a century and a half later. He writes:

> Religion is the grand support of government. The peace, happiness, and prosperity of the secular power depends on that of the spiritual and ecclesiastical.[52]

While churchmen were thus expounding the contribution of religion to the state, there was a general slackness of the clergy in carrying out the duties of their parishes. Moral decay was evident in all classes of the English population. Drunkenness, low forms of amusement, and barbaric criminal procedures characterized the first third of the 18th century.

George II began his 33-year reign in 1727. Shortly thereafter dissenters petitioned Parliament for repeal of the Corporation and Test Acts. The Corporation Act of 1661 and the Test Acts of 1673 and 1678 barred Catholics and Protestant dissenters from holding civil, municipal, and military offices and restricted election to Parliament to members of the Anglican Church. A Tory Parliament refused to repeal the acts but passed annual indemnity acts relieving dissenters from the penalties. This lenience lent aid and encouragement to Methodism, which, developing within the framework of the established church, later broke with it.

Methodism represented an embarrassing threat to the established church. Catholicism and Puritanism had been confronted successfully inasmuch as both were a challenge to Anglican doctrine and ecclesiastical organization. Methodist leaders, however, were staunch churchmen who were a threat neither to the doctrine nor to the organization of the church. Their demand was for moral and spiritual reform in the existing fabric of the church.

Though it must be acknowledged that the church had permitted England to come to a low moral state, it must also be recognized that English bishops and theologians in the 18th century had led a successful attack on the deists and on opponents of the doctrine of the Trinity. Both heterodox views had been supported by Locke's *Reasonableness of Christianity,* which had affirmed that the only requirement for admission to the church ought to be faith and that no formal documents or tests of orthodoxy ought to be required. However, by 1750 the threat posed by these views had subsided, and deism and anti-Trinitarianism ceased to be virile forces in English theological thought.

There were several reasons for the success of the Methodist movement. The first was the magnitude of the moral problems demanding solution. The character, churchmanship, energy, and persistence of the Oxford Methodists, Wesley and Whitefield, were vigorous and persuasive. Methodism was the essence of simplicity. It was adaptable and evangelical in spirit.

On the other hand one must distinguish between the Arminianism of the Wesleyans and the Calvinism of the Evangelicals; the parochial character of Evangelicalism as contrasted with the attitude of Wesley that "the world is the field." It must also be remembered that the Evangelicals were more loyal to the Book of Common Prayer and the Thirty-nine Articles than the Methodists were.

Though there was not a significant agitation toward disestablishment during the reign of George II, when the Methodist and Evangelical movements were a matter of primary concern, P. Skelton wrote *Some Proposals for the Revival of Christianity,* in which he expressed his opposition to the establishment in England: "The greater part of the mischiefs that have fallen out in Civil Society has been owing to the mistake of establishing some religion and mixing government and that together. A more inconsistent compound was never jumbled together. The ingredients are so heterogeneous and incompatible that they ought by all means to be kept asunder." [53]

William Warburton argued the opposite view in his essay on *The Alliance between Church and State* in the same year (1736). He affirmed the necessity of test laws for the security of the church. While he acknowledged the separate function which each serves in the civil and spiritual realms, he said that a union is necessary in order to avoid conflict between church and state. "The church," he said, "shall apply all its influence in the service of the state; the state shall support and protect the church. From this alliance the church receives an endowment from the state and a place in the legislature." [54]

Archbishop Warburton, who wrote so vigorously in the defense of the alliance of church and state, is typical of the 18th-century English church in the age of reason. He was perfectly willing to preside over a latitudinarian church that gave the Evangelicals free rein for preaching within the framework of the establishment.

At the coronation of George III in 1760, English morals were scarcely improved in spite of the work of Wesley and the Methodists. However, the year 1760 marked a turning point in the relations between Methodism and the church. Methodism turned its back on the establishment and began to take out licenses to preach as dissenting clergy. Further, Evangelicalism outside the Methodist fold became more active, showing great vigor in the years 1760–1790. Mrs. Huntington and the Clapham sects reflect the interest of weathy and influential laymen in an Evangelicalism dissociated from the Arminian Wesleyans.

King George III influenced religion very little during his reign. Though he took an interest in Methodism, he did little to further it. Resolved to restore the royal prerogatives in England, however, he opposed repeal of the Test and Corporation Acts and the emancipation of Catholics. The Evangelicals on their part retained the English anti-Catholic prejudice but promoted education, the abolition of slavery, and other social reforms.

Dr. Joseph Priestley, a Unitarian clergyman, remembered for his discovery of oxygen, attacked the establishment in 1768. The following summarizes his views:

1. The rational plea for ecclesiastical establishments is founded on the necessity of them in order to enforce obedience to civil laws.

2. If the expediency of ecclesiastical establishments be allowed, it is allowed on account of their utility only.

3. Investigation will show that states lacking establishment did not suffer the predicted consequences.

4. Though certain inconveniences may follow from disestablishment, this does not prove its [establishment's] necessity. If the support of Constantine had not been given to the church, the popish hierarchy could not have developed. No lack of ecclesiastical establishment can surpass this evil.[55]

Though the debate continued as to the merits of the establishment without any serious approach toward disestablishment,

there was a tendency toward theological modification and toleration. Between 1772 and 1774 some Anglicans tried to abolish
clerical subscription to the liturgy and the Thirty-nine Articles
and to require only profession of faith in the Scriptures as the
Word of God. The king opposed the measure. The most effective opposition in Parliament was that of Edmund Burke, who
argued that there was ample room outside the establishment for
those who found the prayer book and the Thirty-nine Articles
unacceptable.

In 1778 George Saville carried a bill through Parliament for
the relief of English Catholics. It provided that in order to obtain the benefits of this relief, Roman Catholics should take an
oath renouncing the Pretender and the temporal jurisdiction of
the pope. Unfortunately, English feeling against Catholicism
was so strong that riots, beginning in Scotland, spread to England, demanding repeal of the Catholic Relief Act. Even John
Wesley encouraged opposition to the relief act, saying that
a Protestant nation had no obligation to tolerate Roman Catholicism. Actually the English view toward Catholicism had been
expressed nearly a century before in the words of John Locke:
"A protestant state is not bound to tolerate Roman Catholics,
inasmuch as it is one express article of their religion, that faith
is not to be kept with heretics, as they style all denominations
of Christians who are not of their communion; and as they acknowledge subjection to a foreign jurisdiction, viz., the Roman
pontiff; who challenges a power to absolve them from oaths of
allegiance, or any engagements, however sacred, which they may
be under to their own government." [56]

The French revolution tended to create a reactionary spirit
within England, a spirit which in many ways was characterized
by Edmund Burke. Up to the time of the revolution he had
been one of England's great liberals and a friend of the oppressed
everywhere. He supported the abolition of slavery and defended
oppressed colonials in both America and India. However, he
had steadfastly withheld support from those who sought relief
from the regulation of the Book of Common Prayer and the

Thirty-nine Articles. He was also among those who insisted on maintaining the safeguards of the Test and Corporation Acts even though they were not enforced.

When he viewed the French Revolution, he saw liberty threatened rather than supported by the anarchy of the revolutionaries, and as the revolution went on, he saw more and more the need for an established religion to guarantee and maintain morality and order. His *Reflections on the French Revolution* was one of the most influential monographs of the time.

Thomas Paine's attack on Burke in *The Rights of Man* only served to convince England the more of the utility of its establishment. Evangelicalism became strongly antirevolutionary, and the spirit of Methodism favored order and religion. Thus the reaction against the revolution increased the power and prestige of the Church of England, and a spirit of toleration was impeded.

Since the wrath of the French Revolution had fallen with a heavy hand on the Catholic clergy of France and many of them had fled to England, the revolution tended to mitigate feelings against Catholics in England. The passage of a Catholic Relief Bill in 1791 relieved them of numerous disabilities and restored privileges from which they had been excluded since the reign of Henry VIII. No public disturbances ensued.

By the end of the century the number of dissenters in proportion to the number of Anglicans had increased from a ratio of 1 to 24 to that of 1 to 4. No amount of liberalism was able to secure passage of the repeal of the Test and Corporation Acts, though several efforts were made at the close of the century.

A significant element in the reactionary spirit in England after the French Revolution was the view that the Church of England was the bulwark of national stability. The difficulty in maintaining the *status quo* in the establishment was created by the correspondence of the views of the Evangelicals with those of the dissenters. In agreeing on a significant body of social reform they were drawn together in a political arena which was soon to enfranchise the members of religious minorities in England. The most important of these measures were the acts outlawing the slave trade and later slavery itself. It was not long before they were working together in Bible and in religious tract societies as well as in reform and missionary activities.

From the time of its foundation in 1698, the Society for the Propagation of Christian Knowledge was the principal educational agency in England. This organization was a church society that invoked all the privileges given the established church by the Act of Uniformity. The measure of its activity and effectiveness is apparent from the fact that within half a century of its organization the SPCK had established 2,000 schools.[57] Nonconformists established their own schools, of course, but their interest was evangelistic as much as educational. Protected and supported by the establishment, the SPCK had a clear advantage. The assumption was that the church is responsible for education, but a bill introduced in Commons in 1807 to further subsidize parochial education within the framework of the church failed of passage.

Nevertheless, the Sunday school system of Raikes and the Lancastrian system of Bell and Lancaster did reflect a public consciousness of educational needs in England. Two bills were proposed for the establishment of national education. The bill of Samuel Whitbread calling for national support of parochial education in 1807 failed. A second bill was proposed by Brougham in 1820. It outlined the educational needs of England, showing that many children had no educational opportunity at all, and stipulated that only members of the Church of England should be licensed as teachers, with the clergy responsible for designating the curriculum. The bill had a first reading but was dropped because Parliament was not ready to assume religious responsibility for education, and the dissenters, seeing in the bill a possible gain for the state church, opposed it. However, in spite of failure of enactment, the bill did sow the seed which was later to bear fruit in subsequent reforms.

Progress toward Roman Catholic emancipation was made in 1828 with the repeal of the Test and Corporation acts, which had long been nullified anyway by indemnity acts. In 1829, however, the Peel ministry was able to put through the Catholic Emancipation Act that had failed in 1825. The bill was most significant for Ireland, where the Emancipation Act foreshadowed the disestablishment of 1869.

The Extraordinary Black Book of 1831 asserted that "the Church of England cost seven times as much as that of France" and yet "ministered to no more than eight out of twenty-four millions of English and Irish." Stating that the "ecclesiastical revenues of the whole of Europe was less than that of England," it went on to say that these revenues were "spent on a few rich men who neglect their duties." They are "banded against liberal ideas of every kind" and have "no enthusiasm for education." [58]

The author was not advocating the disestablishment of the church but simply pleading for a reform of the admitted abuses present in England's ecclesiastical structure. It was not a protest against tyranny or false doctrine but rather against a church that had lost its sense of a spiritual mission. The outcome of the *Black Book* was the creation of an Ecclesiastical Commission and the publication of the Tamworth Manifesto, which called for reform of the most patent abuses and the restoration of the church to the respect of the people.

Under English common law every parish was bound to maintain the parish church, with the exception of the chancel, which was to be kept in repair by the rector. As the number of dissenters increased, they complained that they were called on to keep in repair churches which they did not enter, while they were making voluntary contributions to the maintenance of their own chapels. The complaint was similar to the objections of some Americans to a double tax for education: one on public schools which they do not use, another on parish schools which they support by voluntary contributions. The final solution was Gladstone's Compulsory Church Rate Abolition Bill, which removed legal enforcement of church rates and made their payment voluntary.

The years 1833–43 saw a measure of progress in public education on the elementary level. In 1835 Lord Brougham brought the matter of education to Parliament, calling attention to the fact that the number of children in voluntary schools had doubled while those in schools endowed by the state had diminished. He urged, therefore, that parliamentary aid be provided for schools supported by voluntary subscription. Proposals for such aid were made in Parliament in 1837 and 1838 but failed of adoption. In 1839 the liberal leader Lord John Russell proposed an Education Committee to create an organized state system of national education. Parliamentary grants were added to voluntary contributions for education, and normal schools for the training of teachers were founded on a nondenominational basis.

The age of reform in England brought into focus areas in which reform might run counter to theological principles and ecclesiastical policies. Among such problems was the question of marriage and divorce. A bill finally passed in 1857 permitting divorce under specified conditions. Pleas that the remarriage of the guilty be forbidden were rejected. This bill represents a milestone in the secularization of the church. The anomaly in the bill of 1857 lies in this, that the state was legalizing an action which the church condemned. When questions of doctrine were referred to Parliament, it usually declared itself incompetent to rule on a doctrinal issue. The worst result was a broadening of the latitudinarianism of the established church. Where cases involving doctrine came before English courts, the judgment was usually inconclusive.

Up to the middle of the 19th century, education in England was supported by voluntary contributions of the church and dissenters. Both were subject to national inspection, which was effective without interfering with freedom of management.[59] Independent teacher training institutions were maintained by the Church of England, Roman Catholics, and dissenters. By 1851 the state was contributing nearly half of the cost of private education in England, and that without an act of Parliament.[60]

In 1853 Lord John Russell proposed the Borough bill which, noting that "the number of church schools was, in round numbers, 17,000 with a million scholars, of other schools of every description, 20,000 with 354,000 scholars," [61] proposed that a school tax be levied to aid the voluntary support of parents for all schools. The bill was not enacted into law, but the suggested tax was later adopted.

Growth in population continued to place a serious strain on the voluntary system of educational support, and it became increasingly clear that a national education system must soon be contemplated. The Revised Code of 1862 had provided for subsidies based on educational results. This unfortunately had the effect of creating a temptation to tamper with "results" for the purpose of securing aid. The Code had worked fairly well, but it was apparent that a more comprehensive national action needed to be taken to supplement the support of voluntary societies.

Both liberals and conservatives had come to the opinion that some form of national and compulsory education was necessary. Their views were to find common ground in the Elementary Education Bill introduced by W. E. Forster on April 17, 1870.

Essentially this bill sought to supplement the existing system of voluntary and state schools. Existing schools were to continue as before. Where needed, new public schools were to be established. There was to be no religious requirement in either secular or religious schools. This made it possible for nonconformists to attend state schools without being subjected to religious instruction. The same was true for members of the Anglican Church who attended nonconformist schools. It was provided that schools which did not accept the conscience clause would receive no subsidy.

This provision made it possible for English schools to provide religious education without compulsion to any who objected to it. The assumption was that the state was responsible for education and would subsidize any private school which was providing an adequate secular education, irrespective of the religious views that were taught in addition to the fundamentals of secular education. All parties in England insisted on religious education. Provision was made in the conscience clause for those who rejected the religious views of a given school. The Education Act of 1944 in effect confirmed these arrangements.

A compulsory Education Act was passed in 1882. The Act of 1870 had made elementary education possible for every English child, but many were simply not coming to school. The Act of 1882 changed that situation. As of that year there were about two million children in voluntary schools and one million in Board schools. Since that time, the advantage in the comparative enrollment has tended toward the Board schools because patrons of voluntary schools had to pay taxes in addition to making voluntary contributions.

In evaluating freedom under English establishment, it must be acknowledged that the English church was established as a defense against foreign interference in religion and religious practice. At a time when the peril of interference was great, there were severe liabilities and restrictions imposed on those who did not accept the religious views of the established church. As that peril diminished, the penalties for dissent and nonconformity were abated until, at the close of the 19th century, they were almost entirely removed.

What remains now is a freedom of worship that permits any religious exercise that is not contrary to the public welfare. An inequality exists, to be sure, in that the established church is supported by public funds. This means that nonconformists must support the state church in addition to making voluntary contributions toward the support of their own religious activities.

This inequality is balanced to a degree by the fact that the English government, acknowledging education as a public responsibility, subsidizes private schools, including those maintained by dissenting religious groups. The so-called Balfour Education Act of 1902 makes possible the allocation of local taxes to church schools except for capital costs.

The outcome of this policy of subsidizing private schools has been that English children have had the advantage of Christian education to a far greater degree than has been possible in the secular schools in the American system. Though English children who desire a purely secular education have that option, the number whose education is purely secular is small in relation to the whole school population.

The anomaly in the situation in England at present is that the established church suffers from lack of freedom. Though it enjoys the prestige of a privileged religion, the Anglican Church is tied to the will and determination of a Parliament whose members are largely drawn from nonconformist groups. In recent years Parliament has been increasingly unwilling and unable to assume responsibility for religious legislation. In 1927 the bishops submitted to Parliament a proposal for the revision of the Book of Common Prayer, which had been 14 years in preparation. A majority of the members of Parliament were not Anglicans, and the proposal was rejected on the grounds that there was not sufficient unanimity in the minds of the churchmen who proposed the revision.

At the time an Anglican churchman said that if Parliament refused the proposal the church ought to ask for disestablishment.[62] Since then the leadership of the Anglican Church is convinced that disestablishment in England would be interpreted by the world as a "national repudiation of Christianity." A commission appointed to study existing relationships between state and church in England reached the same conclusion. In January 1952 this commission recommended more freedom within the church but asserted that "the unique relationship between Church and State in England is regarded by the world as a sign that the country has preserved a continuous Christian tradition" and that if "this relationship were broken it would be considered as a sign that England had abandoned Christianity." [63]

CONCLUSION

The primary factor in European church-state relations in the last two and a half centuries has been the persistent tradition of medieval practice. In Roman Catholic countries the papacy has continued to dominate. Protestant countries, lacking an authority comparable to the papacy, have apparently lost in ecclesiastical virility what they have gained in independence. The Lutheran Church in Norway and the Anglican Church in England are not as strong or as independent as their American counterparts. The same may be said, however, of Catholicism in Spain as compared with the Roman Catholic Church in the United States.

The principal source of friction in Roman Catholic countries has come from an anticlericalism that has nothing to do with a desire for religious liberty. The papal authority, from a purely religious point of view, has tended to be a stabilizing force in the preservation of a uniform theological position.

In Protestant establishments an inability to maintain a religious virility has stemmed from the failure of parliaments to provide a strong religious leadership and to legislate adequately on matters relating to religion.

A study of European countries in the past two and a half centuries reveals the difficulty of maintaining religious equality where one religious group is in an overwhelming majority. It is hardly to be expected that such equality could be worked out in practice. In England, where the established church does not represent an overwhelming majority of the people, the very fact of establishment unavoidably gives some advantage to those who adhere to the religion of the establishment.

It would seem, therefore, that the ideal of religious equality will come nearest to realization in the state that has no establishment and gives preferential treatment to no religious group. The church as a corporate entity also appears to be strongest where it is independent of regulative relations with the state.

European commentators on American church-state relations almost invariably call attention to the fact that "total separation" is an unrealized ideal in the United States.[64] They remind us of salaried Army and Navy chaplains, the name of God on our coinage, and oaths taken on the Bible.

They remind us of what Europeans regard as "the colossal inequity and injustice of a double taxation for all those who want a well-integrated religious instruction." These analysts are unable to sympathize with a concept of justice which declares: "Let's defend the *rights* of parents, but the family must pay for this *privilege*."

Foreign observers suggest that the American system (as that of France) inevitably results in some people drifting away from the church. Religiously inactive parents (especially of mixed faith) tend to send their children to public schools, which do not offer religious instruction, and thus their offspring wander into total disbelief. Public instruction in most free Continental countries imparts at least a minimum of religious values.

The observation is made that the American First Amendment, to the European mind, is clearly directed against "establishment" and not against "cooperation." It is suggested that the American ideal of a wall of separation between church and state is "a current interpretation . . . a hidebound obstacle in the path of equity."

Americans may well study European experiences in church-state relations to discover whether, as Kuehnelt-Leddihn says, the following American ideas are myths: "Separation prevents encroachments of the State on the Church. . . . Separation is necessitated by a 'pluralistic society' . . . that people must pay for their Church in order to feel that they have a stake in her . . . that active State support will automatically result in State control of the Church" and "that great spiritual benefits derive from separation." [65]

FOR A CENTURY AND A HALF of American colonial history, those who came to this country had little choice but to follow the traditions of church-state relations which they had inherited from their European homelands. When the day came that they could adopt their own structure of government, they created something new and different in the relations of church and state. But another century of experience was necessary to determine the full scope and meaning of the arrangement.

In chapter 5 *Carl S. Meyer,* Ph. D., professor of historical theology at Concordia Seminary, St. Louis, sets out to trace the steps which led to our present-day understanding of the relations between church and state. By the time of the Constitution and Bill of Rights, the idea of an independent government with independent churches was commonly accepted. During the subsequent growth of the nation, there were always some efforts to "mold a Christian community." Sunday observances, the temperance movement, and the use of government powers to achieve moral reforms were typical of the problems encountered in making a theoretical pattern fit a practical people.

"Conflict and accommodation, cooperation and contradiction" entered into the dialectics of the period from the Civil War to the first World War. Theocratic thinkers like the Mormons and the Social Gospel preachers were inclined to interpret separation of church and state in the light of their special enthusiasms. At the other extreme were those who wanted separation to be absolute and airtight. By 1914 the pattern called for separation with "sympathy for religion."

Dr. Meyer shows that in the period after World War I all sorts of challenges were presented by issues ranging from censorship of the means of communication to aid for church-supported hospitals. Some of these areas of conflict are treated more extensively in chapters 7 and 8.

Chapter 5

DEVELOPMENT OF
THE AMERICAN PATTERN
IN CHURCH-STATE RELATIONS

Carl S. Meyer

"BUT HOWE FARRE THE BOUNDS of eche doo extende, therein lieth the chief point."[1] Prince or people, Robert Harrison wrote in 1583, ought to take a hand in beginning the reformation of the church. However, the extent of the duties of each in ecclesiastical affairs, he recognized, was one of the great issues of the 16th century.

Almost four centuries later in the United States of America the same question remained an issue, although by that time the pattern had been established. Laws and legal customs, and more especially a *modus vivendi,* denied a strict and absolute separation of church and state, but they brooked no interference in the essential functions of each of the agencies. "The bounds of eche" were respected, although they were vaguely defined.

Perhaps the preoccupation with opening new frontiers removed the need for a sharp delimitation of the functions of the state over against the church. Perhaps the prevailing liberalism, a liberal individualism, which pervaded so much of the 19th century, provided principles for a laissez-faire philosophy. Social circumstances were largely responsibile for the establishment of the pattern.[2] Yet the pattern would not have evolved without the stresses of an expanding territorial state and the strains of

196

increasing governmental functions. The constantly increasing population of the country was matched by an even greater increase in church membership. The churches prospered economically as the nation became wealthier. These parallels, too, contributed to the acceptance of the vague lines of demarcation which seemed to be of mutual benefit to both church and state.

There were spiritual forces, too, which helped to shape that pattern. Puritanism as a movement in idealism [3] may have been dead already by the beginning of the 19th century, but the Puritan hope for "a place of Cohabitation and Consorteshipp under a due forme of Government both civill and ecclesiastical" [4] persisted. Whatever the "errand into the wilderness" may have been, it carried with it the thought of a due form of government in both church and state.[5] Yet Puritanism was modified by a Lockian philosophy. Nor were the multitude of minor sectarians content to permit establishment of a state-favored church. What they might not gain none should gain. Tolerance was more easily advocated by those in less favored positions than by those in positions of influence for the regulation of religion. Necessity, in some instances at least, was made a virtue; the right to existence granted to others was at once a charter of existence for self. Dissenters and Freethinkers were joined by other minorities, among them Roman Catholics and Lutherans, who wanted toleration for themselves and perforce had to allow it for others.

Social, economic, intellectual, and spiritual forces tended to inaugurate the pattern; they were no less potent in shaping the pattern after its basic outline had once been fixed. The legal enactments, both federal and state, together with the interpretations of these enactments as rendered by the courts, provided the larger framework. However, the subtler accommodations within the pattern no legislature nor court could fix. These became the product of historical processes. The shaping of that pattern from the beginning of the national period through the first World War and its aftermath in depressions and more wars is examined in some detail in the subsequent pages.

The separation of church and state was not the pattern which the American compatriots of 1787 had generally experienced, even though a great deal of tolerance was the vogue. Among the colonies before the Declaration of Independence there were only two (Pennsylvania and Rhode Island) which had not known an established religion at one time or another. All the European countries from which their forebears came had established churches.

Evidence of Toleration in Europe

In England the Toleration Act of 1689 had given "some ease to scrupulous consciences." It permitted Dissenters to take the oaths of allegiance and supremacy while retaining their particular religious beliefs.[6] The act excluded the nonconformists from public affairs, yet it marked "the point from which nonconformist life and thought were free to develop without interference from authority." [7] Even so, cases involving burial rights, church rates, and education, alongside the larger questions of disestablishment and disendowment, were bruited about in the England of the 18th and 19th centuries.[8] The English pattern may have been negligible in the establishment of the pattern in the United States of America. It was one factor, however, in the thinking of the citizens of the new nation, who were not ready to permit the federal government to establish an official church.

Nor did they wish a *cuius regio, eius religio* arrangement, such as that sanctioned within the Holy Roman Empire by the Religious Peace of Augsburg (1555), or religious establishments under *Schirm- und Schutzherren*.[9] Even the religious toleration growing out of the religious clauses of the Peace of Westphalia (Treaty of Osnabrück, 1648)[10] was too precarious to become the basis for an enduring arrangement in the New World even if it had been better known and appreciated. Much more was wanted than that the dissenters "shall be allowed patiently and with a free conscience to frequent privately their place of worship . . ."

However, the happenings in France were more important

than those in the Holy Roman Empire. The revocation of the Edict of Nantes (1685)[11] produced periodic persecution and emigrations.[12] The rationalists were strong advocates of toleration. Voltaire, in his *Letters sur les Anglais* (1734) and the *Traité de la tolérance à l'occasion de la mort de Jean Calas* (1763); Marmontel, in his *Bélisaire* (1766); Turgot in his *La tolérance religieuse: project de mémoire au roi* (1775), Condorcet, Malesherbes, and particularly the Marquis de Lafayette advocated the cause of religious toleration.[13] The demands for toleration in France culminated in the "Declaration of the Rights of Man and of the Citizen" (1789) during the French Revolution.[14] "Toleration was in the air, at least in cultured circles, throughout Europe and also in America. It was inevitable that France, the pinnacle of culture and enlightenment of the day, should feel greatly stirred by the movement."[15]

It is difficult to document the influence of European thought on events in the United States of America. Here the readiness to grant toleration to individuals was a necessary step before the disestablishment of state churches and the separation of church and state. In 1774 "the recovery and establishment of their rights and liberties, civil and religious," was listed among the objectives for an intercolonial conference issued by the Massachusetts Legislature.[16] A year later the New York Provincial Congress (1775) declared that "neither the Parliament of Great Britain, nor any other earthly legislature or tribunal, ought or can of right interfere or interpose in anywise whatsoever in the religious and ecclesiastical concerns of the colonies."[17] These pronouncements voice the thinking of the day. They presage the pattern of church-state relations in the new republic.

Early Legislation Promotes the Pattern

The pattern owes much to the Virginia Bill of Rights (1786). It repudiated the idea of coercion in religious matters for any reason whatsoever and set forth the principle of religious toleration.[18] The petitions and memorials which preceded the enactment of this statute had made evident the growing demand for "the free exercise of religion according to the dictates of our consciences." [19] The Virginia statute, the work of Thomas Jefferson, declared these rights to be natural rights of mankind. The law read (in part):

> Be it enacted by the General Assembly, that no man shall be compelled to frequent or support any religious worship, place or ministry whatsoever, nor shall be enforced, restrained, molested, or burthened in his body and goods, nor shall otherwise suffer on account of his religious opinions or belief; but that all men shall be free to profess, and by argument to maintain their opinion in matters of religion, and that the same shall in no wise diminish, enlarge or affect their civil capacities.[20]

The new federal constitution embodied similar principles. A clause in Article VI stated: ". . . but no religious test shall ever be required as a qualification to any office or public trust under the United States." The Bill of Rights provided the guarantees of religious freedom. Its first article read (1791):

> Congress shall make no law respecting an establishment of religion, or prohibiting the free exercise thereof; or abridging the freedom of speech or of the press; or the right of the people peaceably to assemble, and to petition the government for a redress of grievances.[21]

These enactments have been maintained. They belong to the very warp and woof of the pattern of church-state relations in America.

No religious significance was intended in the parenthetical phrase of the constitution which did not include Sunday in the total number of days which might be allowed for a bill to receive the president's signature.[22] Not to be lost sight of, on the other hand, is that the restrictive clauses of the constitution and the First Amendment pertain to the federal government. The federal constitution might become an ideal, a model, for the state constitutions; it did not, however, in the initial stages of its operations presume in any way to encroach on the rights and privileges reserved for the states.[23] There were differences in convictions as there were differences in conditions among the original states regarding religious establishments, the role of the church in education, and the responsibility for maintaining churches and schools. The residual powers reserved for the states included the powers to regulate these affairs.[24]

The Pattern Emerges

What, then, was the pattern of church-state relations among the 13 states which first subscribed to this federal constitution? Virginia had adopted its Bill of Rights (1786). Within two years its legislature voted the formal disestablishment of the Episcopal Church. Then in 1798 formal legislative action reaffirmed the law establishing religious freedom in conformity with the Bill of Rights.[25] Jurisdiction over the property, support of the clergy, management of those phases of church life which had been a matter of state control had to be adjusted. For instance, the state took over glebe lands in 1802, a cause for court contests until 1840, when the Virginia Court of Appeals upheld the 1802 legislation.[26]

The significance of Virginia's action in establishing the pattern on the level of state government is not simply one of priority. Virginia gave an example and her prestige to the movement of disestablishment and of the severance of the churches' dependence on the states.

North Carolina, her immediate neighbor to the south, soon followed her lead. The colonial history of this state reflected the dissent and the desire of toleration common among the English colonies. With the expiration of the Vestries Act in 1773 there were no longer any laws in this state which recognized the Episcopal Church as the established church. The constitution of 1776 provided for disestablishment,[27] yet it did not provide a full measure of religious liberty. Roman Catholics and Jews, atheists and anarchists were denied the right to hold office. Active clergymen were disbarred from the state legislative bodies.[28] After 1835 active clergymen could hold these positions, and Roman Catholics were made eligible for public office within the state. As for religious liberty the Declaration of Rights of the 1876 constitution reaffirmed: "All men have a natural and unalienable right to worship Almighty God according to the dictates of their own consciences, and no human authority should, in any case whatever, control or interfere with the right of conscience." Atheists are still ineligible for public office in this state.[29]

The sequence of events in North Carolina constitutes a pattern discernible in other states. Disestablishment takes place during the period of the emergence of the new nation; most of the clauses restricting civil rights and liberties on religious ground disappear during the Jacksonian era.

North Carolina was only one of eight states which adopted new constitutions in 1776 (three others adopted new constitutions in 1777).[30] Delaware was another. Its charter of 1701 had granted toleration and the right to fill public office to "all Persons who also profess to believe in Jesus Christ, the Saviour of the world." [31] The constitution of 1776 provided for disestablishment and made active clergymen ineligible for civil offices, elective or appointive.[32]

The present constitution of Delaware (adopted in 1897) states that "no power shall or ought to be vested in or assumed by any magistrate that shall in any case interfere with, or in any manner control, the rights of conscience, in the free exercise of religious worship, nor a preference be given by law to any religious societies, denominations, or modes of worship." Religious tests for public office were disallowed.[33]

Religious tests continue to the present day as part of the requirements for public office in Pennsylvania. Public officials must acknowledge "the being of God" and "a future state of reward and punishments." This was set forth in the constitution of 1790 and repeated in the revisions of 1838 and 1873. Moreover, the charter of 1680 provided for complete disestablishment, and the constitution of 1776 reaffirmed it. The constitution of 1873 stipulated: "No appropriations, except for pensions or gratuities for military services, shall be made for charitable, educational or benevolent purposes, to any person or community, nor to any denominational or sectarian institution, corporation or association." [34]

There were variations, of course, in the provisions of the constitutions adopted in 1776 and shortly thereafter. Rhode Island followed the pattern of Virginia in granting full freedom.[35] North Carolina's Protestantism in these early years, insofar as it was required for civic office, was echoed in Delaware.[36] The establishment of the pattern of church-state separation in New York, Maryland, New Hampshire, Connecticut, and Massachusetts shows additional variations. In Georgia[37] and Vermont[38] the early constitutions favored religious freedom and disestablishment.

In Maryland the constitution of 1776 granted religious liberty to all "professing the Christian religion." However, it provided for state support of churches and particularly of the Anglican Church.[39] The Maryland constitution nevertheless restricted gifts of land to ministers or to church organizations.[40] The revision of 1851 retained the restrictions on goods and chattels made after the death of the donor.[41] These provisions were repeated in the constitution of 1864 and 1867, so that these restrictive provisions remain in force.[42] Exceptions can always be granted by the "prior or subsequent sanction of the legislature."

In New York the Constitutional Convention of 1777 heard a debate on the question of granting religious freedom to Roman Catholics. As finally adopted, Article XXXVIII in the constitution on the religious question allowed full religious liberty.[43] This constitution excluded clergymen from all civil and military offices within the state. In 1784 the "emoluments and privileges" which had been granted to the Episcopal Church in New York were repealed. The revisions of the constitution in 1821 and again in 1846 both granted "the free exercise and enjoyment of religious profession and worship, without discrimination or preference."[44]

In New Hampshire the constitution of 1784 had permissive provisions encouraging the establishment of religious organizations and the maintenance of religious teachers. It provided, too, that "no subordination of any one sect or denomination to another shall ever be established by law."[45] The constitutions of 1792 and 1912 repeated these provisions.[46] They have been called "inconsistent with the American tradition of the impartiality of the State in matters involving the religious connections of citizens."[47]

Disestablishment Tested

Two other New England states, however, had the bitterest struggle for the disestablishment of religion. The one was Connecticut, where disestablishment came in 1818; the other was Massachusetts, where the question was not settled until 1833. The pattern was not complete until these two states had granted full religious freedom.

When the federal constitution was adopted with its Bill of Rights, the sovereign state of Connecticut still maintained the Congregational Church as the state church. The "Standing Order" (the ministry of the Congregational Church) led the forces which wanted to restrict the franchise and maintain the tax for the support of this church. In 1784 the Toleration Act was adopted, which permitted dissenters to file certificates that allowed them to pay the tax to their own churches instead of the Congregational Societies. In the years between 1784 and 1818 various measures made for increasing toleration. Then in 1818 a new constitution was drawn up. One article stated: "The exercise and enjoyment of religious profession and worship without discrimination, shall forever be free to all persons in this state . . ." Those who did not wish to be associated with a church had to declare so; all churches were given equal rights and privileges, although none received any special concessions.[48]

Disestablishment came last in the sovereign state of Massachusetts. The constitution of 1780 allowed every citizen of the state to worship God "in the manner and season most agreeable to the dictates of his own conscience." However, this article also stated: "It is the right as well as the duty of all men in society, publicly, and at stated seasons, to worship the Supreme Being, the great Creator and Preserver of the Universe." This article is retained in the constitution of 1920, a remnant of the thinking which regarded the state as the agency which enforced religious observances. The Dedham affair in 1818 and the Constitutional Convention of 1820 preceded the move for disestablishment. In 1833 an amendment to the constitution was adopted (after it had been ratified by a popular plebiscite) which made all churches and denominations within Massachusetts dependent on their members for their support.[49] Complete disestablishment had been achieved.

The Pattern in New States

As new states were admitted to the United States and as they or the original states revised their constitutions from time to time, guarantees of religious freedom and the disassociation of the state and the church were written into them. The constitution of Kentucky of 1792, for example, provided that "no preference shall ever be given by law to any religious societies or modes of worship" and that "the civil rights, privileges or capacities of any citizen shall in no ways be diminished or enlarged on account of his religion."[50] The constitution of Minnesota (1857) provided: ". . . nor shall any control of or interference with the rights of conscience be permitted, or any preference be given by law to any religious establishment or mode of worship . . ."[51] Many of the provisions of the constitutions of the several states regarding religion are borrowed from one another.[52] Alabama's constitution (1867, revised 1875 and 1901 but retaining the same article) says curtly: "No person shall be deprived of the right to worship God according to the dictates of his own conscience."[53] The Bill of Rights of the constitution of New Mexico (1912), the 47th state to be admitted to the Union, uses the same language in more extended form:

> Every man shall be free to worship God according to the dictates of his own conscience, and no person shall ever be molested or denied any civil or political right or privilege on account of his religious opinion or mode of religious worship. No person shall be required to attend any place of worship or support any religious sect or denomination; nor shall any preference be given by law to any religious denomination or mode of worship.[54]

Such is the pattern as it was established in the instruments by which the federal government and the states were to be governed. The guarantees of religious freedom were accompanied with the setting aside of privileges for the churches. None would receive any support from the state or be regarded as the official ecclesiastical arm of the state. Legal equality for all churches, sects, and denominations was written into the constitutions of the states.

Theologians Approve the Pattern

The churches accepted the pattern, and their theologians either found justification for disestablishment in their theologies or repeated expressions from theologians of their persuasions. To Lyman Beecher, as Hudson has shown, "the establishment meant the preservation of true religion, good morals, and sound government." [55] Then came disestablishment, for Beecher "as dark a day as ever I saw." [56] Then he learned from actual experience that disestablishment was "the best thing that ever happened in the State of Connecticut." No longer did the churches depend on the civil law, he says, but they were "thrown on God and ourselves." These were practical considerations, it is true, rather than theological ones for voluntarism in religion.[57] There is little evidence that among the theologians of the Congregationalist churches any attempt was made to formulate the principles of church-state relations in theological terms.[58] Perhaps "the placing of a distinctly Christian stamp upon an entire culture" is "the greatest achievement of the free churches in 'the great century.' " [59] However, this need not be accepted as the outcome of the voluntary principle. At best it remains a practical justification for accepting disestablishment rather than a conviction born from theological principles.

Practically and theologically the adherents of the Anglican churches had even greater difficulty in adjusting to the situation than did the Congregationalists. At the end of the Revolutionary War the problem of a valid episcopacy, of the apostolic succession, and of the forms of the Prayer Book caused grave theological discussions. A theological virtue was made out of the political necessity for disestablishment. For one thing, the dependence on the English crown (as "Supreme Head of the

Church") had to be repudiated.[60] Alterations in the Prayer Book (such as a service for the Fourth of July) were proposed not on theological grounds but "for rendering the Liturgy conformable to the Principles of the American Revolution, and the Constitutions of the several States."[61] God was acknowledged as the Protector of nations and peoples, who in His providence gives the blessings of peace, liberty, and safety; the duty of obedience to the government of the country is to be carried out in "a spirit of love and thankfulness to thee [God]."[62] The reformulations of the Thirty-nine Articles to fit the new conditions in the new nation required a rewording of the article on the power of the spiritual magistrate. Article XXXVII as adopted in 1801 read:

> The Power of the Civil Magistrate extendeth to all men, as well Clergy as Laity, in all things temporal; but hath no authority in things purely spiritual. And we hold it the duty of all men who are professors of the Gospel, to pay respectful obedience to the Civil Authority regularly and legitimately constituted.[63]

The doctrine is stated; its theological basis is not given.

Similarly the Methodist Articles of Religion (1784) have an article (Art. XXIII), "Of the Rulers of the United States of America," which affirms the civil power without stating the theological basis for this affirmation or bringing a declaration of the distinction between the functions of the state and the church.[64]

Some churchmen did express a theological basis for their position. Alexander Campbell drew a sharp distinction between the kingdom of God and an earthly kingdom. He cited the words of Christ, "My kingdom is not of this world." The earth, he said, is for the Christian "the present theatre of war," where he serves as a soldier, equipped and supplied by his Captain. "Christians have nothing to expect from them [the governments of this world] except liberty of conscience and protection from violence."[65]

"My kingdom is not of this world" was also cited by Isaac Backus, the Baptist, in a plea for the separation of state and

church. Freedom from paying taxes for a state-supported
church, according to Backus, is "a right and property granted
us by God." The power to tax in conscience he could not
allow to men but only to God.[66] "Religion," he said, "is ever
a matter between God and individuals; and therefore no man
or men can impose any religious test, without invading the
essential prerogatives of our Lord Jesus Christ." [67] Roger Williams had argued for the cessation of persecution and for religious liberty on theological bases.[68] Perhaps among the Baptists of the early period of the republic more than among any
other religious group of the country the conviction of a separation between the functions of the church and the functions of
the state and the resultant separation of organization was
a theological conviction.[69]

The "free exercise of religion according to the dictates of our
consciences" is a phrase which in many respects can summarize
an important theological and philosophical tenet of those who
favored the disestablishment and sought to find reasonable and
spiritual arguments for it. It is an argument advanced by the
Presbyterians in their memorials to the General Assembly of
Virginia (e. g., 1784). An earlier memorial (1776) had made
theological distinctions between the functions of the church
and of the state.[70]

It appears that the disestablishment of the churches received
some sort of theological justification. This is true especially
after the separation of church and state and the principles of
religious toleration were adopted. Only exceptionally in the
early period do we find a complete theological presentation by
a religious leader of America on the relationship between church
and state. It may be that some of the confused acts of the
religious leaders in the subsequent period resulted from a lack
of theological clarity.

The Formation of Independent Churches

The realization, as indicated, that the churches would have
to be organized entirely independent of the state was a compelling one. "The Nationalization of the American Churches,"

as Sweet called it, was the result.[71] The 1780s saw the organization of the various churches into national bodies independent of state and federal government. The "Christmas Conference" of the Methodists in 1784, the Philadelphia convention of the Episcopalians in 1785, the Presbyterian Assembly of 1789, the revisions of the constitution of the Lutheran Pennsylvania Ministerium in 1792 and 1796, the establishment of the see of Baltimore in 1790, the organization of Baptist associations between 1784 and 1789, and the "constitution-making period" in the Dutch Reformed Church from 1784 to 1792, all show the intense activities of the churches in becoming self-contained entities.

The Presbyterian Church, at the time of its organization and in its constitutional provisions up to the present time, set down the principles of separate functions of church and state, the voluntary character of the church, and the mutual obligations of noninterference.[72] In actual practice during the subsequent years the Presbyterians did not always adhere to the letter and spirit of their constitution. They had nevertheless to a significant degree contributed to the basic pattern of church-state relations in this country by the adoption of these provisions of their constitution.

Less aggressive and less involved in the political activities of the day were the Lutherans of colonial America. In 1748 the first Lutheran synod was organized under the leadership of Heinrich Melchior Muhlenberg, but it was an organization of ministers, a ministerium.[73] The constitution of this body, as printed in 1781, made no mention of the federal government or of the civic order, nor of the relationships between the church and the state.[74] The severance of direct supervision from Europe, especially by the Swedes in Delaware, who broke with the Swedish archbishop in 1789, must be reckoned as a crucial step in establishing the pattern of independence among Lutheran congregations in the new nation.[75] However, this independence did not imply in any way any direct relations with either the state or the national governments in the new nation. A "separation" with nonintervention by either the state or the church was the pattern desired by these Lutherans.

For the Roman Catholics the period from 1784 to 1789 saw "the lessening and gradual extinction of legal disabilities for Americans of [Roman] Catholic faith." [76] Their first bishop, John Carroll, had a clear concept of the relationships between church and state. He recognized alike the limitations of the federal government and the powers reserved for the sovereign states. Writing to a friend in England he rejoiced that "the fullest and largest system of toleration is adopted in almost all American states." [77] He expressed the view that "every denomination of Christians" ought to have equal footing and equal rights.[78] There had been no thought of an American uniate church, independent of Rome as it was independent of the state. The highest jurisdiction would be that of the pope in Rome.[79] Carroll, in writing to the Sacred College of Propaganda (1799), pointed out the need of that body to uphold the authority of the bishop since there could be no reliance on the civil government for the support of ecclesiastical authority.[80] Yet he was not ready to sacrifice the principle of the supremacy of canon law over civil law. This, too, belongs to the pattern of church-state relations which the Roman Catholic Church suggests.

The Baptists were among the outstanding advocates of religious freedom in the early history of our country. They were congregational in polity. "The gradual achievement of religious liberty" was for them one of the outstanding movements contributing to the growth of their denomination.[81] Sweet attributes the formation of associations of Baptist churches to "their leadership in the fight for religious liberty and the separation of church and state." [82] The fear of religious oppression was very real among them; they were therefore "quick to adjust themselves to the new conditions brought about by the Revolution, as the freedom, both civil and religious, involved was most congenial to them." [83]

Thus during the first two generations of American independence the pattern of free churches, disassociated from federal or state governments, became solidified. This pattern, some maintained, is inherent in the First Amendment to the federal constitution; it was written *in explicis verbis* into state constitutions. Theological support was found for it; expediency made it acceptable. The "separation of church and state," or better, the "adjustment to American church-state conditions," brought with it (at least in many instances) the necessity of voluntary support for the churches. It meant, too, that individuals had to rethink their relationships to the basic institutions in society. Preferred status had seemed good for church bodies; the presence of many sects, enjoying equal protection from the government, seemed to militate against the stability of the churches. Insofar as they had to rethink their particular functions and tasks, their conditions for membership, their polity and structure, the churches gained. In many of the denominations it was a period of reorganization and adjustment toward a secure place in the social order. The separation from European ties in most instances (for there were but few churches that did not become entirely independent in this respect too) gave these churches a greater adaptability to American conditions. In ecclesiastical matters democracy was fostered. Certainly the religious freedom and toleration, the freedom of worshiping God according to the dictates of one's own conscience, which were enshrined in the heritage of American liberty, must be counted among the greatest gains of the half century or so between the American Declaration of Independence and the period of Jacksonian democracy.[84]

THE APPLICATION OF THE PATTERN

The first period of nationalization in the United States (1783–1815) saw the constitution of the federal government adopted and the states established within the framework of the union. The relationships between federal and state governments were not settled, however, in all their various ramifications. Areas in which friction might arise remained; one such area involved the larger questions of "states' rights" and "nullification." Before the armed conflict came, the expansion toward the West modified political and social and economic happenings. Canal building gave way to the building of railroads, and personal messengers were displaced by postal services and telegrams. Native-born citizens counted a swelling number of immigrants, and the vast natural resources of the country furthered growing commercial enterprises. By 1815 the general characteristics of a tireless, aggressive, moving, brash citizenry were evident.

The churches, too, had organized and grouped themselves so that (with the immediate exception of two states) by 1815 the voluntary nature of the churches was recognized by the state governments. To most of the churches this was a welcome development. Tolerance and religious liberty were watchwords to which also the theologians paid service. Democracy and liberty in time became firm articles in the American creed. It seems too much, however, to say of the period of the Revolution and the constitution: "The religious ideal of the Kingdom of God was causally related to the secular American Dream." [85]

The letters and journals of foreigners in this country in the years between the War of 1812 and the War of 1861 shed light on the pattern of church-state relationships in this relatively new democracy. Religion, it was said by some of these visitors, had little influence. However, the religious freedom within the country appealed to them.[86] Crevecoeur found this one of the factors which shaped the new America. Francis Grund found the pervading Christianity shaping the very essence of government in this country.

Attempts to Mold a Christian Community

The desire of the frontier preachers to mold Christian communities may be seen from the example of Flavel Bascom. He wrote:

> I had at length reached my own Home Missionary field, away out on the Western frontier. Here I was to have the care of souls, and to test my ability so to preach the Gospel that these pioneer settlers would give heed to it, and be saved; and that all the Institutions of Christian civilization would spring up under its influence, on these Prairies.[87]

Luther Shaw about the same time wanted to establish a colony in Michigan. He wrote:

We hope that we shall form a Settlement of good people who will be decided in the cause of religion & virtue. All who know much of the state of new countries as they are generally settled, are well aware how difficult it is to sustain religious institutions & schools even, not so much for want of funds, as for want of interest & union. We do not intend to exclude all who do not profess religion by any means, but we want those who are decidedly in favor of all good institutions religious, moral, literary & political, & who will readily contribute by example and otherwise to build up a good Society.[88]

In the more settled parts of the country and in the Mississippi Valley, as it filled up, the attempts to mold the nation as such into a Christian community increased. Questions such as national holidays, the Sabbath, Sunday observance and the mail, preachers in politics for moral reform, illustrate how the "separation of church and state" was by no means regarded as absolute.

Some clergymen wished to maintain a "real, though indirect connection between the State and Christianity." [89] Even Alexander Hamilton, the statesman, advocated a "Christian Constitutional Society." This society aimed to support both institutions, the church and the state, and to unite them.[90] Samuel S. Schmucker, the Lutheran, wrote *The Christian Pulpit, the Rightful Guardian of Morals.*[91] Some believed in "perfect free trade in religion," to borrow William Leggett's telling phrase.[92] An Ezra Stiles Ely (1827), however, preached a sermon on "The Duty of Christian Freemen to Elect Christian Rulers," saying that "we have a right to demand that all our rulers in their [official] conduct shall conform to Christian morality." [93]

Zelotes Fuller pleaded that there be no union of any kind between church and state and warned in thinly veiled language against the Roman Catholic Church. "It is the intention," he said, "of certain religious sects in our country, to bring about, if possible, a union of church and state." He asked that "a certain 'Christian party in politics'" should never be encouraged. "The past history of the Christian Church, should be a solemn warning to us, never to permit an alliance to be formed —

between *Church and State powers.*" [94] Even the annual Thanksgiving Day proclamation was decried by William Leggett.

> We regret that even this single exception should exist to that rule of entire separation of the affairs of state from those of the church. . . . The recommending of a day of thanksgiving is not properly any part of the duty of a political Chief Magistrate; it belongs, in its nature, to the heads of the church, not to the heads of the State.[95]

James Madison likewise was not in favor of Thanksgiving Day proclamations. He also opposed chaplains in Congress, as he did Army and Navy chaplaincies, because they violated, in his opinion, "the Constitution and the pure principles of religious freedom." [96]

The question of Sunday observance and the mail, however, aroused much greater controversy than the chaplaincy question. On April 26, 1810, Congress passed an act which directed every postmaster to keep his post office open "on every day of the week" for the delivery of mail.[97] Various petitions against the action of Congress were filed, but to no avail. In 1825 agitation against Sunday mail again came to the fore when the Act of 1810 was rephrased and included in the code for the Post Office Department. A committee of the Senate, headed by Richard M. Johnson, recommended that the petitions against Sunday mail be denied.[98] The report itself showed that basic issues in church-state relations were involved in the controversy, not merely the external ordering of mail deliveries.

This Report of the Committee on Post-Office and Post-Roads of the United States Senate (January 1829) pointed out the religious liberty which the citizens of the United States enjoyed. It held that Congress could not control the consciences of others by legislation in favor of a particular day. "If a solemn act of legislation shall in one point define the God or point out to the citizen one religious duty, it may with equal propriety define every part of divine revelation and enforce every religious obligation, even to the forms and ceremonies of worship, the endowment of the church, and the support of the clergy." The report stated unequivocally: "The framers of the Constitution recognized the eternal principle that man's relation with God is above human legislation and his rights of conscience unalienable." The very practical consideration — the need of speedy mail service for the defense of the country and the common good — was also brought out in the report.[99] The House Report (1830) was very similar in content and in many points borrowed the language of the Senate report.[100] Approval of the Johnson Report was voiced by the legislatures of Indiana, Alabama, and Illinois.[101] The General Union for Promoting the Observance of the Christian Sabbath maintained its opposition, arousing the ire of William Lloyd Garrison and the Friends of Civil and Religious Liberty. "If the Sabbath day be of God, it does not need legislation to uphold it. There is no power which can prevail against it." [102]

The Sunday mail controversy meant indirect rather than direct participation of preachers in politics. Many of the clergy, however, believed that they should participate directly; only the popular aversion compelled them to stay in the background.[103] Even so, there were clergymen who became active politicians. James Garrard, a former Baptist clergyman, was governor of Kentucky from 1796 to 1804. As a member of the Virginia legislature he had actively supported Jefferson's bill for religious liberty.[104] He had been a member of the Elkhorn Baptist Association in Kentucky, which had stated (1785): "It is our opinion that it is lawful for any Christian to bear office either civil or military, except ministers of the Gospel." [105] Peter Cartwright was twice elected as representative to the Illinois legislature from Sangamon County. The slavery issue compelled him, he felt, in his own words, to go "into the agitated waters of political strife." [106] He stated flatly, ". . . I cannot see the impropriety of canvassing for office on Christian principles." [107]

Of greater importance than sporadic preachers in legislative halls or executive mansions were the organized groups dedicated to the cause of religion in politics. In February 1863 representatives of 11 Protestant denominations met in Xenia, Ohio, to lay the foundations for the National Reform Association. Its avowed objective was to make this a Christian nation by means of a constitutional amendment. Moral legislation was to mold the Christian community. Its sentiments are described as "characteristic of the views of conservative religious leaders of the time."[108] They held that the Christian character of this nation demanded the maintaining of Sunday laws, Bible reading in the public schools, prayers in legislative halls, national days for religious observances, and a written recognition of this character in the constitution itself. One objective, in fact, of the National Reform League was "to secure an amendment to the Constitution of the United States as will declare the nation's allegiance to Jesus Christ and its acceptance of the moral laws of the Christian religion, and so indicate that this is a Christian nation, and place all Christian laws, institutions, and usages of our government on an undeniably legal basis in the fundamental law of the land."[109] The persistence of this program rather than the continuance of the organization is of importance. *The Christian Statesman,* a publication begun by this organization in 1867 and still in existence, has had as its purpose "to maintain what it understood to be the Christian ideal of the American republic."[110]

The temperance cause already before the Civil War gave the advocates of promoting Christianity through legislation one of their chief arenas of action. The prevalence of excessive drinking in this country in the period from 1815 to 1860 is evident from the testimony of foreign travelers[111] and the records of frontier society.[112] There was at least one Methodist preacher who never measured his drams but drank as often during the day as he wished, "if I can get it."[113] In 1826 the American Society for the Promotion of Temperance was organized; in 1833 the United States Temperance Union came into being; in 1836 the American Temperance Union resulted from the merger of these bodies.[114] In 1837 the Maine State Temperance Society was organized under the leadership of Neal Dow. In 1851 the Maine law prohibiting the manufacture, sale, or keeping for sale of intoxicating liquors was passed, followed in 1855 by similar legislation in no fewer than 14 states. Although by 1875 only three states retained prohibitory legislation,[115] the role of the clergy in the 1850s in pushing such legislation in the interest of moral reform and for the purpose of molding the Christian community must be recognized.[116]

Roman Catholicism Encounters the Pattern

This Christian community, it must be emphasized, was thought of as a Protestant community. "Puritanism, Protestantism, and True Americanism are only different terms to designate the same set of principles," many believed.[117] In the minds of a majority "the America of today is a country of the Protestant traditions." [118] In these circumstances Roman Catholicism had to adapt itself to political conditions in this country.

This adaptation had to be made in the face of Protestant fears that Roman Catholicism would fill the country and dominate the legislature.[119] "The destinies of the Union will be in their hands." [120] Lyman Beecher, in his *Plea for the West* (1835), asked, "What is required to secure the civil and religious liberty of the West?" The answer lay, he believed, in the establishment of schools and colleges, because the Roman Catholics were establishing educational institutions. He asked whether the nation would "sustain its own institutions for the education of its own people, or depend on the charity of the despotic governments of Europe." [121]

The political implications of acknowledging the bishop of Rome angered the enemies of the Roman Catholic Church. During the 1830s and 1840s a wave of violent demonstrations against Roman Catholicism broke out.[122] "We notice," the Roman bishops stated in a pastoral letter to their people in 1833, ". . . [that] they have even denounced you and us as enemies to the liberties of the republic . . ." [123] Two years later (1835) one of the sharpest attacks came from the pen of Samuel F. B. Morse, *A Foreign Conspiracy Against the Liberties of the United States*.[124] The Roman Catholics felt themselves persecuted in a land which guaranteed religious liberty.[125] They were constrained, therefore, to answer the charge as "notoriously untrue," " 'that we acknowledge the supremacy of a foreign potentate or power,' in that sense which can interfere with our duty as

citizens." No religious allegiance, it was maintained, could be
exacted from them by any civil power. "They and we," the
bishops pointed out, "by our constitutional principles, are free
to give this ecclesiastical supremacy to whom we please, or to
refuse it to everyone, if we think proper: but, they and we owe
civil and political allegiance to the several states in which we
reside, and also, to our general government." The bishops continued by making the very telling declaration:

> When, therefore, using our undoubted right, we acknowledge
> the spiritual and ecclesiastical supremacy of the chief bishop
> of our universal church, the Pope or bishop of Rome, we do
> not thereby forfeit our claim to the civil and political protec-
> tion of the commonwealth; for, we do not detract from the
> allegiance to which the temporal governments are plainly
> entitled, and which we cheerfully give; nor do we acknowledge
> any civil or political supremacy, or power over us in any foreign
> potentate or power, though that potentate might be the chief
> pastor of our church.[126]

Of consequence for the Roman system, even though it raised
no storm of opposition, was the recognition of the seal of the
confessional by the Court of General Sessions in the City of
New York in 1813. The details of the case need not be given.
Its importance, however, must be emphasized. De Witt Clinton
gave the unanimous decision in the case. The guarantee of
religious liberty of the constitution of New York was cited to
support the decision. Since no precedent existed on which to
base the decision, the common law had to be invoked. The
sacramental character of penance, as claimed by the Roman
Church, influenced the tenor of the decision even though it was
rendered by Protestants. They recognized that violation of the
confessional would annihilate penance as a sacrament. The
Roman Catholic priests, therefore, it was stated, "are protected
by the laws and constitution of this country, in the full and free
exercise of their religion, and this court can never countenance
or authorize the application of insult to their faith, or of torture
to their conscience." The enactment of a law in the state of
New York in 1828 which protected the confessional, followed

by similar laws in other states, has served the cause of religious liberty.[127]

Not so easily and amicably solved was the question of the relationship of the Roman Catholic Church to the state-controlled pattern of education. The obligations of parents and of the church for the education of the church's children were stressed in the pronouncements of the Provincial Councils of Baltimore.[128] It was, however, the Fifth Provincial Council that raised the issue of the public schools and their relation to Roman Catholic education.

> We have seen with serious alarm, efforts made to poison the fountains of public education, by giving it a sectarian hue, and accustoming children to the use of a version of the Bible made under sectarian bias, and placing in their hands books of various kinds replete with offensive and dangerous matter. This is plainly opposed to the free genius of our civil institutions. . . . Let them [the parents], therefore, avail themselves of their natural rights, guaranteed by the laws, and see that no interference with the faith of their children be used in the public school, and no attempt made to induce conformity in anything contrary to the laws of the Roman Catholic Church.[129]

The First Plenary Council of Baltimore (1852) admonished parents: "Encourage the establishment and support of [Roman] Catholic schools." [130]

The opposition to the reading of the King James Version of the Scriptures, under the leadership of Bishop John Hughes, involved the Roman Catholic Church in political activities. Attempts were made to get legislative action in various states to do away with the reading of the "Protestant Bible" in public schools. The Supreme Court of Maine (1854) held that laws could not allow "the right of sectarian interference in the selection of books." This view prevailed among legislators and jurists during most of the 19th century.[131]

Throughout this period, as later, Roman Catholics were anxious to be accepted as loyal members of the body politic. They insisted that "the authority and influence of the Church will be found to be the most efficacious support of the temporal authority

by which society is governed." The power of the civil magistracy, however, was recognized only "as subordinate and delegated," to be exercised always "agreeably to God's Law." [132]
The church determined, it was claimed, what is permissible;
it can demand the acquiescence of the state to that decision.

> The Catholic has a guide in the church, as a divine institution,
> which enables him to discriminate between what the Law of
> God forbids or allows; and this authority the State is bound to
> recognize as supreme in its sphere — of moral, no less than
> dogmatic teaching.[133]

The postulate was stated, yet it did not lead to conflict. The
primacy of the spiritual and the need of the state to cooperate
with the church are parts of the underlying principles of church-
state relations held by the Roman Catholic hierarchy. They
played their part for Roman Catholics in establishing the American Pattern.

Public Education and the Pattern

Issues pertaining to religion and the public schools persisted
throughout the history of the nation. The use of tax funds for
the support of church schools and religious instruction in the
public schools are broadly the two main issues in this area.[134]

The concern of the churches for education remained a real
concern. For instance, the report of Abraham Scott, a Presbyterian missionary, to the Connecticut Missionary Society about
conditions in Ohio (1808) showed a solicitude by the people
for education, although there were objections to the use of
Scripture in the schools. He regretted the neglect of instruction
in "the essential and fundamental doctrines of religion." [135] The
philosophy that education should benefit both church and state,
prevalent generally during the Colonial period, was prevalent
also on the frontier during the early years of the first half of the
19th century.[136]

The conviction that education was a legitimate function of
government was growing, although there was, especially in the
academy movement, a greater stress on the establishment of
private schools than public schools. Whether educational func-

tions belonged to the federal government or the state governments was resolved, in the absence of any direct statement in the federal constitution, in favor of the states.[137] This can be seen from the Connecticut Act of 1810, which provided for a commissioner of school funds, the appointment of Gideon Hawley in New York as first superintendent of common schools in 1812, and the granting of state aid for education.[138] However, voluntary school societies were extensively engaged in education in New York City, Philadelphia, Washington, Baltimore, Albany, and Providence among many other cities.[139]

Public education by the establishment of state school systems increased during the period from 1828 to 1860. Humanitarianism and the awareness of the educational needs in a democratic society, the demands of educational reformers, and the pronouncements of prominent public personages, among other factors advancing the cause of free, universal schooling, were aided by the activities of societies such as the Western Literary Institute and College of Professional Teachers and the American Lyceum. Educational journals and the example of foreign schools, not least those of Prussia, had their influence. The influence of "a group of educational reformers who went on to become educational statesmen," among them James G. Carter, Horace Mann, Henry Barnard, Calvin Wiley, and Caleb Mills, was great.[140]

Horace Mann as Secretary of the Board of Education of Massachusetts formulated some telling statements on keeping religion out of the public schools. He pronounced himself fully in favor of religious education,[141] but he did not wish to sponsor a government-established religion. He pointed to the Massachusetts law of 1827, "prohibiting sectarian instruction in our public schools." He advocated Bible reading without comment and the inculcation of moral values in a school system neither "anti-Christian nor un-Christian." [142] Although Mann's personal creed was largely humanitarian, ethical, even naturalistic,[143] he was genuinely concerned for the principles of public education. He pointed out in a letter to the Reverend H. M. Smith (1847) that the state "has only said that no one sect shall obtain any advantage over other sects by means of the school system, which, for purposes of self-preservation, it has established." [144] Smith was only one of the advocates of "local option" for the teaching of religion — that the district should determine, as Mann put it, "what theology shall be taught in school."

This question of religious instruction was enmeshed with the question of the power of the school district or the town and the regulation and supervision of the schools by the state.[145] There seems to be sufficient evidence that "organized and vigorous propaganda" was used for the promotion of state-controlled, "nonsectarian," public schools.[146] "Religious instruction is no part of a common school education," became more and more the accepted view.[147] To this end textbooks were revised, curricula were reorganized, and the virtual elimination of voluntary societies for public education was brought about. "It appeared that, not only in Massachusetts but elsewhere, a strong trend toward the separation of religion and politics in America increased in the Jacksonian period." [148]

The Roman Catholic Church recognized the trend clearly. Under the leadership of Bishop John Hughes this church nevertheless demanded a share of public funds for parochial schools. Its demands and similar demands by others were nullified by an act of the Legislature of New York in 1842. The law stipulated that no public funds were to be given to any school in which the inculcation of denominational beliefs and the teaching of sectarian doctrines were regarded as objectives of the school. A number of privately supported schools continued to receive aid from public funds, but the principle had been established. The Roman Catholics and some other religious bodies were not entirely satisfied, because the nature of "sectarian doctrine or tenet" was not defined more closely and because the Bible (1844) might still be read in the schools without comment.[149]

In other states Roman Catholics attempted to obtain public funds for parochial or church schools. The "Lowell Plan" in Lowell, Mass. (1835–52), tried to give the church a voice in the conduct of the schools.[150] In 1855 a constitutional amendment in Massachusetts made it unconstitutional to give state aid to church schools.

> In fact, no demands to divide the funds made after 1840 were successful anywhere. Between 1840 and the Civil War, six states amended their constitutions to forbid public support of religious schools and three new states made such provisions in their first constitutions. . . . Every state admitted to the Union since 1858, except West Virginia, has erected constitutional safeguards against possible attempts of religious groups to obtain a share of the public school funds . . .[151]

In the period before 1865 many colleges seem to have received state aid at one time or another, sometimes in the form of land grants, sometimes as subsidies. Community support was often solicited for denominational colleges.[152] The support by the state of higher schools under denominational control persisted in a lessening degree throughout the period, although the rise of state universities was one factor in bringing about a decline of such aid. Granting aid to higher schools was not generally thought of as "mixing state and church" or as the support of a "sectarian or denominational" school; instead the support of culture and the raising of the educational level were popular motives.

The uneasiness and internal conflicts of the period exemplify uneasiness and conflicts that emerged in the period after the Civil War and to an even greater extent after World War I. The pretensions of the theocrats did not lessen. "The Kingdom of God" and "the American Dream" must find their nexus. As the years passed, there emerged a glorification of the American way of life that made of it a religion only related to Christianity but one which some churchmen did not hesitate to espouse. Increasingly the demands for moral reforms involved the churches with governmental agencies and officials. Social and economic problems increased with the territorial and economic development of the country. Immigration brought additional problems, some of these problems raised by the Roman Catholic Church, made stronger by the immigration. Not least were the problems connected with education. Also, strict separation of church and state was demanded by others, although the emerging pattern did not show a clear line of demarcation.

ADJUSTING THE PATTERN FOR EMERGING MODERN AMERICA

The pattern of church-state relationships which emerged in the era between 1865 and 1914 is a complex one. The growth of business and industry, the waves of immigrants, the increasing wealth and the evident secularism, uncontrolled and unhampered, pointed up responsibilities for the churches which they had to meet. The territorial expansion that had resulted from the Mexican War now meant further expansion for the churches, in the course of which they grappled with many of the same problems of the earlier frontiers.

In the older sections of the country social problems grew more and more acute by reason of expanding industries. The "Social Gospel" tried to meet some of these problems, although social welfare legislation came much later in America than in Europe.

Public education increased. The high school movement began almost with the closing of the frontier, but any other connection between the two developments must be sought for in the deeper hopes and ambitions that motivated the dynamics of Americanism.

Americanism contained in itself patriotic and religious strains which were taking on the complexion of a nationalistic religion rather than a religious nationalism. Apocalyptic and messianic aspects are found in it. Niebuhr has observed: "From the earliest days of its history to the present moment, there is a deep layer of Messianic consciousness in the mind of America." [153] With it is the concept that America is "the darling of divine providence," favored by God with a manifest destiny and mission of its own.

In addition the fear that foreign ideologies and "un-American" religions might gain too great a foothold in this country clung to that Americanism. The Roman Catholic Church was affected internally by a struggle between American nationalism and Roman internationalism; externally by continued suspicions, misgivings, and even hostility. The question of maintaining the balance between church and state overshadowed most of the other questions in the popular mind. Would Rome seek to dictate to Washington? What about the schools being conducted by the Roman Church? Could the state government regulate them?

The tremendous influx of immigrants into this church body slowed down the process of integration. Accommodation, however, was sought in several areas. Increasingly an emphasis was placed on cooperation and coordination. Humpty Dumpty, sitting on the wall, saw that the wall of separation between church and state was not of equal height throughout. This wall might be straddled.

"Good fences make good neighbours," [154] said the New England poet Robert Frost, but in the American mind church and state were regarded not only as neighbors but also as partners. There were simply too many churches to permit the dominance of any one church or a group of churches. Tolerance had to be accorded even to new sects, for the right of existence could not be denied them. It was easier in popular opinion to grant them that right if they were in the Puritan or Protestant tradition, but that demand was not supported in law.

The majority of American citizens, whether they were church-going or not, seem not to have faced the elementary questions of rights and duties in the orders of society. Under such conditions the question of relationship between these orders was not faced squarely. Ignorance and indifference caused problems to mount. Then, too, there were many different churches and many different levels of government, most of them, like Topsy, just "growin'." Inherent in the changing pattern was conflict. That conflict became sharper in the 20th century than it was in the last half of the 19th.

Conflict and accommodation, cooperation and contradiction entered into the dialectics of the period. The tensions were no greater than they would have been with an established church. Voluntaryism with its problems and dangers was preferred by the

majority of clergy and laity alike. The shadows of the past
seemed at times to form specters; the period itself accentuated
some of the features of those specters.

The Pattern in a Reunited Union

The religious aura of Lincoln's addresses would have seemed
strange in the Washington dominated by Thaddeus Stevens and
Charles Sumner. Nevertheless, Bishops E. R. Ames and Matthew Simpson by their activities in politics [155] etched a design
in the pattern of church-state relations that other preachers would
attempt to retrace. In 1865, however, even the appointment of
a chaplain for the House was governed by anti-Johnson forces.

Meanwhile the problems of the South cried for solution. Congress took up the question of the Freedmen's Bureau, only to
have the bill vetoed by the President. The second Freedmen's
Bureau Bill was passed over the President's veto (1866). The
churches, too, had launched on programs for helping the South.
The American Union Commission claimed to be nondenominational and nonpolitical, yet it combined in its activities religious
and political functions. It merged with the American Freedmen's Aid Commission in 1866 to become the American Freedmen's Union Commission.[156]

Should church groups receive help from the Freedmen's
Bureau? General Howard was ready to grant $5,000 to the Epis-
copalians toward building a normal school in Raleigh, N. C.
Lyman Abbott stated, "The cardinal principle of this country
has been the separation of Church and State." He questioned
the wisdom of making appropriations out of the public funds
*"for the support of schools, avowedly organized to teach de-
nominational tenets."* [157]

Among the problems which the churches of the South faced
was also the problem of the restoration of their property. Here
incidents occurred which illustrate the readiness of churchmen
to become involved in sensitive areas, bordering on "playing
politics," even though they thought these involvements were for
the good of the church.

The impeachment proceedings against President Johnson,

however, are the clearest indication of the concern of the churches, especially of the Methodist Church, in matters of state. Simpson, "the high-priest of the Methodists and a sectarian politician of great shrewdness and ability," was not far from the inner circle working for the conviction of the President. During the days of the trial the Methodist Conference was meeting in Chicago. Four resolutions were presented to this body, aiming at the President's conviction, but all were defeated. A resolution was passed, sponsored by Bishop Simpson, setting aside an hour for prayer, asking God "to save our senators from error." [158]

The activities of the Northern Methodists in the political arena were repugnant to the Methodists in the South. They seemed confirmed in their belief of the strict separation of church and state.

Incidentally, no churchmen or churches seemed to have been involved in the making and adopting of the Fourteenth Amendment. This amendment (1868) guaranteed individual rights which after 1923 the Supreme Court would extend to religious rights and privileges.

Theocracies Within the Pattern

One indigenous religious group, the Church of Jesus Christ of Latter Day Saints, came into conflict with the government and presented problems of church-state relations. The solution of those problems, too, contributed to rounding out the pattern.

This group in the early days of its history aimed at a theocracy.[159] Peter Cartwright reported a statement made directly to him by Joseph Smith (probably in 1843): "I will show you, sir, that I will raise up a government in these United States which will overturn the present government, and I will raise up a new religion that will overturn every other form of religion in this country!" [160] Smith commanded what was in effect a Mormon militia, the Nauvoo Legion. In various ways Smith tried to further his religious body through political means. In 1844, the year of his violent death, he announced his candidacy for the presidency of the United States.[161]

Under the leadership of Brigham Young the Mormons arrived in the Salt Lake Valley in July 1847. Here they established 95 communities within a decade; in 10 years, to 1867, they established another 135 communities; during the third decade they added another 127 communities. In the first period, at least, they hoped to build an independent theocracy. The Territory of Utah was created by Act of Congress in 1851; Brigham Young became territorial governor on the 3rd of February in that same year.[162] Soon thereafter Young advocated separation from the Federal Union. The "Utah War" (1857–58), with its unfortunate Mountain Meadows Massacre, illustrates the tensions that existed.[163]

The more important tensions, however, centered in the question of polygamy. In 1862 Congress passed an act "to punish the practice of bigamy in the territories." [164] In 1878 the Supreme Court decided that polygamy was unconstitutional.[165] In 1890 President Wilford Woodruff as head of the Mormon Church issued a proclamation against "plural marriages." The constitution of the State of Utah, when admitted into the Union in 1896, had an article which read:

> The following ordinance shall be irrevocable without the consent of the United States and the people of the state: Perfect tolerance of religious sentiment is guaranteed. No inhabitant of this state shall ever be molested in person or property on account of his or her mode of religious worship; but polygamous or plural marriages are for ever prohibited.[166]

Other church bodies became involved in this question of polygamy as an aspect of church-state relations. They addressed memorials and petitions to Congress and directed opinions in their religious journals to members of the government. Because of the pressure from the churches some state constitutions expressly stated that polygamy was prohibited, and platforms of political parties included denunciations of polygamy.[167]

While polygamy is the issue which is remembered most easily, the wider question of Mormonism and church-state relations is equally important. "Perhaps no question in the history of Mormonism is more complicated than the Mormon conception of church and state, on the one hand, and the problem of relation-ship between the Mormon community and the United States, on the other." [168] The theocratic concepts inherent in Mormon-ism are fundamental to that faith. "The fact is that a separate community, based on the ultimate authority of the leader of the church and in which church leadership exerted influence and took initiative in fields of endeavor far removed from religion and ecclesiastical affairs, was basic to all Mormon efforts." [169] The Mormons do not deny the legitimacy of civil affairs. They accept American political institutions and regard the constitution of the United States of America as divinely inspired.[170] In a for-mal sense, at least, they recognize the separation of church and state, which came to have meaning after Utah obtained state-hood. However, all male members of the Mormons are members of the priesthood; their important religious leaders, because they follow also secular pursuits for a livelihood, may hold high posi-tions in the state governments. "The fact is that the Mormons never worked out consistently the political implications of their religious philosophy." Ambiguity and ambivalence toward the United States are characteristics of that philosophy.[171]

Another indigenous religious group is the Church of Christ, Scientist, or Christian Science Church. Its members have been called "strong advocates of religious liberty." They maintain that "when the citizen chooses to rely on the practice of a religion to prevent or cure disease, they [his rights] are inseparable from civil and religious liberty." [172] By 1914 there were 26 states or territories in which the practitioners of this group were given legal recognition. In subsequent years all other states of the Union extended such recognition. There are still points, e. g., vaccination, around which controversy is being waged. In gen-eral, however, it seems that the legislatures and courts have been ready to accept the contentions of the Christian Scientists and have provided safeguards for their "religious" liberties.[173]

This broad interpretation of religious liberty characterized the relations between the state and federal governments and religious groups such as the Quakers (Society of Friends), the Moravian Brethren, the Mennonites, the Seventh-day Adventists, the Russellites and Rutherfordites, and other groups.[174] There were others such as the Liberal Church of America. Its "Uncle Sam's religion" claimed that the constitution of the United States of America should be substituted for the Sacred Scriptures.[175] The Christian Catholic Church at Zion City, Ill., founded by John Alexander Dowie and carried forward by Wilbur Glenn Voliva, is a theocracy and within the confines of the city established strict "blue laws." [176] Some of these sects, at least in their readiness to claim religious liberties, have themselves been ready to blur the line of demarcation between church and state by their theocratic notions.

Theocratic notions, sectarian hopes and hesitations were found in many of the political movements of the period without, however, any formal ties between groups identified as political and religious. These notions, common to both, came in part from the same or similar heritages and received divergent emphases. New forces emphasized the material aspects of existence; industrialism and secularization made men seek cures in the economic and social realms. Behind that striving were millennialistic hopes and theocratic visions, most easily discernible in the small sects.

They are discernible, too, in the writings of philosophers and thinkers, even skeptics and rationalists. Not the theologians nor the dreamers, but the economists and industrialists, the prophets and proponents of bigness, the peddlers of "progress," were providing a nostrum which would make financial ease the paradise of American religiosity. The new patterns of thought flared up in Populism and Greenbackism and enlisted the rolling religious imagery of William Jennings Bryan. The passing of the frontier, the rise of labor unions, and the coming of socialism pointed up the proletarian hopes — hopes which combined a mixture of economic and spiritual well-being, the product of a vague Christianity in a democratic state. If religion could not obtain these ends unaided, politics might be of assistance.[177] The millenarian hopes were veiled, for they had been transformed into socio-economic patterns.

The need to subordinate private interests to collective interest was stressed. Within a span of 16 years (1884–1900) 48 Utopian romances were written. Of these, *Looking Backward,* by Edward Bellamy, is one of the most significant. Published in 1888, it soon gave the impetus to a movement which sought social betterment. Taking "nationalism" as its label and *The Nationalist* as the name of its journal, the movement looked for a collective organization of industry — not to be confused with Marxism — that was truly democratic.[178] Bellamy envisioned a new day in which the government would carry out social reconstruction that would embody the best of Christianity. Thus industry and society and government and religion would achieve the "Brotherhood of Humanity." [179]

The Implications for the Pattern of the Social Gospel

In theology the broad movement calling for the fulfillment of a millenarian, Utopian reconstruction of society through the government and with its aid culminated in the Social Gospel. The rise of the Social Gospel was conditioned by liberalism and even skepticism, by the industrial revolution and socialism, no less than by the new science, the doctrine of progress, progressive orthodoxy, evangelicalism, revivalism, and humanitarianism.[180]

The formulation of any theories of church-state relations by the advocates of the Social Gospel is almost in the nature of a by-product of their teachings. The concept of "the kingdom," however, carried with it, as it was used by these theologians, political connotations.

Not every concern for social questions nor every pronouncement on economic and political problems by preachers and theologians, it is true, is a dabbling in political matters or a mixing of church and state. The demand, however, that the government and the church become partners in the solution of social and economic problems is the pattern advocated by the theocrats and social evangelists and has definite political implications.

For instance, the churches must unite in order to carry out a program of poor relief, Gladden taught, in "an organized unity of the Christian elements" within a city.[181] The associated churches in the care of the poor "shall keep themselves in close and sympathetic relation with the public authorities." Some aspects of this relief must be surrendered by the state to the church.[182]

Church and state alike, said Henry King, must be governed by Christian ethics which find their matrix in the concept of the kingdom of God, for the kingdom of God is ethical, as it is spiritual.[183] "The relative independence of the state" is granted.[184] Ely, however, maintained:

> . . . when Christ said, Seek ye first the kingdom of God, and all earthly good things shall be added unto you, He was proclaiming a truth rather of social and national application than of individual application. . . . But it is true today, as in the time of Christ and in all times, that *that nation which in all its laws and institutions seeks first the kingdom of God* shall have all these things added unto it.[185]

Gardner asked for the civil and political implications of Christ's ethical principles. Admitting "the absence in the ethics of Jesus of any teaching concerning the function and value of the state and concerning civic duties" (although the validity of the statement must be questioned), Gardner looked at the ideal state and said: ". . . love will be the informing principle of the organization of the state, as of all other functions of the collective life. . . ." In that ideal society "the state would still be needed as the central institution in which all others would be correlated." [186]

The proponents of progressive orthodoxy, social Christianity, and the Social Gospel — as the movement was labeled at various times — carried on intense efforts for their cause. Josiah Strong wrote, among other things, *Our Country*. Conferences of leaders were held. Reports, bearing titles such as *The National Perils and Opportunities* or, again, *National Needs and Remedies,* were issued.[187] Theological faculties advocated social progress. George D. Herron published *The Christian State*.[188] The Christian Commonwealth Colony was set up in Georgia, in part a result of *The Kingdom,* a weekly paper. For three years in the 1890s a magazine called *The Social Gospel* was published. Christian Socialism was sponsored by *The Social Forum*. *The Christian Patriot* was published by James A. Converse, who also wrote books with titles such as *The Bible and Land* and *Uncle Sam's Bible, or*

Bible Teachings About Politics.[189] The very titles reveal a curious mixture of concepts about the relationships between church and state.

Washington Gladden, however, regarded the state as supreme. He postulated the supremacy of the state on the kingly office of Christ, "as King he is the Head of the state. His kingly office is his supreme office." [190] The functions of the state, he said, are to protect property, to defend the rights of the individual citizen, especially property rights, to maintain public schools, and to restrain monopolies. Any extension of the functions of government, however, require the state to become Christianized. "It is the business of the state to declare and maintain upon the earth the righteousness of God: could there be a more august vocation?" Cooperation will be the watchword and labor will provide Christian leadership and Christian statesmanship.

Cooperation became for Walter Rauschenbusch, too, the answer to the question of church-state relations. He wrote: "Such a cooperation of the religious and political forces of the community furnishes the positive solution to the problem of Church and State." [191] Rauschenbusch was not ready to advocate a union of church and state. However, he spoke of the interpenetration of the life of church and state. He held that Christ condemned those severely who "believed only in the church and kept their hands away from the state." [192]

Rauschenbusch's idea of penetration is not peculiar to him. Though it is not stated explicitly in the "Social Creed of the Churches," adopted by the Federal Council of the Churches of Christ in America in 1908, the idea is implicit in that statement. This creed became part of the pattern of American Protestant thinking and helped to shape legislation in a subsequent period. It embodied the underlying supposition of many theologians that the government would aid the kingdom of God in the realization of its social mission.

Demands for Complete Separation

Alongside the demand for the Christian state of the advocates of the Social Gospel and the National Reform Association (who wanted the adoption of a "Christian amendment" to the constitution) there were those, like Charles Sumner and Francis Ellingwood Abbot, who demanded a complete separation of church and state.

In 1874 Abbot proposed a "Religious Freedom Amendment" to the Constitution. The proposal, although it was not adopted, is noteworthy also because it shows a readiness to increase the Federal jurisdiction in church-state relations.[193] He objected, for example, that the state officials in Georgia, South Carolina, and North Carolina were constitutionally required to be Protestants, that in other states only those who believed in a God could hold office, that oaths were obligatory in courts of law, prayers were said in legislative halls, that days of fasting and prayer were proclaimed, that Sunday laws were on the statute books, that the Bible was used in the public schools, and that the property of religious bodies was tax exempt.[194]

The force of the movement for absolute separation may be gauged from the fact that U. S. Grant in his State of the Union message to Congress on Dec. 7, 1875, voiced some of the "demands of Liberalism." He saw the large extent of the properties of the churches, "receiving all the protection and benefits of Government without bearing its proportion of the burdens and expenses of the same." His recommendation read: "I would suggest the taxation of all property equally, whether church or corporation, exempting only the last resting place of the dead and possibly, with proper restrictions, church edifices."[195] He asked for federal legislation requiring the states to provide "a good common-school education to every child." He recommended, too, that laws be enacted that "no sectarian tenets shall ever be taught in any school supported in whole or in part by the State, nation, or by the proceeds of any tax levied upon any community." A third group of legislative acts should "declare church and state forever separate and distinct, but each free within their proper spheres; and that all church property shall bear its own proportion of taxation."[196]

A Roman Catholic historian, looking at these recommendations, regarded them as "echoes of the Kulturkampf." He cited the circulation of a pamphlet by the Union Republican Congressional Executive Committee with the title *Vaticanism in Germany and the United States.*[197] It would be a mistake, however, to regard all of these demands simply as the backwash of German political currents. There was a genuine tradition in America for as complete a separation of church and state as possible in the interest of religious liberty and freedom of conscience.

James G. Blaine introduced a resolution in the House to amend the constitution in accordance with the recommendation of President Grant, excepting that he would permit the reading of the Bible in the public schools.[198] The Republican national convention of 1876 adopted a plank in its platform recommending a constitutional amendment "forbidding the application of any public funds or property for the benefit of any school or institution under sectarian control." [199]

Although these proposals did not become law, Congress did pass an act which provided that all states accepted into the Union in the future must guarantee religious freedom and provide for public schools "free from sectarian control."

During the 1870s and 1880s the Hoar Bill and the Blair Bill sought to provide federal aid for education, "but the religious issue was inevitably injected." [200] Even a constitutional amendment was proposed that public schools include instruction "in the common branches of knowledge, and in virtue, morality, and the principles of the Christian religion." [201] This proposal, of course, did not carry. In 1896 and in 1897 the appropriation acts for the District of Columbia provided:

> And it is hereby declared to be the policy of the Government of the United States to make no appropriation of money or property for the purpose of founding, maintaining, or aiding by payment for services, expenses, or otherwise, any church or religious denomination, or any institution or society which is under sectarian or ecclesiastical control . . .[202]

Such an enactment did not guarantee a complete separation of church and state, much as it illustrates the demand for such complete separation. For all that, one historian found that "there is a common ideal that state and church are not only separated but that they have an equal interest in remaining separated." [203]

Sunday Laws and "Religion-by-Legislation" as Part of the Pattern

Absolute separation of church and state as the pattern of church-state relations in the United States cannot be postulated in view of the laws in force during the 19th century regulating Sunday observance. Such regulations were but one attempt to further "religion-by-legislation" as part of the pattern. These regulations were made by the federal government and by the state governments; municipalities passed their laws and churches demanded the enforcement of all of these laws. According to Blakely, in the period between 1888 and 1945, 142 religious measures were introduced into the Congress of the United States. Of these bills 93 related to Sunday observance. Not all of them by any means were passed.

The various state legislatures were more ready to enact such legislation.[204] Such laws over the years were observed and they were breached. At times there was greater zeal for enforcement than at other times; in some areas there was greater effort at enforcement than in others, even within the confines of the same state. In Arkansas and Tennessee prosecutions (some would have it "persecutions") were rife in the 1890s for breaking the Sunday laws. Judge Hammond of the Circuit Court of the United States for the Western District of Tennessee, who upheld the decision in the celebrated King case (1891), remarked in his decision: "Nevertheless, by a sort of factitious advantage, the observers of Sunday have secured the aid of civil law, and adhere to that advantage with great tenacity, in spite of the clamor for religious freedom and the progress that has been made in the absolute separation of church and state . . ." [205]

When Sunday legislation has been brought before the courts, conflicting interpretations have been given. The Supreme Court of Missouri (1854), in an opinion delivered by Justice Scott, stated "that there is nothing inconsistent with the Constitution, as it was understood at the time of its adoption, with a law compelling the observance of Sunday as a day of rest." [206] In that same decision it was stated that "our Constitution was framed for a people whose religion was Christianity." The California Sunday Law was held unconstitutional by the Supreme Court of California (1858). The Supreme Court of Colorado declared the Denver Sunday law invalid (1909).

That the enforcement of Sunday laws was often urged by reformers bent on "religion-by-legislation" can scarcely be denied. Even the Supreme Court of the United States delivered itself of an obiter dictum that the United States is a Christian nation.[207]

The growth of the temperance movement after the Civil War is another illustration of the continued attempts to enforce purportedly Christian principles by law. In 1869 the National Prohibition Party was organized. The Women's Christian Temperance Union, organized in 1874 under the leadership of Frances E. Willard, advocated the cause of prohibition in the name of Christianity. An "omni-partisan and interdenominational" organization, the Anti-Saloon League, was organized in 1893 (the "Church at work against the saloons"). By 1918 33 states had become "dry"; on Jan. 16, 1920, the Eighteenth Amendment to the constitution went into effect. The churches played a large role in bringing about this legislation.[208] Abstinence was confused with temperance. Legal enactments were to bring about change in character and a readiness to abstain from evil. Whatever the drive for prohibition may prove or disprove, it does show the readiness of the churches to use the arm of the state to further their aims.

However, there were other areas, notably that of education, in which tensions were evident.

Increasing Tensions in the Pattern Regarding Education

In 1884 the pastoral letter to the Roman hierarchy asked each parish to maintain schools adequate to the needs of its children.[209] In the same year a call was issued for the organization of parish schools in every parish with properly trained teachers.[210] The control of the states in education had been extended, and compulsory attendance laws became general.[211] Now for the Roman

Catholic Church the establishment and maintenance of parochial schools became a problem of huge proportions in the face of the mounting tide of immigration. True, the religious orders supplied some of the needed teachers. If, however, some *modus operandi* might be found which would permit Roman Catholics to use and control public schools, this might redound to the extension of their church.[212]

In Lowell, Mass. (1831–52), and in Poughkeepsie, N. Y. (1875–98), public schools had been used virtually as Roman Catholic parochial schools. The "regular" school subjects were taught during the ordinary hours allotted to a school day; religion was taught either before or after the closing of school. In Poughkeepsie nuns in the habits of their order taught in these "public schools." John Ireland, archbishop of St. Paul, permitted the priests in Faribault and Stillwater, Minn., to lease the parish school buildings to the local boards of education, the nuns to serve as teachers paid from state funds, following the prescribed curriculum of the state. Only during the school hours did the building pass out of the nominal control of the church.[213]

Ireland had advocated this plan in an address to the National Education Association in 1890. He expressed himself as entirely in favor of public schools. However, he favored the teaching of religion in these schools and state subsidies to parochial schools.

> I would permeate the regular state school with the religion of the majority of the children of the land, be this religion as Protestant as Protestantism can be, and I would, as is done in England, pay for the secular instruction given in denominational schools according to results. . . . This is not paying for religious instruction, but for the secular instruction demanded by the State, and given to the pupil as thoroughly as he could have received it in the state school.[214]

Ireland's proposal raised a storm within the Roman Catholic Church. The controversy was brought on not so much because a demand had been made for state funds for Roman Catholic parish schools. In time such demands would become a fixed plank in the Roman platform. Rather it seemed to some of the forces within that church that an attempt had been made to sell out the parochial schools. In a pamphlet, *Education, to Whom Does It Belong?*, Thomas Bouquillon of Catholic University maintained that the state had the right to control education. In the course of the controversy other writings were disseminated. Archbishop Ireland, "to explain his position and to defend himself against the complaints of his opponents," went to Rome to appear before Leo XIII.[215] James Gibbons had written to the Roman officials; in defense of Ireland he cited the agreement of the American archbishops with the Faribault plan.[216] On April 21, 1892, the Sacred Congregation sanctioned the Faribault plan "as long as the decree of the Council of Baltimore was preserved." Then under date of May 31, 1893, Leo XIII wrote a letter to the American hierarchy in which he repeated the necessity of observing the decree of the Council of Baltimore of 1884. "At the same time he observed that it would be most desirable to obtain from the civil government a concession for funds for the parochial schools." [217]

The pope's letter was in line with the 14 propositions of Archbishop Francis Satolli, apostolic delegate in the United States. His propositions permitted the attendance of Roman Catholic children in public schools, "provided these schools were purged of the features that made them objectionable to [Roman] Catholics," [218] or when other plans could not be carried out.[219]

The "school question" (among others) caused a controversy among Roman Catholics. Leo XIII's letter ended the controversy, but by it "Americanism" was condemned and submission to the papacy was enjoined.[220]

In line with the pronouncements of Leo XIII "The Pastoral Letter of 1919" of the American hierarchy indicated that there must be cooperation and a connection between church and state. Governments must appreciate the importance of religion "for the preservation of the common weal."

> *Let them seriously consider whether it be the part of political wisdom to exclude from the ordinance of the State and from public instruction the teaching of the Gospel and of the Church.* Only too well does experience show that when religion is banished, human authority totters to its fall.[221]

Opposition to Roman Catholic schools continued. Already in July 1889, at the annual meeting of the National Educational Association in Nashville, Tenn. (where Cardinal Gibbons and Bishop Kean presented the case of the Roman Catholic parochial schools, and Edwin B. Mead and John Jay presented the cause of the public schools), the statement was made that education would not be safe in the hands of the Roman hierarchy. "The great educational interests of this Republic are of more concern than its tariff or all its material production; but those interests, so vast and so glorious, can never be entrusted safely to the Roman Catholic Church." [222]

The fears that the Roman Catholic Church would encroach on the public schools, by imposing its religious instruction on them, had solid bases. In the Archdiocese of Baltimore a circular letter was prepared (1893) which proposed "that the conscience of parents be respected" and that the public schools system be modified. A bill was prepared for the State Legislature, asking that denominational schools be incorporated by the state, that "each denominational school building should be rented to the city or the state for the annual sum of one dollar," and that the city or state should pay the salaries of the teachers in these denominational schools. [223]

Nevertheless, state constitutional and statutory provisions and judicial decisions have not allowed for state support of church schools. By 1914 the provisions of the various states may be summarized as follows:

1) Thirty States with enactments against the appropriation of public money to denominational or sectarian institutions or to schools under sectarian control.

2) Nine States, providing against appropriations to schools not under the absolute control of the State (not including Massachusetts and North Dakota).

3) Six States with provisions against drawing on the treasury for the benefit of any religious sect, society, or theological institution.

4) Eight States with provisions against appropriations for any sectarian purpose, viz. . . .

5) Four States with provisions against the *control* of school funds by any religious sect. . . .

6) Two States forbidding the acceptance of any gift or grant for sectarian purposes (Nebraska and South Dakota).[224]

It had been true of Maryland, and this holds true of the country in general: "By the close of the nineteenth century two independent systems of education had been established, the one a state system supported by general taxation and the other a church system supported by religious bodies." [225]

It cannot be said, however, that there was absolutely no support of church schools in this country after 1865. Nor were the Roman Catholics the only ones seeking state support of parochial schools. In North Carolina between 1890 and about 1905 there were 17 Presbyterian parochial schools receiving aid from the state.[226] In the New England states there were a few schools, particularly secondary schools, that received state aid during the period from 1865 to 1914. Gabel shows that occasional grants were made to denominational colleges, and in Pennsylvania "quasi-parochial schools — [Roman] Catholic, Lutheran, Quaker — served as district schools" almost until the end of the 19th century.[227] In the South as late as 1914 "some parochial schools or church-controlled academies and normal schools were permitted to receive local or state funds for such education." Also in the Northwest and West instances can be cited of similar support. Such support decreased throughout the period, so that it is evident that the trend has been steadily against any kind of state support of church schools. Patriotism and secularism had their roles in this trend; liberalism and anti-Roman Catholicism played their part.[228] Naturalistic philosophies, a humanitarian religiosity, and a diversity of religious beliefs which scarcely permitted each denomination to erect its own schools all militated against the support of any church schools by the state.[229] "A harmony of views and a fraternity of feeling between different classes of society, who have a common interest in a great public institution of the state," [230] was perhaps an unconscious goal of many. The Protestant churches in general relinquished education to the state because of anti-Romanism and perhaps because of the revivalistic concept of conversion. A lack of trained teachers, a lack of money, a lack of pupils, a lack of strong leadership for parochial schools, and the lassitude of church members were all factors that permitted education to come under the control of the state.[231] These factors, too, account for the decline of state support to church-controlled schools.

Before 1914 the questions of free textbooks, bus transportation, released time, the use of school facilities for religious purposes, funds for lunch programs in church schools or participation in child welfare programs, and similar questions were not raised. Conflict over these arose later.[232] The question of educational support for denominational schools is one of the grave unsettled questions for the church and the state alike. Efforts to establish a cultural monism in the country are contrary to other developments, even though the opposition to pluralism was present.

The Pattern's Shape About 1914

The pattern of church-state relations in the United States about 1914 was neither one of absolute separation nor one of establishment. Churches and ecclesiastical associations were voluntary and free from state control. The governments, federal and state and local, supported religious institutions and enforced laws which aided in religious observances. They gave financial aid to agencies and institutions that were church-controlled in a diminishing degree. The influence of the churches on the governments on various levels was not inconsiderable. Ecclesiastical influence reached its high point in the adoption of the Eighteenth Amendment to the constitution.

Parochial schools gave rise to complex questions of church-state relations in the realm of education, questions which were not solved but multiplied in the subsequent period.

Yet for all the demands of separation of church and state there arose in America a religion that left little distinction between democracy and nationalism and Christianity. "Americans naturalized God," is one statement to explain a regard for religiosity and a disregard for theology. "Religion became increasingly a social activity rather than a spiritual experience." [233] A readiness on the part of many Americans to disregard "the wall of separation" is due to the complexity of social and political and economic forces. Religion reinforced patriotism and aided the reverential cult of the American past.[234] Prejudice against the immigrant had its religious overtones. Currents of protest and reform, looking for a stronger nation endowed with a destiny and a mission, were activated in part by spiritual and religious motives. "The appearance of an aggressive humanism," Gabriel has pointed out, "a new religion of humanity, immediately after the end of the Civil War is one of the more significant events in the history of American democratic thought." [235] Neo-rationalism and a "theology of property" influenced American constitutional law. The far-reaching influences of Puritanism, Protestantism, evangelical reform, and the Social Gospel in the formation of the democratic faith dare not be minimized. The conjunction of the "American Dream" and the kingdom of God [236] could mean only an ultimate fusion of church and state.

The voluntary principle in church-state relations had been one of the glories of this country. At times the glory was obscured; there were forces which would keep it obscured. One demand called for "a type of relationship between church and state that provides for both organic disconnection and sympathetic association." [237] Another said: "I believe America is a faith and its greatness is rooted in Christianity. . . . Christians must play an ever-increasing role in the contemporary American scene, and the Christian Church is the decisive factor in determining the American destiny." [238] Even the call to maintain the voluntary principle and separation of church and state was made in the name of a reasonably Christian democratic society.[239] Separation was combined with sympathy for religion.[240] The problems of church-state relationships were not solved before 1914.

THE PATTERN IN THE 20TH CENTURY

The complexities of life in the 20th century have accentuated the problem of church-state relations in the United States. The unprecedented power and responsibility of this country, the growth in wealth and membership of its churches, and the interaction of the multiphased trends in society complicate the problem. Social welfare and international relations, racial tensions at home and new nationalism in once colonial countries abroad, adjustment to life and pupils' needs programs in schools, post-Protestantism and the religiosity of Americanism are only a few of the forces in the encounter between church and state in America's 20th century.

The heritage of the 20th century was that of disestablishment with some vaguely defined areas on which politicians and churchmen alike poached. Educational issues particularly were not walled up into strict confines. Among them were Bible reading, released time, public aid, religious garb, free textbooks, free transportation. In other areas Sunday legislation, social legislation, war and military measures provided other major issues. Even at the ballot box the religion of a candidate has constituted a consideration for many voters. In spite of "absolute separation of church and state" some areas overlapped and some persons did not recognize any boundaries. Eternal vigilance was still demanded for the preservation of religious liberty.

Roman Catholic Claims

"Cooperation" between church and state is advocated by some Roman Catholic thinkers. The demand has come in strong terms from the National Catholic Welfare Conference in line with the demands of modern popes from Leo XIII to the present. Maritain summarized the Roman position most succinctly when he said: "The things that are Caesear's are not only distinct from the things that are God's; but they must cooperate with them." [241] This cooperation must be "in conformity with Christian principles" [242] — "Christian" here being a synonym for "Roman Catholic." Pius XII made this evident when he said:

> The Church and the State are independent powers, but they must not for that reason ignore one another, still less be in conflict with one another. It is much more in conformity with nature and the divine will that they collaborate in mutual

understanding, since the action of both is applied to the same subject; that is to say, to the Catholic citizen.[243]

This "cooperation" in the 19th century was one which at times (predominantly so in the minds of many Americans) sought favors for the Roman Catholic Church and its members or actively promoted the candidacy of Roman Catholics for public office. It put "the church into politics" (again, in the minds of many) and up to the present time has caused tensions and misgivings. These fears were a powerful factor — but only one factor — in the defeat of Alfred E. Smith, the Democrats' candidate for President, of Roman Catholic persuasion, in the 1928 campaign, and were raised again regarding John F. Kennedy in 1960. The endorsement of a local ward politician by a parish priest, an encyclical letter from the bishop to his diocese on an educational issue in a metropolitan district, or an editorial in a national Roman Catholic journal on a national or international issue have been construed as Roman Catholicism in politics. The broad implications of such "cooperation" have pointed toward an adaptation of Roman claims to dominance over the state without a negation of such claims.

Then, too, cooperation is sought by the papacy by means of concordats or treaties with modern states. No attempt or suggestions have been made to negotiate a concordat between the Vatican and the White House. The ramifications of international politics are such, however, that a concordat between the Pope and Franco has consequences for U. S. troops on overseas bases in Spain. A treaty with Haiti or Colombia might not include guarantees of religious liberty or might come in conflict with an agreement that one of those nations or another nation has with the pope. Pius XII spoke of the "inner meaning" of concordats, which, he said, "may include implications of which the contracting parties are aware." An implication may be the toleration of tolerance.[244]

The practical application of Catholic principles in the field of education has caused major concern in the mid-decades of the 20th century in the United States. The demand has been for "distributive justice," and this demand to "share" in public school

Churchand State Under God*

---

funds has been persistent.[245] Sharing, it has been advocated, may take various forms: bus transportation for pupils to Roman Catholic schools, paid from public funds; federal lunch programs; free textbooks; tuition subsidies to parents whose children attend nonpublic schools; even buildings and equipment and facilities.[246] The question of federal aid to education has been beclouded by these demands.

Among the educational issues raised by the demands of the Roman Catholics is that of "captive schools" or quasi-public schools. These are schools, theoretically public institutions, which are taught by members of Roman Catholic religious orders — *de facto* parochial schools, *de iure* public schools. Modern attempts to transform parochial schools into public schools, while still retaining them under the program of the Roman Catholic Church, are exemplified by the North College Hill case, the Bremond case, the Bradford School case, or the Dixon, N. Mex., case.[247]

The right to maintain parochial schools is not questioned generally. The Oregon case, treated elsewhere in this volume, together with the Nebraska and Michigan "school fights" in the 1920s, definitely established the fundamental principle of parental prerogative in the schooling of children.[248] A prenuptial agreement between a Roman Catholic and a non-Catholic, a New York court held, obligated the non-Catholic party to provide for the Roman Catholic education of a child of such a union. It ruled: "A court and especially the Domestic Relations Court is bound to approve the demand of a Catholic parent that its child be given a Catholic education and a Catholic upbringing in a Catholic home or institution . . ."[249] Illegitimate children of unwed Roman Catholic mothers, when placed for adoption, are placed in Roman Catholic homes, a provision made mandatory by a Massachusetts court.[250]

Religion and Public Education

Litigation in the whole educational area has increased in the period since 1914. Such litigation may be necessary to give legal sanction to, or disapproval of, established practices. It may also be an indication of increased tensions in the church-state relations of this period. Even the question of saluting the flag and reciting the pledge of allegiance to the flag had to be settled.[251] Bus transportation and free textbooks for parochial school children had to be decided by the courts.[252] The use of public school classrooms for released-time religious classes became the issue in the famed Champaign case.[253] Regarded as "one of the most important decisions in American legal history," [254] it did not rule out released time per se. This was definitely stated in the Zorach case. This case was important, too, because of the recognition by the courts that the line of separation between church and state was not absolute.[255]

Dismissed or released time for religious instruction was one attempt to solve the problem of meeting the religious needs of children and youth. This form of religious instruction is entirely under the control of the church, and educational credit is not generally granted for it. In some instances, however, practices have allowed credit for some religious instruction by the churches.[256] In spite of various arrangements, the question of religion in education remained a major concern among educators in the 1940s and 1950s.[257] It was the subject of the reports of several important commissions.

The report of the Committee on Religion and Education of the American Council on Education (1947) stressed the democratic ideal and the religious heritage of this country. Because of the dual importance of these concepts, according to the report, the principle of separation of church and state had to be defined. The committee stated:

> The core of the meaning in the doctrine of the separation of church and state we believe to be this: there shall be no ecclesiastical control of political functions; there shall be no political dictation in the ecclesiastical sphere except as public safety or public morals may require it. This doctrine may not be invoked to prevent public education from determining on its own merits the question how the religious phases of the culture shall be recognized in the school program.[258]

Another pronouncement on religion in public education came from the Educational Policies Commission of the National Education Association of the United States and of the American Association of School Administrators. Its report, *Moral and Spiritual Values in the Public Schools* (1951), advocated the teaching of moral and spiritual values in the public schools "without endangering religious freedom and without circumventing the policy of separation of church and state." [259] Teaching objectively *about* religion, in the thinking of the committee, did not mean teaching denominational beliefs. Its advocacy of dealing with religion in the public school instruction may nevertheless be regarded an important modification of the complicated question of church-state relationship as it pertains to education. An overwhelming majority of public schoolmen and Protestant religious leaders favored the teaching about religion in the public schools. This was evident in another report by the American Council on Education (1953). It stated: "The public school shares responsibility with home and church in developing the awareness of the importance of religion in human affairs." [260]

A staff associate of the American Council on Education has summarized his findings on religion in public education:

1. Much more is being done in the public schools to teach religion than is recognized.

2. There is no consistent policy among states, among communities within a state, or even among public schools within a single public school system.

3. In the public schools, little is known as to the best means of teaching religion or even of teaching *about* religion.[261]

Such is the pattern of church-state relations in this area.

Dispute concerning Bible reading in public schools reached its climax with major Supreme Court decisions in 1962 and 1963, as will be shown in succeeding chapters. Meanwhile, there was no consistent policy in the issue of the teaching of religion in public schools. The fact that Bible reading has been permitted and legislated and forbidden and tolerated in the public schools of this land demonstrates the fears and concerns about the relationships between church and state.

Underneath, there has been a concern, too, for religious liberty. Wilbur Katz pointed out that "separation is a subordinate concept, instrumental to the maintenance of religious liberty." He came to the conclusion that "the basic American principle of church-state relations is not separation but religious liberty." [262]

Religion and Free Communication

Freedom of religion and freedom of speech have generally been regarded as corollary. "In this country the full and free right to entertain any religious belief, to practice any religious principle, and to teach any religious doctrine which does not violate the laws of morality and property, and which does not infringe personal rights, is conceded to all." [263] Related to the general question of religious liberty has been the question of the rights of minority groups, such as the Jehovah's witnesses, to propagandize their religious views. The rights of this group (and others) to engage in house-to-house solicitations and distributions of literature setting forth their cause or religious views have been the subject of several court cases in this period. [264]

Freedom of speech has involved also the control of modern means of communication, such as radio and television, problems unknown to the pattern of church-state relations before 1914. Broadcasting and televising are important media of mass education; the churches would be less than alert to their responsibilities were they not interested in these media. The Federal Communications Commission, created in 1927, has tried to be objective in its policies in granting latitude in freedom of speech consonant with the public good. Points of difference and occasionally friction have arisen between the churches and the federal agency. The churches have complained about advertising on these stations and the adequacies of the time for presenting religious views.

The United States is the only country in the world, it has been pointed out, "in which any religious topic may be presented provided the speaker can persuade a station to sell him time." [265] However, two of the three nationwide broadcasting systems have not sold time to religious groups; almost all local and regional chains have. Whether the time is purchased or donated, it may not be used by any group for a direct attack on another religious group. The policy may be illustrated from the code of standards of the National Association of Broadcasters:

> Radio, which reaches all men of all creeds and races simultaneously, may not be used to convey attacks upon another's race or religion. Rather it should be the purpose of the religious broadcast to promote the spiritual harmony and understanding of mankind and to minister broadly to the various religious needs of the community.[266]

The rule has caused cries of censorship, as, for instance, when the *Martin Luther* film was withdrawn from a scheduled showing over a Chicago TV station. Roman Catholics have exercised a close vigilance in some parts of the country and at least an indirect pressure on radio and television. Occasionally other denominations, too, have been involved in questions of limitations or censorship, especially on the local level. The possibilities of extensive censorship through governmental policies, or indirectly in support of a given denominational group, remain. In the area of radio and television – through censorship – the likelihood of conflict between church and state is continually present.

Censorship of motion pictures has also involved religious denominations in questions of governmental policies. The churches have attempted to influence public opinion so that their voice may be heard in the regulation of the motion picture industry.

The Neely Bill, for instance, in 1938, which prohibited "block booking" and "blind selling," was supported by the Federal Council of Churches of Christ in America, separate Protestant denominations, and organized groups within the Roman Catholic Church. The restrictions adopted were due largely to the efforts of church groups. The motion picture industry endeavored to meet some of the objections of the churches by including a section dealing with religion in its code.

Among the groups for the regulating of motion pictures one must number the National Legion of Decency as the most effective. This organization within the Roman Catholic Church reviews films and grades them on a scale of objectionableness. Some films which have been permitted for showing by governmental committees have been found unfit by the National Legion. Cardinal Dougherty of Philadelphia demanded in 1948 that theater owners desist from showing two films and threatened that Roman Catholics would boycott "all productions at *both* theaters for a year." [267]

Closely related to the censorship of motion pictures is the censorship of books. Unchaste, indecent, impure, corrupting literature has been condemned by the churches, which have called upon the federal and state governments to suppress and ban all forms of pornography. Only insofar as some church organizations have doubted the effectiveness and extensiveness of governmental control has there been an area of conflict. Censorship of theological works and religious writings has not been practiced on the part of governmental agencies.

Religion and Family Life

The dissemination of birth-control information has raised questions of interference by some churches. The Roman Catholic Church in November 1959 pronounced through the National Catholic Welfare Conference its judgment on a foreign-aid program that might include the dissemination of any family-planning information. One editor has contended: "Birth control is becoming the world's number-one church-state problem." [268] The regulation of birth-control instruction in municipal hospitals of New York City in accordance with Roman Catholic teachings was ended in 1958. In Massachusetts and Connecticut it is still illegal for a doctor to give advice on birth-control to his patients.

The issue involved the larger question of the right of the Roman Catholic Church to make pronouncements on what she regards as moral issues and making these pronouncements binding on the state. Regarding sterilization the pope has said that "even the public authority" has no right to permit or to enjoin it.[269] Of greater consequence are the far-reaching claims of the Roman Catholic Church to regulate marriage, divorce, and sex education.

The Roman Catholic Church has taken the position that sex

education is a matter for the home and the church but not for the state and its public schools. Blanshard says:

> An important corollary to the Catholic sexual code is that all sexual education should be under priestly control. The state is not competent to educate in such matters because it may disregard Catholic fundamentals.[270]

The all-inclusive claims of the Roman Catholic Church to regulate marriage include "the legislative, judicial, and coercive power." [271] In its teachings on divorce it has been at divergence with the practices of the state and has opened areas of conflict. A Roman Catholic judge, Pius XII declared, "may not pronounce, unless for motives of great moment, a sentence of civil divorce (where it exists) for a marriage which is valid before God and the Church." [272]

The extent of forbidden degrees of marriage, mixed marriages, annulments, impediments, and similar questions present large areas for possible conflict between this church and the government. Recognizing that there are possibilities, one must also recognize that actual clashes in this country in a legal sense have been infrequent. The lax divorce laws of some states have caused alarm among Protestants and Roman Catholics alike. Marriage and divorce laws have been within the jurisdiction of the states, not the federal government. It is doubtful that the churches will agree among themselves or that the Roman Catholic Church will try to obtain uniform laws on marriage and divorce or federal jurisdiction in these matters. The practice of Roman Catholics in an "overwhelming number of summary cases" to obtain inexpensive annulments [273] may be noted, however, as an impediment to harmonious church-state relations unless marriage were to be placed entirely under the jurisdiction of the Roman Church in this country.

Social Welfare and the Churches

Churchmen and church groups, traditionally directing the dispensation of charity and providing for the needs of the poor and the unfortunate, have seen the state take over the main responsibility for social service since 1914. Especially the impact of the Great Depression of the 1930s and the sweep of social legislation under the New Deal amplified the Social Gospel. Co-operation has resulted between the churches and the state. Views that proclaim that "state welfare programs are inherently anti-Christian" [274] have not gained general acceptance.

Nevertheless, federal aid for the construction of denominationally owned hospitals has been opposed, among others, by the Baptists. The Hill-Burton Act (1945) is one of the clearest instances of church-state cooperation. An allocation of $424,000,000 from federal funds for the benefit of hospitals, according to one authority, resulted in grants of $58,000,000 to Roman Catholic hospitals and $16,000,000 to Protestant hospitals.[275]

Religion in Military Life

Cooperation between church and state is evident, again, in the chaplaincies which the states and the federal government support in prisons, reformatories, and corrective institutions. State hospitals for mental patients and municipally owned hospitals, county homes, and similar state-controlled establishments have found the ministrations of the servants of the church most welcome.[276]

The chaplaincies established by the federal government in the Armed Services are another example of church-state cooperation. The Army, the Navy, the Air Force, the Marine Corps, the Coast Guard, the service academies, and the legislative halls of Congress have their chaplains. Stokes's observations summarize well the view which has made these chaplaincies an acceptable trait of the church-state pattern in this country.

> The government's attitude toward religion and religious denominations as shown in the Army and Navy is, speaking generally, characteristic of the fundamental American position. It is sympathetic with the cause of religion; appreciates its significance in individual and national life; and encourages provisions for worship in all branches of military service, while at the same time retaining an impartial attitude toward the various denominations. An individual's religious creed is not considered in matters of enlistment and promotion; the only recog-

nition of creedal differences is the attempt to distribute chaplaincies fairly, and the custom, for the guidance of chaplains, of having the identification tag worn by a soldier or sailor indicate whether he is Catholic, Jewish, or Protestant, and the indication of this fact on admission blanks to army hospitals.[277]

At the service academies chapel attendance on Sundays is compulsory. Although the practice has caused some adverse comments, criticism has not been severe enough to cause a discontinuation of the practice. Congressional chaplaincies, chaplaincies in the Veterans Administration, and related practices, too, have generally become acceptable. They belong to the pattern of church-state relations which disavows absolute separation.[278]

It may be pointed out, too, that the problem of the conscientious objectors in wartime was made more acute by the pacifist movements which had gained ground in the two decades between the two World Wars. The continuance of universal military training, the Korean conflict, and the "cold war" aspects of international relations have made for almost bizarre cases of protest in individual instances, although the principles of traditional pacifist groups were usually safeguarded.[279]

The Pattern Persists in America

Sunday legislation, tax exemption for church properties, incorporation of churches (and even the question of trusteeism), the seal of the confessional, privileges for clergy, and related points belong to the complete picture of the pattern of church-state relations in contemporary America. Stokes has pointed up four major considerations in evaluation of such aspects of the pattern.

1. That Church and State both function effectively.

2. That Church and State observe their functional limitations.

3. That peace and mutual sympathy be maintained between them.

4. That freedom of thought and worship be maintained for all.[280]

In the pattern of church-state relations as it developed in America in the 1940s and 1950s the rise of what Marty has called American Shintoism is particularly significant. This pattern blurs the distinction between the functions of church and state. It is a "religion of democracy," or "a temporalization of religion in the democratic structure." [281] The phenomenon has its roots deep in the history of our country. The multistrand aspects of those roots need not concern us now, important as they are for an adequate understanding of that phenomenon. Success and bigness, liberty and security, creature comforts under a high standard of living, peace and prosperity, the good life with respectability without spoiling our fun — these have been the ideals of a religiosity that found expression in the glorification of the American way of life and the philosophy of patriotism that has become the *Ersatz* of the theology of Puritanism or Calvinism or Lutheranism. Stated more simply: "Piety, comfort, and the good American life are sometimes mixed together and served." [282]

> So we swing between nationalism and one-worldness, between capitalism and socialism, never quite sure when the line is crossed, or between *the search for God and the idolatry of nation worship*, or between the desire for freedom and security, half conscious that conflicts exist, unable to make up our minds.[283]

Spiritual conformity to the common denominator of American nationalism has been the trend, which has resulted in a confusion between the tenets of Christianity and the American way of life. "America's dream" has ingredients of individualism and religion, the concept of the covenant nation and freedom under God.[284]

The extent to which politicians and governmental officials have used this mixture of patriotism and religiosity has raised serious questions in the minds of some students of the contemporary scene. "Piety on the Potomac" can make for closer ties between church and state, an increase in what the present study has demonstrated to be a blurring of the distinctions between the functions of the church and the state in this country. Prot-

estant clergymen only to a limited degree have seen these ramifications; many of them have not been alarmed by them.

> It is at least probable that most Protestant clergymen and
> organizations approve the recent overt manifestations of reli-
> giosity on the part of government in the United States. More-
> over, even among the minority that disapproves, disapproval is
> predicated not so much on considerations of church-state rela-
> tions as on the questionable value and sincerity of such super-
> ficial verbalizations. A few Protestant voices, however, have
> indicated uneasiness on constitutional grounds.[285]

Many others instead will agree with the sentiment which urges:

> The belief may well be cherished that the American Common-
> wealth was not erected for itself alone but for the glory of
> God and to make manifest his purpose, which is that all men
> shall live together on this earth as brothers, in peace and free-
> dom, enjoying together the fruits of good things of the earth,
> not some as masters and the rest as slaves, but with equal
> rights and equal opportunities for all.[286]

Such pious hopes will not obscure the tensions in the pluralistic society, the complexities of the pattern of church-state relations in this country, and the need to maintain eternal vigilance
for the cause of religious liberty.[287]

A KEYSTONE IN THE STRUCTURE of American church-state relations is freedom of religion. The significance of religious liberty is the theme of the chapter by *Roy C. Frank,* A. B., LL. B., a Washington, D. C., attorney and former Solicitor of the Post Office Department, a member of the bar of the Supreme Court of the United States.

Mr. Frank begins by analyzing the provisions of the Constitution and the First and Fourteenth Amendments as they relate to freedom of religion. The guarantees against arbitrary action by the states over religion were slow in appearing and were established, says Mr. Frank, "only after a long road of judicial construction." A substantial definition of religious freedom began in 1940 and continues to the present day.

The meaning of the "establishment of religion" clause was scrutinized in several notable cases during the past two decades. The Supreme Court's increasingly inflexible concept of a wall of separation between church and state has been only partially ameliorated in recent decisions. In fact, recent Supreme Court rulings against religious exercises in public schools have again aroused concern about the absolute nature of separation.

The meaning of the clause in the First Amendment assuring the free exercise of religion has likewise been interpreted by the Court. The result in this instance has been that a balance has been struck between liberty and license which is essential to the American pattern.

Mr. Frank concludes that absolute separation of church and state is impossible, and state subsidization of the church is unwise. He feels that by mutual respect and cooperation both institutions should assist in the preservation of the American spirit of religious freedom.

Chapter 6

RELIGIOUS LIBERTY
IN THE CONSTITUTION

Roy C. Frank

"THE CROWNING GLORY of American freedom is absolute religious liberty; and that every American has the unquestioned and untrammeled right to worship God according to the dictates of his own conscience, without let or hindrance from any person or any source." [1] This liberty is, in the words of Thomas Jefferson, "the most inalienable and sacred of all human rights." [2]

Constitutional guarantees of religious liberty are found exclusively in Article VI of the Constitution of the United States,[3] the First Amendment to the Constitution,[4] and the due-process clause of the Fourteenth Amendment,[5] as applied to the First Amendment by judicial construction.

The guarantees of the First Amendment are twofold: (1) "Congress shall make no law respecting an establishment of religion" or (2) "prohibiting the free exercise thereof." Simple and clear though this language is, its application has given rise to storms of controversy and bitter recriminations, particularly with respect to the meaning to be attributed to the words "an establishment of religion."

The legal relationship between church and state in its present posture derives its force from two sources: (1) the accepted practices of church and state which have not been subjected to the challenge of judicial scrutiny and (2) concepts estab-

258

lished by judicial interpretation of the First and Fourteenth Amendments. It is with such concepts, particularly those established by the Supreme Court of the United States, that this chapter is concerned.

THE CONSTITUTIONAL PROVISIONS

Religious Guarantees in the Original Constitution

Study of the proceedings and debates of the Constitutional Convention of 1787 compels the conclusion that the delegates to the convention were not particularly concerned with guarantees of religious freedom on a national level. These were deemed to be matters of state concern. The chief desire of the convention was the creation and establishment of a strong and vigorous central government rather than a loosely knit federation of states. In the opinion of many of the delegates the ratification of the proposed constitution would be endangered if the convention entered into the field of human rights. The delegates knew that the states were already jealous of the national government and fearful that it would usurp what the states considered to be their natural rights and privileges. The convention sought to allay these fears and suspicions by limiting the authority of the national government to those powers specifically granted it by the Constitution, reserving for the states all powers not specifically granted to the national government.

However, some of the delegates, including Charles Pinckney of South Carolina, were of a different frame of mind, particularly with respect to the right to hold public office. They believed that all citizens had the inherent right to hold public office regardless of their religious beliefs. They were well aware of past and existing religious discriminations. Accordingly, Pinckney proposed to the convention that there be inserted in the proposed constitution language providing that "no religious test or qualification shall ever be annexed to any oath of office under authority of the U. S." [6] Subsequently, Pinckney amended his proposal to read: "But no religious Test shall ever be required as a Qualification to any office or public Trust under the United States . . ." [7] This language was adopted unanimously by the convention, ratified by the states, and now forms an integral part of Article VI of the Constitution of the United States. This clause of Article VI is the only provision of the original Constitution which affords protection against religious discrimination.

Limited as it is in its area of protection, Article VI was of utmost significance in that it placed the federal government firmly on the side of religious liberty. From that time, in the words of Joseph Story, "The Catholic and the Protestant, the Calvinist and the Arminian, the infidel and the Jew may sit down to the Communion-table of the National Council without any inquisition into their faith or mode of worship." [8]

Adoption of the First Amendment

Subsequent events demonstrated that the delegates to the convention had underestimated the true wishes of the people. Upon return to their homes the delegates soon discovered that the people wanted a total bill of rights in the Constitution, including the right of religious freedom on the national level. It was obvious that Article VI did not provide the desired protection.

Thomas Jefferson, minister to France during the convention, expressed his dissatisfaction in a letter to James Madison. He wrote Madison that what he did not like about the proposed constitution was "the omission of a bill of rights providing clearly, without the aid of sophism, for freedom of religion . . ." [9]

Five states proposed amendments in the form of a bill of rights simultaneously with their ratification of the proposed constitution. New Hampshire, New York, and Virginia, closely followed by North Carolina, included declarations of religious freedom in their proposed amendments. [10] Virginia proposed that "no particular religious sect or society ought to be favored or established by law in preference to others," [11] a proposal which North Carolina followed word for word. New York used identical language, omitting only the word "particular." [12] Only New Hampshire, fearing for its established church, wanted restrictions which would exclude Congress entirely from the field of religious enactment. It proposed that "Congress shall make no laws touching religion . . ." [13]

The First Congress considered several proposals containing various degrees of religious freedom before the First Amendment in its present wording was adopted and submitted to the states for ratification. Madison, one of the leaders of the First Congress, although strongly in favor of a bill of rights, considered specific prohibitions not "essential" but had no objection to them since they were "neither improper nor altogether useless" [14] and were "anxiously desired by others." [15] In deference to the fears and demands of several of the ratifying states, Madison presented to Congress an amendment which he thought incorporated the desires of these states: "The civil rights of none shall be abridged on account of religious belief or worship, nor shall any national religion be established, nor shall the full and equal rights of conscience be in any manner, or on any pretext, infringed." [16] This amendment was referred first to the Committee of the Whole of the House of Representatives [17] and then to a specially appointed Committee of Eleven of which Madison was a member. [18] The Committee of Eleven, after careful consideration of Madison's amendment, reported the following proposed amendment to the full House: "No religion shall be established by law, nor shall the equal rights of conscience be infringed." [19] After some debate the House changed the Committee's proposed amendment to read: "that Congress shall make no laws touching religion, or infringing the rights of conscience." [20] This wording proved to be unsatisfactory to many of the members of the House and was changed to read: "Congress shall make no law establishing religion, or to prevent the free exercise thereof, or to infringe the rights of conscience." [21]

When this amendment reached the floor of the Senate, it was replaced by language which provided: "Congress shall make no law establishing articles of faith or mode of worship, or prohibiting the free exercise of religion . . ." [22] The two versions of the amendment were then referred to a Joint Conference Committee. [23] There emerged from this committee the religious freedom guarantees of the First Amendment in their present wording.[24]

The absolute guarantees of the First Amendment reflected the keen awareness of the people of the experiences with religious persecution and bigotry suffered by the early colonists, and "of conditions and practices which they fervently wished to stamp out in order to preserve liberty for themselves and for their posterity."[25] The basic premise of the amendment was rooted in the deep belief that the legitimate areas of influence of church and state can best be served if each is "free from the other within its respective sphere."[26] There was also the desire in the minds of the people that no one denomination or any combination of denominations would ever become strong enough to exercise undue influence on the state or on persons of conflicting opinions and beliefs.[27]

APPLICATION OF THE FIRST AMENDMENT
TO THE STATES

Initial Efforts

Sensitive to the strong states-rights sentiment of the people, the Constitutional Convention had rejected all attempts to write into the proposed constitution restrictions on the powers of the states. As a result the document, as submitted to the states for ratification, contained no restrictions on them in relation to their own citizens other than "on subjects entrusted to the government of the union, in which the citizens of all the states are interested."[28] This pattern was closely followed by the First Congress in its consideration of the demands of the states for more stringent prohibitions against federal encroachment on the basic rights and privileges of the people. Until the adoption of the Fourteenth Amendment, the Bill of Rights (the first ten amendments to the Constitution) operated only as a restriction on national action. The individual states were left free to impose such restrictions on their people as the consciences of the people would permit. Despite this clear intent of Congress and of the people repeated attempts were made to persuade the courts to declare invalid state legislation which imposed restrictions forbidden the federal government. Of major interest is *Permoli v. First Municipality of New Orleans*.[29] In this case the religious liberty guarantees of the First Amendment were invoked as the vehicle to invalidate a municipal ordinance prohibiting the burial of a corpse from a Roman Catholic church. The Supreme Court of the United States refused to apply the amendment because "the Constitution makes no provision for protecting the citizens of the respective states in their religious liberties; this is left to the state constitution and laws . . ."[30] By 1868 this principle was so well established that the scope and application of the Fifth and Sixth Amendments to the Constitution as limitations on the First Amendment were "no longer subjects of discussion."[31]

The Fourteenth Amendment

At the close of the War Between the States, the problems of reconstruction faced Congress. The first of the War Amendments, the Thirteenth,[32] adopted Dec. 18, 1865, freed the slaves. Within the approximate period of the amendment's passage by Congress and its ratification by the states the First Supplemental Freedmen's Bureau Bill[33] and the First Civil Rights Act[34] were enacted by Congress. Both bills were directed to the objective of securing for all of the people the full and equal benefits of law. The Freedmen's Bureau Bill was limited in its application to states that had seceded from the Union, while the First Civil Rights Act was applicable to all states. This was the only major difference. The First Civil Rights Act defined citizenship in the United States and provided that all such citizens were entitled to equal rights in every state with respect to certain specified conduct, and were entitled also to enjoy the full and equal benefits of all laws and proceedings for the security of their persons and property.

Proposals to amend the Constitution of the United States had been submitted from time to time to Congress, but action thereon had been deferred. However, after it enacted the First Civil Rights Bill, Congress entertained serious doubts with respect to its power to enact legislation of such drastic nature which would be applicable to all states. It further feared that even though it had such power, future Congresses might not be in sympathy with the policies expressed in the act. These factors stimulated Congress to expedite action on pending proposals to amend the Constitution. Eventually there emerged from Congress the Fourteenth Amendment, the second of the War Amendments, which was subsequently ratified by the states. The amendment followed in essence the provisions of the Freedmen's Bureau Bill and the First Civil Rights Act.

The initial sentence of the amendment provides that "all persons born or naturalized in the United States, and subject to the jurisdiction thereof, are citizens of the United States, and of the States wherein they reside," thereby disposing of the troublesome problem of citizenship in the United States. Prior to the adoption of the amendment, citizenship in the United States was considered to be a mere derivative of state citizenship.[35] By virtue of the definition contained in the Fourteenth Amendment national citizenship assumed dominant importance; state citizenship was relegated to a position of secondary importance. In addition the constitutional scope of the national government was enlarged to encompass powers never contemplated by the framers of the Constitution.[36]

The adoption of the Fourteenth Amendment placed the protections afforded by the Bill of Rights, including the First Amendment, in an entirely different perspective. The immediate purpose of the amendment was to secure for the Negro the full enjoyment of the freedoms of the white race.[37] It soon became apparent, however, that the amendment has a real impact on the liberties of all citizens, regardless of race, color, or creed.

The federal courts for the first time were empowered to review the legislative enactments of the states and the judicial decisions of state courts which were alleged to infringe on the "privileges or immunities" of citizens of the United States or to deprive them of their "life, liberty, or property without the due process of law." A new era of freedom to enjoy the inherent and fundamental rights of free men was inaugurated with the consent of the people who but three quarters of a century before had persistently and vehemently refused to extend the blanket of federal protection to arbitrary and capricious state action. Reflected in the amendment was a growing national pride, so lacking during the days of the Constitutional Convention. The infant nation of the days of the First Congress developed national stature with the adoption of the Fourteenth Amendment.

The States and Religious Freedom

The Fourteenth Amendment serves to restrain the states in their regulation of the free exercise of religion on a state level to the same degree as the First Amendment restrains the federal government on the national level.

This truth is so ingrained in the minds of the people that they tend to forget that religious freedom from state action was attained only after the adoption of a historical concept of freedom of other fundamental liberties and that religious liberty was the last of the guarantees of the First Amendment to receive judicial blessing. To trace the development of religious liberty by judicial interpretation is to trace the development of the concept that all fundamental and inalienable rights of free people are included within the framework of the Fourteenth Amendment.

Religious freedom against arbitrary and capricious state action is of but recent attainment. It was established only after a long road of judicial construction, commencing with the first Slaughterhouse Cases in 1873 [38] and ending with *Cantwell* v. *Connecticut* in 1940.[39] During the intervening years the area of application of the Fourteenth Amendment to the freedoms expressed in the Bill of Rights of the Constitution of the United States was the subject of various hypotheses.[40] There eventually evolved, in the historical development of the word *liberty*, the doctrine that no state can arbitrarily or capriciously violate "the fundamental principles of liberty and justice which lie at the base of all our civil and political institutions" [41] and which are "implicit in the concept of ordered liberty . . ." [42]

The Fourteenth Amendment was initially subjected to the

test of judicial interpretation in the first Slaughterhouse Cases. These cases involved the constitutionality of a Louisiana statute which created a monopoly in the slaughterhouse business of certain favored companies. The opponents of the law advanced the thesis that the dual citizenship recognized by the Fourteenth Amendment secured for all citizens the protection of the federal government against state deprivation of their fundamental "privileges and immunities" of state citizenship and that the statute under consideration deprived them of their fundamental right to engage in their occupation and trade, contrary to the protection afforded them by the Fourteenth Amendment. The Supreme Court carefully distinguished between the inherent nature of citizenship in the United States and citizenship in a state and between the relative rights of each. The court then held that the Fourteenth Amendment had no application to "privileges and immunities" which are inherently the creation and concern of a state but was applicable only to citizens of the United States by virtue of their relationship to the national government, or to "privileges and immunities" which had been specifically granted or secured to all citizens or persons by the Constitution of the United States. The slaughterhouse business was held to be subject to the exclusive regulation of the state. The effect of the decision was to leave the states "free to abridge, within the limits of the due process clause, the privileges and immunities flowing from state citizenship." [43] It also reinforced the constitutional doctrine of federalism "by leaving the states the responsibility of dealing with the privileges and immunities of their citizens except those inherent in national citizenship." [44] This limitation has never been relaxed.

Having thus disposed of the hypothesis that all privileges and immunities of the citizens of a state are protected by the "privileges and immunities" cause of the Fourteenth Amendment, the Supreme Court was next confronted with a limited version of the same argument. It was contended that all of the guarantees contained in the Bill of Rights of the federal Constitution were "privileges and immunities" protected by the Fourteenth Amendment from state regulation. This contention was rejected in a line of decisions commencing in 1874 with *Edwards* v. *Elliott*,[45] which held that the amendment applies only to those provisions of the Bill of Rights inherent in national citizenship. The Supreme Court has consistently refused to enumerate all of the rights inherent in national citizenship since "there is no general rule." [46]

The third contention advanced was that the due-process clause of the Fourteenth Amendment incorporated all of the rights contained in the Bill of Rights. This proposal met the same fate as the others.[47]

Emphasis on the word *liberty* as used in the due-process clause of the Fourteenth Amendment first appeared in Justice Field's dissenting opinion in the first Slaughterhouse Cases. He protested that the slaughterhouse monopoly restrained the butchers "in the freedom and liberty they previously had, and hinders them in their lawful occupations." [48] This same emphasis appeared in Justice Bradley's concurring opinion in the second Slaughterhouse Cases [49] and in Justice Field's dissenting opinion in *Powell* v. *Pennsylvania*.[50]

The application of the Fourteenth Amendment to the protection of religious liberty against unwarranted state action was first suggested by Justice Field when he stated in his dissenting opinion in *Ho Ah Kow* v. *Numan:* "In our country hostile and discriminating legislation by a state against persons of any class, sect, creed or nation . . . is forbidden by the Fourteenth Amendment." [51]

Liberty as originally conceived was freedom from physical restraint. Broader meanings were gradually attributed to the word, including not only the right to be free from arbitrary and capricious physical restraint but also the right, subject to the police power of the state, to enter into contracts, to engage in lawful occupations, and, in brief, to enjoy all privileges "essential to the orderly pursuit of happiness by free men." [52]

One of the great decisions embodying the broad definition of *liberty* is *Meyer* v. *Nebraska*.[53] This case involved a Nebraska statute which imposed criminal sanctions on the teaching of any subject, in private, public, denominational, or parochial schools, in a language other than English (by interpretation of the Supreme Court of Nebraska, Latin, Greek, and Hebrew were not proscribed), and the teaching of a foreign language to any pupil who had not passed the eighth grade. The Supreme Court of the United States declared the statute invalid for the reason that it constituted an infringement on the fundamenal liberty of a teacher to pursue a lawful occupation and on the right of a parent to control the education of his children. The court found that the statute was not an exercise of the legitimate police power of the state since the study of foreign languages by an average child is not injurious to his health, morals, or understanding.

This case is of particular interest since it contains language illustrative of the ultimate pronouncement of the court when it was called on to render a direct decision on the right of religious liberty under the Fourteenth Amendment. In touching on this liberty the court, gratuitously as a matter of dictum, stated that the liberty guaranteed by the amendment is the right of an individual "to worship God according to the dictates of his own conscience." [54]

Two years later the parental right recognized in *Meyer* v. *Nebraska* was reaffirmed by the Supreme Court when it declared unconstitutional an Oregon statute which made it mandatory for children of compulsory school age to attend public schools because the law "unreasonably interferes with the liberty of parents and guardians to direct the upbringing and education of children under their control." [55]

The views of the Supreme Court with respect to the inclusion of religious liberty within the ambit of protection afforded by the Fourteenth Amendment were made abundantly clear by its several dicta in adjudicated cases. However, it was reluctant to apply the same reasoning to the other freedoms of the First Amendment. The one exception was "the right of the people to assemble, and to petition the Government for a redress of grievances." At no time did the court refuse to apply the

Fourteenth Amendment to this liberty. On the other hand, as late as 1922 the court declined to include freedom of speech within the protection of the Amendment,[56] despite the vigorous and well-reasoned arguments advanced by Justice Harlan, as early as 1907, in his dissenting opinion in *Patterson* v. *Colorado*,[57] wherein he stated that freedom of speech and freedom of the press were essential ingredients of every man's liberty. Progress, however, could not be denied, and three years after the court had refused to accept freedom of speech as an essential liberty, it "assumed" that this freedom and that of the press "are among the fundamental rights and 'liberties' protected by the due process clause of the Fourteenth Amendment." [58] Two years later, in 1927, this assumption ripened into acceptance with respect to freedom of speech [59] and in 1931 with respect to freedom of the press.[60] Thereafter, religious liberty was the only freedom of the First Amendment which had not been judicially incorporated into the word *liberty* under the due-process clause of the Fourteenth Amendment, although its ultimate acceptance was in little doubt.

Any doubt in this respect was laid to rest by the court in *Hamilton* v. *Regents of the University of California*,[61] decided in 1934. The court held that compulsory military training did not infringe on the liberty of students who were opposed to war on religious grounds. Of interest is the court's statement, by way of dictum, that the liberty protected by the due-process clause of the Fourteenth Amendment included the "right to entertain the beliefs, to adhere to the principles, and to teach the doctrines on which these students base their objections . . ." [62] Of clearer import was Justice Cardozo's "assumption" that "the religious liberty protected by the First Amendment against invasion by the nation is protected by the Fourteenth Amendment against invasion by the states." [63]

Thus, when in *Cantwell* v. *Connecticut* the application of the word *liberty* in the due-process clause of the Fourteenth Amendment to the religious freedom guaranty of the First Amendment was before the Supreme Court for direct decision for the first time, the ruling of the court was in the nature of an anticlimax.

It did, however, have the practical effect of placing the religious guarantees of the First Amendment in their proper setting within the protection afforded by the Fourteenth Amendment.

Cantwell v. *Connecticut* ushered in an era of repeated appeals to the Supreme Court for definitions of the areas of application of the religious freedoms of the Constitution. For the first time since the ratification of the First Amendment the meaning of "an establishment of religion" received the careful and exhaustive attention of the court.[64] In a series of decisions involving the religious practices of the Jehovah's witnesses, principles were evolved which endeavored to delineate the nature and extent of the protections afforded by "free exercise of religion."

Review of these cases graphically illustrates the extreme difficulty of drawing precise and clear dividing lines between the legitimate spheres of influence and activity of the church and those of the state. Application of the constitutional protections to specific facts has uncovered marked areas of disagreement, particularly with respect to the "establishment clause" of the First Amendment. A bitterly divided Supreme Court has sharply curtailed long-established practices accepted by both church and state as being within the framework of the Constitution. Confusion has been created by the failure of the court to follow consistently its own rationalizations with respect to the nature of the protection afforded by the Constitution.

It is in the light of these conflicts that an attempt is made to analyze the foundation on which the basic reasoning of the Supreme Court is premised; first, with respect to the constitutional directive that "Congress shall make no law respecting an establishment of religion," and, second, with respect to the directive that "Congress shall make no law . . . prohibiting the free exercise [of religion]."

"Establishment of Religion" Clause

Respected constitutional students and writers almost uniformly have assumed, as self-evident truth derived from a reading of the First Amendment and a study of the circumstances surrounding its adoption, that the total effect of the establishment clause is solely to prohibit preferential treatment of any religious group or sect. Such prohibition would of course encompass the establishment or recognition of a national church and, by virtue of the Fourteenth Amendment, the establishment of a state church. The learned constitutional student Thomas Cooley clearly enunciated this concept as follows:

> By "establishment of religion" is meant the setting up or recognition of a state church or at least the conferring upon one church of special favors and advantages which are denied to others. It was never intended by the Constitution that the Government should be prohibited from recognizing religion where it might be done without drawing invidious distinctions between different religious beliefs, organizations, or sects.[65]

Justice Story, another eminent authority on constitutional law, writing in the period immediately following the adoption of the First Amendment, expressed the same understanding of the "establishment clause."[66] Edward S. Corwin[67] summarizes the views of constitutional students as follows: "In a word, what the 'establishment of religion' clause of the First Amendment Clause does, and all that it does, is to forbid Congress to give any religious faith, sect or denomination, a preferred status."[68]

The limited application of the "establishment clause" so expounded by constitutional students has not met with favor in the judicial thinking of the Supreme Court. Supporting its reasoning with (1) Madison's *Memorial and Remonstrance Against Religious Assessments* in 1785,[69] (2) Virginia's Bill for Establishing Religious Freedom[70] and its own version of the import of Jefferson's highly controversial "wall of separation between church and state" letter to the Danbury Baptist Church Association on Jan. 1, 1802,[71] the court initially extended the application of the "establishment clause" to prohibit all laws which seek to set up a church or which "aid one religion, aid all religions, or prefer one religion over another."[72] After further reflection the court partially relaxed such an inflexible concept of the clause.[73]

"Wall of Separation" Doctrine

Jefferson's "wall of separation" was first cited with approval, not with reference to the "establishment clause" but as a premise on which to hold that federal legislation prohibiting the practice of polygamy in a Federal Territory was not a deprivation of the "free exercise of religion" since the police power of the government was paramount to religious freedom of action.[74] The first indication of the Supreme Court's leaning toward strict neutrality between the religious and the irreligious appeared some years later in *Davis* v. *Beason*.[75] In that case the court, in sustaining the constitutionality of an Idaho statute prohibiting polygamists from voting or holding public office, said that the First Amendment "was intended . . . to prohibit legislation for the support of any religious tenets, or the modes of worship of any sect." [76]

Thereafter, more than half a century elapsed before the court was required to establish definite concepts of the implications of Jefferson's "wall of separation." During this interim the question was presented to the court in oblique fashion only, and there was no need for detailed examination. In *Bradfield* v. *Roberts* [77] the court held that the appropriation of money to a hospital operated under the auspices of the Roman Catholic Church was not in violation of the "establishment clause" as aid forbidden to a religious society. There the hospital was a separate corporate entity and as such a creature of the state not subject to the control of the church authorities, although members of the corporation could also be members of the church or of a monastic order or sisterhood of the church. The court concluded that the influence of the church over the corporation was not sufficient to convert the corporation into a religious or sectarian body.

Similarly, in *Aver* v. *United States*, commonly referred to as the Selective Draft Law Cases, the contention that the exemption of ministers from the Draft Act resulted in the "establishment of religion" was summarily rejected "because we think its unsoundness is too apparent to require us to do more." [78]

The doctrine of "public purpose" or "public welfare" came into play in *Cochran* v. *Louisiana State Board of Education*.[79]

In that case the Supreme Court held that children attending parochial schools could be made the beneficiaries of the state's free textbook law without offense to the Fourteenth Amendment as taking property for a private purpose. The case did not involve the application of the First Amendment but is significant in that it was used as a vehicle by the court in *Everson* v. *Board of Education* [80] to justify the payment of transportation expenses of children attending parochial schools as serving the public welfare. This conclusion is open to serious question.[81]

Everson v. *Board of Education* involved a New Jersey statute which authorized local school districts to adopt rules and make contracts for the transportation of children to and from schools. The Board of Education of Ewing Township, purporting to act under this authority, adopted a resolution which authorized the reimbursement to parents of money spent by them for the transportation of their children on public buses to and from public and Roman Catholic parochial schools. The validity of both the statute and the resolution was challenged on the ground that they were in contravention of the "establishment clause." Curiously, no attack was made on the resolution for the reason that it preferred one church over all others. The court refused to pass on this aspect of the resolution since the question was not presented to it for determination. It would seem that this preferment would have rendered the resolution invalid.

For the first time the "establishment clause" received the full and careful study of the Supreme Court. The court discussed the religious discriminations and persecutions of the colonial era and the fight for Virginia's Bill for Establishing Religious Freedom and reached the conclusion that the provisions of the First Amendment "had the same objective and were intended to provide the same protection against governmental intrusion on religious liberty as the Virginia statute." [82] It cited *Reynolds* v. *United States* as authority for this conclusion, although in that case, as we have seen, Jefferson's "wall of separation" was used, not in connection with the "establishment clause" but with respect to the "free exercise of religion clause." The court commented: "The First Amendment has erected a wall between church and state. That wall must be kept high and impregnable. We could not approve the slightest breach." [83] The court then promptly proceeded to puncture this unbreachable wall by applying the rule of "public purpose," which consisted of supposedly getting children safely and expeditiously to school. The court completely disregarded the fact that the "expenditure of the tax funds has no possible effect on the child's safety or expedition in transit" [84] since the children were ordinary fare-paying passengers on regular public transportation buses.

Snyder v. *Town of Newton* [85] placed in its final resting place any doubt as to the right of the state to provide free bus transportation to pupils of parochial schools. In placing its approval on a Connecticut statute which permitted a city to decide by referendum whether buses should be provided for pupils of nonprofit schools, the court brusquely disposed of objections by stating that "no substantial federal question was involved . . ." [86]

Full application of Jefferson's metaphor was accorded in *McCollum* v. *Board of Education.*[87] *McCollum* is noteworthy, among other things, as the first decision of the Supreme Court to declare a legislative enactment, federal or state, to be violative of the "establishment clause." Held to be unconstitutional was an arrangement of the Champaign, Ill., school district whereby religious instruction was given in school buildings under a released-time arrangement. Public school pupils, at the request of their parents, were permitted to attend religious instruction classes taught by outside teachers. These teachers were provided by a religious council representing various faiths subject to the approval and supervision of the superintendent of public schools. Although, in the words of Justice Reed, "it [is] difficult to extract from the opinion any conclusions as to what it is in the Champaign plan that is unconstitutional," [88] the aspects of the plan which apparently rendered it objectionable to the majority of the court were (1) "the use of the tax-supported property for religious instruction" and (2) "the close cooperation between the school authorities and the religious council in promoting education." [89] This meant that the operation of the state's compulsory educational system thus assists and is integrated with the program of religious instruction carried on by separate religious sects. Pupils compelled by law to go to school for secular education are released in part from their legal duty upon the condition that they attend the religious classes. This is beyond all question a utilization of the tax-established and tax-supported public school system to aid religious groups to spread their faith.[90]

The far-reaching effects of a literal application of *McCollum* are readily apparent. If the use of tax-supported facilities is to be the dominant test, then no public property can be used by a religious body if such use furthers its teachings. On the other hand, if the use of the state's compulsory-attendance laws is the controlling factor, no released-time program for students of compulsory school age can be valid whether the religious instruction be provided on public property or at any other place. Indeed, it could be argued that if a partial released-time program is prohibited, no student of compulsory school age could attend a parochial school full-time during public school hours. Application of this rule would necessarily reverse *Pierce* v. *Society of Sisters* and destroy the salutary doctrine that a parent has the right to direct the education of his children under the word *liberty* in the due-process clause of the Fourteenth Amendment — this even though *Pierce* was not discussed or even mentioned in *McCollum*.

Also significant is Justice Jackson's fear that a literal application of the decision may ban the teaching in public schools of any subject which includes within its reference the influence of religion, particularly with respect to the arts and sciences, music, literature, and history. This could be the case despite Jefferson's admonition that "the relations which exist between man and his Maker, and the duties resulting from these relations, are the most interesting and important to every human being, and the most incumbent on his study and investigation." [91]

Five years later, in *Zorach* v. *Clauson*,[92] the court executed a significant partial retreat from its previous inflexible concept of a high and impregnable wall between church and state, and the concept that the state should be strictly neutral not only between religious groups but between religion and irreligion as well. *Zorach* v. *Clauson* involved a released-time program of New York City. The program permitted the release of public school children during school hours, at the request of their parents, for religious instruction on nonschool property. The court distinguished between the facts of this case and those in *McCollum* on the ground that in *McCollum* school property was turned over to religious groups for use in religious instruction while in *Zorach* the religious instruction involved neither the use of public property nor the expenditure of public funds.

The court reiterated the philosophy expressed in both *Everson* and *McCollum* that church and state should be completely and unequivocally separated and that the First Amendment does not permit any exception. It significantly declared, however, that the First Amendment "does not say that in every and all respects there shall be a separation of church and state." [93] Rather it studiously defines the specific ways in which there shall be "no concert or union or dependency one on the other . . ." [94] This is to say there shall be free exercise of religion and no establishment of religion. The court came very close to adopting the concept of Cooley and other constitutional students that the First Amendment merely prohibits the preferment of one religion over all others, although not without vigorous and caustic dissents by four of the nine Justices. The court abandoned its previous position that the use of the state's compulsory school attendance laws to aid religious groups to spread their faith constituted an establishment of religion. It retained, however, its displeasure with the utilization of tax-supported property for such purpose.

The court's deviation from its previously expressed neutrality toward the religious and the irreligious was stated in its expression of belief:

> We are a religious people whose institutions presuppose a Supreme Being. . . . When the state encourages religious instruction or cooperates with religious authorities by adjusting the schedule of public events to sectarian needs, it follows the

best of our traditions. . . . To hold that it may not would
be to find in the Constitution a requirement that the government show a callous indifference to religious groups. That
would be preferring those who believe in no religion over
those who do believe.[95]

The bitterness marking the conflicting views of the Justices
is illustrated by Justice Jackson's caustic dissent:

A number of Justices just short of a majority of the majority
that promulgates today's passionate dialectics joined in answer-
ing them in Illinois ex rel. McCollum v. Board of Education. . . . The distinction attempted between that case and
this is trivial, almost to the point of cynicism, magnifying its
nonessential details and disparaging compulsion which was the
underlying reason for invalidity. A reading of the Court's
opinion in that case along with its opinion in this case will
show such difference of overtones and undertones as to make
clear that the McCollum case has passed like a storm in a tea-
cup. The wall which the Court was professing to erect between
Church and State has become even more warped and twisted
than I expected. Today's judgment will be more interesting
to students of psychology and of judicial processes than to
students of constitutional law.[96]

Zorach v. *Clauson* having demolished *McCollum's* interdic-
tion against the use of the state's compulsory school attendance
law to promote released-time programs as aids to religious training, the court next destroyed the ban on the use of tax-supported
property for religious purposes. In *Poulos* v. *New Hampshire*,[97]
decided one year after *Zorach* v. *Clauson*, the court adopted the
opinion of the Supreme Court of New Hampshire that a municipal ordinance making it obligatory on a municipality to grant
a license for religious services in a public park was constitutional.
Emphasis was placed on the public character of parks. However, if the criterion for prohibition, as enunciated in *McCollum*
and *Zorach,* is the use of tax-supported property, it must follow
that under *Poulos* the use of a public school, or any other tax-
supported property, cannot be characterized as "an establishment of religion."

History Interprets the Premise of the Supreme Court

Of what force are the historical data on which the Supreme Court so strongly relies to erect its interpretation of Jefferson's "wall of separation between church and state," and its refusal to give to the "establishment clause" the meaning attributed to it by constitutional scholars and commonly accepted practices?

As is usual, historical data lend support to varying interpretations and inferences. A detached examination of the historical data surrounding the adoption of the First Amendment impels the conclusion that the Supreme Court has erroneously given too much weight to Madison's *Remonstrance,* Jefferson's "wall of separation" letter, and Virginia's Bill for Establishing Religious Freedom. Studied in the light of accepted practices this conclusion is all the more evident.

Little weight can be attached to Madison's *Remonstrance.* Although Justice Rutledge points out in *Everson* v. *Board of Education,* "As the Remonstrance disclosed throughout, Madison opposed every form and degree of official relation between religion and civil authority. For him religion was a wholly private matter beyond the scope of civil power either to restrain or support," [98] the application of the *Remonstrance* cannot be so easily accepted. In addition to the circumstances that the *Remonstrance* was written four years before the First Amendment was drafted, its context does not wholly substantiate Justice Rutledge's interpretation. The *Remonstrance* says: "Who does not see that the same authority which can establish Christianity, in exclusion of all other Religions, may establish with the same ease any particular sect of Christians, in exclusion of all Sects?" [99] It is evident that the document was directed against the establishment of one religion, in that case the Christian religion, to the exclusion of all others. It is significant that each time the word *establishment* appeared in the *Remonstrance,* its use was to describe exclusive recognition and preferment of one religion over others. This concept underlies all but one of the proposed religious freedom amendments submitted by the states to the First Congress — that of New Hampshire. It must be remembered further that the *Remonstrance* was directed to Madison's conception of what the law of Virginia should be and not to what the law of the federal government should be. Madison wanted to put to an end the established church of Virginia. In like manner, as is shown by all of his actions and utterances, Madison's aim in the First Congress was limited to dispelling the fears of the states with respect to the establishment of a national church.

In the light of the Supreme Court's statement that the First Amendment was conceived in the pattern of Virginia's Bill for Establishing Religious Freedom it is of particular significance to note that Virginia, in ratifying the original Constitution, proposed an amendment which did not contain the wording of her bill but provided "that no particular religious sect or society ought to be favored or established by law, in preference to others." [100] Other states concurred in this proposal almost word for word.

It must be accepted that the amendments proposed by Virginia and other states are more indicative of the intent of the states than was the purpose of the Virginia Assembly in enacting its Bill for Establishing Religious Freedom. This premise was conceded by Madison since the amendments proposed by him were not his own and did not reflect his personal views but were drafted by him to conform to the demands of other states.

From the beginning to the end of the debates on the various proposed versions of the freedom of religion amendment, in both House and Senate, the legislative intent that there was to be no one national religion was clear. When the Committee of Eleven's revised draft of Madison's proposed amendment reached the floor of the House of Representatives for consideration, two questions were propounded: (1) Was the amendment necessary? (2) Was the draft too radical? Roger Sherman of Connecticut thought that the amendment was not necessary "inasmuch as Congress had no authority whatever delegated to them by the Constitution to make religious establishments." Peter Sylvester of New York was troubled by the fear that the wording of the draft "might be thought to have a tendency to abolish religion altogether . . ." Elbridge Gerry of Massachusetts urged that it be made entirely clear "that no religious doctrine shall be established by law." [101]

Madison answered these comments by stating that his interpretation of the draft of the amendment as revised by the Committee of Eleven was "that Congress should not establish a religion, and enforce the legal observance of it by law, nor compel men to worship God in any manner contrary to their conscience." [102] He believed that the people feared one sect might obtain a preeminence, or two combine together and establish a religion to which they could compel others to conform.[103] Thus, in Madison's view, "to establish a religion" was to give one religion a preferred position over all others.

Madison's personal philosophy with respect to the relation of church and state is well known. No one carried the principles of separation to more extreme lengths than he. For him "religion was wholly a private matter . . ." [104] He opposed exemption of religious institutions from taxation of any kind as well as the incorporation of religious bodies in order that they might hold legal title to property. He also opposed the appointment by Congress of chaplains paid from public funds, which he stated "is a palpable violation of equal rights as well as constitutional principles." [105] As President he issued proclamations for days of thanks only at the insistence of Congress.[106] However, his personal views concerning the undesirability of governmental aid to religion did not influence him in the preparation of his proposed religious-freedom amendment nor in the debates which followed. Nowhere do we find him expressing his personal beliefs that aid should be prohibited to all religions. His every action as a member of the First Congress confirms the conclusion that his sole purpose was to prohibit preferential treatment of religious groups, in accordance with the demands of the states.

Additional evidence of Madison's views dates back to June 1788, when, during the debates on Article VI by Virginia's Ratifying Convention, he stated: "I confess to you, sir, were uniformity of religion to be introduced by this system, it would, in my opinion, be ineligible; but I have no reason to conclude that uniformity of government will produce that of religion." [107]

Virginia's Bill for Establishing Religious Freedom provided: "No man shall be compelled to frequent or support any religious worship, place, or ministry whatsoever, nor shall be enforced, restrained, molested, or burthened, in his body or goods, nor shall otherwise suffer on account of his religious opinions or beliefs . . ." [108] Citing *Reynolds* v. *United States* and *Davis* v. *Beason,* the Supreme Court in *Everson* v. *Board of Education* concluded that the provisions of the First Amendment "had the same objectives and were intended to provide the same protection against governmental intrusion on religious liberty as the Virginia statute." [109] This conclusion hardly takes sufficiently into account the stringent opposition which the amendment encountered in the Virginia Senate because of its inadequacy in comparison with the Virginia statute. This opposition delayed Virginia's ratification of the First Amendment for almost two years.[110] The reasons for this determined opposition were concisely stated by the majority of the members of the Virginia Senate to be:

> The Amendment does not prohibit the rights of conscience from being violated or infringed; and although it goes to restrain Congress from passing laws establishing any National religion, they might, notwithstanding, levy taxes to any amount for the support of religion or its preachers; and any particular denomination of Christians might be so favored and supported by the general government, as to give it a decided advantage over the others, and in the process of time render it as powerful and dangerous as if it was established as the national religion of the country.[111]

This contemporaneous construction by persons who were most familiar with Virginia's Bill of Establishing Religious Freedom lends little support to the finding of the Supreme Court that the First Amendment was designed in the image of the Virginia bill.

Jefferson's "wall of separation between church and state" is hardly more appropriate material from which to fashion a rigid separation of church and state. Read in its proper context, this statement refers only to freedom of religious opinion and belief. This was confirmed by the Supreme Court in *Reynolds* v. *United*

States when it adopted the metaphor, not to define the prohibition of the establishment clause but to affirm the protection afforded by the First Amendment to religious belief and action. This protective shield could be penetrated only when the welfare of the state was endangered by action in the name of religious freedom. An examination of Jefferson's Danbury letter reveals that his statement was not only prefaced with a statement of his belief that government reaches "action only and not opinion . . ." [112] but was also followed by a description of the religious guarantees of the Amendment as the "expression of the Supreme will of the Nation in the rights of conscience." [113] Added emphasis to this conclusion is found in Jefferson's Second Inaugural Address, wherein he stated: "In matters of religion, I have considered that its free exercise is placed by the constitution independent of the powers of the general government." [114]

The best interpreter of the "wall of separation between church and state" must be Jefferson himself. In his *Annual Report as Rector to the President and Directors of the Literary Fund of the University of Virginia,* dealing specifically with the use of state-owned and tax-supported property for religious education, Jefferson wrote:

> It was not, however, to be understood that instruction in religious opinion and duties was meant to be precluded by the public authorities, as indifferent to the interest of society. On the contrary, the relations which exist between man and his Maker, and the duties resulting from these relations, are the most interesting and important of every human being, and the most incumbent on his study and investigation. The want of instruction in the various creeds of religious faith existing among our citizens present, therefore, a chasm in a general institution of the useful sciences. . . . A remedy, however, has been suggested of promising aspect, which, while it excludes the public authorities from the domain of religious freedom, will give to the sectarian schools of divinity the full benefit of the public provisions made for instruction in the other branches of science. It had, therefore, been in contemplation, and suggested by some pious individuals, who perceive the

advantages of associating other studies with those of religion, to establish their religious schools on the confines of the University. Such establishments would offer the further and greater advantage of enabling the students of the University to attend religious exercises with the professor of their particular sect, either in the rooms of the building still to be erected . . . or in the lecturing rooms of such professor. . . . Such an arrangement would complete the circle of the useful sciences embraced by this institution, and would fill the chasm now existing, on principles which would leave inviolate the constitutional right of freedom of religion.[115]

This *Report* was approved by the Visitors of the University, of which Madison was a member.[116]

It would appear that to Jefferson his "wall of separation between church and state" was not so impenetrable as to exclude all governmental aid to the propagation of religious beliefs, provided that neither the church nor the state infringed on the prerogatives of the other.

That the "establishment clause" merely forbids preferential treatment to one or more religious groups and not aid to all religions was given further contemporaneous expression when the First Congress provided for tax-paid chaplaincy services in both Houses of Congress [117] as well as in the armed services.[118] Additional contemporary evidence to illustrate this interpretation is found in the practices of the individual states and their political subdivisions existing at the time of the ratification of the amendment, in tax exemption for religious institutions, and in the use of town halls and other public buildings for religious purposes during off hours [119] — practices which have continued to the present day. That such aids are accepted as being within the framework of the Constitution and that the verdict of public opinion has been contrary to the Supreme Court's edict of no aid to any religion, is illustrated further by repeated legislative aids to religion. These aids are chaplaincy services and compulsory church services on Sunday in the United States Naval, Military, and Air Force Academies; [120] subsidized lunch programs for schoolchildren, including those attending parochial schools; [121] payment of training of veterans for the ministry in denominational schools; [122] aid for enlargement of denominational hospitals; [123] and numerous other well-recognized forms of aid and assistance subsidized with funds raised by taxation.[124]

In addition to monetary aids, other forms of governmental aid to religion are found expressed in oaths of office containing the words "so help me God"; the opening prayers of both Houses of the Congress and of the Supreme Court; the words IN GOD WE TRUST inscribed on our currency, and in numerous other affirmations of our belief and trust in the Creator found in oaths of allegiance, patriotic exercises, and other forms of public life.

Some of these aids commonly accepted as being within constitutional limitations have been justified under the "public welfare" doctrine enunciated in *Cochran* v. *Louisiana* and *Everson* v. *Board of Education*. Others will be justified on the theory that the religious meaning of the expression or affirmation has given way to secular purpose. In *McGowan* v. *Maryland*,[125] the Supreme Court combined this theory with that of "public welfare" and upheld the validity of a Maryland statute establishing Sunday as a compulsory day of rest. The court held that the original religious purpose of Sunday closing laws has given way to secular purposes of health and welfare of the people and consequently such laws do not constitute a violation of the "establishment clause." Speaking through Chief Justice Warren, the court stated:

> Throughout this century and longer, both the federal and state governments have orientated their activities very largely toward improvement of the health, safety, recreation and general well-being of our citizens. . . . To say that the states cannot prescribe Sunday as a day of rest for these purposes solely because centuries ago such laws had their genesis in religion would give a constitutional interpretation of hostility to the public welfare rather than one of mere separation of church and state.[126]

In *Engel* v. *Vitale* the court held that the state could not prescribe an official prayer for use in the public schools. Under attack was a law of the State of New York and a directive of the

Board of Education of a New Hyde Park school district. The law authorized school districts to provide for the recitation of a prayer, composed by the New York State Board of Regents, at the commencement of each school day. The prayer, nondenominational in character and content, read: "Almighty God, we acknowledge our dependence upon Thee, and we beg Thy blessings upon us, our parents, our teachers and our country." [127] No student was compelled to take part or to be present when the prayer was recited, and comment upon such failure was forbidden.

In upholding the contention that the law and directive were in conflict with the "establishment clause" of the First Amendment, the court, speaking through Justice Black, stated:

> We agree with this contention since we think that the constitutional prohibition against laws respecting an establishment of religion must at least mean that in this country it is no part of the business of government to compose official prayers for any group of the American people to recite as a part of a religious program carried on by the Government.[128]

If the court had been content to rest on this enunciation of the "establishment clause" — one to which there can be no objection — *Engel* would not have been the subject of the violent reception which it received. However, broader issues were interjected, issues which did disturb the American religious community. Particularly disturbing was Justice Douglas' statement: "The point for decision is whether the Government can constitutionally finance a religious exercise. Our system at the federal levels is presently honeycombed with such financing. Nevertheless, I think that it is an unconstitutional undertaking whatever form it takes." [129] This reasoning, carried to its logical conclusion, would invalidate all forms of aid even though the aid was incidental to the secular purposes of the enactment providing such aid. Instead of "freedom of religion" this country would then have "freedom from religion." [130]

Although *Engel* did not establish any principle beyond that which forbids the state to compose and prescribe forms of prayers for recitation in public schools, it was a vehicle for the court, in

School District of Abington Township v. *Schempp* and *Murray* v. *Curlett* [131] to proscribe all forms of prayer, Bible reading, and other exercises partaking of a dominant religious flavor, in public schools.

School District of Abington Township involved a Pennsylvania statute which required that each public school day commence with the reading of 10 verses from the Bible, without comment and with voluntary attendance. *Murray* involved a rule of the Board of Education of the city of Baltimore, Md., which provided for the holding of opening exercises in the public schools of that city consisting primarily of reading, without comment and with voluntary attendance, of a chapter from the Bible and/or the recitation of the Lord's Prayer. Different versions of the Bible were permitted to be used by the pupils. The two cases were the subject of one opinion by the court.

Speaking for the majority of the court, Justice Clark declared that the provisions for voluntary attendance were in effect shams, and held both the statute and the rule to be unconstitutional since they provided for religious exercises in public schools in contravention of the "establishment clause." The doctrine of strict neutrality set forth in *Everson* v. *Board of Education* was restated by Justice Clark in the following words: "In the relationship between man and religion, the State is firmly committed to a position of neutrality." [132]

The court clearly defined what it meant by "neutrality" when it said:

> The test may be stated as follows: What are the purposes and the primary effect of the enactment? If either is the advancement or inhibition of religion then the enactment exceeds the scope of legislative power as circumscribed by the Constitution. That is to say that to withstand the strictures of the Establishment Clause there must be a secular legislative purpose and a primary effect that neither advances nor inhibits religion.[133]

This rule of "primary purpose and effect" must necessarily render some aids, financial and otherwise, unconstitutional. There can be no other purpose than to advance religion in the inscription of IN GOD WE TRUST on our currency despite the suggestion of the court that the original religious purpose of such a motto has given way to a secular purpose. Other examples could well be cited where the only purpose of the aid can be of a religious character.

On the other hand, where the mention of the Creator is incidental to the complete text in which it appears, such as in the pledge of allegiance or an oath of office, the prime purpose and effect of such reference obviously is not to promote religion. The "primary purpose and effect" doctrine places each aid on its own merits, and it will be interesting to observe the treatment accorded each by the court in future cases.

Of more significance is the possible conflict between the "establishment clause" and the "free exercise of religion clause." This possibility was raised by Justice Brennan in his concurring opinion when he stated:

> There are certain practices, conceivably violative of the Establishment Clause, the striking down of which might seriously interfere with certain religious liberties also protected by the First Amendment.[134]

This conflict could well rise in the construction of statutes providing for chaplaincy service to members of the armed services who, through action on the part of the government, are deprived of the free exercise of their religion.

The court, in *School Board of Abington Township* and *Murray,* studiously endeavored to avoid the violent repercussions which *Engel* v. *Vitale* was subject to. Great care was exercised to emphasize the religious nature of our people, the concern of the court that no hostility towards religion be tolerated, and the specific enumeration of aids and practices which could well be held to be in accord with the "establishment clause." Typical of the solicitude shown by the court is the following statement of Justice Goldberg:

> Neither the state nor this Court can or should ignore the significance of the fact that a vast portion of our people believe in and worship God and that many of our legal, political and

personal values derive historically from religious teachings.
Government must inevitably take cognizance of the existence
of religion and, indeed, under certain circumstances the First
Amendment may require that it do so. And it seems clear to
me from the opinions in the present and past cases that the
Court would recognize the propriety of providing military
chaplains and of the teaching *about* religion, as distinguished
from the teaching of religion, in the public schools. The examples could readily be multiplied, for both the required and
the permissible accommodations between state and church
frame the relation as one free of hostility or favor and productive of religious and political harmony, but without undue
involvement of one in the concerns or practices of the other.[135]

Other aids which are probably permissible within the framework of the First Amendment were stated by Justice Brennan
to be: "the excusal of children from school on their respective
religious holidays; and of the allowance by government of temporary use of public buildings by religious organizations when
their own churches have become unavailable because of a disaster or emergency";[136] nondevotional use of the Bible in public
schools;[137] and uniform tax exemptions which benefit churches
and religious institutions as well as charities and nonprofit organizations.[138]

The only discordant voice was that of Justice Douglas, who
did not try to soothe the public but resolutely adhered to his
basic philosophy, expressed in *Engel* v. *Vitale,* that no aid to
religion is in harmony with the "establishment clause." He stated
that the First Amendment "does not say that some forms of
establishment are allowed; it says that 'no law respecting an
establishment of religion' shall be made. What may not be done
directly may not be done indirectly lest the Establishment Clause
become a mockery." [139]

FREE EXERCISE OF RELIGION

Implications of Freedom

Separate from the "establishment clause," but serving as
a complement thereto to complete the absoluteness of the re-

ligious guarantees of the First Amendment, is the right of the free exercise of religion. This freedom encompasses a larger area than does the "establishment clause," although its application has been less difficult. It acts as a restraint on the federal government and, through the Fourteenth Amendment, on the states, preventing both from interfering with religious beliefs and opinions, practices and conduct.

The purpose of the "free-exercise clause" and the distinction between it and the "establishment clause" is stated by Justice Clark, in *School District of Abington Township,* as follows:

> The Free Exercise Clause . . . withdraws from legislative power, state and federal, the exertion of any restraint on the free exercise of religion. Its purpose is to secure religious liberty in the individual by prohibiting any invasions thereof by civil authority. Hence it is necessary in a free exercise case for one to show the coercive effect of the enactment as it operates against him in the practice of his religion. The distinction between the two clauses is apparent — a violation of the Free Exercise Clause is predicated on coercion while the Establishment Clause violation need not be so attended.[140]

Religious belief and opinion are absolute — they cannot be restricted. Thus, in *United States* v. *Ballard* [141] the Supreme Court held that religious beliefs, whatever their nature, could not be made the subject of inquiry as to their truth or falsity because:

> Freedom of thought, which includes freedom of religious belief, is basic in a society of free men. . . . It embraces the right to maintain theories of life and death and of the hereafter which are rank heresy to followers of the orthodox faiths. Heresy trials are foreign to our Constitution. Men may believe what they cannot prove. They may not be put to the proof of their religious doctrines or beliefs. Religious experiences which are real as life to some may be incomprehensible to others. Yet the fact that they may be beyond the ken of mortals does not mean that they can be made suspect before the law. Many take their gospel from the New Testament. But it would hardly be supposed that they could be tried before a jury charged with determining whether those teachings contain false representa-

tions. The miracles of the New Testament, the Divinity of
Christ, life after death, the power of prayer are deep in the
religious convictions of many. If one could be sent to jail
because a jury in a hostile environment found these teachings
false, little indeed would be left of religious freedom.[142]

Conversely, the freedom to refuse to avow what is contrary
to one's religious beliefs is equally sacred in the eyes of the Constitution. In *West Virginia State Board of Education* v. *Barnette*
the court upheld the right of a child of a member of Jehovah's
witnesses to refuse, under parental direction and for religious
reasons, to salute the flag of the United States, stating: "If there
is any fixed star in our constitutional constellation, it is that no
official, high or petty, can prescribe what shall be orthodox in
politics, nationalism, religion, or other matter of opinion or force
citizens to confess by word or act their faith therein." [143]   The
difficulty experienced by the court when engaged in applying
spiritual principles to specific facts is well illustrated by the circumstance that this case reversed a contrary opinion handed
down by the same court just three years before under an identical
factual situation.[144]

While the constitutional umbrella of protection is complete
with respect to entertaining and expressing religious beliefs and
opinions, its absoluteness does not extend to conduct and practices. Conduct is and must remain "subject to regulation for the
protection of society." [145]   Justice Black aptly stated this principle
in *West Virginia State Board of Education* v. *Barnette* in the following language: "Religious faiths, honestly held, do not free
individuals from responsibility to conduct themselves obediently
to laws which are either imperatively necessary to protect society as a whole from grave and pressingly imminent dangers or
which, without any general prohibition, merely regulate time,
place or manner of religious activity." [146]   The refusal of a school-
child to salute the American flag did not, in the opinion of the
court, constitute such a clear and present danger as would permit a state to punish the child. Carrying this thought further
the court in *Taylor* v. *Mississippi* held that since schoolchildren
cannot be compelled to salute the flag, the Fourteenth Amend-

ment a fortiori "prohibits the imposition of punishment for urging and advising that, on religious grounds, citizens refrain from saluting the flag." [147] On the other hand, as we have seen, in *Hamilton* v. *University of California* [148] the right of the state to impose military training on all students of the university regardless of their religious beliefs was upheld by the court.

Controls and Licenses

The doctrine of clear and present danger invoked by the Court in *West Virginia State Board of Education* v. *Barnette* was extended in *Prince* v. *Massachussets* [149] when the court held that minors could be prevented from distributing religious tracts on public streets under the broad generalization that such conduct was inherently dangerous to minors although no clear and present danger was shown to exist. Admittedly such prohibition would have been invalid if applied to adults.

Present in these cases is the struggle between the liberty of the parents to exercise control and direction over the activities of their children as contrasted with the power of the state. We have seen in *Meyer* v. *Nebraska* and *Pierce* v. *The Society of Sisters* that parental control over the education of their children was paramount. In *West Virginia State Board of Education* v. *Barnette* this control and direction was applied to the refusal to avow beliefs contrary to the religious beliefs of the parent and child. Since these rights were personal and not in conflict with the public safety, morals, or well-being, the court recognized the exclusive right of the parent to prepare his child for obligations and responsibilities which the state could not provide. However:

> The family is not beyond regulation in the public interest, as against the claim of religious liberty. . . . Acting to guard the general interest in youth's well-being, the state as *parens patriae* may restrict the parent's control by requiring school attendance, regulating or prohibiting the child's labor, and in many other ways. . . . A democratic society rests, for its continuance, upon the healthy, well-rounded growth of young people into full maturity as citizens. . . . It is too late now to doubt that legislation appropriately designed to reach such

evils is within the state's police power, whether against the parent's claim to control the child or one that religious scruples dictate contrary action.[150]

It has long been held that the regulation of religious practices such as polygamy by federal [151] and state [152] enactments constitutes a legitimate exercise of the police power of the state for the protection of public morals. Similarly the cursing of a public officer by a member of a religious sect was held not to be an exercise of religion within the meaning of the constitutional guarantees of religious worship; [153] and the Mann Act [154] has been held to apply to the interstate transportation of plural wives notwithstanding religious beliefs to the contrary.[155]

More recent cases involving the interpretation of areas of coverage of free exercise of religion have contained attacks on municipal and state licensing and taxing regulations. Certain well-defined principles with respect to the validity of such regulations have been established by the Supreme Court. Ordinances and statutes which prohibit the solicitation, sale, or distribution of religious matter without first securing a license or permit have been held uniformly to constitute an unconstitutional invasion of the free exercise of religion where the issuance of the license or permit is within the unlimited discretion of the licensing authority. On the other hand, where the issuance of the license or permit involves mere administrative action on the part of the licensing authority, the ordinance or law will be declared valid. Ordinances and laws requiring the payment of a tax for the privilege of sale or distribution of religious material are invalid. Likewise, ordinances or laws prohibiting the use of public parks for religious purposes, or public streets for the dissemination and sale of religious tracts, are invalid.

The first license case was *Cantwell* v. *Connecticut,* which case blanketed the religious guarantees of the First Amendment under the protection of the Fourteenth. In that case the Connecticut law vested in the Secretary of Public Welfare the sole right to determine whether an applicant for a license to solicit was representing a religious cause. If he found in the negative, he had the exclusive power to refuse to grant the license. The court declared the statute invalid because it deprived members of religious sects of their liberty of soliciting money for a religious cause. The court stated: "But to condition the solicitation of aid for the perpetration of religious views or systems upon a license, the grant of which rests in the exercise of a determination by state authority as to what is a religious cause, is to lay a forbidden burden upon the exercise of liberty protected by the Constitution." [156]

The court explained in some detail, however, that the state could legitimately regulate the times, places, and manner of solicitation and could safeguard the peace, good order, and comfort of the community. The statute under scrutiny did not purport to impose any such restraints, and once the license was issued, there were no limitations with respect to the conditions of solicitation.

Affirmation of this principle is found in *Largent* v. *Texas*.[157] In that case the court declared unconstitutional a municipal ordinance which made it unlawful to solicit orders for, or to sell, books and other merchandise within the residential area of the municipality without first obtaining a permit from the mayor. The mayor had the sole discretion to grant or deny the permit. The action of the court was premised on this reasoning: "Dissemination of ideas depends upon the approval of the distributor by the official. This is administrative censorship in an extreme form. It abridges the freedom of religion . . ." [158]

Where, as in *Cox* v. *New Hampshire*,[159] the licensing authority did not possess arbitrary power but was limited to the determination of when a public highway could be used to assure the safety and convenience of the public, an ordinance requiring a license to hold a parade on the public streets was held to be valid. In upholding such an ordinance the court stated: "The authority of the municipality to impose regulations in order to assure the safety and convenience of the people in the use of public highways has never been regarded as inconsistent with civil liberties but rather as one of the means of safeguarding the good order upon which they ultimately depend." [160] This principle was reaffirmed in *Poulos* v. *New Hampshire,* when the court held that the use of a public park for religious services was subject to the obtaining of a license since the power to refuse arbitrarily such license was not in the licensing authority. The court further held that when such license was obtained the state could not refuse the use of the park for religious purposes. In like manner, in *Jamison* v. *Texas,*[161] the Supreme Court held that a municipality cannot prevent the use of its streets for the distribution of religious handbills. The fact that the distributors of such handbills solicited the purchase of religious books while distributing the handbills did not affect their right of free exercise of religion.

The validity of the imposition of a license tax as a condition of solicitation and sale of religious matter was considered in *Murdoch* v. *Pennsylvania.*[162] In that case members of a religious sect went from door to door distributing religious tracts and soliciting contributions in the form of purchases of the tracts. Argument was made that the solicitation constituted a commercial enterprise for which the municipality could exact a reasonable canvassing fee. The court characterized the distribution of religious literature as a form of missionary evangelism "as old as the history of printing presses," [163] which holds the same privileges under the First Amendment as worship in churches and preaching from the pulpit. The sale of religious tracts, in the opinion of the court, cannot constitute a commercial enterprise any more than can the passing of the offering plate in a church. "The constitutional rights of those spreading their religious beliefs through the spoken and printed words are not to be gauged by standards governing retailers or wholesalers of books." [164] The court then declared that the license tax imposed by the municipality was not a nominal fee designed to defray the expense of policing the licensee's activities. Rather it was a flat fee attached to the pursuit of the free exercise of religion. As such the ordinance was unconstitutional since it compelled the licensee to pay for a privilege guaranteed by the First Amendment and: "The power to tax the exercise of a privilege is the power to control or suppress its enjoyment." [165]

This principle was reaffirmed the following year in *Follet v. Town of McCormick* [166] when the court held a town ordinance requiring agents selling books to pay a license fee unconstitutional as an improper restriction on "freedom of religion" when applied to a minister who earned his living by the sale of religious books.

A different approach looking to the suppression of the distribution of religious matter was attempted in *Martin* v. *City of Struthers*.[167] There the municipal ordinance was premised on the supposed power of the city to protect householders from inconvenience and annoyance. Door-to-door solicitation or distribution which in any manner caused the householder to come to the door was prohibited. The ordinance was set aside as being an unconstitutional invasion of the right of free speech and freedom of the press. Justice Murphy, however, extended the prohibition of the court to include the free exercise of religion when he commented: "Freedom of religion has a higher dignity under the Constitution than municipal or personal inconvenience." [168]

The Supreme Court went even further in *Marsh* v. *Alabama*.[169] That case involved the right of Alabama to impose criminal sanctions on a person who distributed religious literature on the streets and sidewalks of a town wholly owned by a private corporation without first securing a permit. Application for such a permit was denied. The court held that, since the property was used for general public purposes, the fact that it was privately owned did not give the owner the right to prohibit distribution of religious literature. The court significantly held that "when we balance the Constitutional rights of owners of property against those of the people enjoying freedom of press and religion, as we must, we are mindful of the fact that the latter occupy a preferred position." [170]

CONCLUSION

Inevitably as new factual situations are presented to the Supreme Court for consideration and determination, additional concepts of church-state relations will be formulated, or present concepts revised. There will continue to be challenges not only by those who sincerely and honestly believe that absolute separation in every respect expresses the philosophy of the framers of the First Amendment, but also by those who feel that such principle is necessary to preserve the independence of the church. At the opposite pole will be those who sincerely and honestly believe that it is the duty of the state to subsidize in every manner the promotion of religious activities. Neither appears to express the correct answer.

As creatures of God the church and the state can never be separated absolutely. This is an impossibility. Neither can subsidization, with all of its connotations and implications of state control, be the true answer. The philosophy of the First Amendment must necessarily require an interdependence of church and state expressed in terms of mutual cooperation, assistance, and friendly understanding without the interference of either in the legitimate affairs of the other. Both church and state are under mandate to assist actively in framing principles and concepts which will best preserve and nourish the spirit of religious freedom in the United States. "In these days free men have no loftier responsibility than the preservation of that freedom." [171]

PART III

Tensions in the Interaction
of Church and State

ARNOLD C. MUELLER
AND ARTHUR L. MILLER
WITH JOHN H. STRIETELMEIER

EUGENE F. KLUG
AND JAMES S. SAVAGE

THE AMERICAN PEOPLE have always had a pragmatic approach to their political and social theories. The principles which govern our church-state relations are therefore most adequately understood in their practice. Part III concerns itself with the practical application of the theoretical pattern. It is here that the tensions are real and the issues are posed for decision. The major area of tension is, of course, education. But other areas, such as the chaplaincy and Sunday laws, are also frequently in the news as sources of community disagreement.

In chapter 7 the problems of educational tensions in the relations of church and state are brought out in detail. *Arnold C. Mueller*, M. S., D. D., of the editorial staff of the Board of Parish Education, The Lutheran Church — Missouri Synod, who has long been a student of church-state issues, takes up the complications presented by various religious observances in the public schools. *Arthur L. Miller*, Ph. D., executive secretary of the Board of Parish Education, The Lutheran Church — Missouri Synod, reviews the place of the church school in American society. Since the Synod maintains the largest of the Protestant systems of full-time Christian day schools, its view deserves to be heard. *John H. Strietelmeier*, M. A., Litt. D., university editor at Valparaiso University, has supplied editorial touches to the chapter as well as some of his own insights.

In public education the difficulty of reconciling moral indoctrination with freedom of conscience is pointed out in the chapter as a unique American problem. Religious activities were once very prevalent in the public schools of the land, but recent Supreme Court decisions have sharply curtailed them. In church education the right to existence of Christian day schools is now well established. The debate centers on the kind of government aid, if any, which such schools are entitled to receive or in good conscience may accept.

Chapter 7

CHURCH, STATE, AND EDUCATION

Arnold C. Mueller and Arthur L. Miller
with John H. Strietelmeier

I

RELIGION IN THE PUBLIC SCHOOLS
Arnold C. Mueller

AS RECENTLY AS 150 years ago, education on all levels in Europe and the Americas was almost entirely church-controlled. The American public school came upon the educational scene in the first half of the 19th century, largely through the efforts of a small, dedicated group of educators whose most eloquent spokesman was Horace Mann. The need which called the public school into being was obvious and urgent. Democratic government, which vests sovereignty in the voting citizen, presupposes an informed citizenry. Private schools, which were beyond the financial means of many people and were objectionable on denominational grounds even to many who could afford them, were obviously not equal to the enormous job of educating all of the children of a religiously pluralistic nation. To Mann and his associates it was obvious that the American experiment in popular government could succeed only if it were undergirded by a new kind of school — a publicly owned and operated school which would offer free education in the common branches of learning to all of the children of the community with no tinge of sectarian bias.

300

It is important to note, though, that while the early public school movement was vigorously opposed to any form of denominationalism it was by no means antireligious. Mann himself approved of Bible reading and other nonsectarian religious exercises in the public school. The McGuffey Readers, which for so long set the tone of public-school education, were almost sermonic in style and content. The public school teacher was expected to be as much an exemplar of morality as was the clergyman. It was the common practice to recruit public school teachers and administrators from among graduates of seminaries and denominational colleges.

For approximately the first half century of its existence, the public school was able to engage unhindered in what we today call moral indoctrination simply because it did not have to contend with the kinds of religious and moral pluralism which were introduced into American society by the immigrant throngs which shortly after the Civil War began to convert the United States from a Protestant, Anglo-Saxon, English-speaking nation into a melting pot of many religions, many nationality groups, and many tongues. It is true that, beginning with the large Irish migrations of the 1840s, a sizable Roman Catholic minority began to assert its own particularity against the generality of Protestant America, but since Roman Catholics chose to establish and maintain their own schools, they did not greatly disturb the consensus of the constituency of the public school. This consensus, essentially Protestant in its presuppositions, asserted a belief in God, in the Scriptures of the Old and New Testaments as the revelation of God, in a moral law rooted in the Ten Commandments and the Sermon on the Mount, and in a moral order which rewarded virtue and punished sin.

The latter half of the 19th century was a time of revolutionary changes in the constituency of the public school. Beginning shortly after the Civil War, immigrants began pouring into the United States, large numbers of them from southern, eastern, and southeastern Europe. By the end of the century, Roman Catholics, Jews, and Eastern Orthodox were as vocally a part of the American scene as were Congregationalists, Methodists,

Baptists, and Presbyterians. More than that, new philosophical systems (e. g., Hegelianism) and apparent conflicts between science and religion began to make agnosticism a tolerable if not perhaps altogether respectable point of view. Industrialization and the mushrooming of large cities began to break down family and community solidarity, creating the rootless individual. For millions of people the ideal of democracy or the mysteries of secret orders became adequate substitutes for traditional religion. And the multiplication of goods that could be bought by anyone who had the money to afford them made Mammon an exceedingly attractive alternative to God.

These changes greatly narrowed the area of consensus within the constituency of the public school. Believer and agnostic claimed equal rights to define the limits of moral indoctrination. Christian and Jew wrestled with the hard question of how the schools could transmit their common ethical heritage without exposing their profound disagreement on the nature and authority of Jesus Christ. Protestant and Roman Catholic found it impossible to agree on which version of the Bible was to be read in the schools if indeed it was to be read at all. A small but influential atheist minority demanded respect for their right to have their children uncontaminated by the "superstition" of religion. Among the almost 40 percent of the nation's population who claimed no church membership the prevailing attitude was that religion is a private matter and that the best way to settle the question of religious or moral instruction was to leave this sort of thing to the family and the church and to let the schools restrict themselves to the transmission of information and the development of skills.

In the midst of this confusion Professor John Dewey, then a member of the faculty of the University of Chicago, wrote *The School and Society* (1899). In this and in his numerous other writings during a long lifetime Dewey strongly influenced both the philosophy and the practice of American education. He gave expression to a set of views which were congenial both to the spirit of the age and to the pragmatism of the American mind. Any attempt to reduce the broad range of his thought to a few sentences runs the risk of oversimplifying and possibly even distorting them. For our purposes, however, it is important to note certain elements of his philosophy which are still being adhered to by many educators.

Dewey held that man is a purely biological organism engaged, like all organisms, in a struggle to survive and to evolve. He found in him no trace of a mind or a soul in the traditional sense of something separate or apart from his body. Man's highest good he defined as the creation and sharing of happiness, not in any merely private or personal sense but in the sense of removing those social and personal evils which produce unhappiness. Dewey did not altogether deny the existence of eternal truths or fixed moral laws; he merely asserted that, if there were such things, man had no way of knowing it. Religion he defined as the belief in and the effort to secure the conservation and the enhancement of socially recognized values. Practically speaking, therefore, man could test the truth of an idea only by its consequences in life, and he could validate an alleged moral law only by demonstrating its necessity for human happiness.

Dewey's *instrumentalist* philosophy found expression in *progressive* education, the most influential spokesman for which is Professor William Heard Kilpatrick, for many years a member of the faculty of Teachers College, Columbia University. A recent biographer of Professor Kilpatrick has this to say about his theory of education:

> In Kilpatrick's thinking there was no predestination, no pre-determination; man's decisions and efforts mattered, for good or for ill. There was no limit, no boundaries to this expanding, evolving, "unlidded" universe. There was no stop, no end, no finality; improvement should only lead to more improvement and growth. The final resource for all good is the free, roaming, unfettered mind dedicated to the highest common good.[1]

Contemporary public education may best be described as a blending of the methods and certain philosophical assumptions of progressive education with a modified form of the old, deep-rooted Protestant ethic. In its present form this ethic holds that

there is a good God Who is the father of all men and that
under his fatherhood all men are brothers; that the whole duty
of man is comprehended in the Golden Rule; that God deals
with men and their societies under a system of reward for good
behavior (or at least good intentions) and punishments for
violations of His law, i. e., the Ten Commandments; and that
the chief objectives of religion are personal happiness and
social justice.[2]

Religious practices as such are generally frowned on. The observance even of those religious holidays (such as Christmas)
which are widely celebrated in the community at large becomes
a "touchy" matter and in numerous cases has had to be abandoned. Textbooks scrupulously avoid the name of God and
touch lightly, if at all, on any ideas that might seem to be
expressive of a sectarian point of view. Motivational appeals
are made to good citizenship rather than to the will of God.
The "Pledge to the Flag" has supplanted the morning prayer
as a devotional exercise. And the pantheon of national secular
heroes (Washington, Jefferson, Lincoln, Lee, Theodore Roosevelt) plays much the same example-setting role which in Jewish
or Christian education had been played by the prophets and
the saints.

The foregoing are presented as statements of fact, not as
criticisms of the public school. The unique problem of American
public education is to provide as much moral indoctrination
as is possible without violating consciences which have been
shaped in the most pluralistic society, as to religion, the world
has known since at least the days of the Roman Empire. This
means that of necessity the moral content of public education
must be set at the level of whatever least common denominator
actually exists within the society at any given time. Moreover,
this content must be transmitted without reference to any
specifically religious sanctions. Ethics must therefore necessarily be defended on purely utilitarian grounds ("Thou shalt
not steal because no one can be secure in his property if any
man is free to take whatever he wants"). And morality can be

defined only within the context of the working mores of the community without reference to any supernatural origin.

In recent years, especially since World War II, certain symptoms of moral decay have become so evident that they have produced insistent demands for a shoring-up of the nation's foundations. Juvenile crime, for instance, has increased dismayingly since 1945. Sex mores have undergone a revolutionary change. Early marriage, often followed by quickie divorce, has become commonplace. Cases of narcotics addiction and social disease have increased alarmingly in the high-school-age group. Whatever the causes of these trends may be, criticism has focused on those institutions which are chiefly responsible for the education of the young: the home, the church, and the school.

In the case of the school, this criticism has taken the form of a demand for greater discipline and a more intensive indoctrination in religious and moral values. Critics of the schools contend that if students really are "whole persons" their learning experiences must be whole as well, and that to exclude the religious from education is to give the child a distorted view of life.

At the same time another substantial segment of the American public has not been so ready to concede that the separation of religious learning from secular education is altogether bad. In the first place, they contend, there is no way to introduce any religious instruction worthy of the name without offending religious and nonreligious minorities. In the second place, they argue, any attempt to do an adequate job of religious instruction in the classroom would require special training for teachers and, if given at a least-common-denominator level which would not offend denominational sensibilities, would probably leave a poorer impression on the children than no religious instruction at all. Those who hold this position maintain that the problem of providing any substantial religious instruction in the public schools of a pluralistic society such as ours is intrinsically insoluble and should be referred to the church and the home.

Against this background we shall describe and evaluate some of the ways which have been suggested for bringing religious instruction or activities into the public school classroom. The most common of them are Bible reading, religious exercises, the teaching of moral and spiritual values, and provision for released-time, dismissed-time, and shared-time programs.

BIBLE READING IN THE PUBLIC SCHOOLS

The practice of reading a portion of the Bible in public schools each day goes back to the very beginnings of the American school system. The educational reformers of the early 19th century took no exception to the practice so long as the Bible was read without comment. By the beginning of 1963, Bible reading in public schools was required by law in 13 states and permitted in another 25 states. Most of the school districts where Bible reading was part of the daily school routine were in the South and the East, but they included many districts with large school populations.[3]

The King James Version of the Bible, irrespective of one's views of its authorship or authority, is universally recognized as a masterpiece of English literature and the source of so many expressions and allusions in writers from Shakespeare to the moderns that it would be hard for any English-speaking person to escape its influence. Indeed, college and university instructors frequently complain that their students' lack of acquaintance with the King James Version handicaps their understanding of English literature.

It appears to be general practice that certain of the most eloquent portions of the King James Version must be included in any respectable survey of English literature. Its use for specifically religious purposes — especially as devotional literature or as a source book of moral instruction — has, however, been definitively forbidden by the United States Supreme Court in the case of *Abington School District* v. *Schempp,* decided on June 17, 1963. The court seems to invalidate every argument that has been advanced for the constitutional permissibility of Bible reading in the public-school classroom. Speaking for the eight members of the court who concurred in the opinion, Justice Clark wrote:

Applying the Establishment Clause principles to the cases at bar we find that the States are requiring the selection and reading at the opening of the school day of verses from the Holy Bible and the recitation of the Lord's Prayer by the students in unison. These exercises are prescribed as part of the curricular activities of students who are required by law to attend school. They are held in the school buildings under the supervision and with the participation of teachers employed in those schools. . . . The trial court in No. 142 [*School District of Abington Township, Pennsylvania, et al., Appellants,* v. *Edward Lewis Schempp, et al.*] has found that such an opening exercise is a religious ceremony and was intended by the State to be so. We agree with the trial court's finding is [as?] to the religious character of the exercises. Given that finding the exercises and the law requiring them are in violation of the Establishment Clause.

There is no such specific finding as to the religious character of the exercises in No. 119 [*William J. Murray III, etc., et al. Petitioners,* v. *John N. Curlett, President, et al., Individually, and Constituting the Board of School Commissioners of Baltimore City*], and the State contends (as does the State in No. 142) that the program is an effort to extend its benefits to all public school children without regard to their religious belief. Included within its secular purposes, it says, are the promotion of moral values, the contradiction to the materialistic trends of our times, the perpetuation of our institutions and the teaching of literature. The case came up on demurrer, of course, to a petition which alleged that the uniform practice under the rule had been to read from the King James version of the Bible and that the exercise was sectarian. The short answer, therefore, is that the religious character of the exercise was admitted by the State. But even if its purpose is not strictly religious, it is sought to be accomplished through readings, without comment, from the Bible. Surely the place of the Bible as an instrument for religion cannot be gainsaid, and the State's recognition of the pervading religious character of the ceremony is evident from the rule's specific permission of the alternative use of the Catholic Douay version as well as the recent amendment permitting nonattendance at the exercises. None of these factors is consistent with the contention that the Bible is here used either as an instrument for nonreligious inspiration or as a reference for the teaching of secular subjects.

The conclusion follows that in both cases the laws require religious exercises and such exercises are being conducted in direct violation of the rights of the appellees and petitioners. Nor are these required exercises mitigated by the fact that individual students may absent themselves upon parental request, for that fact furnishes no defense to a claim of unconstitutionality under the Establishment Clause. . . . Further, it is no defense to urge that the religious practices here may be relatively minor encroachments on the First Amendment. The breach of neutrality that is today a trickling stream may all too soon become a raging torrent and, in the words of Madison, "it is proper to take alarm at the first experiment on our liberties." [4]

RELIGIOUS EXERCISES IN PUBLIC SCHOOLS

The broad sweep of the court's opinion in *Abington School District* v. *Schempp* determines the unconstitutionality of religious opening exercises in public schools, previously permitted in 38 states. It also casts grave doubt on the constitutionality of other exercises of a religious nature not specifically at issue in that case.

In many communities it is customary for the schools to observe Christmas with some sort of program which may include dramatizations, carol singing, recitations, and the construction of creches. In some schools, Jewish children enact the festival of Hannukah at the same season of the year. There appears to be a trend toward combining the celebration of these two holidays in one observance organized around some such theme as hope or brotherhood or joy.

Most public high schools arrange baccalaureate services for their graduates. Attendance is of course optional, but group pressure usually results in the attendance of most graduates. Clergymen of churches which forbid pulpit and altar fellowship across denominational lines have frequently been embarrassed by invitations to participate in such services, which violate both their own convictions and the polity of their church. The alternative which is sometimes offered them — of having complete charge of the service — is equally embarrassing because their adherence to a confessional principle is almost certain to be widely misinterpreted as a mere "dog in the manger" attitude and because it places them in the awkward position of having to lead the worship of a group which is not agreed on the object or nature of worship.

The position taken by the court is that the First Amendment commands "that the Government maintain strict neutrality, neither aiding nor opposing religion" in the public schools. Applied to the exercises just cited, this position would seem to rule out even those religious exercises which are deeply rooted in tradition and custom. And while there will undoubtedly continue to be those who complain that the court has in effect delivered the schools over to a religion of secularism, many more will agree with Walter Lippmann that the decision in *Abington School District* v. *Schempp* "closed a blind alley that led nowhere. The forbidden religious exercises would not and could not have dealt with the great moral and intellectual deficiencies of American education. The exercises were harmless and negligible. But had they been allowed to evolve, they could have led only to religious quarrels." [5]

TEACHING MORAL AND SPIRITUAL VALUES

While divergent points of view will continue to exist regarding the means by which the schools may exhibit an active interest in character building and conduct consistent with high moral standards, there is substantial unanimity in the expectation of the American people that the public schools will somehow inculcate those values and standards which for most people draw their sanctions from religion.

Reflecting this concern, the Educational Policies Commission of the National Education Association concluded, in a report published in 1951, that the schools must teach the accepted standards of conduct. This report climaxed a series of endeavors to establish morality codes which might be taught in the public schools. Already in the early 1920s teachers had begun experimenting with "direct" and "indirect" methods of character education; right conduct was taught as part of the curricular subjects and in extracurricular activities. In Nebraska, Florida, and some other states, efforts were made to provide guidance for the teaching of moral values; often the approach was through a study of the Declaration of Independence, the federal and state constitutions, famous addresses, and the national anthem. Stress was laid on good citizenship and on the moral and spiritual values underlying democracy.

One of the best-known efforts in this direction was that of the Regents of the University of the State of New York.[6] After citing evidence to support the point that "we are a religious people whose institutions presuppose a Supreme Being," the Regents recommended a study of great American documents to develop in the pupils an understanding and appreciation of their role as individuals endowed by the Creator with rights, and to stimulate respect for others and reverence for Almighty God. These objectives were to be achieved "through all the activities and lessons of the school day and particularly by the good example of the school staff." It was hoped:

> Thus, our children, inspired by the example of their ancestors, guided by the faith and love of their parents and encouraged by their spiritually sensitive teachers, will renew in their daily lives America's Moral and Spiritual Heritage: Liberty under God . . . Respect for the Dignity and Rights of each individual . . . Devotion to Freedom.[7]

A recent study document prepared under the direction of the Department of Religion and Public Education of the National Council of the Churches of Christ in the U. S. A.[8] distinguishes those aspects of religion which may be dealt with in the public schools from those which are the concern of the home and the church. To the latter belong worship and commitment to a particular denominational faith. To the school — along with the home and the church — belong ethical codes. "Developing acceptable ethical judgments and conduct is the joint concern of home, church, public school, and community.

Each should reinforce the other in helping the pupil develop the kind of behavior necessary to the development of a free society." [9]

The committee which developed this study document concluded that it would be impossible to find a "common core" of religious understandings which might be included in the school curriculum. It stressed the fact, however, that certain common goals in individual and group behavior are recognized by school and church, and expressed its conviction that these goals can and should be taught. "The public school has long taught ethical and moral values," the study document asserts. "Plans for teaching these should be encouraged and strengthened." [10]

Since democratic government presupposes some commonly accepted set of moral principles and values, the importance of developing such a moral consensus in the future citizens of the nation is universally admitted. Disputes arise principally over the question of motivation. Who decides what is right and what is wrong? And assuming there is essentially unanimous agreement on the answer to that question — or that it is a question that need not be answered — why should a man do what is right (especially when it is also hard) and eschew what is wrong (especially when it is attractive)?

Practically speaking, all of the great world religions give essentially the same prescriptions for right conduct: reverence for God, respect for parents and superiors, respect for life and property, respect for the family and the marriage relationship, honesty in speech and behavior, a positive concern for the welfare of other people. The most eloquent Christian statement of this "natural knowledge of the moral law" is that of Paul in Romans 2. By virtue of this natural knowledge of the Law, man is held to be capable of achieving a high degree of civil righteousness. Thus, though many Christians would hold that the teaching of moral and spiritual values independently of the motivation of the Gospel of Christ is inadequate, they favor the teaching of such values in all of the public schools on the grounds that civil righteousness is vital to the health of the state, which must depend primarily on the goodwill and voluntary obedience of its citizens for the maintenance of law and order. It is not necessary to know who wrote the rules of a game so long as all of the participants in it agree that the rules are necessary to the playing of it and must therefore be obeyed.

The principal objection to the teaching of moral and spiritual values in the public schools is that these values cannot, as a matter of fact, be taught effectively without getting into the question of motivation. Roman Catholics maintain that only the church can speak authoritatively on morals. Lutherans are fearful of any teaching of right conduct that might leave the impression that "good works" justify man in the sight of God. Jews would be obviously disturbed by any such motivation as: "It's the Christian thing to do," or: "This is a Christian country." But children will ask "Why?" and in practice the teacher is more likely to attempt to answer the question than to refer it to the pupil's parents or spiritual adviser. Such attempts, however nobly motivated, are intrusions into matters which cannot be dealt with in a non-sectarian way.

THE STUDY OF RELIGION

It would seem to be impossible to understand any culture, including our own, without trying to determine what religious concerns shaped the pattern of its thought and activity. Yet the absence of religion from the public school curriculum is so conspicuous that the place which it should occupy has come to be known as a "blind spot."

Certain anthropologists and theologians have insisted that man's various religious beliefs can be presented and examined as objectively as his rules of logic or his systems of philosophy. Churchmen and educators have therefore cooperated in seeking ways to bring the objective study of religion into the school curriculum without infringing on religious freedom. The American Council on Education, in its 1948 report,

> contended vigorously for including in the public school program for objective study, religious subject matter wherever it is intrinsically related to a given school discipline. This would mean that the study of literature should take in our religious classics; the study of history should include the religious aspects

of the period studied; the social studies program should provide for visitation and observance of religious institutions as well as those related to business, industry, and social welfare; and so on.[11]

A similar position has been taken by the Educational Policies Commission of the National Education Association:

Although the public schools can not teach denominational beliefs, they can and should teach much useful information about the religious faiths, the important part they have played in establishing the moral and spiritual values of American life, and their role in the story of mankind. The very fact of the variety of religions represented in this country increases the relevance of this suggestion. How many adults could state with reasonable clarity, regardless of agreement or disagreement, what the chief tenets of the various great religious faiths are? How many non-Catholics know what a Catholic believes? How many Catholics really know where Protestant views differ from their own? What are the essential elements of the faith of Islam or of the other major creeds held by the inhabitants of this shrinking world? The unity of our own country, our understanding of the other nations of the world, and respect for the rich religious traditions of all humanity would be enhanced by instruction about religion in the public schools. Like any other teaching in which deep personal emotions are involved, such instruction should, of course, give due consideration to the varying degrees of maturity of the students.[12]

The study document *Relation of Religion to Public Education,* previously referred to, agrees that "the role of religion in contemporary culture is an essential element in general education." [13] It encourages teacher-training institutions to prepare teachers to deal with religious aspects of the various subjects. "Belief in God and in unalienable rights stemming from God," the document asserts, "is taken for granted in our cultural life, and in our public institutions."

The effort to restore some measure of instruction about religion to public schools is fraught with difficulties. Few teachers have had anything comparable to a course in comparative religions. In most cases the courses which they had in college did not prepare them to teach the religious classics, to explain the religious aspects of historical periods, to outline the chief tenets of the various great religious faiths. Moreover, objectivity is a difficult thing to attain even in matters where emotions are not involved. What is objective fact to one man seems mere denominational opinion to another. The Roman Catholic Church would almost certainly oppose teaching "about" religion in the public schools, and it is possible that other churches — especially those of a conservative Protestant orientation — would do so also. Attempts to deal with these objections by providing for exemption for those who object may be interpreted as admission that even its champions recognize teaching "about" religion as a trespass into the area of conscience.

Presenting the facts of religion and discussing its role in human culture is perhaps less difficult in the high school than in the elementary school and could perhaps be done in such a way as not to violate the principle of voluntarism. The high school student is more mature than is the elementary school pupil, and the secondary curriculum provides more points of contact for the consideration of religion and its influence on individuals, communities, and nations. Moreover, the diversity of the high school curriculum allows for the possibility of elective courses and their corollary, nonattendance, without embarrassment.

RELEASED TIME, DISMISSED TIME,
SHARED TIME

The almost unanimous insistence of the constituencies of the public schools that pupils be given an appreciation of moral and spiritual values has for a long time conflicted with an equally strong insistence that the schools avoid even the appearance of sectarian indoctrination. Educators, recognizing their responsibility to "the whole child," have at the same time been aware of constitutional and legal limitations on what they can do in the way of meeting the spiritual needs of public school pupils. In an attempt to meet these needs without subjecting the schools to charges of sectarian teaching, a growing number of communities have experimented with arrangements under which some portion of the child's school time is "released" to the churches.

While the several variations on the "released time" arrangement do not admit of precise definition, the two most common are "released time" and "dismissed time." A typical released-time plan provides for pupils being excused from regular school programs during school hours on certain days in order to attend classes in religion taught by representatives of their own denominations. Usually attendance records are kept, and nonparticipating pupils are kept busy with other activities in their regular classrooms. Under the "dismissed time" plan, all of the pupils in the same grade or class are excused at the same time — typically the last afternoon period one day a week — and those who wish to then attend a religion class taught by representatives of their own denominations.

In the early days of these experiments the schools themselves frequently made space available for these weekday religion classes. In its decision in the McCollum case, however, the United States Supreme Court ruled that the use of tax-supported public school buildings for this purpose is in violation of the First Amendment and therefore unconstitutional.[14] The court also declared the enforcement of compulsory-attendance requirements for religion classes unconstitutional. Four years later the court reviewed a New York City plan which provided for religious instruction on school time but in buildings away from the school.[15] Under this plan, parents had to authorize their children to attend, and the churches maintained attendance records. This plan was upheld because public school rooms were not used and public funds were not expended. The court went out of its way to declare that "when the state encourages religious instruction or cooperates with religious authorities by adjusting the schedule of public events to sectarian needs, it follows the best of our traditions." The minority opinion held, however, that an element of coercion was still involved.

It is estimated that between a million and a half and two

million Protestant children are receiving religious education on time shared by the public schools.[16] The typical arrangement provides for one period of religious instruction a week, conducted off the school premises and under the complete supervision of the churches. Advocates of the "dismissed time" arrangement assert that it not only supplements the Sunday school but gives religion its proper emphasis in the educational life of the child. They believe that the courses can be so planned as to supplement some of the school subjects, such as the social studies, and thus be more effective than they have been in the past. They also maintain that weekday religious classes reach children who would not ordinarily be brought within the scope of Sunday school activities.

Critics of released- and dismissed-time programs contend that they are in themselves violations of the principle of separation of church and state and that they constitute an opening wedge for more serious violations. Besides, they argue, such arrangements defeat their own stated purposes; the lack of high-quality instructional material and the impression which such arrangements may give children, that religion is something "tacked on" to the curriculum, can do positive damage to religion and the church.

There are other criticisms of these programs which betray an aggressively secularistic orientation. Such criticisms are directed not so much at the arrangements themselves as at the very idea of sectarian religious instruction. It is alleged that such instruction, by its very nature, emphasizes religious differences and is thus a divisive influence in our society; that in many cases it encourages religious prejudice, particularly anti-Semitism; and that, in any case, the pupil's time could be spent more profitably on subjects taught in the regular school curriculum than on religion.

A substantial number of Protestant denominations have expressed themselves in favor of released-time classes. The Lutheran Church — Missouri Synod, for example, which operates the largest Protestant parochial school system, has actively encouraged the program. Its Board of Parish Education recommended to the denomination's 1947 convention: "Where released-time instruction is permitted, our Church should seize the opportunity to make use of this additional time for religious instruction." The Synod went on record as encouraging its congregations to develop this part-time agency for Christian education and took the same position at each subsequent convention.[17]

Both released time and dismissed time presuppose that the child's educational working day belongs to the school, which may then, if it chooses, allot a portion of the day to other institutions for other purposes. The very recent suggestion of a "shared time" arrangement presupposes that the child's working day belongs to his Creator, in whose representatives — i. e., the child's parents — its allocation is properly vested. This means that at their discretion the parents may choose to make use of the services of a variety of institutions in the education and nurture of their children, also during the school day.

"Shared time" recognizes the existence of public schools and church schools side by side. The courses to be offered in each church school would be determined by its supporting constituency. Thus one school might offer only courses in the Bible or in religious doctrine. Another school might offer courses in religion, in literature, in history, in civics. In either case the child would take as much of his work as his parents chose in the church school and the rest of his work in the public school. He would thus be enrolled simultaneously in a church school and in a public school. Some adherents of the "shared time" idea would not limit it to the church and the public school; they would allow for other agencies, also, to offer courses in which, at the discretion of parents, the child might be enrolled. Thus a labor union or a chamber of commerce might offer a course in economics. The American Legion might offer a course in civics. In any case the parents would decide what courses their children would take and where they would take them.

Under the "shared time" proposal the public schools would

continue to receive tax support from the whole citizenry. Other educational agencies would have to finance their own programs. The advantage to the churches of the "shared time" arrangement would be that they could offer substitute courses under their own direction in areas where they believe theological differences strongly affect value judgments, without having to support a whole program of education parallel to that of the public schools, much of which — such as reading, arithmetic, art, and geography — by its very nature seems to be nonreligious.

It is difficult to envision the practical workings of the shared-time arrangement. The single problem of coordinating class schedules, for instance, so that children from perhaps half a dozen nonpublic schools could take a specific course at a specific time would seem to be a formidable one. Even more vexing would be the problem of assuring that the child in a nonpublic school was receiving adequate instruction from a qualified teacher in courses which, whatever their religious implications, are also deemed to be essential to training in good citizenship. Perhaps most troublesome of all is the question of how to allow for the presence of so many cooks without ruining the educational broth. Well-structured curricula provide for continuity from course to course and from year to year. Without the most meticulous co-ordination of work among all of the educational agencies involved in a shared-time arrangement the educational program could become a kind of uncoordinated arrangement with no clear goals and with no logical progression in the learning process.

LUTHERAN VIEWS ON RELIGION
IN THE PUBLIC SCHOOLS

The polity of the Lutheran bodies in the United States and Canada does not permit them to give definitive answers to questions which are not clearly answered in the Scriptures or the historic Lutheran Confessions. Neither the Scriptures nor the Confessions speak directly to the problem of education in a religiously pluralistic state. They do, however, speak to certain questions which bear on that problem, and it may be assumed that the answers which they give provide an area of consensus from which individual Lutherans and Lutheran bodies approach the problem. Some of these areas of consensus are the following:

1. "The power of the Church and the civil power must not be confounded" (Augsburg Confession, Art. XXVIII, par. 12). There is a "difference between the power of the Church and the power of the sword," and "both of them, because of God's commandment, are to be held in reverence and honor, as the chief blessings of God on earth" (ibid., par. 4). Lutherans therefore concede to the state a right in the area of education to ensure public order, national security, and intelligent participation in public affairs by requiring the kind of education which in its judgment will produce good citizens. Lutherans do not conceive of the state as a mere handmaiden of the church but as an agency possessing God-given authority in its own area equal to, but different from, the authority which the church possesses in its proper area.

2. Subject only to the limitation, "We ought to obey God rather than men" (Acts 5:29), Christians are to "be subject to every ordinance of man for the Lord's sake" (1 Peter 2:13). Unless it can be shown that the First Amendment to the Constitution and the judicial interpretations which have broadened its meaning to imply a "wall of separation between church and state" interfere with their obligation of obedience to God, Christians are obliged to be subject also to these ordinances of man for the Lord's sake. It is not therefore permissible for the Christian to disobey these ordinances or to attempt to circumvent them by subterfuge. It is permissible for him to seek to have them changed either by constitutional amendment or by attempting to persuade the courts to reinterpret them.

3. There is something approaching a universal moral consensus among men which is not the peculiar teaching of any denomination or even of Christianity. As St. Paul says: "The Gentiles, which have not the Law, do by nature the things contained in the Law" (Rom. 2:14). The demands and prohibitions of this Law can be taught by Christian and non-Christian alike as "rules of the game" which, however much men may

disagree about their origin, are necessary for good order in society. Questions of the authorship of these rules or of the motives which should prompt men to obey them are, however, religious questions and must be referred to religious organizations.

4. The apostolic command: "Be ye not unequally yoked together with unbelievers" (2 Cor. 6:14), clearly implies, in the area of education, that there are occasions when the Christian cannot in good conscience participate in rites or activities which require a false or distorted confession of his faith. He cannot, for instance, join in a prayer which is addressed by implication to "whatever god may be." He cannot join with non-Christians in addressing God as "Father" when the circumstances imply a denial of Jesus Christ as the "Son." By the same token, Christian charity forbids him to put the non-Christian in the position of either having to assent to what he does not believe to be true or to make an embarrassing scene by dissenting.

5. Our Lord's words: "He that is not with Me is against Me; and he that gathereth not with Me scattereth abroad" (Matt. 12:30), would seem to leave no room for the argument which is often advanced by good people that education can be religiously neutral. Taken in their strict sense, they would seem to say that any education which is not specifically Christian is, at least in some sense, anti-Christian. But the fact that non-Christian education is in itself anti-Christian does not mean that it is the worst alternative among sub-Christian alternatives. In the area of education, as in every other area of life, the practical choice is often limited to a number of objectionable alternatives, and it is morally defensible to choose the alternative which is least objectionable. Thus individual Christians may judge a non-Christian educational system to be less objectionable than a system which attempted to force or insinuate Christian teaching into the children of non-Christian parents.

6. The First Amendment, which Lutherans consider themselves bound to obey as a lawful ordinance of man, cuts both ways. Too often the amendment is invoked to justify a secularization of education which in effect relegates religion to the

position of private opinion, having no relevance to the questions, problems, and techniques which are the concern of the schools. Wrongly understood, the assertion that education is concerned with "the whole child" poses a threat to the First Amendment at least as serious as any posed by attempts to favor religion. Lutheran theology is as opposed to the idea of an omnicompetent state as it is to the idea of an omnicompetent church.

7. That a Christian may not want or need particular services provided by the state does not relieve him of the obligation to support them with his prayers, his taxes, and his active participation in the political process, if these services are required by considerations of the general welfare. Those Lutherans who maintain their own schools claim no legal or moral right to exemption from taxes for the support of the public system, nor do they seek to justify the existence of their schools by undermining confidence in, or respect for, the public system.

Outside these areas of consensus, Lutherans differ on many of the particular questions of church-state relations in the area of education. The Missouri Synod, for instance, has been committed for well over a century to the ideal of parochial schools. With only a few exceptions its responsible spokesmen have opposed any proposal for government assistance to its schools. In contrast, the churches adhering to the National Lutheran Council — with a few exceptions in the premerger American Lutheran Church — have not considered it desirable to establish their own schools, and some churchmen in the NLC see in the parochial school a divisive influence in American society. Lutherans generally have opposed all attempts to introduce sectarian teaching and specifically religious rites into the schools but have not disapproved of such practices as Bible reading without comment, Christmas observances, and the pledge of allegiance to the flag. The major Lutheran church bodies have strongly endorsed released-time and dismissed-time plans. The shared-time plan is still too new to have been given consideration by any Lutheran church body.

II

CHURCH SCHOOLS AND
THE CHURCH-STATE ISSUE

Arthur L. Miller

Nonpublic school enrollments have risen considerably in the past 20 years, not only in the aggregate but also in proportion to the total school population. The following summary of enrollments from kindergarten to grade 12 will serve to point up this development:

	Total Enrollment All Schools	Enrollment Public Schools	Enrollment Nonpublic Schools
1939–40	28,044,589	25,433,542 (90.69%)	2,611,047 (9.31%)
1949–50		25,111,427 (88.14%)	3,380,139 (11.86%)
1959–60*		36,200,000 (86.8%)	6,500,500 (13.2%)

* Estimates, U. S. Office of Education

Roman Catholic schools account for about 92 percent of the nation's nonpublic school enrollment; Lutheran schools, chiefly those of the Missouri Synod, for another 2 percent; nondenominational schools for about 4 percent. In the light of these percentages it is easy to see why questions of public vs. nonpublic education are often stated in the form of criticisms or defenses of the Roman Catholic school system and the educational philosophy underlying it. That Protestant churches — particularly the Lutheran — justify the maintenance of their schools on grounds which are not identical with those of the Roman Catholic Church is understandably too little recognized. The rationale of The Lutheran Church — Missouri Synod has been treated at length in various articles in *Lutheran Education* and the *Concordia Theological Monthly*.

There is also the widespread misconception that the nonpublic school, particularly the church-supported school, is an entirely autonomous agency, free from all public controls and answerable only to its own constituency. The fact of the matter is that the state exercises a large measure of control, direct and indirect, over the nonpublic school and assists its work with a wide range of benefits and services.

GOVERNMENT CONTROLS OVER
NONPUBLIC SCHOOLS

The broad areas of proper state control over nonpublic schools have never been subjects of significant dispute. They are referred to as matters of consensus in a unanimous opinion of the United States Supreme Court in the case of *Pierce* v. *Society of Sisters:*

> No question is raised concerning the power of the State reasonably to regulate all schools, to inspect, supervise, and examine them, their teachers and pupils, to require that all children of proper age attend some school, that teachers shall be of good moral character and patriotic disposition, that certain studies plainly essential to good citizenship must be taught, and that nothing be taught which is manifestly inimical to the public welfare.[18]

The constitutional question before the court in this case was the question of the right of private individuals and private corporations to maintain schools. The court's ratification of this right was grounded in the doctrine of the fundamental right of the parent to direct and control the education of his children. But the court takes for granted that the government, too, has its rights in education, certain of them deriving from the police power, which is an essential attribute of government, and certain others deriving from the "general welfare" clause in the Preamble of the Constitution. In its exercise of the police power, government may require that "teachers be of good moral character and patriotic disposition" and that "nothing be taught which is manifestly inimical to the public welfare." Under the general-welfare clause, government may require that the schools train children for good citizenship, and to that end it may regulate, inspect, and examine the schools, their teachers, and their pupils; may require that all children of school age attend some school; and may require that certain studies which it believes essential to good citizenship be included in the school curriculum.

While the general-welfare clause may be interpreted to imply some proper concern of the federal government in education, the ownership and control of public schools is reserved to the states.

Federal government intervention in questions affecting the public schools most commonly takes the form of court decisions in cases where questions of the rights of citizens are involved. Thus, when the people of Oregon adopted an initiative measure which would have required all children between the ages of 8 and 16 to attend a public school, the Supreme Court, in the case of *Pierce* v. *Society of Sisters,* held the measure unconstitutional, asserting that "the fundamental theory of liberty upon which all governments in this Union repose excludes any general power of the State to standardize its children by forcing them to accept instruction from public teachers only." This decision has become a kind of magna charta of the parochial school, the legal basis of its right to exist.

When, on the other hand, the American Socialist Party challenged the constitutionality of a New York licensing law stipulating that no license would be granted to any school which proposed to give instruction in the doctrine that organized government shall be overthrown by force, violence, or other unlawful means, the Supreme Court held that the statute was a valid exercise of the police power.[19] Similarly, the court has held that the state has power to impose minimum secular standards on all schools.[20] However, that there are limits to the state's right to prescribe in curricular matters was made clear in the historic case of *Meyer* v. *Nebraska.* Robert T. Meyer was tried and convicted in the District Court for Hamilton County, Nebr., of having violated a state law which provided:

> Section 1. No person, individually or as a teacher, shall in any private, denominational, parochial, or public school, teach any subject to any person in any language other than the English language.

> Section 2. Languages, other than the English language, may be taught as languages only after a pupil shall have attained and successfully passed the eighth grade as evidenced by a certificate of graduation issued by the county superintendent of the county in which the child resides.[21]

Meyer's conviction was upheld by the state supreme court, where the law was declared constitutional. But on appeal to the

United States Supreme Court the law was declared unconstitutional, Justice McReynolds asserting for the court:

> The problem for our determination is whether the statute, as construed and applied, unreasonably infringes the liberty guaranteed to the plaintiff in error by the 14th Amendment. "No State . . . shall deprive any person of life, liberty, or property without due process of law."
>
> That the State may do much, go very far, indeed, in order to improve the quality of its citizens, physically, mentally, and morally is clear; but the individual has certain fundamental rights which must be respected. The protection of the Constitution extends to all — to those who speak other languages as well as to those born with English on the tongue. Perhaps it would be highly advantageous if all had ready understanding of our ordinary speech, but this cannot be coerced by methods which conflict with the Constitution — a desirable end cannot be promoted by prohibited means.[22]

Thus, so far as the federal government is concerned, the relationship between church and state in education is primarily a matter of state concern except in cases where the national welfare or safety is at issue or where there is a question of the violation of rights under the Constitution.

Subject to these limited areas of federal review, the states have exercised varying degrees of control over the nonpublic schools. In general this control is exercised indirectly by establishing standards which schools must meet in order to qualify their pupils to satisfy the state's compulsory-attendance law or to enter high school without examination. Typical of state regulatory statutes is the Rhode Island law, which provides:

> For the purposes of this Chapter the school committee shall approve a private school or private instruction only when it complies with the following requirements, namely: That the period of attendance of the pupils in such school or on such private instruction is substantially equal to that required by law in public schools; that registers are kept and returns to the school committee, the superintendent of schools, truant officers, and the director of education in relation to the attendance of pupils, are made the same as by the public schools;

that reading, writing, geography, arithmetic, the history of the
United States, the history of Rhode Island, and the principles
of American government shall be taught in the English language substantially to the same extent as such subjects are
required to be taught in the public schools, and that the teaching of the English language and of other subjects indicated
herein shall be thorough and efficient . . .[23]

Briefly summarized, the Rhode Island statute claims for the state
the right to determine the length of the school year, to prescribe
specific courses of instruction, to require records and reports, and
(by implication) to ascertain whether the instruction is "thorough
and efficient." Few states are so specific in the definition of their
regulatory powers. Most states merely require in general terms
that the education given in parochial schools be equivalent to
that offered in the public schools. "Supervision" in many cases
involves nothing more than the registration of private schools
with the state department of education.

There are other states, however, which require the nonpublic
schools to meet all or most of the standards set for the public
schools, and authorize representatives of the state department
of education to ensure compliance. Thus the school laws of
Michigan state: "It is the intent of this act that the sanitary conditions of such nonpublic schools, the courses of study therein,
and the qualifications of the teachers thereof shall be of the same
standard as provided by the general school laws of the State." [24]
Nebraska not only requires that "all private, denominational, and
parochial schools shall have adequate equipment and supplies"
but also provides:

The county superintendent in first class school districts, or the
superintendent of schools in all other districts, where any private, denominational, or parochial school is located, shall inspect such schools and report to the proper officers any evidence
of the use of any textbooks or of any activities, instruction,
or propaganda therein subversive to American institutions and
republican form of government or good citizenship or of failure
to observe any of the provisions of sections 79-1701 to 79-1707.
The superintendent of public instruction (commissioner of edu-

cation) shall require the several county superintendents and superintendents of schools to make such inspections at least twice a year, and the school officers of such schools and the teachers giving instruction therein are required to permit such inspection and assist and cooperate in the making of the same.[25]

Furthermore, any state in the exercise of its police power may establish and enforce building standards, zoning regulations, and fire-prevention rules for the nonpublic school as well as for the public school. It may order schools closed in times of epidemic or civil disorder. It may requisition the use of school property in times of flood or other disaster.

Thus it is hardly in accord with the facts to say that the nonpublic school is a free and autonomous institution. It is subject to numerous public controls. That many states have not chosen to exercise the powers which they possess does not invalidate the general statement that the states may, if they choose, exercise almost as effective control over the nonpublic schools as over the public schools in all matters relating to their specifically educational function and to their functions as places of public assembly.

GOVERNMENT ASSISTANCE TO NONPUBLIC SCHOOLS

According to the First Amendment to the Constitution and the explicit prohibitions in state constitutions, direct financial support of sectarian schools is forbidden. Except under specific arrangements or certain conditions in special cases, this same prohibition extends to privately controlled schools. However, in all states the properties of religious and educational institutions are exempt from taxation, and in some states certain types of aid are provided to pupils attending nonpublic schools for certain auxiliary services such as pupil transportation, health services, textbooks, and school lunches. Moreover, teachers in denominational schools who are classified by their denominations as ministers of religion are exempted from service under the Selective Service Act.

It would seem to be flogging a dead horse to raise the question of the propriety of exempting religious and educational institutions from real estate and personal property taxes. The practice is rooted in a tradition which antedates the Constitution and is specifically reaffirmed in several state constitutions. Only occasionally does anyone challenge the legality or constitutionality of the practice, and then usually in cases where the properties of such institutions are used for some nonreligious, noneducational, income-producing purpose. But it was not always so. James Madison criticized a proposal in Kentucky to "exempt Houses of Worship from taxes" as a case of "encroachment by Ecclesiastical Bodies" which violated the constitutional "separation between religion and government." [26] President Grant in a message to Congress in 1875 noted that the value of tax-exempt church property had increased in a quarter of a century from $83,000,000 to approximately a billion dollars and expressed fears that taxpayers would not indefinitely put up with the exemption of this property from taxation. He therefore suggested "the taxation of all property equally, whether church or corporation, exempting only the last resting place of the dead, and possibly, with proper restrictions, church edifices." [27]

Despite attitudes as critical as these and despite the self-evident fact that the exemption of religious and educational institutions from taxation constitutes a kind of subsidy, in most states property passes from the tax roll whenever title to it passes to a religious, educational, or charitable institution. In some states (e. g., New York) mere ownership of property by such organizations does not in itself furnish grounds for exemption; it must also be used for religious, educational, or charitable purposes. Attempts to apply this criterion of use in states where it had not previously been applied meet with strong opposition, particularly from the Roman Catholic hierarchy.

With the growing importance of the income tax as a source of state and federal revenue, exemptions for gifts to religious, educational, and charitable purposes have come to constitute another very sizable subsidy to churches and church schools. Arguments over the constitutionality of such exemptions bog down in an impasse between those who contend, on the one hand, that they breach the "wall of separation" and those who, on the other hand, contend that government's power to tax is a power to destroy and could thus effectively prohibit the free exercise of religion by draining off the funds which citizens have available for voluntary giving.

Another indirect but very significant form of government assistance to parochial schools has been the granting of exemption from military service under the National Selective Service System to those teachers who are classified by their denominations as ministers of religion. The chief denominational beneficiary of this exemption is The Lutheran Church — Missouri Synod, whose male teachers, unlike most male teachers in Roman Catholic schools, are not members of religious orders. This exemption raises no constitutional question since it is not based on any constitutional pronouncement with respect to church and state but on the power of Congress to determine where individuals or groups of individuals can best serve the national interest in time of war or national emergency. The courts have repeatedly refused to review congressional decisions in these areas even where violations of constitutional rights were alleged.

Of the more direct forms of government assistance to nonpublic schools, the most common are transportation of children to nonpublic schools, various types of health service, the provision of textbooks, and the subsidization of school lunch programs. All of these have occasioned considerable controversy.

Transportation of Children

The past quarter century has seen a growing trend toward school consolidation. As one rural school after another has been closed, more and more children in rural areas and in places of less than 10,000 population have depended on the school bus to take them to the nearest consolidated school. The most recent figures available indicate that almost 30 percent of the nation's public school population in elementary and secondary schools are transported by school bus.[28] In predominantly rural areas the percentage is even higher.

With the large-scale development of pupil transportation to public schools came a demand for similar service for pupils attending nonpublic schools. At the present time the statutes of 16 states — Alabama, California, Illinois, Indiana, Kansas, Kentucky, Louisiana, Maryland, Massachusetts, Michigan, New Hampshire, New Jersey, New Mexico, New York, Oregon, and Rhode Island — authorize free transportation for children attending nonpublic schools. Typical of such statutes is that of Illinois, which provides:

> If children who attend any school other than a public school reside on or along the highway constituting the regular route of any public school bus or conveyance provided by any school district for transporting pupils to and from the public schools, the school board of such district shall afford transportation, without cost, for such children from their homes or from some point on the regular route nearest or most easily accessible to their homes, to such school, or to the point on such regular route which is nearest or most easily accessible to such school.[29]

A number of these 16 states (e. g., Kentucky) provide that the cost of this transportation shall come out of funds other than educational budgets, thus avoiding any implication of direct assistance to sectarian schools. Transportation paid for out of general funds can be justified on the grounds that it is a benefit to the children (rather than the schools which they attend) or that it is a means of protecting children against the hazards of walking on busy roads. Several of these 16 states limit free transportation of nonpublic school children to those who attend state-approved schools.

The policy of transporting nonpublic school pupils has been attacked in a number of state courts. In three states — California, Maryland, and New Jersey — the policy has been upheld. In seven — Delaware, Missouri, New York, Oklahoma, South Dakota, Washington, and Wisconsin — it has been ruled unconstitutional. Following the decision in New York, the state constitution was amended to permit the practice as an exception to the prohibition respecting the use of public funds for sectarian purposes.

One of the basic decisions on the bus transportation issue arose out of litigation over a New Jersey law which provided:

Whenever in any district there are children living remote from any school house, the Board of Education of the district may make rules and contracts for the transportation of such children to and from school, including the transportation of such children to and from school other than a public school, except as is operated for a profit in whole or in part.

When any school district provides any transportation for public school children to and from school, transportation from any point in such established school routes to any other point in such established school routes shall be supplied to school children residing in such school district and going to and from school other than a public school, except such school as is operated for profit in whole or in part.[30]

The constitutionality of this law was contested before the New Jersey Supreme Court by a taxpayer, Arch R. Everson. The State Supreme Court held that the legislature could not constitutionally authorize such payments. The New Jersey Court of Errors and Appeals, however, reversed this decision, holding that the law violated neither the state nor the federal constitution. On appeal to the United States Supreme Court, the decision of the Court of Appeals was upheld in a five-to-four decision, the majority opinion holding:

The establishment of religion clause of the First Amendment means at least this: Neither a State nor the Federal Government can set up a church. Neither can pass laws which aid one religion, aid all religions, or prefer one religion over another. Neither can force nor influence a person to go to or remain away from church against his will or force him to profess a belief or disbelief in any religion. No person can be punished for entertaining or professing religious beliefs or disbeliefs, for church attendance or non-attendance. No tax in any amount, large or small, can be levied to support any religious activities or institutions, whatever they may be called, or whatever form they may adopt to teach or practice religion . . .[31]

Finding nothing in the New Jersey statute which was in conflict with these limitations, the court then went on to point out that other language of the amendment commands that New Jersey cannot hamper its citizens in the free exercise of their own religion. Consequently, it cannot exclude individual Catholics, Lutherans, Mohammedans, Baptists, Jews, Methodists, Nonbelievers, Presbyterians, or the members of any other faith, because of their faith or lack of it, from receiving the benefits of public welfare legislation . . .[32]

The court ruled that New Jersey was doing no more than providing a general program to help parents get their children, regardless of religion, safely and expeditiously to and from accredited schools and for that reason held that the state had not exceeded its constitutional power.

It is interesting to note that six states which have similar laws — Illinois, Indiana, Louisiana, Massachusetts, Michigan, and New York — filed briefs in support of the constitutionality of the New Jersey law. No state filed an opposing brief, although attention was called to the fact that in at least seven states laws similar to the New Jersey law had been held invalid. It is even more noteworthy that the supreme courts of two states — Washington and Missouri — later held laws providing for the free transportation of children attending nonpublic schools unconstitutional despite the decision in the Everson case.

Health Services

A number of states have enacted legislation empowering their state departments of education and/or health departments to administer and supervise health and safety programs in nonpublic as well as public schools. The extent of this authority varies considerably from state to state, but among the powers thus granted are the following:

1. To conduct physical examinations of children attending nonpublic schools (New Hampshire, New York, Pennsylvania, Rhode Island);

2. To insure that persons suffering from communicable tuberculosis are not employed in public or nonpublic schools (Illinois, Maine, Massachusetts);

3. To insure that nonpublic school buildings meet minimum health and safety standards (Maine, Michigan);

4. To see that fire drills are held in nonpublic schools (Oregon, Pennsylvania, Rhode Island);

5. To establish school safety patrols in nonpublic schools (Washington.)[33]

Free Textbooks

In the states of Louisiana, Mississippi, and New Mexico free textbooks are provided by law for the use of the schoolchildren of the state, including those enrolled in nonpublic schools. The Louisiana law provides:

> The state board of education shall exercise administrative control and supervision over the adoption, distribution, and use of free textbooks as provided by R. S. 17:351 through 17:353, and shall adopt such rules and regulations governing their use by schools, parish [i. e., county] school boards, and superintendents of education as may be necessary. The state board of education shall adopt lists of basal textbooks. In its administration of textbook regulations, the said state board shall enforce uniform use of the books from the adopted lists . . .[34]

This statute was challenged as unconstitutional but was upheld by the court for the following reasons: "(a) the law did not provide for the purchase of books for sectarian schools; (b) by providing for free books for the children of the state the law was obviously enacted for the benefit of the children and the 'resulting benefit of the state'; (c) the schools are not the beneficiaries of the statute; (d) the books furnished by the state are not sectarian books; (e) none, it is to be expected, would be adapted to religious instruction."[35]

The issue was appealed to the Supreme Court of the United States, which affirmed the decision of the Louisiana court in the following words:

> Viewing the statute as having the effect thus attributed to it, we cannot doubt that the taxing power of the State is exerted for a public purpose. The legislation does not segregate private schools or their pupils as its beneficiaries or attempt to inter-

fere with any matters of exclusively private concern. Its interest
is education, broadly; its method, comprehensive. Individual
interests are aided only as the common interest is safeguarded.[36]

The Mississippi statute was also subject to a suit brought by
taxpayers against the practice. The court again upheld the
statute. The court said:

> The religion to which children of school age adhere is not sub-
> ject to control by the state; but the children themselves are
> subject to its control. If the pupil may fulfill its duty to the state
> by attending a parochial school it is difficult to see why the
> state may not fulfill its duty to the pupil by encouraging it
> "by all suitable means." The state is under duty to ignore the
> child's creed, but not its need. It cannot control what one
> child may think. The state which allows the pupil to subscribe
> to any religious creed should not, because of his exercise of
> this right, proscribe him from benefits common to all. . . . The
> narrow construction contended for by complainants would
> compel the pupil to surrender use of his books when and
> because he elected to transfer from a public school to a quali-
> fied parochial school. Such would constitute a denial of equal
> privileges on sectarian grounds.[37]

An earlier attempt to distribute free textbooks to parochial
school pupils in New York was not upheld by the court. The
argument that such textbooks were a benefit to pupils and not
aid to sectarian schools was countered with the following statement by the court:

> The school is not the building and its equipment; it is the
> organization, the union of all the elements in the organization,
> to furnish education in some branch of learning — the arts or
> sciences or literature. It is the institution and the teachers and
> scholars together, that make it up. The pupils are part of the
> school. . . . It seems to us to be giving a strained and unusual
> meaning to words if we hold that the books and the ordinary
> school supplies, when furnished for the use of pupils, is a fur-
> nishing to the pupils, and not a furnishing in aid or main-
> tenance of a school of learning. It seems very plain that such
> furnishing is at least indirectly in aid of the institution, and

that, if not in actual violation of the words, it is in violation of the true intent and meaning of the Constitution and in consequence equally unconstitutional.[38]

The states distributing textbooks to pupils attending non-public schools construe this as an aid to the child rather than as aid to the school. This is termed the "child benefit" theory.

School Lunches

One of the best examples of an attempt to put the "child benefit" theory into practice is the National School Lunch Act (Public Law 396, ch. 281) which provides for the distribution of certain surplus agricultural commodities to the schools. The purpose of this act is to improve the general level of nutrition among school-age children. The schools enter the picture not so much as the recipients of these commodities as the channels through which they may most conveniently be distributed to the children.

Law and practice regarding the eligibility of nonpublic schools to benefit under this act vary from state to state. In three states — Indiana, Oregon, and Vermont — the law specifically authorizes their departments of education to accept and direct the disbursement of funds appropriated under this act to all non-profit schools eligible to receive them. In 10 other states the statutes are construed as conferring authority to administer such funds to eligible nonprofit schools. In Pennsylvania and Wisconsin the statutes are construed as applying only to those non-profit schools which are also nonsectarian. In certain other states (e. g., Minnesota) the law does not permit the disbursement of funds under the act to nonprofit private schools or does not permit the matching of federal funds made available by the act.[39]

The two opposing views reflected in these divergencies of practice have been expressed in opinions by the attorneys-general of two neighboring states, Idaho and Wyoming. On Aug. 27, 1946, the attorney-general of Idaho ruled: "Federal monies contributed to a state agency under the National School Lunch Program become public monies of the state upon receipt by the state agency and cannot be distributed to parochial or private schools under the state constitution." Six months later, on April 4, 1947, the attorney-general of Wyoming ruled: "The School Lunch Program is not a direct contribution to the school but merely a general program to promote the health and well-being of the children. Therefore, the state may enter into a contract with the U. S. Department of Agriculture to administer the program in sectarian and private schools." [40] The attorney-general of Massachusetts goes beyond his Wyoming colleague to assert that "even funds appropriated by the Commonwealth for the school lunch program may be used to pay for the lunches of children who attend private or parochial schools since under the theory of the Everson and Cochran cases, the welfare benefits are directed to the child and not to the institution." [41]

Many of the vexing questions that are raised when a particular kind of assistance to education is proposed come down finally to this question: Is the proposed assistance a form of subsidization of sectarian education and thus inimical to freedom of religion, or is it merely a form of assistance to school-children and their parents, channeled through the schools simply because they happen to be the most convenient conduits through which to channel it? The separation of the two elements of this question is easy enough in theory. It is very difficult in practice.

THE PLACE OF THE NONPUBLIC SCHOOL IN AMERICAN EDUCATION

The public school and the nonpublic school have coexisted on the American educational scene for well over a century. Each has had its fervent protagonists and its equally fervent opponents. There have been attempts in the past to legislate the nonpublic school out of existence. More recently there have been attempts, motivated chiefly by a desire to avoid desegregation, to abolish the public school systems in certain states. There seems little likelihood that either the public school or the nonpublic school will in fact disappear from the scene, whether by legislative action or otherwise.

Although the private and church-sponsored school represents the older tradition in American education, the public school has won such overwhelming acceptance in its relatively short history that for many people the public school is the "normal," or "American," educational institution and the parochial school is to greater or lesser degree an "offbeat" or possibly not quite American institution which is looked upon with some degree of suspicion. Criticism of the public school seldom raises the question of its right to exist. Criticism of the private or parochial school often raises the question of its right to exist.

The coexistence of these two kinds of school has therefore been made possible by the general acceptance of certain broad areas of consensus. It has been attended by certain tensions, not all of which have been resolved. The major areas of consensus would seem to be the following: (1) that the nonpublic school has a legal right to exist; (2) that the state has a legal right to supervise at least certain aspects of the administration and work of the nonpublic school; and (3) that both systems benefit from the cultivation of the friendliest possible relations between them. The major point of tension, apart from the fundamental question of whether the nonpublic school has a right to exist at all, would seem to lie in the area of state support for the nonpublic school.

Legal Rights

Although education in the United States is a power reserved to the states and although it is conceded that the state may control the education of its own citizens, the legal right of the nonpublic school to exist has been commonly accepted by the American people. This right has been buttressed by numerous court decisions which in effect establish nonpublic schools as a basic feature of American education. Five court decisions have been especially significant in establishing this right against the efforts of hostile individuals to abolish the nonpublic schools or to set arbitrary and unreasonable restrictions on their operations. These five are the Meyer Case, the Pierce Case, the Farrington Case, the Packer Collegiate Case, and the West Case.

Reference has already been made to the Meyer Case and the Pierce Case. For our present purposes the significance of the Meyer Case is that, in forbidding arbitrary and unreasonable restrictions on the curriculum of nonpublic schools, the Supreme Court of the United States did not even question the right of such schools to exist. In the Pierce Case the court in a unanimous decision excluded "any general power of the State to standardize its children by forcing them to accept instruction from public school teachers only" and asserted "the liberty of parents and guardians to direct the upbringing and education of children under their control" as a matter of "right, coupled with high duty."

The Farrington Case *(Farrington* v. *Tokushige)* involved an attempt of the governor of Hawaii to place the privately controlled foreign-language schools under strict and detailed government control. The court held that no facts had been presented to warrant such extreme regulations which in effect entrusted the control of such schools to public officials. While this case did not involve religious schools, the effect of the court's decision was to extend strong constitutional protection to nonpublic schools against possible state legislative or executive action that would be inimical to parochial schools.

The Packer Collegiate Case arose out of a paragraph in the New York educational law which provided that no organization or individual other than public school authorities or an established group might establish or maintain a nursery school, kindergarten, or elementary school unless the school was registered under regulations prescribed by the Board of Regents. The New York courts found this act unconstitutional because it attempted to delegate legislative power to the Commissioner of Education as the chief administrative officer of the Board of Regents. In the course of its decision the court said:

> This is no small technical matter we deal with here. Private schools have a constitutional right to exist, and parents have a constitutional right to send their children to such schools. The Legislature, under the police power, has a limited right to regulate such schools in the public interest. Such being the fundamental law of the subject, it would be intolerable for the Legislature to hand over to any official or group of officials, an unlimited, unrestrained, undefined power to make such regu-

lations as he or they should desire, and to grant or refuse
licenses to such schools depending on their compliance with
such regulations.[42]

The West Case was an attempt by Emory West and other
heirs of one L. J. Murray to terminate a testamentary trust created
in Murray's will for the purpose of "establishing and forever
maintaining and conducting a permanent common school for
the education in the common school branches of an English
education of the poor white children of Buncombe County,
North Carolina, living anywhere within said county." It was
the contention of heirs that the expansion of the state school
system and the enlargement of opportunity to benefit from it
adequately met every educational demand of indigent children
provided for in the will and therefore destroyed the object of
the trust. In deciding against the heirs the court stated:

> The State maintains no monopoly in the education of its
> citizens. It neither requires nor expects that its youth receive
> tuition exclusively within the State-sponsored public schools.
> The compulsory attendance law recognizes the private schools
> teaching comparable branches and gives credit for attendance
> there. Neither the school law nor the educational policy of
> the State excludes private educational enterprise patently con-
> ducive to the public welfare. The reasons are cogent and too
> numerous for discussion here. So long as there remains the
> liberty to attend the schools it provides, there remains the
> *raison d'être* of a charitable trust of this character, no matter
> how adequate the public school system provided by the State
> may become.[43]

The North Carolina court in 1944 thus again emphasized that
the state maintains no monopoly in education and recognizes
private schools teaching comparable branches.

In view of these multiple court decisions, it seems clear that
the courts have established the rights of parents in the choice
of educational agencies as included in the general exercise of
their civil liberties. The rights of private and parochial schools
have thus been defended by the courts, and there are legal
precedents that buttress the continuation of such rights.

The Right of the State to Regulate and Supervise

The right of the state to regulate and supervise nonpublic schools is another point of common agreement. Since the compulsory-attendance laws of the several states recognize the nonpublic schools as a means of satisfying the attendance requirements of such laws, it is natural that regulations be developed by the state requiring such things as reports, safety and health measures, minimum curriculum requirements, and evidence of teacher competency. In the period 1918 to 1925 there was a definite trend toward increasing state regulation of private schools. Since 1925, however, there has been a decrease in particularized state regulation of nonpublic schools, at least beyond these basic matters.[44]

As in the case of the legal right of a nonpublic school to exist, the right of the state to regulate and supervise nonpublic schools has been stressed in numerous court decisions and state actions. To be sure, this right is limited; it does not entitle the state to set arbitrary regulations or to act arbitrarily in administering them. But subject to these limitations, it is a right which nonpublic school authorities, whether sectarian or nonsectarian, have been willing to concede. With only rare exceptions the nonpublic schools have fully cooperated with the states in maintaining educational programs equivalent to those which are required by state compulsory-education laws.

Friendly Relations Between Public and Nonpublic Schools

Since public and nonpublic educational institutions exist side by side in the United States at all levels of education, it is important that the leaders of both types of institution have an understanding of the nation's total educational effort. This assumes, on the part of the leaders in public education, a recognition of the important role that administrators, teachers, and other leaders of nonpublic education play in shaping the educational opportunities of American youth. At the same time it requires that the leaders of nonpublic education keep in proper perspective an appreciation of the importance of the public education effort at all levels of education.

These several concerns were significantly brought out in an address given by William G. Carr at the 75th-anniversary celebration of Marquette University. Speaking on the topic "The Partnership of the Independent and Public Schools in the Future of America," Carr stated frankly that there existed, among some Roman Catholics and among some public school spokesmen, a spirit of militant hostility and mutual distrust. He argued that such a spirit could only create increasing problems, and he made a plea for considerate restraint, courteous words, and a basic shift in the controversy. He offered the following suggestions to the leaders of the public and nonpublic schools:

1. That the public schools are necessary and respected institutions in these United States and that concern for their improvement and support is a general public responsibility of each citizen.

2. That such terms as "secular" and "pragmatic" as applied to education be restored to their normal descriptive purposes, and that the use of these words as vehicles of abuse and opprobrium be discontinued.

3. That, insofar as schools of any kind are responsible for the imperfections of our society and for evil behavior in general, that responsibility is shared by all schools, unless it can be shown that the graduates of private schools or of public schools are substantially more free of the particular faults than other persons.

4. That when school people disagree — as they surely will — on some basic issues of human life as well as of educational policy and political theory, they endeavor to exchange evidence rather than epithets and endeavor to persuade rather than to wound.

The foregoing suggestions were addressed to the leaders of the nonpublic schools. To leaders of the public schools Carr offered the suggestion that they refrain from such statements as these:

1. That private schools are less democratic and less American than public schools.

2. That individual members of the Catholic church who

attack the public schools are invariably speaking officially for the church as a whole.

3. That Catholics want to destroy the American public-school system.

4. That all the misfortunes of public education are due to the machinations of the Catholic clergy.[45]

Points of Tension Concerning Nonpublic Schools

Large as these areas of consensus may be, there exist a number of problems and points of tension arising out of this dualism of approach to education. Particularly in recent years the whole theory of public education has come under vigorous attack, and both popular and professional magazines and books have shown an inclination to make the public school the scapegoat for everything from Russian space successes to the increase in illegitimate births. These criticisms have sometimes been accompanied by invidious comparisons between allegedly inferior public education and allegedly superior private education.

While most of this criticism has been directed against the public school, the nonpublic school has come in for its share of censure. There are still those, notably James Bryant Conant, former president of Harvard, who consider the nonpublic school a "divisive influence," incompatible with American democracy. The best single catalog of charges that have been leveled against nonpublic education can be found in Anson Phelps Stokes, *Church and State in the United States*, pp. 659, 660. While these criticisms are directed chiefly against Roman Catholic schools, they could in most cases be just as validly (or invalidly) directed against Protestant schools.

The most common objection to church-related elementary and high schools is that they tend to accentuate differences in our society, which is already pluralistic enough, and to create divisiveness. That there is some substance to this charge is self-evident; a minority segment of the school-going population is separated in the nonpublic school from the majority attending public schools. Whether this separation is as undesirable as some allege is another question. Individual liberty presupposes a fair degree of cultural heterogeneity. It is a strange contention that there must be a monopolistic, largely homogeneous educational program in order to foster the personal individualism and the cultural pluralism which are among the glories of a free society. Strangely, this demand for an educational monopoly comes most frequently from persons who on most other matters maintain a liberal position.

A second very common objection to church-related schools is that they weaken public education by fostering among their supporters a hostility or indifference to the public school. It would have to be admitted that there is some substance to this charge also — although there is as yet no strong evidence that the typical Roman Catholic or Lutheran is any less interested in the public schools than is his neighbor who does not support a denominational school. At any rate such attitudes run counter to the official attitude of both the Roman Catholic and the Lutheran churches.

Even less valid is the objection that teachers in nonpublic schools are detached from the mainstream of American life. While this may be partially true of teachers who are members of monastic orders, it hardly applies to most teachers in Protestant schools. Lutheran teachers, for example, are for the most part men and women with families who participate as fully as do most business and professional people in the social and cultural life of the community. Outside a few metropolitan areas they send their children to the public high school, and in most communities they maintain professional contact of one sort or another with their colleagues in the public school system.

Least valid of the criticisms that are directed against the nonpublic schools is the charge that teachers of the church are by their training and by their commitment to a denominational "line" discouraged from independent thinking or a democratic outlook. This supposed narrowness is allegedly reflected in their failure to prepare pupils to discuss impartially and independently the great social and political problems which face the nation.

This charge can be refuted on two counts. The first is of a philosophical or theoretical nature. It is obvious that the real

point at issue here is whether a man can acknowledge any super-
human authority and be credited with intellectual honesty and
loyalty to the ideals of democracy. Lutheran teachers, at least,
are trained in colleges which meet all of the academic standards
of the recognized accrediting associations. Whatever supposed
narrowness of view they may have developed in the course of
their training would therefore presumably have to be ascribed
to their training in Christian doctrine — a criticism which would
logically have to be extended to any Christian who knows and
accepts the teachings of his church. As for commitment to a denominational position, no teacher in any school system is wholly
free to state his private opinions on all matters whatsoever (e. g.,
economic, political, ideological). It could be argued with considerable validity that the Lutheran teacher, bound only to the
authority of the Scriptures, is at least as free as his public-school
colleague to arrive at his own judgments on matters on which
the Scriptures do not speak authoritatively. He may be even
freer from political and social pressures than is the public-school
teacher.

In everyday life this charge is daily refuted by the attitudes
and activities of parochial school graduates, from high federal
and state government officials down to ordinary citizens, who
hold as great a diversity of views on social and political problems as does the citizenry at large. Impartial and independent
discussion is a rare thing at best; there is no evidence to suggest that it is any rarer among graduates of nonpublic schools.

It would seem fair to say that much of the criticism which
has been directed at the parochial school reflects the development of a mystique which has begun to surround the public
school and which carries certain quasi-religious overtones. Thus
a recent pronouncement of the National Education Association
contains the following statements which are in their essence
a confession of faith: "Faith in public education rests ultimately
on two beliefs: that a particular kind of education must be designed to support a particular way of life, and that public education will best support the American way of life." [46]

This statement could obviously be used in support of the

contention that the churches, of all institutions, ought to be most concerned to maintain schools, for every church contends that it is, among other things, inculcating a way of life. The implication of the statement would seem to be that a particular association of ethics and behavior known as "the American way of life" is normative. This is a religious claim and could be accepted only partially and with many reservations by most Protestants, Catholics, and Jews. No one seriously proposes that the state abandon its system of public schools, but exclusive claims of this sort can only lead to misgivings concerning the willingness of the schools to respect the proper spheres of influence of such institutions as the home and the church.

The parochial school permits the achievement of the legitimate objectives of education quite as much as does the public school. It can and does foster love and respect for democracy as a political system without elevating democracy to the rank of a religion. It can and does teach love of country, obedience to law, and participation in the political process without deifying the state. Thus the parochial school at its best can foster both that unity which is essential to national security and stability and that pluralism which is inseparable from freedom.

It was to alleviate some of the tensions arising out of misunderstandings of the relationship between public schools and parochial schools that The Lutheran Church — Missouri Synod expressed its position in the following statement adopted at its convention in 1959:

> Both the state and the church are concerned about the education of children and youth. The state requires that children and youth be educated for civic, social, and vocational responsibilities. The Christian church has the responsibility of teaching children and youth to become disciples of Jesus Christ.
>
> The effort of the state in public education is a community effort and therefore the responsibility of every citizen. The Lutheran Church — Missouri Synod recognizes the responsibility that every citizen has to support and uphold the public schools. The Synod continues to encourage its members to interest themselves in the welfare of the public schools through

personal participation on school boards and committees and financial support of the schools.

The church provides Christian education through various agencies — some part-time schools, others full-time schools. The Lutheran Church — Missouri Synod encourages its congregations to establish Lutheran elementary schools and high schools. In the school year 1958–59 there were 1,268 Lutheran elementary schools, with an enrollment of 138,338, and 16 community Lutheran high schools, with an enrollment of 7,748. These schools are founded because of deep religious convictions as to the desirability of combining religious education with the teaching of the regular school subjects.

The Synod emphasizes that the development of Lutheran elementary schools and high schools is not to be misinterpreted as a criticism of the public school, disinterest in the public school, or unwillingness to support the public school. Lutheran schools are not in competition with the public schools; they are established to provide a specifically Christian education, which the public school cannot supply.[47]

Federal Aid in Education

Even more controversial than proposals for state aid to parochial schools have been the various suggestions for some form of federal aid to schools. Proponents of federal aid have pointed to the manifest disparities of educational opportunity from state to state and contend that the only effective way of equalizing these opportunities is to provide federal funds to states which for one reason or another seem unable to develop and maintain good schools out of their own resources. Opponents of federal aid insist that federal aid necessarily implies federal control and thus constitutes another intrusion into areas of responsibility constitutionally reserved to the states.

The issue has been complicated by the insistence of influential Roman Catholic spokesmen and a few Protestants that, if the federal government is to assist education on the elementary or secondary level at all, this assistance should be offered in the same amount and on the same terms to the nonpublic school as well as to the public school. A bipartisan coalition of statesrighters with northern Roman Catholic Democrats has effectively blocked any bill calling for federal aid to public schools on the elementary and secondary level.

Efforts to secure federal aid to education date back to 1919, when a committee of the National Education Association recommended the establishment of a federal Department of Education, the head of which would have cabinet rank. The committee suggested that appropriations amounting to $100 million be made for the general improvement of schools. As a result of this campaign launched by the NEA a number of bills were introduced into the Congress, including the Smith-Towner, the Sterling-Towner, and the Sterling-Reed bills. All of these proposals failed to pass.

The NEA renewed its activity for federal aid to education in 1936 by sponsoring the Harrison-Black-Fletcher bill, which would have provided financial assistance to all of the states, beginning with $100 million and reaching ultimately $300 million. The Senate failed to consider the bill. In the same year President Roosevelt appointed an Advisory Committee on Education headed by Floyd W. Reeves. This committee in its 1938 report recommended two types of federal grant:

1. General appropriations for elementary and secondary education up to a figure that would ultimately reach $140 million a year.

2. The establishment of special federal funds to aid the states in improving teacher training, constructing public school buildings, administering state departments of education, aiding adult education, extending rural library services, and carrying on educational research.

From 1943 on, a number of bills providing for federal aid to education were introduced in Congress. Some of them specified very clearly that federal funds would be available only to public schools. Others, such as the bill sponsored by Senator Robert A. Taft in 1947–48, would have authorized the states to use federal grants as they used other state funds for education. In 1952 a proposed bill provided for grants-in-aid amounting to

$9 billion over a 10-year period for public school construction. Failing to pass Congress at that time, it was reintroduced in 1956 and in 1957. None of these efforts succeeded. In fact an increasing opposition to the whole concept of federal aid became evident. To a very large extent this opposition had its roots in a concern that no bill be passed which provided — or could be interpreted as providing — federal aid to nonpublic schools. Paralleling this concern was the concern of most Roman Catholic churchmen and congressmen that no bill be passed which would deny federal assistance to nonpublic schools.

On the very last day of the congressional session in 1958 the National Defense Education Act was approved and sent to the President for signature. This bill provided for a 4-year program of special aids, fellowships, and language and science institutes. Sections of the bill which called for negotiations between the U. S. Office of Education and institutions of higher learning went into effect rather quickly. Other sections of the law waited for legislation in the various states to authorize the necessary machinery and matching funds.

The National Defense Education Act had two specific provisions dealing with nonpublic schools:

1. Nonprofit, private elementary and secondary schools were offered loans for the acquisition of laboratory or other special equipment for the improvement of teaching in fields deemed important to national security: science, mathematics, and modern languages. The bill also made loans available for minor remodeling of laboratory or other space suitable for such equipment.

2. Nonpublic schools were also included in a 4-year program of grants for the identification and encouragement of able students. In states that had the legal authority to test in nonpublic schools the state educational agency could include nonpublic schools in its own testing program and would be reimbursed for half the cost of the program. In other states the U. S. Commissioner of Education was authorized to arrange for tests in nonpublic schools so that students in both public and nonpublic schools would be tested in comparable ways at the same grade

levels and under the same conditions. In each state where the commissioner arranged for testing in nonpublic schools he was authorized to pay the first year's cost of such testing out of the state's allotment; in the following three years he would pay half the cost.

The presidential campaign of 1960 and the subsequent election of the nation's first Roman Catholic President raised the federal-aid controversy to the level of a national debate. Both as candidate and as President, Mr. Kennedy took the position that any form of direct assistance to sectarian education was unconstitutional. This position was clearly contradictory to the stated views of the overwhelming majority of the American Roman Catholic hierarchy. As President, Mr. Kennedy twice sent to the Congress recommendations for the spending of something in excess of $5½ billion over a 5-year period for buildings, scholarships, and increases in teachers' salaries in public elementary and secondary schools. Bishop Lawrence J. Shehan of Bridgeport, Conn., chairman of the department of education of the National Catholic Welfare Conference, found fault with the President's recommendations for containing "no recognition of the contribution of private elementary and secondary schools to the critical needs of the country." Francis Cardinal Spellman, archbishop of New York, called omission of parochial schools from the President's aid bill "a terrible crime," "a dagger threatening our very existence," and warned a gathering of nuns, brothers, and lay teachers that "if the Federal Government should favor the public schools and put an additional tax on us, from which we would receive no benefit, then, my dear friends, it is the eventual end of our parochial schools." [48] Dissenting, as they often do, from the political, social, and economic views of the hierarchy, the editors of the lay weekly *Commonweal* held that "emotional descriptions of the President's bill as a threat, a crime, an attack which means the end of the parochial school system" were "misleading and exaggerated, and likely to do much harm." [49]

Protestant reaction to the President's recommendations divided along three lines: (1) general agreement with the President's program, coupled with vigorous support of his "no aid to nonpublic schools" position; (2) disapproval of federal aid to education on political, economic, or social grounds having no direct bearing on the church-state issue; and (3) disapproval of the President's recommendations because they did not include provisions for assistance to nonpublic schools.

Representative of the first of these reactions — which would appear to be by all odds the general Protestant reaction — is the comment of the *Christian Century:*

> Each child has a basic human right to receive all the education his capacities permit. Our nation will be better served if he receives that education than if he does not receive it. These personal and national concerns outweigh the objections to President Kennedy's well rounded plan of federal aid to education. With the exception of the proposed grants to private and sectarian universities and colleges, his plan has our support.[50]

The Board of Parish Education of The Lutheran Church — Missouri Synod, in a carefully worded statement of March 21, 1961, on "Federal Aid to Church Schools," made a distinction between social services such as library service, the school lunch program, health services, and transportation, all of which the board believes should be made available to all children of school age, and facilities and personnel required for the teaching program, which it believes should be excluded from federal aid. Specifically the board registered its opposition to federal aid for teachers' salaries, buildings, and equipment; loans to church-related elementary and secondary schools; and tax credits for the full cost of tuition in nonpublic schools. The board's opposition to these forms of assistance was grounded in its belief that good stewardship would demand that the government "concern itself with the use of these funds and . . . control their use"; that "the church would through such aid become obligated to the federal government, and yet it could not in good conscience submit its teaching program to a secular authority"; that the acceptance of such aid "would have a tendency to interfere with the mission and purpose of the church"; that loans "may provide an opening wedge leading to outright grants to church-related schools"; and that tax credits for the full amount of tuition "would mean that in many cases the federal or state governments would pay for all or a part of the student's education in nonpublic schools." The one form of aid which the board found unobjectionable is the inclusion of tuition paid to nonpublic schools under contributions to religious, charitable, and educational purposes in federal and state income-tax returns.[51]

Protestant objections to federal aid in principle are deserving of consideration but are not germane to our present discussion. It should be noted, however, that a small minority of Protestants have objected to federal aid which is restricted to public schools. Professor Marion Snapper, of the education department of Calvin College, contends that "all education — including Christian day schools — is not merely an activity of government; it is of the essence of government"; and: "If Christian day school education is governmental activity, and if such education is controlled by the state, either by direction or indirectly, because it is governmental activity, then it would appear that it ought to have financial support from the state." Snapper then goes on to say:

> There is rapidly growing evidence to indicate that the question of federal aid to private and parochial elementary and secondary schools will not be answered on the basis of the superficially neat logic of "separation of church and state"; or "Education is the responsibility of the parent rather than of the state"; or "This is good for Roman Catholicism and therefore bad for us"; or "Federal support means federal control."
>
> These neat logical distinctions are crumbling under the pressure of national and world events and under the growing realization that private and parochial education is an integral, vital activity of the body politic . . .
>
> The most rapid crumbling of the old categories is taking place in relation to education at the college level. . . . In my opinion it is only a matter of time until the logic of human and world affairs forces the same approach to secondary and elementary private and parochial education. . . . One or two more hitches in the American belt and the 15 per cent of America's children being educated in private and parochial schools will

be as critical to the national welfare as the 40 percent being educated in nonpublic colleges today.

This argument rests on the assumption that in the years ahead elementary and secondary nonpublic schools will not be able to continue to provide a comparatively high-quality education without being subsidized in some form or other by the state . . .

The cause of Christian education must learn how to preserve its uniqueness while accepting the state subsidy necessary to its continuance. . . . We hold to the principle that education is the responsibility of parents. But we must learn to understand that this principle does not proscribe support from sources other than parents' pocketbooks . . .[52]

A somewhat similar view — this one from an unofficial Lutheran source — was expressed by the editors of the *Cresset* in an editorial entitled "Prohibiting the Free Exercise Thereof":

The First Amendment not only forbids Congress to make any laws respecting an establishment of religion; it also forbids Congress to make any laws prohibiting the free exercise of religion . . .

That raises a vexing question: Where are the bounds of this freedom, and who determines them? For a Roman Catholic and for many Lutherans, the free exercise of their religion involves, among other things, the religious education of their children in schools organized around a particular theology. If, for any reason, they were forced to abandon their schools, they would not be wholly free to exercise their religion, for in both churches all of learning is conceived of as religious and the schools are conceived of as seed-beds not only of the state but also of the church.

Of course, no one expects Congress to enact legislation which would have, as its direct purpose, the outlawing of parochial schools. But Congress may enact, and has enacted, various types of legislation which have this unhappy side-effect. A citizen may be effectively prohibited from doing all sorts of things simply by siphoning off, through taxation, the funds that he needs to do them . . .

Groups of people may be denied the free exercise of their religion if the institutions which they maintain (schools, hospitals, benevolent societies, social welfare organizations) are forced out of existence by the preferential treatment of competing secular institutions. The allocation of federal funds to public schools can hardly fail to achieve the laudable objective of improving the quality of facilities and personnel in those schools. The denial of such assistance to private and parochial schools must therefore, however unintentionally, place these schools at an even greater competitive disadvantage than is presently the case.

We ought, in any case, to be clear about what we are doing. Massive Federal aid to public schools accompanied by a denial of equivalent assistance to private and parochial schools means, whether we intend it or not, the end of non-public schooling. It won't happen suddenly and it may not happen soon, but it will happen. If this is what we want to happen, well and good and hang the First Amendment. But then let's be honest about it and not delude ourselves with pious hopes that the systematic starvation of private education will somehow strengthen and invigorate it.[53]

The views of these two Protestant journals, like those of *Commonweal,* are worth noting chiefly as dissents from nearly unanimous Protestant and Roman Catholic positions. To place the controversy in its proper focus, it need only be said that Roman Catholics overwhelmingly support the demands of their leaders for some form of direct federal assistance to private and parochial schools. Protestants just as overwhelmingly oppose it.

The present state of the controversy has been summarized by John D. Eusden, associate professor of religion and chaplain at Williams College. He notes that arguments for aid to nonpublic schools have to do with considerations in at least four areas: (1) Educational. "Parochial schools are engaged primarily in the task of general education, and they are good schools. . . . Financially, the parochial schools save taxpayers millions of dollars each year. It is time for the government to assume responsibility toward these schools." (2) Sociological. "Roman Catholics now number approximately 23 per cent of our population. It cannot be contended that provision of a public school system vaguely Protestant or secular equitably serves the needs of the nearly one-fourth of our people who desire religious schools." (3) Legal. "A fundamental legal principle, a matter of basic human rights, is at stake in the matter of aid: the right of parents to choose that education which is, in their judgment, best suited for their children. . . . Supporting the right of parents to choose in the matter of education is the ancient principle of distributive justice. Father John C. Murray points out that this principle requires that in distributing burdens and benefits within the community the government should have in view the needs and desires of all groups of citizens." (4) Religious and moral. "The religious pluralism that exists in the United States makes it impossible to teach religion in public schools. Roman Catholic leaders argue that education which leaves out religious truth and moral values is not education at all; further, it contributes to the collapse of moral fibre in individuals and organizations, and adds to the senseless relativism of our time."

Professor Eusden summarizes the arguments against federal aid to nonpublic schools under four major headings: (1) The nature of parochial schools. "Parochial schools are intimately associated with the church. . . . As Mr. Justice Jackson said in his dissent in the New Jersey school bus case, 'The parochial school is a vital, if not the most vital, part of the Roman Catholic Church.'" (2) The meaning of the First Amendment. "The Constitution guarantees that no one shall be called upon to support a particular faith with which he does not agree, but in the current demand for federal aid to parochial schools the approximately 77 per cent of our population which is not affiliated with the Roman Catholic Church is being asked to give such support." (3) The promise of the public schools. "The beneficial effect of Roman Catholic schools on our national life is open to question. Certainly it can be said that the growth of Catholic schools tends to increase our social divisiveness. Public and parochial school children are set apart from each other in local communities; they even dress differently. . . . The public school system is conceived in community even as a parochial school system is conceived in division. The right to do something — to establish a separate religious school — is not to be equated with the wisdom of doing it."

(4) The problem of religion and education. "The word 'secular' is more appropriate for the public schools than 'secularistic.' Secular means 'of the age.' Given the religious pluralism of the age, the public schools cannot teach the doctrine of any particular faith. To say that they are secular, however, is not to say they are godless or secularistic. Most of the teachers in the public school system today are members of religious groups — Protestant, Catholic or Jewish — and they attempt to make spiritual and moral values relevant amid the pluralism of their classrooms." [54]

President Kennedy based his opposition to extending federal aid to nonpublic schools on the contention that to do so would simply be unconstitutional. In view of the Supreme Court's decision in *Massachusetts* v. *Mellon,* it is hard to see how the constitutional question could even be presented to the court for consideration. At this point no party to the controversy has shown any strong inclination to settle the constitutional question by placing aid to nonpublic schools before the nation in the form of a constitutional amendment, although Father John P. Leary, president of Gonzaga University, has suggested that within 50 years Roman Catholics will constitute a majority in the United States and can then amend the Constitution to permit federal aid to their schools. With the constitutional question set aside, therefore, as a moot point, the question would seem to resolve itself into a controversy which is as old as our country — how to permit individuals and groups to retain their identities and to practice their peculiarities within the framework of some sort of national and cultural unity.

One of the many glories of the American Constitution is that it has never prevented the sovereign people from doing what in their considered judgment they wanted to do or needed to do. The extremists in the controversy over federal aid to nonpublic education are, on the one hand, those who can barely conceal their irritation at scruples of conscience which stand in the way of a national homogenization process and those, on the other hand, who only grudgingly accept the idea of a secular state and openly champion some legal or quasi-legal establishment of re-

ligion. Between the two poles represented by these extremists
lies a broad area of cooperation and tension between church and
state. The two cannot simply be kept separate so long as both
claim the loyalties of the same people. In practice — whatever
the theory may be — the rival claims of church and state are decided as are all great issues in a democracy, by public debate
leading either to consensus or to compromise. Once a verdict
has been reached in the forum of public debate, the courts find
"constitutional" grounds for its validation, and it takes its place
in that broad stream of custom and tradition which we call "the
American way."

This being the case, the question that needs to be answered
is not so much what is constitutional as what we want to be constitutional. That delicate balancing of loyalties which is reflected
in the phrase "separation of church and state" has served us well
in the past and ought not be recklessly upset. If the traditions
of the past can be shown to be outmoded by present necessities,
comprehensive adjustments rather than revolutionary change
would seem best calculated to preserve a balance between the
demands of church and state. The maintenance of such a balance will require those at both poles of the controversy to prepare themselves to accept considerably less than the whole loaf,
perhaps even less than the half loaf, that they are demanding.

A reasonable compromise at this moment would seem to be
that nonpublic elementary and secondary schools might be made
eligible for all of those social services, apart from instruction as
such, which the government offers children through the schools.
Under such a rule of thumb, grants for such purposes as transportation, physical examinations, aptitude testing, and civil defense measures would be permissible; grants for teachers' salaries,
textbooks, the purchase of real property, and building construction would not. Interest-bearing government loans for nonpublic
school construction would seem to suggest no sectarian favoritism,
although they would probably be of little practical use and might
be criticized as a form of governmental competition with private
lending agencies. Remission of taxes or the granting of tax exemption for tuition paid to nonpublic schools is probably a greater

concession than our national consensus would at present be will-ing to support.

Whatever the constitutional issue and however far the na-tional consensus might move in the direction of federal aid to nonpublic schools, the churches have good reason to move cautiously in the direction of its acceptance. In Lutheran the-ology, at least, church and state are both God's instruments, relatively autonomous within their own areas and operating with different means under different laws. Confusion of the Kingdom of Power with the Kingdom of Grace usually produces much unforeseen and unforeseeable mischief, almost inevitably to the disadvantage of the church. Thus before the church chooses federal assistance as the best solution to the problem of increas-ing teachers' salaries (which, admittedly, are still too low), it would do well to consider the practical classroom implications of the warning: "No man can serve two masters." Before the church accepts federal money to build schools, it would do well to ask what implied "service charges" are involved. Before it asks for assistance for its own schools, it would do well to con-sider what stake it has in the maintenance and strengthening of a strong public-school system. Before the church proposes any breach in the "wall of separation," it would do well to reflect on Robert Frost's line that "good fences make good neighbors."

MAINTAINING CHURCH-RELATED COLLEGES

The focus of this chapter has been on church-state relations in elementary and secondary education because it is at this level that the tensions have been particularly acute. On the college level these tensions are considerably less acute for many reasons, among them the following:

1. Attendance at a college or university is optional; atten-dance of educable children and youth below certain specified ages at elementary and secondary schools is compulsory under the basic minimum-education requirements of the various states.

2. Numerous administrative regulations of state educational authorities apply to both public and nonpublic schools on the

elementary and secondary levels; nonpublic colleges and universities are, at least in theory, free of such administrative control.

3. Instruction on the elementary and secondary level necessarily involves a considerable element of indoctrination; instruction on the college or university level presupposes both the opportunity and the duty of the student to make his own free choice among conflicting ideas and views.

4. The typical parochial school is an integral part of a particular parish or congregational structure and is closely supervised by the parish pastor or priest; the typical denominational college or university is very loosely — often only nominally — attached to a denomination and is for all practical purposes an autonomous institution.

To these distinctions must be added a very practical consideration. While the parochial school represents an exception to the general pattern of American secondary and elementary education, the private or church-related college or university has a long, secure, and honored tradition in the American higher educational structure. Few publicly supported colleges or universities are "national" institutions in the same sense as are Harvard, Yale, Princeton, Johns Hopkins, Chicago, or Northwestern, all of which are "private" or even, in two cases, technically church-related institutions.

In its dealings with colleges and universities the government, with the practically unanimous support of the people, has been willing to look beyond appearances to realities. No one sees any implications of federal assistance to the Methodist Church in a research grant to a Jewish member of the Northwestern Medical School faculty who is engaged in cancer research, nor would any such implication be likely to be drawn if the researcher happened to be a Methodist. Some eyebrow raising occurs when substantial grants are made to more obviously denominational institutions such as Notre Dame or Valparaiso or Asbury or Calvin, but the special competence of particular faculty members who are the beneficiaries of the grant is usually answer enough to such criticism.

Federal assistance to nonpublic colleges and universities has grown both in range and in volume since World War II. The first major step in this direction — and a giant step it was — was the passage in 1944 of Public Law 346, the "G. I. Bill." This law provided tuition payments for veterans to the college or university of their choice. Many veterans chose nonpublic colleges — fortunately, for public institutions would have been altogether incapable of receiving the whole influx of veterans. Similar benefits were extended to veterans of the Korean "police action," thus reinforcing a precedent which has since been broadened to support the granting of a wide variety of scholarships at the college level for both public and nonpublic schools.

The National Defense Education Act of 1958, Title 2, authorized loans to students in institutions of higher education, again without discrimination between public and nonpublic institutions. Scholarship programs for students engaged in particular courses of study deemed to be in the national interest (e. g., language development and certain areas of the natural sciences) have also made no distinction between public and nonpublic institutions.

Faced with the practical problem that many colleges and universities have not been able to finance necessary plant expansion out of their own resources, the federal government in recent years has offered low-interest loans to nonpublic colleges and universities for the construction of noninstructional buildings, chiefly dormitories. Through the passage of the Higher Education Facilities Act of 1963 this form of assistance has been broadened to include grants and loans for certain instructional buildings. Thus on the college level federal assistance on a rather large scale to private and denominational institutions is not only a reality but in some cases a very significant consideration in institutional planning for development. Although numerous responsible voices have been raised in warning of possible federal control, there is as yet no reported instance of any attempt on the part of government to interfere in the business of any institution which has benefited from its assistance.

That no such attempt has yet been made does not, of course,

mean that it could not be made. Moreover, it must be said that the availability of federal money for certain purposes and not for others has played an important, if not decisive, role in influencing the policies and orientations of many nonpublic institutions. In general the physical, natural, and technological sciences have benefited greatly from the willingness of government to underwrite research, purchases of equipment, and scholarships in those areas. The social sciences have benefited considerably less, and often at the expense of sacrificing "pure research" for more "practical" projects which the government was willing to support. The humanities have benefited very little, the arts even less, and religion not at all.

The step-by-step extension of federal aid to college-level institutions provides some reinforcement to the argument of those who contend that the only way to prevent a similar development in elementary and secondary education is to "resist the beginnings." At the same time it offers, at least for the present, little support to the contention that "federal aid necessarily means federal control." It may be that experiments in federal aid on the college level can serve as pilot projects which, with such modifications as experience may suggest, could be applied to the problems confronting the nonpublic school on the secondary and possibly even the elementary level.

SUMMARY

From the point of view of religion, the United States is a pluralistic country in which the radical differences of belief are obscured by a remarkable consensus on matters of morals. What a man should do is not a matter of serious disagreement among the people of this country. Why he should do it is a question on which their disagreements are many and profound.

The people of the United States are committed to a policy of universal, free, and compulsory education on the elementary level and increasingly on the secondary level. Overwhelmingly they agree that education on these levels must include a considerable element of moral indoctrination. There is almost equally general agreement that moral indoctrination is ineffectual unless it is grounded in some kind of religious conviction. It is understandable, therefore, that concerned people have felt that there must be some common core, some least common denominator of religion which would be inoffensive to religious and nonreligious people alike and at the same time effective as a foundation of morality.

It is time to ask whether the search for this kind of inoffensive religion is not perhaps only a modern version of the ancient search for a universal solvent. Every religion is, at its base, dogmatic, and the honest atheist or agnostic will admit that he, too, proceeds from certain dogmatic assumptions. If the public school is to be kept truly public, it must be free from denominational dogma. In effect this means that, however much practice may vary from community to community, there should be no compromise with the principle that the public schools are nonreligious without being antireligious. Morality taught for what it is — i. e., the rules of the game to which practically all subscribe — is a necessary and desirable element in public education. But any attempt to lay a religious foundation for morality in the public schools can only result in promulgating denominational dogmas. There simply is no least common denominator of religion to which we subscribe as a people.

Those who believe that religious instruction is an indispensable part of education have the alternative of maintaining their own schools. The choice of this alternative does not exempt them from meeting the proper objectives of the state in education, but it does allow them to do more than the state requires. The private school shares with the public school the responsibility of preparing children for responsible citizenship in a free society and must therefore concede the right of the state to set reasonable academic standards, to require reasonable evidences of competence in its teachers, to set and enforce minimum standards of health and safety, to require a minimum number of school days, to enforce compulsory attendance laws, and to require records, reports, and other reasonable accountings of its activities.

In return it would seem fair to expect the state to recognize the important contributions which the nonpublic schools make to the public welfare and to assist them in their work within the limitations of the First Amendment. The use of tax moneys for teachers' salaries or for school construction can hardly be rationalized as anything else but a grant in aid of religion, for it involves direct and substantial assistance to the churches in carrying on what they themselves have described as essential elements in their total work as churches. On the other hand, benefits intended primarily for children of school age and channeled through the schools largely as a matter of convenience should be made available to all children irrespective of whether they attend a public or a nonpublic school. Among these benefits would be bus transportation, state-approved textbooks, health programs, aptitude and achievement tests, the hot-lunch program, and perhaps others.

The existence of public and nonpublic schools side by side in the United States is not a matter of accident, nor is it merely an evidence of the willingness of the American people to tolerate eccentricity. The two types of school reflect basic and probably irreconcilable differences among them on such fundamental questions as the nature of God, of man, of truth, and of knowledge. Totalitarian societies see differences as threats and endeavor to minimize or eliminate them. Free societies see differences as colorings which brighten the social fabric, and they endeavor to protect and even foster them. The tension between church and state in the area of education has been a wholesome tension, beneficial both to the public and to the nonpublic school. The maintenance of this fruitful tension would seem to hold the promise of greater benefits to both the church and the state than any attempt to resolve the tension by making the public schools more "religious" or by allowing the nonpublic schools to die by a slow process of economic suffocation.

THE FORCE OF CUSTOM is strong in well-settled societies. It has a profound effect on those activities which occur where church and state have interests in common. But it may also become evident in the multitude of adjustments, large and small, which are part of daily living over a long period of time.

The chaplaincy is an institution which represents the common interests of both government and ecclesiastical organizations. It is explored in this chapter by *Eugene F. Klug*, M. A., assistant professor of systematic theology at Concordia Theological Seminary, Springfield, Ill., formerly a chaplain in the United States Navy. He shows how the military chaplaincy predates the establishing of our nation, was accepted after some debate in the middle 19th century, and has by now a fairly fixed role in the armed services of the country. Modern regulations, according to Professor Klug, provide for adequate guarantees "fully in harmony with the word and intent of the First Amendment . . . and the confessional platforms of the churches." The assistance which government gives to the churches through the chaplaincy is justified on the government's part by its own needs and on the church's part by its obligations to witness to the Word.

In the second section of the chapter, *James S. Savage*, LL. M., professor of law at Valparaiso University, engages in the task of assessing the role of the church as a legal entity. Of special interest are the issues raised by the exemption of churches from taxation, the subjection of churches to zoning laws, and the whole controversy over the closing of business establishments on Sunday, the grounds for which were once religious but more recently have become social and humanitarian.

Chapter 8

CUSTOM AND LAW
IN CHURCH-STATE PRACTICES

Eugene F. Klug and James S. Savage

THE ACTIVITIES of church and state touch each other in many ways. While education is the area where church-state relations are most frequently in the public eye, there are other aspects of American life in which church and state must establish a working accommodation.

Sometimes custom provides a pattern. A relationship develops in one era of national history to meet a certain need and is continued for so many years that it becomes a traditional way of doing things. Questions about it are no longer accepted for debate. The practice exists because it has always existed. Any effort to change it inevitably meets with stiff resistance.

Such is the situation of the chaplaincy in America. It has been a part of our way of life since the national beginnings. It has served a useful purpose so long that attempts to modify it are seldom successful. Some church bodies disagree with it in principle. Some critics challenge it as a contradiction to the policy of the separation of church and state. In certain ways it may even be inconsistent with other American practices in church-state relations. But the fact remains that the chaplaincy is embedded in our usages.

Other examples of the binding character of custom can also be cited. The observance of Sunday as a holiday and the exemption of church property from taxes are two instances. But these also involve the legal associations which church and state may have. When churches become legal entities, the state regards them much like any other nonprofit corporations. The law rather than custom defines this sort of relationship.

In the following pages an effort will be made to show how custom and law affect church-state practice. The unique and interesting structure of the American chaplaincy is analyzed in some detail. Legal aspects of church-state relations, exemplified in various ways, will also be explored.

I

THE CHAPLAINCY IN AMERICAN PUBLIC LIFE

Eugene F. Klug

Implicit in the First Amendment is the guarantee that religion in its various denominational forms may be freely exercised and propagated. Though keenly aware of the loss of liberty which is at stake when state and church are mingled in their functions, our government has not hesitated to encourage its citizens to support religion, because of the benign effect which it has on the lives of individual citizens, families, and the whole common-wealth. Almost without exception the relationship of government to the churches in the land has been friendly. This sympathetic attitude is especially reflected in the area of the chaplaincy.

The development of the chaplaincy program in the Armed Forces, as well as in various federal and state institutions, grew out of a concern of government for the general welfare of its citizens and the recognition that ours was a nation of people who worshiped and depended on Almighty God. The development has been gradual, dating back in the case of the military chaplaincy to the Continental Army and Navy, and to the time of Lincoln for federal institutional chaplaincies. The United States government frankly acknowledged that it had no right and no ability to sustain the spirit of man and that this properly was the sphere of the churches. Therefore the establishment of the chaplaincies followed. Government has shown itself willing to meet the churches part way by employing as chaplains the clergymen they supply.

The role and function of the chaplain today are reflected in the regulations of the Armed Forces, the Veterans Administration, and the federal and state welfare codes. Basically the statements of purpose are the same in all of these codes. A chaplain's duties are usually described as being analogous to those of a civilian parish minister. The only real difference is to be found in the modifications imposed by military or institutional life and exigency. When for doctrinal reasons the chaplain cannot serve certain individuals or groups, he is at liberty to make alternative arrangements through clergymen of other and more mutually acceptable beliefs. The chaplain conducts worship, administers the sacraments of his church, instructs for church membership, teaches Bible classes, solemnizes marriages, conducts funerals, ministers to the sick, imprisoned, and distressed, and offers counsel to those who need help or guidance. By precept and example he sets the moral tone for the "community" of his ship, station, base, regiment, or institution. In his position as spiritual leader the chaplain usually serves the commanding officer or superintendent as adviser on religious, moral, and morale matters. The emphasis is strictly on the spiritual side.[1] In all his activities the chaplain has a remarkably free hand, and he is excused, for the most part, from collateral duties which do not directly fit into the area of his professional calling.[2]

The chaplaincy is a ministry which finds its justification in the commission of Christ to go into all the world and preach the Gospel to every creature (Mark 16:15) and its example in the ministry of the apostle Paul, who became all things to all men for the sake of the Gospel. (1 Cor. 9:22, 23)

DEVELOPMENT OF THE CHAPLAINCY

The Beginnings of a Chaplaincy Program

Chaplains were a traditional part of the American military scene even before the Revolution of 1776. In this respect the colonies simply followed the example of the mother country in its armies and navies. On Sept. 23, 1756, at the time of the French and Indian War, Col. George Washington addressed a letter to Governor Dinwiddie of Virginia in which he requested appointment of a chaplain for his regiment. Along with pointed military strategy, Washington detailed at some length the morale situation of the troops under his command. Food costs, he explained, were beyond the individual soldier's ability to pay, and tippling houses in the vicinity of the camp were far too many and liquor flowed too freely. In summary he made this plea:

> The want of a chaplain, I humbly conceive, reflects dishonor on the regiment, as all other officers are allowed. The gentlemen of the corps are sensible of this, and proposed to support one at their private expense. But I think it would have a more graceful appearance were he appointed as others are.[3]

Failing to get a chaplain appointed through Governor Dinwiddie, Washington in a letter to the president of the Virginia Council on April 17, 1758, expressed the hope that this need could now be supplied since the assembly had ratified the expenditure:

> The last assembly, in their Supply Bill, provided for a chaplain to one regiment. On this subject I had often without any success applied to Governor Dinwiddie. I now flatter myself, that your Honor will be pleased to appoint a sober serious man for this duty. Common decency, Sir, in a camp calls for the services of a divine, which ought not to be dispensed with, although the world should be so uncharitable as to think us void of religion, and incapable of good instructions.[4]

Undoubtedly the request was for an Anglican clergyman, for that was the established church in Virginia. But in that same year, 1758, provision was also made for Dissenting (Baptist) clergymen to serve with the troops when requested.[5]

When the colonies resorted to arms in their fight for justice and freedom, many of the troops had their ministers with them. A diary entry by President Ezra Stiles of Yale for Nov. 17, 1774, tells how Col. Israel Putnam's letter concerning the earnestness of the situation in Massachusetts was read "publickly in most of the Congregations in Connecticut"[6] and how thereupon response was immediate, with various contingents being formed under the instigation of and in company with their pastors. Early in 1775

the Provincial Congress of Massachusetts approved the appointment of chaplains for the army.

An act of the Continental Congress, dated July 29, 1775,
established the military chaplaincy as a legal entity.[7] The individual colonies, however, followed various methods of procuring
chaplains. Some were appointed by the governor, some by the
legislature, others by the established church of the colony, and
still others by the commanding officers of the regiments or ships.
The chaplains appointed were regularly of the denomination to
which the majority of the men to be served belonged. Even
language was a criterion in some cases. In the summer of 1776
a German Lutheran, Christian Streit, was appointed chaplain for
the German-speaking Eighth Regiment of Virginia.[8]

There were some problems for the Continental Congress on
the chaplaincy question, not the least of which was the perennial
low pay for men of the cloth. In a letter addressed to the president of the Congress on the last day of 1775, Washington, as
general of the army, observed that the chaplains' pay was "too
small to encourage men of abilities." With deft and ironic thrust
he paid tribute to the self-sacrificing devotion of the chaplains
by adding that "some of them, who have left their flocks, are
obliged to pay the parson acting for them more than they receive."
To his way of thinking, "advancement of their pay" was the only
way to remedy the situation, even if the number of chaplains had
to be reduced by half, from one for every regiment to one for
every two.[9]

On July 9, 1776, with the fledgling nation still in its infancy
but with its military task more clearly defined, General Washington made the following entry in his orderly book:

> The honorable Continental Congress, having been pleased to
> allow a chaplain to each regiment, the colonels or commanding
> officers of each regiment are directed to procure chaplains
> accordingly, persons of good characters and exemplary lives,
> and to see that all inferior officers and soldiers pay them a suit-
> able respect. The blessing and protection of Heaven are at all
> times necessary, but especially so in times of public distress
> and danger. The General hopes and trusts, that every officer

and man will endeavour to live and act as becomes a Christian soldier, defending the dearest rights and liberties of his country.[10]

Less than a month later, in the orderly book entry for Aug. 3, 1776, the general stated that troops were to have opportunity for worship and were to cease from profanity.[11] The frequency with which references to the chaplaincy, to worship, and to religion in general occur demonstrates the concern for the subject in official quarters.

The Army set a precedent which was followed almost immediately by the Navy. On Nov. 28, 1775, when the Navy regulations were first adopted, the second article provided for religious worship in the following statute:

> The commanders of the ships of the Thirteen United Colonies, are to take care that divine service be performed twice a day on board, and a sermon preached on Sundays, unless bad weather or other extraordinary accidents prevent.[12]

The Reverend Benjamin Balch, a Congregationalist, was the first Navy chaplain on record. He had fought with the Minute Men at the Battle of Lexington and later served as Army chaplain during the siege of Boston. On Oct. 28, 1778, Balch reported for duty as chaplain aboard the frigate *Boston*.

The new nation on Sept. 20, 1776, had already adopted the "Original Rules and Articles of War," which in Article IV provided for the commissioning of brigade chaplains.[13] By the end of the war there was an organized system of brigade chaplains who were reimbursed for their services on a pay scale comparable to that of a colonel. Almost all of the chaplains were Protestant since the colonies themselves were predominantly so.[14] The need for the services of these wartime chaplains ceased in 1783 when the Continental Army was all but disbanded.

The Middle Period

From the end of the Revolutionary War until the Civil War the military chaplaincy was a chapter marked by uncertainty. The country itself was going through the struggle of growth and survival as a nation. In 1791 the office of chaplain was formally established as part of the new nation's Army, which had been organized two years before. At first there was only one chaplain, an Episcopalian. As time went on, the number increased in keeping with the needs of the Army. Acts of Congress in 1788 and again in 1808 made provision for brigade chaplains, and in the War of 1812 there were at least 12 regularly appointed chaplains, besides an uncertain number of volunteers. Navy chaplains also served on the frigates during these years, but their appointment was a haphazard affair. It was while Samuel L. Southard was Secretary of the Navy (1823 to 1829) that the ruling was made requiring prospective chaplains to be properly ordained ministers in fellowship with a recognized denomination.[15] Evidently before this time they often were merely petty officers who aspired to the office, having had little or no specific theological training. The policy adopted by the Navy was not formally expressed in Army regulations until 1861–62.[16] After 1818 and until 1838 the only official chaplain in the Army was a civilian clergyman employed on a contract basis at West Point.[17]

In 1838 an Act of Congress established a system of post chaplains, providing budget funds for a total of 20 chaplains and giving the right to post commanders to employ "such person as they may think proper to officiate as chaplain, who shall also perform the duties of schoolmaster at such post."[18] A description of Army and Navy chaplaincies before the time of the Mexican War is contained in a book by the Reverend Robert Baird, *A View of Religion in America,* published in 1844. He indicates that conditions were still somewhat confused and deplores, for one thing, the arrangement whereby the Secretary of the Navy was responsible for the appointment of Naval chaplains, contending that this should be delegated to a missionary society or some similar organization.

During the period from 1838 to the time of the Civil War, the Army quotas for chaplains were not always filled. In part this was because of the shift in concept of what the chaplain's function was to be, whether strictly a spiritual leader or a kind of catchall for various peripheral duties. Then, too, "the institution itself fell into disfavor because appointment as a chaplain was considered by many as a political plum, to be held along with a civilian job." [19]

A more serious threat to the continued existence of the military chaplaincy came in the late 1840s, when critics began pointing to it, as well as to chaplains in the Congress and at Indian stations, as unconstitutional on the grounds that these arrangements effected a mingling of the functions of church and state. These charges continued to mount through the following years, until finally in 1852–53 sharp and articulate opposition was mustered against the government chaplaincies, particularly in Congress.

The advocates of reform spoke from diverse convictions. Some were radical freethinkers, others were concerned Protestant sectarians. The core of the problem, as they saw it, was that church and state were not being kept absolutely separate. Their thinking, however, seemed to be characterized more by prejudice than by insight into the principle. They were so unrealistic in their views that they would have the two realms not only separate but each also with no responsibility for the welfare of the other. It is possible to see now that this was a posture which in the future was to characterize the assaults against any working arrangements between church and state on the grounds that an establishment of religion was being effected. The opposition has never succeeded in convincing the legislative or judicial branches of our government that the chaplaincies were unconstitutional.

The opposition, however, was not to be taken lightly. Included in the argument against the chaplaincies were the significant opinions of James Madison, who had since the time of his presidency changed his mind on the legality of the arrangement. His *Detached Memoranda* contains this paragraph:

> The establishment of the chaplainship to Congress is palpable violation of equal rights, as well as of Constitutional principles:
> The tenets of the chaplains elected (by the majority) shut the

door of worship against the members whose creeds and consciences forbid a participation in that of the majority. To say nothing of other sects this is the case with that of Roman Catholics and Quakers who have always had members in one or both of the Legislative branches. Could a Catholic clergyman ever hope to be appointed a Chaplain? [20] To say that his religious principles are obnoxious or that his sect is small, is to lift the evil at once and exhibit in its naked deformity the doctrine that religious truth is to be tested by numbers, or that the major sects have a right to govern the minor.[21]

The judiciary committees of both houses considered the matter very carefully. The verdict, as given in the Senate committee report, was that neither the letter nor the spirit of the First Amendment of the Constitution of the United States was violated by the chaplaincies. The reply included the opinion that there had been no establishment or endowment of a particular religious society; no privileged or preferred status had been granted to any religious denomination; and no penalties had been inflicted on any dissenting individual or group for failure to participate. "It is not seen, therefore," the report concluded, "how the institution of chaplains is justly obnoxious to the reproach of invading religious liberty in the widest sense of the term." [22]

The challenge had been presented primarily as regards congressional chaplaincies. Accordingly the decision made by the judiciary committees of the 32nd Congress was a key factor in all future judgments involving chaplains. Madison's serious doubts had been weighed, judged, and answered with forthright support for the chaplaincy idea.

The year 1854 saw additional attempts at eliminating chaplaincies on constitutional grounds. The new tack was an appeal to Article Six of the Constitution, which required that "no religious test shall ever be required as a qualification to any office or public trust under the United States." Congress, however, could not be convinced that this in any way involved the position of the chaplains. The reply of the Judiciary Committee of the House of Representatives in 1854 is significant in this connection:

While your committee believe that neither Congress nor the army and navy should be deprived of the service of chaplains, they freely concede that the ecclesiastical and civil powers have been, and should continue to be, entirely divorced from each other. . . . There is a great and very prevalent error on this subject in the opinion that those who organized this government did not legislate on religion. They did legislate on it by making it free to all, "to the Jew and the Greek, to the learned and unlearned." The error has risen from the belief that there is no legislation unless in permissive or restricting enactments. But making a thing free is as truly a part of legislation as confining it by limitations; and what the government has made free, it is bound to keep free.[23]

The argument went on, however, and Congress continued to be pressed for rulings on the issue. On March 13, 1859, the House Judiciary Committee added this opinion to what had previously been stated:

The spirit of Christianity has ever had a tendency to mitigate the rigors of war, if as yet it has not been entirely able to prevent it; to lend to acts of charity and kindness; and to humanize the heart. It was true philanthropy, therefore, to introduce this mitigating influence where, of all other places, its fruits were to be more beneficially realized, namely into the Army and Navy, and to abolish it, in this Christian age of the world, would seem like retrograding rather than advancing civilization. While much good and no perceptible evil has resulted from the practice; while no constitutional prohibition exists in relation to it, and no tendency to a "religious establishment" is discernible under it; while diversity of truth is tolerated as freely as the constitutional requirement, in the minister, as well as in those for whom he officiates; and while the expense is so small as not to be felt by any one, your committee do not think it necessary to interfere with the office of chaplain, as it exists at present, in the Army and Navy.[24]

This is an excellent summary of the position which our government has continued to hold to the present. However, the criticism against the chaplaincies continued into the first years of the Civil War and was not quieted until the House Judiciary

Committee drew up another opinion reaffirming the previous stand and giving unqualified support to the chaplaincy.[25]

There were also those who agitated for the continuance of the chaplaincies. One of the chief spokesmen in their support was Lorenzo Dow Johnson, an Episcopalian layman of Washington, D. C. In 1856 he published a pamphlet entitled "Chaplains of the General Government, with Objection to Their Employment Considered." This was followed in 1857 by another, "An Address to the Pastors and People of These United States on the Chaplaincy of the General Government." Though Johnson was frank to point out the weaknesses which then existed in the chaplaincy, he contended that its chief opponents were "those who avowed their disbelief in all revealed religion."[26] With his arguments in favor of the chaplaincy system, Johnson had also compiled the first, though brief, history of the chaplains' corps. Undoubtedly his efforts were important in defeating the move to have Congress abolish all government chaplaincies. Moreover, a number of his recommendations were of sound value, antedating by years their final adoption into the chaplaincy program. Among these, for example, were the setting up of an examining board for the processing of applications of new chaplains, appointing chaplains on the basis of ability and merit, and requiring annual reports from the individual chaplains to the supervisory board. These have since become standard items of the military chaplaincy.

The Civil War brought a large number of chaplains into military service[27] and with them also a more spiritualized type of ministry. Chaplains for the Army posts, regiments, and hospitals were provided by both federal and state legislation. An Act of 1861 established regimental chaplains for the Regular Army, specifying that they be duly ordained ministers of a Christian denomination.[28] This was expanded the following year to include the presentation of "testimonials of his good standing" in his denomination, as certified by either the denomination or five accredited ministers thereof.[29] The Army obviously was concerned about keeping undesirable chaplains out of the service and thought this safeguard sufficient. It was during the Civil War that the title "chaplain" first came into general use.[30] As for pay and other allowances, military chaplains were placed on the same level with cavalry captains.

In the Navy at this time important changes also took place, notably the provision of 1860 which specified that each chaplain be permitted to conduct worship according to the forms of his own church and that attendance at worship be voluntary in keeping with the Constitution. At this time (1862), too, Lincoln was granted authority to appoint chaplains for every general hospital at the same rate of pay as post chaplains.[31]

Demobilization at war's end naturally brought a sharp reduction in the number of chaplains. Those who were retained with their regiments were now placed on a permanent basis. Provision was also made for each Negro regiment to have its chaplain. By 1877, however, the position of chaplain had again reverted to little more than schoolteacher and librarian of the army post. For about 25 years the situation remained static, although on larger posts other personnel were gradually drawn in to take over the chaplain's peripheral duties. The war against Spain in 1898, primarily a naval affair which involved a relatively small army, brought little change or improvement in the chaplain's position. Chaplains did serve with both the Navy and the Army of Occupation in the Philippines during this time.

The Modern Concept of the Military Chaplain

The present-day status of the military chaplain dates from between 1899 and 1901, when Congress enacted legislation calling for chaplains who were qualified clergymen of their respective denominations and were duly endorsed by their ecclesiastical boards.[32] In a sense this merely served to underscore a policy which Civil War days had shown to be necessary. To meet the government's new set of standards, several churches now set up commissions for the procurement of chaplains. The Episcopal Church led the way, followed closely by the Roman Catholic Church. However, the ecclesiastical endorsement for new applicants was not required of the various denominations as routine procedure until 1913.[33] In accord with this requirement the Protestant churches set up the Protestant Committee on Army and

Navy Chaplains in 1917.[34] In this year also the chiefs of chaplains
were first vested with examining authority on the admission of
new chaplains,[35] and the Congress provided for the appointment
of chaplains from minority groups, such as the Jews.[36]

When World War I began, the Army had 74 regular chaplains,
the National Guard 72. By the end of the war more than 2,300
had been commissioned for military service.[37] The goal was one
chaplain for every 1,200 men, but this ratio fell short by half.
To help orient the many new chaplains to their military ministry,
an Army chaplains' school was established for the first time in
1918 at Fort Monroe, Va. The school had various locations
thereafter, and during the period 1928–42 it was inactivated,
and chaplains were prepared for military service through correspondence courses. Early in 1942, soon after the onset of
World War II, the school was reactivated at Fort Benjamin
Harrison, Ind. When this post proved inadequate to the size of
the operation, a shift was made to the campus of Harvard
University, where most World War II Army chaplains received
their training. After the war the school was moved to Carlisle
Barracks, Pa., where it continues today.

In the Navy a total of 203 chaplains saw service during World
War I, some of them with the Marines along the Western Front.[38]
At this time, too, the Chaplains' Division with a Chief of Chap-
lains was established in the Bureau of Navigation.

The scope and intensity of this first world conflict called for
immediate and adequate realignment in many departments of
the Armed Forces. In this the chaplaincy was no exception; the
war helped it grow to full stature. Better organization and supervision of the chaplains' departments in both Army and Navy
grew out of the demands laid on them. In the Defense Act of
1920 the office of Chief of Chaplains was set up for the Army, and
the duties of the incumbent were specified to "include investigation into the qualifications of candidates for appointment as
chaplains, and general coordination and supervision of the work
of the chaplains." [39]

The period between the two world wars was not without
difficulties for the military chaplaincy. The drastic demobiliza-

tion of the Armed Forces brought about by the Kellogg-Briand Pact, the movement toward pacifism in some American churches,[40] the criticism of incumbent chaplains for their lack of spirituality — these were factors that combined to all but undo the military chaplaincy.[41] Sentiments toward a civilian-type chaplaincy were strong in some of the major denominations during the early 1930s.[42] One of the leaders in this crusade was the *Christian Century,* which editorialized: "We look with shame upon the blind servility with which the Christian church gave itself to the government of the United States in 1917 and 1918." [43] The editor expressed the hope that the churches would disavow their connections with the military chaplaincy program.

Under this pressure the military chaplaincy was subjected to renewed scrutiny by various denominational assemblies and especially the Federal Council of Churches. The outcome of this concern and study was the consensus that "the way for the churches to deal with the problem of the chaplaincy was not to separate themselves from their involvement in our national defense but to strengthen their spiritual ties with chaplains and to work for a greater spiritual vitality in the chaplaincy." [44] Thus it was that the General Commission on Chaplains of the Federal Council of Churches and the commissions of other church bodies were ready to meet the extraordinary demands laid on them for the procurement of chaplains during the world conflict which was soon to follow.

During World War II the military chaplaincy expanded rapidly, counting at its peak over 8,000 chaplains in the Army and almost 3,000 in the Navy.[45] Most important of all was the generally high level of respect and efficiency of operation to which the military chaplaincy had risen. Chaplains had gone with their troops and ships to the ends of the earth and distinguished themselves with faithful, altruistic service in behalf of their men. The Korean War told a similar story of accomplishment.

In 1950 a study of the chaplaincy program was made by a committee appointed by President Harry S. Truman. The findings of this committee were published in the report known as *The Military Chaplaincy.*[46] In general the report voiced strong and unqualified words of commendation for the services rendered by the chaplains. The chief shortcoming in the opinion of the committee was that the quota allotment for all denominations was too conservative, often not up to the required level, and that consideration ought to be given toward the procurement of more chaplains. The report also took cognizance of the fact that this was a problem related to the prevailing shortage of trained ministers in most church denominations.

Meanwhile, after World War II, far-reaching changes were taking place in the Air Force. Up to 1947 the Army Air Corps had existed as a department under the Army. Chaplains serving with the Air Corps were drawn from among Army chaplain personnel on a 4-year rotation basis. With the adoption of the National Security Act in 1947 the United States Air Force became a distinct and separate department of the Armed Forces, along with the Army and the Navy. By May 1949 the Chaplains Service of the Air Force was constituted as a separate unit. In organization and purpose it paralleled closely its Army and Navy counterparts.

The continuing tensions in the world have called for unusual measures in our country's life and policies. National defense and worldwide treaty commitments have required that relatively large armies, fleets, and air forces be maintained even in peacetime. Never before in our country's history has it been necessary to continue compulsory military training so many years after hostilities ceased.

These are factors which have also effected changes and development in the military chaplaincy. For one thing, there still are about 3,000 clergymen on active duty. They serve a widely scattered host in every area of the globe, wherever our government has deployed its military installations and manpower. At many bases, including those overseas, the family dependents of servicemen have become a part of the government's concern. About 60 percent of the military personnel are married.

The peacetime concept of military ministry has of necessity

had to be geared to meet these changes. At many military bases a typical parish program has come into being. In addition to preaching, teaching, and counseling, many chaplains now have the usual diversified parish responsibilities, youth and adult programs, Sunday schools, weekday and vacation Bible schools, teacher training programs, and men's and women's organizations.

The physical properties or facilities employed in this ministry have of necessity also changed and improved in recent years. Many new chapels have been built at bases in our country and abroad, some are still being built or renovated, and a growing number of educational buildings are rising alongside some of these chapels.

Obviously our government has poured a considerable amount of tax money into the military chaplaincy program. The cost today, however, is but a small fraction of the total military outlay. The government's thinking on the arrangement is basically still the same. In return for the many benefits which accrue to it, government is ready and happy to assume the financial cost of the spiritual ministry which the chaplains render to its citizenry under arms.

THE CHAPLAINCY AND THE CHURCH-STATE ISSUE

The Chaplaincy and Military Regulations

The regulations of all three branches of the Armed Forces have become more and more explicit in defining the position and duties of the chaplain and in setting up proper safeguards for his conscience and the rights of the denomination he serves. The ecclesiastical position of a chaplain is conceived of as deriving solely from the church body which endorses him.[47] There is no such person as a nondenominational or interdenominational chaplain. The wording in the manuals varies, but basically all three branches of the Armed Forces agree that ecclesiastical endorsement is the *sine qua non* of the chaplain's position. For the Army chaplain this requirement is stated as follows:

A principal requirement to qualify for appointment as chaplain in any compound of the Army is an ecclesiastical indorsement. This indorsement is submitted by the applicant's denomination

to the Office of the Adjutant General. The withdrawal of
a chaplain's ecclesiastical indorsement by the denomination
which he represents is basis for action by the Adjutant General's Office to terminate his commission and separate him from
the service.[48]

Similar provisions and conditions are stated in the manuals
of the Navy and the Air Force.[49] The chaplain depends for the
continuance of his position on fraternal relations between himself
and his sponsoring denomination. Without this no clergyman
can be accepted into the chaplains' corps, and without it he
cannot remain.[50] Thus the churches, not the government, are
looked on as the calling as well as the disciplinary agents in the
ecclesiastical standing of the chaplains. No longer can it be
claimed, as was true before World War I, that the military chaplains are the "forgotten men" of their denominations. Today they
represent a large bloc of professional workers whose needs and
work must be duly considered in each church denomination.

The regulations of the Armed Forces regarding the chaplain's
duties under the commanding officer of a ship or station have at
times been misinterpreted to mean that the Armed Forces themselves are sponsoring religious worship and practice.[51] Actually
all regulations which provide for the scheduling of religious services are simply the safeguards which have been set up to provide
the climate or sanction for the duly appointed chaplain to go
about his professional duties, similar to the authorization which
is given to the medical officers to perform their functions. Commanders of ships and stations therefore have as little power in
themselves to practice religion as they have to perform surgery
and administer medications except in emergency situations. The
churches alone, through their chaplains, provide the spiritual
content and activation of the government's regulations. Without
the churches the regulations on the chaplaincy would mean
nothing.

The Chaplain's Dual Task

Every chaplain has a dual capacity: to foster morals and high
morale in the Armed Services and to provide for military person-

nel the rights and privileges of religious worship. To this end commanding officers are instructed to make provision for religious worship and to encourage attendance at the same by all men under their command.[52]

The government does not imply by these regulations that it has an interest and in any way seeks to meddle in the church's prime work of saving souls for heaven. This is recognized as the chaplain's proper sphere. His call, mission, message, and ecclesiastical responsibility are entirely under the church of which he is a continuing part. Thus, as an officer the chaplain fulfills one function for the government and another simultaneously for the church, carrying out the vows of the ministry which he made to God and church.

It might be debated whether military rank as an officer is essential to a clergyman's status as a chaplain. The fact is that a chaplain is part of a military establishment governed by specific laws and regulations. Commanders are the legally responsible officers in the component parts of this vast military machine. Authority rises through various command positions with increasing rank and responsibility. But ultimate authority and sanction reside in the American people. In this structure, as a loyal citizen of his country, the chaplain must take his place, either with rank or without, with military status or as a civilian. The tradition of giving the clergymen military status as commissioned officers goes back, as has been shown above, to the earliest history of our nation. Long experience has demonstrated that the arrangement is good. The chaplain is not expected to assume command functions like those of the line officers. Ministry to the spiritual needs of the officers and men is his responsibility. And it has never been shown that his rank as an officer in any way influences his effectiveness adversely. The people he serves are aware that his rank is chiefly an honor bestowed on his office, needed for proper integration and deployment in the organization and in determining a pay scale commensurate with his office.

In the fulfillment of his duties a chaplain is free to proceed, speak, interpret, and motivate in accord with the dictates of his conscience and the principles of his church. In the conduct of worship he has this kind of guarantee:

> As provided by public law and *Navy Regulations,* the chaplain shall conduct public worship according to the manner and form of his own church, and, on occasions requiring it, may wear the vestments of the church to which he belongs.[53]

Respect for Religious Particularity in Doctrine and Practice

In a day when ecumenical movements have almost become a fetish to some Protestants, it is conceivable that the military chaplaincy could be regarded as a great opportunity for putting a form of united Protestantism into operation. Some might consider it a desirable goal to procure and develop chaplains according to a kind of poured-in-the-mold procedure. Even Canon Stokes shows the confusion which results on the question when the regulations as stated in the service manuals are not taken at their face value. He states:

> On the whole the present system seems to meet the needs of the Army better than any other plan proposed. But still more care should be used to *eliminate from eligibility those men* in all denominations *who because of rigid views* or personal idiosyncrasies *are not able or willing to cooperate with other groups.* It seems essential, owing to the very nature of the Army, especially in times of war, that chaplains should be subject to its control *in all except spiritual matters.*[54]

To say, on the one hand, that chaplains should have perfect liberty in spiritual matters, and on the other hand, that rigid views should bar candidates from appointment, is palpable double-talk. The military establishment has no direction or sanction to work toward the removal of the particularity of the various denominations represented through the chaplains. Such sentiment points up the continuing concern which the churches must have to keep any policy from developing within the respective chaplains' corps which would eliminate from consideration candidates of conservative religious position and approve only those who measure up to norms adopted by a group with vested interests in a liberal position, or vice versa.

Government's chief concern, as seen in the regulations governing the chaplaincy, is that there must be equal opportunity for all, within the bounds of the reasonable, and that none be made to conform to any establishment of religion, however benign and well-intentioned it may be. The standard policy and practice of Army, Navy, and Air Force have been in accord with these principles.

One of the good fruits of the participation of conservative church bodies in the chaplaincy program during the past 20 years is that their doctrinal position and practice have become generally known and respected. The result has been that the regulations themselves have been expanded to include additional safeguards for churches and chaplains with strongly confessional standards and practices. One of the regulations, for example, which has been added to the Navy manual since World War II is the following on Holy Communion:

> The Navy Department allows chaplains perfect freedom of conscience with respect to the matter of "closed" ["close"] or "open" communion. In order to meet the religious needs of officers and men, it is expected that the chaplain will provide opportunity for them to partake of communion, or, when this ministry is limited either by the chaplain's own conscience, the regulations of his church, or by the custom or conscience of officers and men, he will exercise every effort to arrange for the service of communion to be conducted by chaplains or civilian clergymen of other faiths.[55]

Similar provisions are made in the Army and Air Force manuals.[56]

Another item of concern has been the question of so-called unionistic worship practices. Among some denominations joint worship and prayer fellowship are common occurrences, particularly where doctrinal differences are viewed as of minor importance or concern. Certain chaplains, however, e. g., those in The Lutheran Church — Missouri Synod, are compelled by conscience and oath of office to avoid unionistic practices. The regulations of the Armed Forces provide the necessary safeguards for every chaplain's conscience and the proper conduct of his office under denominational rules. The Army manual

states: "No chaplain is required to conduct any service or rite
contrary to the regulations of his denomination." [57] Specifically
on the matter of union services there is this ruling: "The chaplain may officiate jointly in a religious service with a chaplain
or civilian clergyman of another denomination, unless forbidden
by laws and practices of his own denomination. Freedom of
worship in our democratic way of life is recognized by the
military establishment." [58] A similar guarantee is plainly expressed in the Navy and Air Force manuals. [59]

In the light of these examples of the regulations governing
military religious life, it is hard to conceive of a fairer and freer
arrangement under which chaplains might operate. These guarantees appear to be fully in harmony with the word and intent
of the First Amendment of the country's Constitution and the
confessional platforms of the churches.

The Institutional Chaplaincy — a Parallel

If the story of government-supported chaplaincies is to be
complete, a brief reference must be made to the institutional
chaplaincies, federal and state, which have multiplied rapidly
in recent years.

The Veterans Administration is responsible for the hospital
and institutional care of veterans who require medical, surgical,
psychiatric, or nursing care. There are some 176 of these establishments throughout the United States. [60] Under the Civil Service Act the Veterans Administration employs chaplains to minister to the spiritual needs of the patients under the government's care. Clergymen who have had military service as chaplains receive preference in the appointment to these institutional
posts. In general the Veterans Administration chaplaincies are
modeled after and receive their sanction from the military concept of spiritual care of citizens. Federal prisons follow similar
policies.

State and local institutions of all kinds are also in this pattern. There is recognition here, too, that public institutions must
initiate and implement a program of spiritual care for the growing number of patients who are the wards or responsibility of

the state. Churches for many years have provided such ministry to patients in their own institutions and on a voluntary basis at their own expense; they have also rendered similar service through full- or part-time chaplains to patients in state institutions. But the increasing number of these institutions in recent years has emphasized the need for having many more clergy, clinically trained, for this specialized ministry. As a result the chaplaincy programs established in institutions on the local and state levels are comparable to those of the Veterans Administration.[61]

The problems of procurement, control, support, and equitable distribution of institutional chaplains must all be met and resolved by the local or state legislatures or welfare boards. The questions, however, which are basic to the church-state issue may be evaluated along with the military, congressional, and Veterans Administration chaplaincies.

The Chaplaincy Tested Under the Separation Principle

There are those who look upon these involvements as violations of the Constitution. Among these are such groups as the American Association for the Advancement of Atheism, extreme church pacifists, and a conscientious minority who believe that chaplains, if there are to be any, should be supported by the churches themselves and carry no rank. Virtually the same group also opposed the Navy's V-12 program during World War II, under which the Navy gave financial support to theological trainees who later were to become Navy chaplains. This arrangement also caused the *Christian Century* to become quite exercised and to editorialize:

> Well here it is — the United States navy stepping in to control the education of boys as Christian ministers, with their training for that holy calling fixed by the navy's judgment as to what will produce officer material! Not in the 150 years of the nation's history has the issue of state control of the functions of the church been raised in such aggravated form. And this by a government which professes to be fighting for freedom of religion! The Christian Century has long opposed the inclusion of chaplains, with military and naval rank, among the

commissioned officers of the army and navy. We have always believed that ministers could render more effective spiritual service to the enlisted men simply as chaplains, bearing only the commissions of the churches which send them to this particular task.[62]

The debate was carried over into the pages of *Christianity and Crisis,* where an opposite view was defended:

The Church does not surrender a single right within the sphere of her own jurisdiction. . . . If it is right for the Church to permit her ministers to render spiritual service to American soldiers, sailors, and airmen at the expense of the State, it is not wrong for the Church to permit future chaplains to accept financial assistance from the State while they are preparing themselves to render a service which the State is eager that they should render, and in the rendering of which they are granted complete spiritual freedom.[63]

No branch of the Armed Forces any longer gives financial assistance to prospective military chaplains. In order to fill their quota allotments for the future, however, both Army and Navy encourage qualified theological students to apply for commissions while still at the seminary.[64] The only compensation which the student receives under such arrangement is that normally given to a reserve officer for the time he spends with a reserve training unit or on temporary tour of duty.

The dispute over the V-12 chaplaincy training program serves as a case in point to illustrate how the question of the military chaplaincy has periodically been dragged into the arena of contest on the subject of religious freedom and the separation of church and state. Critics of the chaplaincy have seen in it, as well as in similar arrangements where the efforts of church and state run a closely parallel course, a serious threat to our heritage of freedom. Public sentiment, however, and legal opinion have consistently supported the chaplaincies and their constitutionality on the grounds that equal opportunity is guaranteed to each denomination and no establishment of religion by the government can be shown to have occurred.

The friendly dependence of the government on the churches

in the attainment of certain goals has not been confined merely to the military chaplaincy. It is apropos to remember that the clergy have always held a unique position in the consideration of our national and state governments as a result of their sacred calling and devotion to the religious needs of the people. While these professional servants of the churches have not been exempted from any of the laws which apply generally to the populace of the land, they have consistently been accorded respect, even certain privileges, because of their position. Thus, for example, ministers have regularly been excused from jury duty and military draft. They have also been looked on as public officers in being legally authorized to perform marriage ceremonies. In addition the federal government has exempted clergymen from including in their total reportable income for tax purposes the home which is furnished them by the church. There are exemptions, too, from ordinary restrictions of immigration laws, so that bona fide ministers are not subject to quota allotments. Certain travel privileges and rates for clergymen have also reflected government's friendly intervention. The Interstate Commerce Act of 1887 specifically exempted the clergy from its prohibitions designed to eliminate abuses in the issuing of free passes. During World War II clergymen were granted special ration privileges for gasoline and tires because the government did not want their ministry to the populace restricted in any way. All of these considerations demonstrate the favorable attitude of government toward the churches, as well as its policy of utilizing to the fullest, within the limits of the Constitution, the salutary influence of clergymen.

In the minds of our forefathers no breach of religious liberty ensued from the activity of chaplains appointed and supported by the government, military or congressional. Yet in that day the concept of religious liberty and the separation of church and state were uppermost in their minds. Because all denominations were regarded impartially, the consensus prevailed that there was no violation of the First Amendment in establishing the chaplaincy, since Congress was not thereby establishing a national religion.

Military chaplaincies and all other chaplaincies supported by the government have their sanction from the laws of our land because of the government's interest in the service of the church to the needs of society. The courts and the Congress have stood behind this interpretation, judging the position and the employment of chaplains to be analogous to tax exemption, a privilege accorded the churches for valuable and distinctive social contributions.

The question was publicly debated in the years before the Civil War.[65] The charges of violation of the First Amendment and the principle of the separation of church and state were carefully studied and discussed over a long period by the judiciary committees of Congress. In the days of Lincoln (1863) the House Judiciary Committee handed down the opinion which has stood ever since: that no violation of the Constitution was involved. "It was pointed out that chaplains were in the Army before the adoption of the Constitution; that the First Congress had appointed chaplains; that the expense of the chaplaincy was slight; that the need for religious guidance was necessary for the 'safety of civil society.'"[66]

This judgment has never been reversed in any way by later judicial opinions. Its most recent challenge was brought in a suit against the Treasurer of the United States by Frank C. Hughes of Minneapolis, a professed atheist who repeated the charge (advanced on several earlier occasions by the American Association for the Advancement of Atheism) that it was unconstitutional to pay the salaries and allowances of chaplains out of tax money. The case was dismissed by Judge Edward A. Tamm in December 1955 in the Federal District Court at Washington, D. C., on the grounds that the plaintiff "does not have status to maintain the action" and that, moreover, his plea failed to "set forth a cause of action."[67]

Carl Zollmann, in his valuable compilation of legal opinion involving this issue, cites quite a number of court decisions in support of his summary:

> The consequences of this situation stand out clearly and well defined. "No principle of constitutional law is violated when

thanksgiving or fast days are appointed; when chaplains are designated for the army and navy; when legislative sessions are opened with prayer or the reading of the Scriptures." [68]

In line with these judgments the government chaplaincies exist and function today. Government has not proposed to take over the work of the churches. Nor is it concerned with the salvation of souls. But government recognizes two facts realistically: men in military service and patients in public institutions are no exceptions in their need and desire for religious ministration, and churches must provide the answer to this need. Only thus is religious freedom not inhibited and a high level of morality and morale maintained in the land.

Government is being realistic, therefore, when it makes available the chaplaincy program to the churches. It has its own purposes in view and expects that these purposes will be achieved more or less as side effects of the work which the churches are primarily interested in doing through their own clergymen and in their own way. Hence that it is paying for and supporting these efforts is considered to be merely incidental to achieving its own stated ends.

While this attitude may seem to reflect adversely on government, as if it after all is merely "organized selfishness," [69] the fact remains that the assistance which government gives to the churches in the form of the chaplaincies can be justified under the Constitution in no other way. Zollmann has given an excellent summary of this position in the light of civil law and Scriptural principle:

> Though Christ, the founder of the Christian religion, did not intend to erect a temporal dominion but to reign in the hearts of men by subduing their irregular appetites and propensities and by moulding their passions to the noblest purposes, though he did not make any pretense to worldly pomp and power, his religion is calculated and accommodated to meliorate the conduct and condition of man under any form of civil government. The services of religion to the state indeed are of untold value. To it we are indebted for all social order and happiness. Civil and religious liberty are due to it.[70]

Special Problems and the Chaplaincy

There is no need to minimize the dangers that attend an arrangement like the chaplaincy, military or institutional, when supported by public funds. This is spelled out by the criticisms, not all invalid, which persist even after all legal difficulties have been resolved to the satisfaction of the parties involved.

Is there threat, for example, that a militarized church will result from the cooperation of the church and state through an institution like the chaplaincy? Does the church by its loan of chaplains to the government cast a vote in favor of militarism? That depends to a great extent on the vitality of the American churches, especially Protestant, which have a long history of enlightened and critical interaction with government.

The soldier under arms owes obedience to his government in support of its stated aims of protecting life, liberty, and property, of maintaining peace, and of quelling aggression. The chaplain is no more a militarist than his civilian counterpart when he leads those under his care to assume gladly their part in government's task. At the same time the churches through their chaplains must always remain alert to the threat of the militaristic way of thinking, which exalts power and its exercise for its own sake. Chaplains and chaplaincy boards dare never be swept away by any riptide of militaristic fervor to the extent that they no longer speak out against the unforgiving and intransigent spirit in men and nations wherever and whenever it appears. The freedom to speak and preach the Gospel with its fullest application remains a right for clergymen in uniform as well as out.

At the same time and on the other side of the coin, chaplains can do much to forestall the opposite attitude which, especially in peacetime, leads to a condemnation of the military man and military power. Neither Christ nor His apostles ever spoke against the office of the soldier but only against the abuse of that office. Obviously, for both purposes — to prevent militarism and to quash unjustified condemnation of military power per se — it is of strategic importance that there be clergymen within the military machine, as well as out of it, to aid the citizenry to view its task rightly under God.

The chaplaincy, more than any other institution in our national life, has demonstrated that rather than a wedding between two diverse partners, whose rights, privileges, and functions are quite distant and not to be fused, there can be continuing enlightened interaction by church and state on matters that concern them both, each fostering the other's wellbeing and prosperity, each respecting and observing the other's proper sphere of activity, each firmly resisting any deviation from constitutional norms, each also ready to explore new approaches to old problems.

Chaplains and denominational chaplaincy boards also have the responsibility for preserving intact the particularity of religious expression, if this indeed is conceived as being basic to religious freedom. Government, as Luther foresaw, tends all too easily to appropriate to itself the shepherd's role, even as the church in times past has sought to control the hangman's noose.[71] Neither must ever happen. It is conceivable that the chaplaincy could be made into an instrument of the state to serve the state's own ends. To prevent this the churches must continue to stress the purely ecclesiastical functions which through the chaplains they are willing to assume in behalf of the government in military or institutional situations. Chaplains themselves must especially conceive of their status as deriving first and foremost from the call or endorsement they have received through their church. The government is not in position to issue such tokens of vocation, nor indeed can it, if it is to avoid the onus of inciting the establishment of national military religion.

Recognition of these basic truths underlying the relationship of church and state through the chaplaincy is vital also in another direction. Whatever support government has rendered religion by assuming the cost of the chaplaincies must always be conceived of as brought about by the peculiar demands of military life and as an expense rightfully incurred for the incidental benefits that accrue. Government must therefore not propose, nor ought the churches agitate for, additional and more generalized subsidy of religion through public funds.

Eternal vigilance is the price of a basic right also in another matter. Men in the Armed Forces, especially those in the early stages of their training, can by injudicious use of military law be easily made into "captive audiences" for religious purposes. Such trespass of the individual's rights occurred during World War II, and undoubtedly some commanders will continue to exceed their responsibility to make church available to all hands in the future by requiring recruits to attend worship services whether they so desire or not. However benign and well-intentioned the motives, it would be shortsighted and contrary to basic principles of the Reformation heritage for churches to tolerate any arrangement whereby men are involuntarily placed into a worship setting. The chaplaincy must have as its basic rationale the readiness to serve and minister the Gospel to all men who voluntarily desire such service.

Freedom, however, has an ambivalent meaning in some people's definition. What they demand for themselves they often would deny to another. Thus, when freedom of religion is at issue, there are some reactionary minds who agitate strongly for the complete exclusion of religion from the government's concern. The courts have never agreed that freedom of religion means the lack of it, nor the denial of its free use, nor even the refusal to encourage its practice. While government must recognize the right of the agnostic or atheist not to worship God if he so chooses, it at the same time is fully within the limits of the Constitution when the courts resist the motions of groups or individuals who seek to make the man who believes most conform to the way of thinking of the man who believes least or nothing at all. The chaplaincy, especially in the Armed Forces, exists as a continuing evidence of the government's attention to this inalienable right of men to worship God freely and as a bulwark against the inroads of atheistic materialism and nihilism, which could spell ruin not only for our country but also for civilization.

Concluding Thoughts

The state and the church have their God-appointed spheres.[72] It is vital to the welfare of both that the respective realms not be confused. Safeguards which the state must always defend appear to be fourfold: that no church be given preferential treatment over another; that worship be maintained always as a voluntary privilege; that no penalties be meted out for non-participation in religious exercise; and that there be no taxation for direct support of religion. In the light of these principles and aware of the concessions which it has granted to the churches in the matter of the chaplaincies, military and institutional, government must conscientiously avoid all semblance of being a minister of religion and the Word rather than a minister of discipline and the sword.[73]

On the other hand the churches must endeavor just as conscientiously, through their military and institutional chaplains, to abide by the God-given task of ministering the Word and of preaching it to the ends of the earth. This they can do without fear and favor under the guarantees for freedom of expression and freedom of religion inscribed in our Constitution. They must expect and demand no favor from government beyond that which it is reasonable for government to give in pursuit of its own ends for the public weal.

To know the dangers attendant on mixing of church and state and to avoid them is incumbent on both institutions. But folly it would be, especially for the churches, for fear of the dangers involved, to be struck with apathy and inaction, to forgo privileges within the bounds of God's law and civil authority, and thereby to fail to become all things toward all men that some might be saved.[74] When the cautions are properly observed and the duties properly fulfilled, then both, the state and the church, will not be "turned upside down"[75] but will be able to serve the people with much good and blessing in their respective spheres.

II

LEGAL CONTACTS OF CHURCH AND STATE

James S. Savage

Church and state have numerous contacts. The state, of course, is concerned with the church in its socially organized form as well as with individuals. Church bodies and congregations are recognized as legal entities. The state adopts an attitude toward them which reflects, in the laws of the state, the custom and accepted practice of the people. This attitude includes a favored tax treatment, special application of zoning regulations, and certain privileges. From time to time the prevailing pattern of the state's treatment of churches is challenged, and friction occurs between church and state. Some of these areas which have become taut with tension in recent times are important measuring sticks for the extent of the separation of church and state as well as for the scope of religious freedom enjoyed by church groups.

THE CHURCH AS A LEGAL ENTITY

Incorporation

In all of the states and in federally governed territories, churches and religious institutions have the privilege of incorporation. As corporations they enjoy legal status and protection greater than that given to an aggregate of individuals: they have perpetual existence, and freedom from personal liability for corporate acts. Most religious bodies take advantage of this privilege. Most congregations, presbyteries, conferences, synods, colleges, seminaries, publishing houses, etc., maintained by churches are incorporated.

It should be noted that a religious corporation is customarily formed to handle the property of the religious body and is not to be confused with the "church" itself. The "church" is a spiritual body and is not subject to civil power, while the society which becomes incorporated is a temporal body and therefore subject to civil law. Membership in the "church" according to the requirements of the "church" is a prerequisite to membership in the society. When the temporal society is incorporated, it is endowed with substantially the same rights and privileges as are other private corporations.

Almost all state constitutional and legislative provisions for the incorporation of religious bodies limit the activities of the corporation so formed to those which naturally tend to carry out the purposes of the religious group. A religious body may not

form a corporation to engage in an activity that is not germane
to the purpose of the body, particularly if that activity is in competition with a corporation formed for the purpose of profit making. An incorporated religious society cannot, for example, enter
the banking field. Corporations formed for profit, in contrast with
those not formed for profit, are subject to different laws and taxation.[76]

Corporations formed by religious bodies may own property,
both real and personal. In general most states impose restrictions
on the type of real property that may be owned by such corporations. Usually it must be real property used in carrying on the
work of the organization. No similar restrictions apply to the
ownership of personal property, and an incorporated religious
society may purchase such property, e. g., shares of stock in
a commercial corporation, as it chooses.

Church corporations may enter into binding contracts with
other persons, both natural (i. e., human beings) and artificial
(i. e., corporations and institutions created by law), and may seek
the aid of a court in the enforcement of such contracts. They
may make their own bylaws, receive voluntary contributions,
enter into contracts, and merge or consolidate with other corporations formed for the same or similar purposes.[77]

The Church in Court

A church body or its incorporated society may find itself
going into court, either voluntarily as a complainant or involuntarily as a defendant, in a variety of situations. The most troublesome and complex of these situations is the court action that
arises from an intrachurch dispute resulting in a schism.

It should be noted that a church dispute that does not involve
either the property of the church or some aspect of the corporation will not ordinarily involve court action. Most courts in the
United States, federal and state, follow the ruling of the United
States Supreme Court in *Watson* v. *Jones:*

> Whenever the questions of discipline, or of faith, or ecclesi-
> astical rule, custom, or law have been decided by the highest
> church judicatory to which the particular congregation is sub-

ject, and to which the matter has been carried, the legal tribunals must accept such decision as final and as binding on them in their application to the case before them.[78]

Where a church dispute involves property or some aspect of the corporation, it may not be possible for a court to avoid litigation. Property may be held by the corporation under an expressed or implied trust, or the charter of the corporation may limit or prescribe the uses to which the property owned by it may be put. In such cases it may be necessary for the court, in protecting temporal property and legal rights, to examine the entire dispute and to make final disposition of the problems involved in the light of the law of property and of corporations in that jurisdiction.

The church may find itself in court as a complainant, attempting to secure enforcement of police regulations designed to protect all persons from harm, e. g., statutes against burglary; or to protect all persons in a given neighborhood against a given type of harm, e. g., zoning restrictions; or to protect the church itself, e. g., against disturbances of religious meetings. The church may find itself in court as a defendant. It may be charged with violating a police regulation, e. g., excessive ringing of church bells, impeding traffic, creating a disturbance at unreasonable hours. In all cases of this sort the church appears in much the same way as any other person, real or artificial (e. g., a corporation), and will normally be afforded or denied protection as the law and the facts of the case warrant. No special consideration will be given the church as church, nor should it be expected. In these situations the church appears merely as another citizen to enforce its rights or defend them as the case may be.

EXEMPTION FROM TAXATION

Exemption from taxation afforded to religious institutions and property used for religious purposes is such a well-established part of the American tradition that it would hardly seem necessary to do more than note its historical origin and continued existence.[79] Some post-World War II developments, however, have focused considerable attention on the whole matter of aid to religious activities by the government. If exemption from taxation is regarded as a form of aid, then the important thing today is not that the pattern exists — a fact conceded on all sides — but whether it can and should be continued.

Origins of Tax Exemption

The early settlers in our country brought with them from Europe the concept of an "established" church, as noted in a previous chapter of this book. The church so established was regarded as a division of the government, and taxing it would have been considered a self-defeating practice. The established churches in England and on the continent could look back to many centuries of tradition in this practice, reaching as far into antiquity as the reign of Emperor Constantine. Even in the pre-Christian era, exemption from taxation for the representatives of the church was a part of Judaic thinking.[80]

The wave of "disestablishment" that swept the colonies and early states culminated in the adoption of the First Amendment to the Constitution. It was not intended by this measure to demonstrate hostility to religion or the churches. The "disestablished" churches and the "dissenting" churches alike were granted immunity from taxation as a matter of course. In the original colonies it was not thought necessary to write a special exemption clause into the state constitutions. Most of the states admitted to the Union after the first 13, however, did make that provision. Periodically, opposition to exemption from taxation was voiced, but it has become significant only in recent years.[81]

The present pattern of exemption from taxation by the federal government may be sketched in broad terms. Religious bodies and churches are not required to pay income taxes, but Social Security taxation may be provided in given optional situations. Church property in the District of Columbia is not taxable if used for religious purposes. The government permits individuals and corporations to deduct contributions (subject to certain mechanical limitations) to churches and religious institutions from the amount of income subject to federal income tax. It also permits individuals and trusts to deduct such contributions in the computation of federal gift and estate taxes. Bibles, regalias, gems, and furnishings intended for religious purposes are exempt from import duties.[82]

Every state in the Union provides in one way or another for property tax exemption for church edifices, parsonages, buildings used for a church school, and cemeteries. The general basis is humanitarian. There are some mechanical limits and qualifications, but these vary so much from state to state that it is difficult to generalize regarding them. In about two thirds of the states the basic exemption is provided in the state constitution. In about half of these states the constitutional provision is self-executing, and in the other half it is simply a grant of authority to the legislative body. In those states without constitutional provision, the exemption is based either on legislative enactment or on historical practice and custom.[83]

Pros and Cons of a Change in Pattern

There are a number of factors which could bring about a reconsideration of tax exemption for the churches.

If population grows in the United States without a corresponding growth in the number of people belonging to churches, the unchurched might become the large majority. Even now the unchurched constitute a sizable proportion of the population. If they should become convinced that exemption from taxation is a form of establishment of religion forbidden by the First Amendment, they may succeed in eliminating exemption through democratic processes.[84]

Most commentators agree that the economic loss to various governmental bodies involved in tax exemption is not at present significant. But in recent years increases in governmental costs have forced a reappraisal of tax sources. The voters might conceivably decide that even the elimination of an "insignificant loss" can afford some relief. The multiplication of new and elaborate church edifices and church-school plants may hasten that conclusion.[85]

The phenomenal rate of growth of the Roman Catholic Church could also become provocative. Its expanding educational system is expensive, and the Catholic interest in subsidy for church schools is already well known. Agitation for such support might well result in a determined reaction that would not only deny aid to parochial schools but sweep away existing exemptions for the substantial property holdings of the church.

Recent decisions of the Supreme Court regarding religion and education lean toward a stricter interpretation of the "wall of separation" doctrine.[86] This view has a strong following which can easily be encouraged to reevaluate tax exemption for religious purposes in the light of the court's conclusions. Determined efforts toward removal of church privileges as potential breaches in the "wall" could well follow.

These are possible future developments unfavorable to the continuation of the current pattern. But there are good prospects that the present status of tax exemption will be unaltered for a long time to come.

In the first place the force of history and tradition is on the side of exemption. The pattern is well established. Charitable institutions, colleges, and other nonprofit ventures are also tax exempt, presumably because they contribute to the well-being of society.

Thus far there has been no "establishment" of religion with the exemption pattern. Hence it is hard for most Americans to see in it a violation of the First Amendment. Any privilege granted is shared without discrimination by all churches, and church activity is regarded as important to the American way of life. There would therefore seem to be nothing improper about the exemption.

The enormousness of the job involved in changing the pattern can be a strong deterrent to even the most zealous of reformers. Public debate on any proposed change in constitution or law would involve the issue of "secularism" versus "religion." Many persons who honestly oppose tax exemption would be reluctant to appear to be on the side of secularism. Judges, legislators, and other officers of government are not prone to seem hostile to religion. It would not be easy, for example, to amend a state consti-

tution so as to eliminate exemption, without the cooperation
of the legislature and governor.[87]

A more telling argument for retention of the practice is derived from the American concern for religious liberty. Some
believe that the power to tax churches and religious institutions
may be an opening wedge for the curtailment of religious freedom. Chief Justice John Marshall said: "The power to tax involves the power to destroy." [88] The point is made by those
in favor of the pattern that it is better to allow exemption than
to run the risk of infringement on religious liberty.

The chief stumbling block in the path of those who want to
stop tax exemption for churches lies in the complications of the
amending process. To amend the federal Constitution requires
ratification by three fourths of the states. A sizable mobilization
of opinion is required for that purpose. A similar problem exists
in the states which have exemption embodied in their constitutions.

The possibility of securing a state amendment always exists,
of course. California is a case in point. In 1951 the legislature
voted overwhelmingly to grant tax exemption to church-related
elementary and secondary schools, following a California policy
for church-related colleges which had existed since 1914.[89] By
petition the matter was submitted to the voters and approved.
It was subsequently upheld by both state and federal supreme
courts.[90] Opponents of exemption for parochial schools then
sought to forbid the practice by constitutional amendment but
were defeated in 1958.

California's experience also provides an example of how the
issue might be approached on a technicality. In a taxpayer's
suit against Alameda County government challenging the validity
of exemption provided under the state law of 1951, the claim
was made that the law was an establishment of religion and
therefore unconstitutional.[91] Although the trial court held the
exemption invalid on the basis of other claims the challenger
had raised, thus avoiding the First Amendment problem, the
California Supreme Court reversed the trial court on the grounds
that the exemption promoted general welfare by encouraging

education and that it applied without discrimination to all non-profit private schools. The court held therefore that any benefit received by a religious denomination is "incidental to the achievement of a public purpose." The court then added:

> Secondly, even if we regard the exemption as benefiting religious organizations, it does not follow that it violates the First Amendment. The practice of granting tax exemptions benefiting religious sects began in the colonial period. . . . Today, at least some tax exemption for religious groups is authorized by statutory or constitutional provisions in every state and the District of Columbia, as well as by federal law. . . . No case has been found holding that the granting of such exemption is contrary to state or federal constitutional provisions prohibiting the support or establishment of religion, and where the matter has been raised, the exemptions have been upheld. . . . The United States Supreme Court, in discussing the prohibition of laws respecting the establishment of religion, recently stated that the standard of constitutionality is the separation of church and state, and that the problem, like many others in constitutional law, is one of degree. . . . The principle of separation of church and state is not impaired by granting tax exemptions to religious groups generally, and it seems clear that the First Amendment was not intended to prohibit such exemptions. Accordingly, an exemption of property used for educational purposes may validly be applied to school property owned and operated by religious organizations.[92]

After this decision, the case was appealed to the United States Supreme Court. On Dec. 3, 1956, the court in a *per curiam* decision (rendered by the whole court as distinguished from a single judge) dismissed the appeal for "want of a substantial federal question." [93] Two justices dissented and one justice took no part in the consideration on the case. The decision seems to afford support to those who claim that tax exemption is constitutional.

An interesting approach to the problem is voiced by Dr. Eugene Carson Blake, stated clerk of the United Presbyterian Church in the U. S. A. He contends that churches are acquiring by gift and bequest considerable unrelated business ventures and that these should not be tax free. In time the churches could conceivably control the economy. Further, churches and religious institutions, such as colleges and seminaries, ought to make voluntary contributions to state and local governments in order to help share the cost of public services.[94] The editor of the magazine in which Dr. Blake's views were expressed subsequently commented that almost all of the letters received favored the proposal to tax unrelated business enterprises, but there was a divided opinion about the voluntary contributions. Those who opposed the latter believed that to make such contributions was to concede that exemption might be wrong. The editor felt obliged to note that "many clergymen reflected an enthusiasm for tax levies based on anti-Catholic feelings more than on views of Church and State."[95]

ZONING AND THE CHURCHES

In the early history of the United States, local governments sought to control the use of property situated within their boundaries, mainly in order to protect it against fires. The first comprehensive zoning regulation was adopted by New York City in 1916.[96] In 1926 the United States Supreme Court gave its full approval to such land-use programs.[97]

Most of the initial zoning regulations contained some restrictions on churches. Little or no litigation has grown out of them. Comprehensive zoning regulations usually include requirements concerning fire protection, sanitary conditions, and building specifications. In addition there may be requirements pertaining to effective land use, such as setback lines, or requirements based on local traffic situations, such as off-street parking for buildings used by a large number of people. These regulations apply to all buildings, and churches have generally not found them unreasonable.

But some zoning codes have recently followed a trend toward restricting or excluding churches in residential areas. On such cases brought before them, most state courts have refused to allow the exclusion,[98] on the grounds that exclusion is either a violation of the "due process" clause of the Fourteenth Amendment [99] or of the "equal protection" clause of the same amendment.[100] Not all courts agree, however, and a number have upheld exclusionary zoning.[101]

Under the "due process" approach, the court seeks to discover whether the exclusion of the church has a substantial relation to public health, safety, morals, or the general welfare. If the relation cannot be found, then the court rules there is a violation of the church's rights. Under the "equal protection" approach, the court seeks to know whether the exclusion is arbitrary or unreasonable when considered in relation to other uses permitted in the area. If it seems to the court that the excluded use for a church building has an undesirable characteristic connected with it (e. g., traffic congestion) and if there is a permitted use in the area (e. g., theater or ball park) with the same undesirable characteristic, then the court will deny the exclusion.

This has been particularly applicable with respect to zoning ordinances excluding parochial schools from areas where public schools are permitted. Generally, such exclusions have been invalidated on the ground that, since both types of buildings have the same undesirable characteristics, they must be treated alike.[102] In 1954, however, the Supreme Court of Wisconsin upheld the exclusion of a church school from an area where public schools were permitted. The court professed to find a distinction in benefit derived from a parochial school as opposed to the benefit derived from a public school, since the former is selective in its choice of pupils and the latter is open to all.[103]

Perhaps the most significant cases under either the "due process" or the "equal protection" approach were the appeals taken to the United States Supreme Court by the losing party in *Corporation of the Presiding Bishop* v. *Porterville,* and the losing party in the case of *State ex rel. Wisconsin Lutheran High School Conference* v. *Sinar.*[104] The Mormon Church in the first case and a Lutheran high school in the second case were excluded from a residential area. In both cases the United States Supreme Court dismissed the appeals "for want of a substantial federal question." The federal court's refusal to consider the cases was no doubt because the state courts did not decide them squarely on the issue of violation of the First Amendment as made applicable by the Fourteenth Amendment. It must be assumed that the federal court does not consider the infringement on the First Amendment in these cases to be serious, if indeed it took place at all. Commenting on a case before it in 1950, the court said:

> When the effect of a statute or ordinance upon the exercise of First Amendment freedoms is relatively small and the public interest to be protected is substantial, it is obvious that a rigid test requiring a showing of imminent danger to the security of the Nation is an absurdity. We recently dismissed for want of substantiality an appeal in which a church group contended that its First Amendment rights were violated by a municipal zoning ordinance preventing the building of churches in certain residential areas.[105]

It should be noted that in these cases the exclusion was from an area. What might happen if the exclusion were from the entire community would be another story. The best opinion is that such an exclusion would not be maintained unless the community could show there were reasonable alternative locations for such a church in close proximity to the community.[106]

SUNDAY CLOSING LAWS

Sunday laws trace their origins back to the time of Emperor Constantine, A. D. 321.[107] In later generations, restrictions were imposed on the activity of Christians on the Lord's day. By the Middle Ages work was forbidden on Sunday, and fines were collected for violations of the law.

The American colonies inherited the English prescriptions against Sunday activity. Sabbath laws were based on the laws of God. They were concerned with a purely religious institution and not a civil one.[108] The underlying idea was that the sabbath of the Christians was not to be desecrated even if the state had to exercise its authority to make sure. Almost all of the states enacted Sunday legislation in the interest of religion. The courts generally upheld the constitutionality of these laws despite their religious intent.[109]

In the past century, defense of Sunday observance laws took

a new turn. The Supreme Court in 1885 held them constitutional on the ground that such laws protected the public health. This was a legitimate exercise of the state's police power, according to the court.[110] The same line of argument was followed by the court in hearing another case a few years later.[111] Sunday as a civil day of rest has received widespread support in state court decisions as well.

There are signs, however, that Sunday observance restrictions are beginning to break down. A few state court cases have supported the view that a legal observance of Sunday is inimical to the religious freedom of groups which observe another day of the week as sacred, and that Sunday laws cannot therefore be enforceable.[112] Furthermore a number of activities formerly prohibited by state law on Sunday have become permissible, especially in the field of recreation and entertainment. A handful of states in the Far West have even repealed their Sunday laws altogether.

In the spring of 1961 the United States Supreme Court took under consideration four cases involving Sunday laws. It was generally expected that the court would reaffirm its earlier position (Sunday laws are secular) or that it would break with this line of authority and hold them to be religious laws and therefore in violation of the First Amendment, either in its "establishment" provision or in its "free exercise" provision (in the case of Sabbatarians). In two of the cases [113] the court by a 6–3 vote upheld the Sunday laws of Maryland and Pennsylvania against the contention that these laws involved an establishment. The complainants argued that the tenets of Christianity were being imposed on them. The Chief Justice, in speaking for the majority, said that the laws are secular and bear no relationship to establishment.

In the other two cases [114] the complainants were of the Orthodox Jewish faith, and they contended that their free exercise of religion, guaranteed by the First Amendment, had been infringed. Their argument was that their faith did not allow them to work on Saturday, and the law did not allow them to work on Sunday to compensate for the loss of Saturday's business.

The court rejected their argument on establishment on the basis of the two cases previously mentioned. With regard to the religious-freedom argument, the court split more drastically. A detailed explanation of the complex vote and the various opinions would unduly lengthen this account, but it should be noted that there was no clear majority opinion. Four of the justices, speaking through the Chief Justice, rejected the argument of the complainants, stating that the Sunday laws did not make any religious practice of the complainants unlawful but only made the practice of their religious beliefs more expensive. One other justice concurred in the result, and there were vigorous dissents in all four cases. It appears that the Supreme Court has not yet spoken the final words on Sunday laws.

The habit patterns of the American people are very strange. Even though Sunday laws were originally intended to support the work of the churches, it is likely that Sunday will continue to be observed, more or less, as an expedient to provide a necessary day of rest each week. Most Christians do not need Sunday laws as a reinforcement of religious conviction. They find it convenient to have Sunday as one day each week for common worship with fellow Christians. The problem here is the possible infringement of the rights of conscience of those who for religious reasons prefer to observe a different day of the week.

CONCLUSION

The relationships between church and state become very practical when seen from a legal point of view. The state must give the outward organized form of the church appropriate consideration, even as it must regard all other social groups within its jurisdiction. The corporate structure which church organizations adopt is an indication of how complex the relationship of church and state can become. In effect the incorporation of the church group is the state's acknowledgement of the church as a legal entity with which it or other persons can deal even in a court of law. Exemption from taxation constitutes one kind of special treatment of the incorporated church organization. If the churches contribute to the moral and cultural foundations of organized society even as schools, cultural organizations, and eleemosynary institutions which are also tax exempt, then there seems to be no reason why they should not continue to enjoy that privilege. More careful delimitation of the property and activities of churches which are classified as tax exempt would seem to be reasonable and might well be anticipated. Zoning codes thus far have not proved to be a major point of friction. In a few instances church organizations appear to be discriminated against, and these developments will need to be watched with concern. The issue of Sunday laws, although reviewed by the Supreme Court in 1961, still needs clarification.

PART IV

Application of Principles
in Church-State Relations

MARTIN E. MARTY

ALBERT G. HUEGLI

THE FIRST THREE PARTS of this book have brought out many problems which must be faced in the relationships of church and state. The solutions to these problems will take the best efforts of theologians, lawyers, and plain honest citizens. In Part IV are identified the directions to which we ought to look for guidance in this quest.

Chapter 9 provides an overview of the several forms which the resolution of conflicts in church-state relations could take. It is written by *Martin E. Marty*, Ph. D., associate professor of church history at the University of Chicago Divinity School and an associate editor of the *Christian Century*. Beginning with the assumption of pluralism in American religious life, he suggests that there are three basic choices in church-state relations available to Protestants, Catholics, Jews, and secularists.

The first alternative is radical separation. "It is . . . the alternative which most Americans, if they do not think twice, would describe as their own." The second is the overlapping of spheres of church and state. It is a nostalgic dream of many Protestants and, in a sense, of some Catholics. The third is an interpenetration and tension between church and state. This, says Dr. Marty, is becoming a more significant option to people in all religious groupings.

He feels that we need to realize old slogans are no longer as meaningful as they once were in defining the relationships of the church and the state. American practice is not always consistent with American theory. Somehow new formulas to meet realistic situations must be — and are being — devised as the need for adjustment of conflict in this aspect of contemporary life becomes more apparent.

Chapter 9

ALTERNATIVE APPROACHES
IN CHURCH-STATE RELATIONS

Martin E. Marty

ONE OF THE BASIC FACTS of American religious life is pluralism. Whether we like it or not, the cards of history are so dealt that we must play our hands as pluralists. Varying and opposing approaches to ultimacy compete for attention. It is beside the point to discuss Lutheran views of church-state relations, therefore, without attempting to see them against the background of varying and competing approaches. The moment we introduce this complicating feature we have cast the problem in a mold which transforms every aspect of it. We see that there is no single and simple Lutheran view which is held by all Lutherans or held decisively by any of them. We must speak of *a* Lutheran view or of Lutheran *views* of church-state relations. And when we begin to contrast our tenuous hold on an elusive and ill-defined reality with its alternatives, we begin to live out the uncomfortable but never dull parable of American political and religious life.

This complexity might spare us from becoming involved in an illusion which oversimplifies many other Americans' interest in this subject. Much of the tension over the relation between religious and political concerns grows from assumptions about masses, monoliths, and monopolies of interests. This tension grows whenever we talk about the Catholic vote, the Protestant legislation, the Jewish interest, the secularist impulse as if they were clearly definable and passionately held views. Life is never so simple for Lutherans or their fellow participants in a free society.

This becomes obvious if we begin to picture the variety of decisions that go into political action. I cannot conceive of a Lutheran carting *The Book of Concord* into the voting booth, and I suppose few besides Paul Blanshard and the P. O. A. U. visualize Roman Catholics operating with intimate awareness of papal encyclicals as they push the lever. The average Irish precinct captain would no doubt greet one with a confused stare and an invitation to "go out and have a beer" if he were asked about the *Syllabus of Errors*. Few secularizers or secularists carry around *The Age of Reason* or John Dewey's *A Common Faith* as a manual of arms. To suppose something other than this is to be captive of an intellectualizing naïveté.

Political interests are primarily decided politically. For millions of Americans, affiliation with a party is largely determinative. Backgrounds, family, education, class, status, wealth, personal preference and interest are other factors which complicate the bearing of religious involvement on political decision. Were we able to outline a consistent theory of Lutheran church-state relations that might be tenable on the American scene, we would be a long way from determining whether a Lutheran Indiana farmer of Republican lineage and a sour experience in public schools would vote against free bus transportation on public vehicles to parochial schools. At the same time this consistently Lutheran theory would at so many points overlap other positions held by Baptists, Democrats, Roman Catholics, populists, royalists, "wobblies," and Leagues of Women Voters that it would be difficult to insist on a monopoly of intention or interest on any subject.

Yet the alternatives to ill-defined Lutheran theories exist, and there is no particular virtue in not knowing either or in relishing confusion of definition. This understanding increases in importance as we see the degree to which any sort of Lutheran view makes its way against the grain of American life.

Reformation Day tracts to the contrary, American democracy is not the simple creation of blessed Martin Luther, and the over-simplified yet often-touted proclamation of Lutheran interest in "absolute separation of church and state" is not the same thing that Thomas Jefferson or his descendants meant by a "wall of separation between church and state." There may be coincidences of viewpoint and instances of common origin and influence, but the historical argument becomes very thin when Lutherans try to appropriate the American experience as their own.

Indeed, North American societal life was, after several false starts, largely shaped by interests which grew out of the Reformation of the church. But in the forms in which the Reformation encountered America, Lutheranism was long an insignificant minority. John Calvin and John Wesley and the myriad translations and transformations of their witness had more to do with America than did the impulses that flowed from Wittenberg and Augsburg. This Reformed Christianity fused at many points with other stances which might loosely be associated with "the Enlightenment," an episode in history with which most Lutherans are or should be quite uncomfortable, however eager they are to appropriate and capture its political fruits. America was not Roman Catholic in its national life. It was not Jewish or Protestant or secular and certainly not Lutheran. It was complex and pluralistic, with a Protestant-Enlightened matrix and afterglow.

To point to all of these complicating features is wearying and may serve to frighten the student of church-state relations away from a necessary task. The alternatives must be traced and strained and understood and related in new ways and with new urgency today because America has recently entered a new age. It has always been pluralistic, but it has only recently *realized* its incipient pluralism. Realized pluralism is the result of the almost total breakdown of meaning applied to spatially segregated assumptions about American life. When there were valleys of Scandinavians in Minnesota and Wisconsin, islands of Presbyterians off the shores of Canada, Italian and Polish

Catholic wards, German Lutheran midwestern towns or Southern Baptist southern towns or Congregationalist New England villages, one was still granted the luxury of cultivating illusions. Then one could still pretend that he was allowed to develop and hold to a specific religious theory of political life and need never sharpen it against others.

This spatial metaphor of colony and island and hamlet and ghetto and ward is today disrupted. The diagrammatic solution of separating ideas by separating peoples is waning and doomed; any strategy based on it is certain to fail. This is why old formulas about "two realms" and "walls of separation" are becoming less meaningful every year. The reasons for the change are obvious. America is running out of space for these luxuries. The population explosion is bringing citizens into closer relation to one another. "Togetherness," so carefully manufactured, brings new but temporary intimacies. Mobility on the social scale and horizontal mobility as Americans move from place to place in the age of corporate life; predominating intermarriage; the interruption of every man's sanctuary by values beamed over mass media of communication — all these render some understanding of alternatives to each religious or political option vital to survival and freedom.

This understanding of American life as somehow captive of a new interpersonal, dialogic situation will prevent another illusion from developing: the idea that alternative theories of church-state relations appear in hundreds of live-option varieties along, as it were, a cafeteria line. If there is a Lutheran view, or *the* Lutheran view, would there not then be for the dilettante of theories a view for the other 250 denominations and for each brand of philosophical interest current on our shores? Cannot one simply walk down the line and pick the dish of his choice? Instead the walker in the line observes that Americans have already made a salmagundi or a hash of most of these theories and are content to gulp and sometimes to relish it.

Take the Lutheran. He may sometimes want "walls of

separation" breached. He likes tax-exemption for churches, government-paid military chaplains, aid to veterans who are theological students, and maybe even indirect aid to parochial education and "Christian" prayers in public life. He may then turn around and want the walls restored against Roman Catholics when their tax-exempt properties grow, when G. I. Bill money goes to train priests, or when aid to parochial education helps the Catholic monolith come toward monopoly. He may be "correct" in both sets of views, but he is not consistent. He has, either primitively or with some sophistication, worked out a rationale that finds him falling somewhere between the varieties of theories.

We can now begin to retrace our steps and at last to simplify the picture. Though there may be over 250 denominations and even more philosophies in America, an instinct and insight has led Americans to do their own fairly accurate simplifying. By the middle of the 20th century the division of American religious life into "Protestant-Catholic-Jewish-'Secularist'" was so much a part of common parlance that we would merely waste words if we tried to redefine the pools of interest. Let us, for the purposes of this chapter, welcome them and see how three fairly consistent alternatives are operative within each.

THREE BASIC ALTERNATIVES

The basic alternatives are not simply religious. The three central options are held by people within the four religious pools, or "conspiracies" (in the positive sense of that term). The first alternative is an honored and ancient diagrammatic picture of *radical separation of church and state*. This assumes the spatial metaphor which we have described as being in jeopardy. It is, however, the alternative which most Americans, if they do not think twice, would describe as their own. Most of them probably feel that they have Moses or the popes or Luther and Calvin or Thomas Jefferson on their side as they see it.

The Jew, faced by Christian majorities in American religion, fears that he will be assimilated, dissolved, or mistreated if

Protestants and Catholics are given predominance in church-state interests. Looking for an ally he will find it among "secularists" and with them will insist on radical separation of the two spheres. The Roman Catholic layman in political life, whether he be symbolized ruggedly by Al Smith or with sophistication by John Kennedy, finds it possible or necessary to insist as well that his religious decisions are purely religious and his political decisions are political; the two shall never likely overlap or conflict. He is for separation of church and state.

Protestants glance over their shoulders at a growing Catholic minority and hurriedly rush back to their religious roots in American life to prove the variety of ways in which they have always favored "absolute separation." And secularists, heralded by anti-Catholics and prodded by urbane reflectors on the American experience, can point to the dangers of priestly politics; they add their bricks to the walls. Diagrammatically everything is neat. Few people live out their lives between such cozy walls, however.

A second diagrammatic picture appears within each of these four clusters and can be symbolized by the *significant overlapping of the spheres of church and state*. This should come most easily to Jews, with their theocratic lineage. But American Jews are sufficiently realistic about their minority status in America to have thoroughly revised their dreams. The theocratic ideal has largely dissolved or been transformed, and the doctrine of "significant overlapping" has perhaps its fewest supporters among those who should find it most congenial. Roman Catholics, if they are doctrinaire about their dogmas and experience, will often express themselves in favor of this approach; that they do not do so oftener is perhaps because of a desire not to "push their luck" in American life. We shall see that a basic assumption of Roman Catholic alternatives in political life pulls Catholicism toward the doctrine of significant overlapping of spheres (though few would recognize it under this name). We shall return to this and other alternatives later.

Meanwhile, as we shall also see, Protestantism is not without

its fusers and theocrats either. Its nostalgic historians and its
visionaries remember and hope for the day when America was
or will be Protestant and thus somehow fused in church-state
relations. Even secular proponents of a religion of democracy
yearn for overlapping of spheres.

The obsolescence of the spatial metaphor and of diagrammatic
illusions has led an increasing number of Americans, last of all,
to the situation of realized pluralism: a permanent if never
relaxing at-homeness with *dialogic interpenetration and tension
between church and state.* This alternative is based on the idea
that all people, including religious people, have bodies and souls;
that each lives simultaneously and all his life as one person in
two realms; that the drawing of diagrams or verbalizing of
dogmas based on them will be unrealistic in today's world. In
such a setting people are in quest of kinetic, dynamic, interactive
views which permit affairs of state to come under judgment of
the church and which force the church to recognize its political
setting; which allow for pragmatic and temporary intrusions of
realm upon realm and sphere upon sphere because this is what
life is and because corollary interpenetrations and tensions are
creative and healthy.

This alternative permits Jews to participate in National Councils of Christians and Jews to promote Biblical views against
secularism and to safeguard against warfare among partisans of
Biblical religion. It will allow for some give and some take in
church-state relations. Thoughtful Roman Catholicism recognizes
the fruitfulness of dialogic interpenetration; it is coming to see
pluralism as a more or less permanent state of affairs in America.
The less edgy Protestants, no longer reluctant to see dreams of
monopoly go, have learned that they must share the American
experience with three other kinds of religious interest and with
Christian realism are exploring theories which are at least poten-
tially coexistent and compatible with the facts of American life.
Meanwhile people of secular orientation are finding many kinds
of roots in the American past for dialogical interaction between
church and state. We can now examine the three alternatives
in the life of the pools of interest.

JEWS

We have said that Jews for the most part have a great interest in fostering separation of church and state. As a 1—35 minority they have least interest in fusing church and state, as their interests would assuredly be swallowed. Their more articulate and careful spokesmen today are pleading the third alternative. In many respects Jews appear to be the most monolithic group on the American scene, but this is less true of religious parties within Judaism than it is for a recognizable stance in church-state affairs. In this matter, as Leo Pfeffer points out, even though American Judaism is largely of Orthodox (and theocratic) descent, it has taken on much of the coloration of Protestant secular humanism.

> Of all the major religious groups, American Jews are probably the most secularist in the sense of being most concerned with this life and its affairs and problems. They probably have the greatest faith in democracy, not only in political society but in the world of religion and morality. All in all, they are quietly happy with the way the American political system and American culture have developed and are no less than the Protestants concerned about the challenge to that culture posed by the rising tide of Roman Catholicism. It is for that reason that the Jewish position on public issues far more often coincides with the Protestant than the Catholic position. This is another reason why interreligious conflicts and tensions in the United States revolve largely around Catholic-non-Catholic relations rather than Christian-Jewish relations.[1]

Mr. Pfeffer, by his participation in various legal suits in behalf of total separation of church and state, has come to be one among many symbols of Jewish interest in "high walls." He finds distinguished company in the Synagogue Council of America, which consists of and represents the six national organizations that make up American Judaism and which issued statements in support of extreme interpretations of the First and Fourteenth Amendments in favor of "strict separation."

Will Herberg, himself no doctrinaire separationist, describes this as the characteristic Jewish position. He traces it to a widely held view that, because the Western Jew became emancipated with the secularization of society, he has a vested interest in preserving it. As religion gains a place in the formal life of the community, the minority Jew will be crowded out. "The intrusion of religion into education and public life, the weakening of the wall of separation between religion and the state, is feared as only too likely to result in situations in which Jews would find themselves at a disadvantage — greater isolation, higher 'visibility,' an accentuation of minority status." [2]

If we look for traces of theocratic afterglow in Judaism, we must content ourselves with obscurantist and sectarian dreams and not with any live options among numbers of thoughtful Jews. The nearest instance we see of this memory in American national life is in the interest in a pro-Israel foreign policy as somehow an American duty — a decision which obviously has more heavy religious overtones than political.[3]

The third alternative is typified by men like Will Herberg, who have gone so far as to argue for public support of parochial education, at least in theory, on political and religious grounds of "right." [4] As such he would be opposed to the court decisions for the separationist view in the *Everson* and *McCollum* cases. Those who share his view are interested in finding middle ground between Catholic monopolistic interest and Protestantism's newly expressed obsessive interest in diversity for diversity's sake. Herberg says: "I find the Jewish position, somewhere between the Catholic emphasis on unity and the liberal-Protestant worship of diversity for the sake of diversity, more plausible, more viable, and more realistically related to the interests of religion and society." [5] As such he would be interested in interpermeation of creative influences, balanced by creative tensions, between the spheres of church and state as they are personified in the lives of Americans.

For the most part, American Judaism serves as the only substantial *religious* reminder that Americans cannot assume in public discourse and action that this is a "Christian" nation; that when Roman Catholic and Protestant noses are counted, millions of their compatriots, not necessarily "secularist" in orientation,

must still be accounted for. In religious terms, Jews are coming
to translate once again their hopes and dreams in their newest
setting:

> [They have faith] that Israel is not merely an ethnic group,
> a racial entity, or some historically conditioned society, but is
> indeed a servant of God — destined, it may be, to much more
> suffering, but destined also to live so that it may play its
> appointed role in establishing God's Kingdom upon this earth.[6]

And as they see it, this will be in America with its complex
church-state relations.

ROMAN CATHOLICS

Roman Catholics offer by far the most explosive and controversial option in contemporary American church-state relations.
The largest single American religious group under one jurisdiction
and the only substantial competitor with Protestantism for
America's religious heart, Roman Catholicism has grown from
a small minority in colonial times and an isolated minority in
later times to a position of responsibility and often dominance
in American life. It presents a paradox to its contemporaries.
Obviously Catholicism has adapted itself for the most part
congenially to the Protestant-secular environment. It has apparently accepted the semipermanent resolution which we have
been calling realized pluralism. It has allowed its adherents
a wide variety of political options. All the while it has been
mistrusted for its history and its dogma. Both informed and
uninformed non-Catholic Americans tend to become uneasy in
the presence of the Catholic "system." They fear the ultimate
impact, as Catholicism gains in size and influence, of a system
of authority which has made it clear that it regards both pluralism
and separation of church and state as provisional, tolerable, but
never ideal situations. They tend to become uneasy as, one
after another, new areas of tension develop: in parochial appeals
for public funds for education, in arguments over birth-control
legislation, and in other realms which secularists and many Protestants and Jews regard as intrusions on areas once assumedly
settled under the term "separation."

Roman Catholicism may present one ultimate intention in religio-political life, but this is so remote from realization in the present American constellation that we do best to explore Catholicism also along the three lines we have been seeing as alternatives. First, most Roman Catholics in America would say — and mean it when they say it — that they are for separation of church and state. Through long participation in urban politics, thousands of Catholic laymen have acquired a thoroughly secular approach to political affairs. They tend to compartmentalize, bringing piety to bear on certain aspects of life but granting a great deal of autonomy to purely political choice on purely political grounds. The growth of this interest is what lends plausibility to scholarly and hierarchical protests that to talk of imperial Roman Catholic efforts in America does not do justice to things as they are.

This assumes that American Catholic laymen are turning their backs on European history; they are glossing it over or are merely forgetful or publicly repudiative. Rarely is their expression so blatantly anarchic that it calls for official condemnation. No realistic approach to American church-state life that does not do justice to this growing secularized Catholicism in political life will be recognizable to the average Catholic layman as voter or precinct captain. However remote this may be from official teaching and actual experience, it is here to stay. It is in this setting that even the Paul Blanshards may conceivably perform some service when they point out the disparity between contemporary expression and the recorded and professed intention of Catholicism.[7]

From the side of Catholic apology, eloquent men like Jacques Maritain serve to remind that "to make the Church and the body politic live in total and absolute isolation" is not a real choice in American Catholic profession, and to use this phrase in American life: "separation between Church and State," is to mean something different than it does to Europeans and others.[8] "Absolute separation" is therefore more an unthinking political phrase picked up by unthinking Catholic laymen. However many hold it, it has no major theorists and is not likely to find any.

The second alternative is one which many Protestants and other Americans are convinced lurks just around the corner behind every Catholic intrusion on their domain: the overlapping of church and state to the profit of Catholicism. It takes no acute student of history to see that ancient Catholic aspiration is still prevalent in many modern states in Latin America, or in Spain. It takes no profound understanding to see Catholic reluctance to be content with a world that has come of age and has expressed itself in secular political terms. It takes but little more ability to exhume documents that still retain official character and that are embarrassing to American Catholics. Its takes a good deal more subtlety to strain out the ways in which Roman Catholics here make their actual peace with the environment. "The Catholic Church is divided from top to bottom in this country and abroad on matters of principle in regard to religious liberty." [9]

The alternative of significant overlapping or fusion of church and state is represented by the ancient view of the confessional Catholic state which would limit rights of minorities. This union of state and church is often described as the "thesis" which permits adjustments such as those made in America. The most famous expresser of the "thesis" in velvet-gloved ways for American consumption was Father John A. Ryan, who defended it and then said:

> While all of this is very true in logic and in theory, the event of its practical realization in any state or country is so remote in time and in probability that no practical man will let it disturb his equanimity or affect his attitude toward those who differ from him in religious faith.[10]

Few Catholics realize how unreassuring such expressions are; they give rise to the more blatant and strident anti-Catholic expressions in the political order. It is this that prompts them to do research in the documents of states that are dominated by Catholics. Thus the Spanish constitution, Article 6:

> The profession and practice of the Catholic religion, which is the religion of the Spanish state, will enjoy official protection.
>
> No one shall be disturbed by reason of his religious beliefs or of the private observance of his form of worship.

Ceremonies and public manifestations, other than those of the religion of the state, are not permitted.

Fearful Americans perform a not always accurate but usually understandable translation of this approach to an America with a virtual Catholic majority, and tremble. They take no more comfort from expressed contentment, a century later, with the *Papal Syllabus of Errors* of 1864, which pronounces it an error to assert that "it is no longer expedient that the Catholic religion shall be held as the only religion of the State, to the exclusion of all other modes of worship" or "that the church ought to be separated from the state and the state from the church." So long as Americans are document-conscious or authority-conscious and so long as such documents by such authorities exist and remain unchallenged within Roman Catholicism, uneasiness will persist. The advocacy of expediency in application of the thesis to American life, as typified by Ryan and Boland and by Heinrich Rommen, may not excuse the Blanshards and the P. O. A. U. and anti-Catholicism in general, but it goes a long way to explain them. The thesis remains, in other words, the official Catholic teaching, however it be softened.

But a licit and unofficial other side of this approach has begun to take form against the American environment, and this third alternative must also be dealt with fairly. It accepts pluralism. It need not prefer it, as John Courtney Murray says, but it must accept that this is woven into the fabric of history. What to do with pluralism in American life is then the basic problem for the American Catholic whose literate spokesmen are Murray, Gustave Weigel, or Walter Ong. Murray, in a brilliant series of essays in *Theological Studies,* has worked out these dialogic theories better than others. They have been summarized somewhat as follows:

The idea of a Confessional Catholic state belongs to an earlier period in European history; it is now obsolete and has become an irrelevancy under contemporary conditions.

Anglo-Saxon democracy is fundamentally different from the democracy of the French Revolution in that the latter was totalitarian in its tendency.

The state in this country is by its nature limited and in principle the Church does not need to defend itself against a limited state as was necessary in the case of European revolutionary states which were the foil to Pope Leo's thinking when the embarrassing documents were prepared.

The American constitutional provisions for separation of church and State are not motivated by anti-clericalism or anti-religion; the Church therefore does not need to enter into dogmatic encounter with the resolution as a doctrine.

The Church in America has, as a matter of fact, enjoyed greater freedom and scope for its witness and activities than it has in the Catholic states of the traditional type. It is important to emphasize the rights of the state in its own sphere in this setting; it is also necessary to emphasize the freedom of the church from state control, and the influence of Catholics as citizens on the state. One cannot separate religious freedom from civil freedom; there can be no democracy if the freedom of the citizen is curtailed in religious matters, for such curtailing can often take place as a means of silencing political dissent.

Error does not have the same rights as truth but persons in error, consciences in error, do have rights which should be respected by the church and the state. The church should not demand that the state as the secular arm enforce the church's own decisions in regard to heresy. It does more harm than good to the church for the state to use its power against non-Catholics.[11]

Obviously this approach fits into the dialogic, or interpersonal, situation which we have described. The focus is on the Catholic citizen and the person who holds error and not on two competing, abstract, impersonal power systems. Murray's views have received slight implicit official sanctions from time to time, and many American Catholics pin their hopes on these. The newer Catholic position could be summarized as follows: it expresses itself with more open congeniality in favor of the Protestant-secular milieu; it is less uneasy with pluralism; its "public relations" about "thesis" and "hypothesis," about intention and expediency have improved; most Catholics would desire nothing more than creative coexistence with their contemporaries.

We shall postpone discussion of Protestant alternatives to the end and next discuss the alternative which we shall label as "secularist," attaching no judgment or invidium to the term, as the quotation marks are intended to show. Again, the alternatives of the spokesmen of the secular order do not follow one single predictable pattern. Some are for separation (most are); some are for fusion; more and more are for creative interplay in the lives of persons.

As an example of the first we would take the man on the street who fears the mixing of religion and politics, who does not want Catholics or anybody else getting sanctions from public life and public funds. He will find noisy prophets among the smaller and obscure secularist groups, the rationalist and humanist and atheist associations, the American Association for the Advancement of Atheism and the American Humanist Association — groups so small and insignificant that few Americans would know how to go about finding a local cell if one exists. But this ferment cannot easily be dismissed, as it has a place in national life in the courts, particularly in reaction against religious intrusions on public life. The *McCollum* decision illustrates the extent of this secular orientation in the courts. Incidentally, legal guardians of this tradition provide happy allies for each religious group against each other intruding group. This is secularism's most sanctioned function. But this emphasis represents also the most consistent advocacy of "absolute separation of church and state" and picks up a great deal of inconsistent and unthinking support from varieties of Protestants, among them many Lutherans.

Is the second alternative, significant overlapping or fusion, present among secularists? It may seem strange to speak of people of naturalistic or humanistic orientation desiring any form of union of church and state. Yet in effect this is a widespread option. It appears whenever Americans, not content with the religions of a democracy, try to make a religion of democracy. Whenever ultimate values are attached to the democratic process and the particularities of other religious impulses are blunted, the state in effect becomes a church. The attempt to bring meta-physical sanction and ceremonial reinforcement to democratic values, thus making of it a religion, is a frequent attempt by partisans of democracy on the lines of secularism.[12] The battle-ground for this view exists in the area of education, where opponents of sectarian teaching in public schools stress that secular-democratic teaching produces ultimate values, is spiritual, and is the "established religion" of American democracy.

The third alternative, here again, seems to be more productive. "Absolute separation" does not allow for the ways in which church and state are both symbolized in the lives of over a hundred million Americans who can separate parts of themselves from other parts of themselves. Fusion of church and state in the form of a political religion does violence to particularity of revelation and response. The mainstream American secular position is more congenial to the part religion plays in shaping American life but wants to see this congeniality brought to bear to keep balances of power, to prevent establishment of a particular religion, and to help justice and fairness prevail.

This may involve a certain theologizing of the basic documents of the American experience, as Ralph Henry Gabriel has done.[13] It need go no further than a recent student has done in countering claims of historic Roman Catholicism that only the church has competency to judge in matters of church-state conflict:

> Those who believe in separation, then, must go a step farther. The two possible judges in case of conflict are necessarily the parties to the dispute, for there are no higher agencies to which to turn. Modern Roman Catholic political theory seems to assert the right of the church as the divine agent of God on earth to make the decision. Secular political philosophy, especially in America in the hands of Jefferson and the "Roosevelt Court," maintains the opposite: the state is of right the judge. Those of us who agree with the Jeffersonian tradition have no reasoned philosophical basis for our position, for the writer of the Act for Religious Freedom and our modern court justices seem to have arrived at the concept almost intui-

tively. . . . [The state] is the only social agency which properly has jurisdiction of all citizens and institutions within the society.[14]

Such a position forces its holders to argue against the idea that a "godless society is a doomed society" and conclude from this premise that state power should be used to reinforce religious belief. Some sort of "partial separation" and "partial overlapping," in constant dialog and tension, remains the alternative for such advocates of a secular position that is congenial to religion. This theory has attracted many adherents among religious people as well.

PROTESTANTS

Protestants of various communions also hold the varieties of views described above. Some of their motives or doctrinal bases are different. Some of them are similar, and the practical grounds are often identical. As an example, witness the prevalence of Protestant expression in favor of "absolute separation of church and state." Most Protestant laymen, if confronted with a question concerning their views on the subject, will answer in terms somehow approximating this one. And if the "absolute" is tempered in a nation that deals clumsily with absolutes, they will still insist that the wall be built as high as possible. Yet when the surface is scratched and the consequences of this simple-sounding theory are explored, they are likely to retreat from a position which they find theoretically difficult to defend and practically impossible to live with. The "high wall" approach has been converted into a convenient phrase, but its meaning in mid-century America was blurred.

There are Protestants who come by the phrase naturally and with honesty. Baptists, whose roots go back to Isaac Backus, John Leland, or (with some revisions) to Roger Williams as advocates of radical separation, are enduring champions of this view and worthy judges of religious groups — Protestants or otherwise — who seek sanctions from the state for their churchly endeavors. Another example would be groups with special defensive interests. The Seventh-day Adventists, for instance, to protect themselves from legislation favoring Sunday, have extended this interest and formed protective societies for religious liberty and complete separation. It would be safe to say that most Protestants join most Jews, Catholics, and secularists in self-identification along the "wall of separation," though few are willing to carry out the logic of the premises. Walls are spatial symbols that have been battered in the new setting of American life.

Some Protestants support the opposite option and speak wistfully of a Christian America in which the state is somehow fused with the public profession and sanction of the Christian faith. This theocratic tendency has roots in the past in New England particularly and dies hard with the realities of pluralism. For the most part, theocratic tendencies have become the property of "sects" which have virtually no hope of seeing their dreams realized. In most cases, were they realized, the "state" would be obliterated in the name of the "church" — or the "kingdom" as in the case of the aspirations of Jehovah's witnesses. Already 125 years ago "Christian" parties in American politics were proved to have little cohesion and significance, and legal sanctions applied to Christianity were seen to be unfair even if theoretically somehow justifiable. Yet as late as 1955 the "Christian Amendment" movement through Senator Ralph Flanders introduced a constitutional amendment which reads: "This nation devoutly recognizes the authority and law of Jesus Christ, Savior and Ruler of nations, through whom are bestowed the blessings of Almighty God."

Both of these diagrammatic solutions, separate or overlap, have been threatened in the kind of age we described above. It is in this period that creative and critical Protestant leaders have been learning how to live with realized pluralism; how to be faithful to their own truths and fair to others. In theological terms, most of this redefinition, of the type we associate with names like Reinhold Niebuhr or John Bennett, is of Reformed rather than Lutheran orientation, though the two have many points of confluence. Whereas Lutherans find a fruitful distinction between state and church along lines of Law and Gospel (whether in the archaic diagrammatic patterns or as two words of God applied to individual and collective lives in the personal situation), the Reformed tradition is less careful with the distinction. It is as reluctant as Lutherans to see law and justice removed from the realm of the state, but it is more ready to speak of the Christian Gospel interpenetrating the realms of the state or the earthly city.

In any case this approach to church-state relations recognizes that real people with real bodies inhabit one order which must relate itself to the realities symbolized by both church and state. Walls of separation do not speak of the unity of this life; fusion does not allow for its complexity and the potential clash of the two realities. Some, Winthrop Hudson among them,[15] have argued that the great tradition of American churches, separation of church and state, is being worn down by growing dependence of Christians on the state for religious sanction. Yet Hudson would by no means argue against all forms of interaction between church and state. Most, with Robert McAfee Brown, would remind Christians where their ultimate allegiances lie:

> The Protestant must never give his final allegiance to the *state*. Nothing a nation does can rightly receive uncritical and absolute loyalty, but must always stand under the judgment of a higher loyalty. Nor may final allegiance be given to a *church*, since a church is composed of human beings who err and whose judgments are always something less than divine truth.[16]

With ultimate allegiance given only to God, both church and state are seen in different perspectives.

SOME CONCLUSIONS

We have tried to show that *alternatives* do not mean simple ideologies simply held by simple people. Significant alternatives somehow thrust themselves upon us and become limited according to our experiences and a few basic philosophical or theological commitments. Among them America's four religious conspiracies offer alternatives; the practical effects of none of these alternatives differ radically from the practical effects of others.

The old formulas have little meaning today. "Walls of separation" may be a convenient historic symbol; "union of church and state" has become unacceptable to almost everyone. To say that one is for separation or for union has not yet said whether he is Christian or non-Christian, Protestant or Catholic. We have to know more about his hopes and dreams and memories. Even when we know this, we often find that as an American citizen he may have more in common in his aspirations in the political order with other people as citizens than with them as sharers of hopes for a heavenly city, however defined. Definition of both cities becomes a major task in an age when *diagrams* and *spatial models* mean little and *persons* mean much.

TO THE EDITOR BELONGS not only the responsibility for initiating and directing the writing of the contents of this book but the obligation to report where all of the thinking comes out. In chapter 10 he attempts to show what conclusions have been reached from the studies of his colleagues.

This requires more than a summary which gathers together all that has been said in some meaningful fashion. The entire subject of church-state relations is too volatile, too dynamic to allow any conventional filing of data among comfortable pigeon-holes. The American pattern in this field of cultural adjustment is an ongoing experiment, subject to new interpretations with each new cycle of our national life. The Christian approach to government recognizes that, except for the verities of God's revelation, there can be nothing completely static in the day-to-day contacts of church and state.

Chapter 10 is therefore pointed toward the new dimensions which are already discernible in church-state relations. It shows how Scriptures are being studied again for guidance and what attitudes in this matter the churches are discovering they have in common. The rethinking of basic American principles is bringing new insights. Even the tensions which can be so perplexing may be regarded as a sign of health in the condition of our church-state pattern. Since all of us have so much at stake in the resolution of current issues, the fact that the area of church-state relations is more familiar to more of us augurs well for future adjustment of conflicts.

It is the editor's opinion that while this book presents no easy answers for church-state problems, it does offer bases for thought out of which such answers can be constructed.

Chapter 10

NEW DIMENSIONS
IN CHURCH-STATE RELATIONS

Albert G. Huegli

IN THE PLAY *Becket,* Jean Anouilh portrays Thomas à Becket, archbishop of Canterbury, locked in ideological combat with his former friend, King Henry II. Becket finally concedes a number of points for the sake of peace and the king's right to be king. He is ready to yield amost everywhere — "in all save the honor of God." There he holds his ground.[1]

This is the time-honored theme in the story of church-state relations. Christians recognize the claims of the state at every turn in their lives. But at some point they draw the line and stand fast. The honor of God will not permit them to yield any further. They feel compelled to contend for the rights of the church over against the state.

Previous chapters have illustrated how the relationships of church and state have been affected by the pull and tug of these two forces in human destiny. Sometimes the church has not only resisted the inroads of the state into its jurisdiction but even aggressively invaded the realm of Caesar itself. This is most dramatically illustrated by the famous decree *Unam Sanctam* of Pope Boniface VIII, which boldly asserted the church's claims to the earthly as well as the spiritual swords.[2] Sometimes the state's proclamation of power has reached into the very core of the church's existence. The Russian criminal code of 1923, restated in 1938, made it a crime punishable by forced labor for up to a year if anyone gave religious instruction to children and minors in state or private educational institutions.[3] Generally the relationships of church and state have moved back and forth between these two extremes.

On the midground there are many variations in the patterns of church-state relations. State churches of Europe have one form of association with the government.[4] It seems to be satisfactory for them. The independent churches of the United States have another pattern, and they apparently thrive under it.[5] There are even within our own country differences in application of principle and practice. A Christmas creche on the courthouse square may be acceptable in a small Protestant Iowa community but indignantly challenged in the Bronx, New York. All of these variations make it difficult for the thoughtful observer to come to fixed and final conclusions about what is proper and universally applicable in the relationships of church and state.

There are other complicating factors. If the organized Christian church were a single visible entity and if all of its members agreed on one perspective in church-state relations, issues could be more readily defined and problems simplified. But the Christian church is divided into many bodies, whose members do not see eye to eye on these things. There are innumerable religious groups — not all of them Christian — which must have the attention of the state. In a democratic society even the rights of non-church members have to be considered in church-state questions. In actual practice, problems involving church and state in this country are problems which the state has with *churches* or with *churchmen* rather than with the *church* as such.

To add to the confusion, the term *state* has various meanings. In the United States it implies a representative government at the national, state, or local level. Sometimes there are differences among the levels of government as to the proper relationships of state and church. For example, while the federal court has sanctioned public bus transportation for church school pupils, the state court of Wisconsin refused to approve it.

At every level the government as representing all the citizens has a hard time asserting a consensus in the relations of church

and state. For as citizens, apart from church affiliation, we have
many opposing views on these matters which seem irreconcilable.
In a sense, problems of church-state relations are problems be-
setting the churches or churchmen in their dealings not with
a theoretical state but with those who are the duly constituted
officers at any time in any one area of our governmental structure, charged with interpreting and carrying out the law of
the land.

These complexities therefore lead us back to fundamentals
in church-state matters. We must begin as Christians with what
God has to say to us in our perplexities. The manner in which
the church of God has understood His Word and applied it to
changing times and conditions also becomes important. This the
authors of the chapters in Part One of this book have sought to
tell us. As citizens we have an obligation to study and understand the pattern provided by the state in its relations with the
church. It will be a pattern based on both law and custom.
Part Two and to some extent Part Three have supplied us
with guidance for our thinking in this direction. In the last
analysis, however, there can be no definite rules and roles for
all of the changing circumstances where church and state are
jointly involved. The judgment of the individual Christian, enlightened by the wisdom of God and the experience of men,
must finally shape the action to be taken.

In the whole area of church-state relations we are probably
too prone to think in terms of groups. We evaluate the issues
from the point of view of one group or the other, as if in this
way answers based on numbers would give us greater soundness
in judgment and provide the final solution. Instead we probably
should return to the one-to-one relationship characteristic both
of Christian doctrine and of democratic theory. It is the individual soul which stands humbly before its Maker, pleading the
merits of the cross. To a lesser but still important extent it is the
individual citizen for whose rights and security the democratic
society exists. In his role as a Christian the Christian citizen in
a democracy confronts himself in his role as a citizen.

If there is to be any solution to the problems of church-state relations in the United States, therefore, the individual must become very much involved. Ultimately these are issues for each Christian wherever the power of the sword is exercised over him. The situation may call for obedience, even to the headsman's ax, as in the case of Paul. Or it may call for resistance to governmental encroachment on sacred things as in the case of Peter and John before the Jewish Sanhedrin. The final determinant is Christian judgment. Each of us shall be called to give account — not churches as such nor states as such. Each of us has a responsibility as a citizen — not aggregates of us as political parties or pressure groups or residents in a particular locality.

It would be helpful to us as individuals therefore to know as much as we can about the course of events in church-state relations. The historical past should be useful as a guide. The present provides a mold for the shape of the future. New directions are discernible in church-state relations for us in America. It is to these we turn for some understanding of current developments and for intelligent and thoughtful decision on the issues they present to us.

SCRIPTURAL PRINCIPLES IN NEW APPLICATIONS

There is a renewed interest today in the study of the Word of God. Our age of increasing uncertainty has brought a fresh appreciation of the eternal truths of divine revelation.

But Holy Scriptures do not pinpoint solutions for every concrete problem arising in the relations of church and state. We shall discover nothing there about chaplaincies, prayers in Congress, or the zoning of church property. Government aid to church schools has little parallel for or against it in God's teachings to His people of the old or the new covenant. However, what we do find in the Word of God is a clear statement of principles governing the life of man in relationship to his Maker and to the lives of other men.

Organized churches and states, so familiar in our time, did not exist when our Lord walked the paths of Palestine. Church and state are referred to under the terms of *God* and *Caesar,* or *the body of Christ* and the *king*. Nevertheless three basic theological presuppositions derived from the New Testament have become more significant today for their relevance to our problems of church-state relations.

The first theological presupposition is this: Both the church and the state are the instruments of God. The church — God's Right Hand — is the consequence of Jesus' Great Commission to preach the Gospel, and His promise of the coming of the Holy Spirit. The purpose, nature, and tools of the church center in the redemption of men through the Word and sacraments in the all-encompassing love of God. The church exists in the hearts of God's people.

The description and manifestation of the life of the church are being restudied by present-day theologians. Luther saw the church as an active group of believers.[6] Christians, he felt, were not to withdraw into caves and monasteries and so await the end of time. They were to have a direct relationship with life around them. They were to submit to the state and yet chastise it whenever it needed correction. They were to be obedient but also take their part in political life.

While most streams of Christendom would follow this general direction for the civic lives of their people, they have differed in their interpretation of how far Christians organized into church groups should go in relating to their political environment. Roman Catholics have traditionally held that the state must be subject to the church's direction. Yet in our day Catholics seem to be shifting their ground in the practical situations of democratic societies.[7] The Calvinist churches admit the subordination of the church as an institution to the state but allow for large spheres of ecclesiastical influence in social and political affairs.[8] Lutherans, who became quietistic in the centuries immediately after the Reformation, are moving back into assertions of a relevance of the churches to the life of the state. The sobering example of Nazi Germany, where most churchmen in times of violence to the human spirit kept their hands folded, has not been without some effect on all of Christendom.[9]

The state — God's Left Hand — is again being soberly appraised in the light of God's purposes. With so much of the world ruled by wicked men, it is hard to see how God could have anything to do with government at all. Yet, as we have noted in a previous chapter, the state is the product of God's creative act. It is the "minister of God" with a prescribed responsibility for order, justice, and the public welfare. It rules by the sword and, the Scriptures tell us, it warrants our obedience.

The state was clearly evident and personified in the Rome of Paul's day, but it is less well defined in our own. As citizens of a democracy we are obedient to government and we are the source, means, and concern of political power. Our kind of state is concerned with mobilizing majorities, giving ear to minorities, expressing and shaping opinion in newspaper editorials and letters to congressmen. The United States belongs to international organizations which bind and commit us as much as the laws of our own land. New insights are needed to make clear our civic responsibility. The idea of law and order through government remains a blessing of God. But in an age of living at the edge of thermonuclear war, when men are preparing to leave earth for outer space, we shall require new meanings for God's instrument, the state.

The second theological presupposition is: Both the church and the state have separate spheres of activity marked out for them. Jesus directed His followers to render to Caesar and to God their respective dues. The differences between the church and the state have become very obvious.

The things of Caesar are concerned with law and order and justice. The ruler is the "minister of God to thee for good" as well as the punisher of evil. The things of God are concerned with the souls of men and their lives of dedication to the lordship of Christ.

The state is temporal and limited in its functions. Many nations which existed before World War II have disappeared or have been significantly changed. Since 1945 about 50 new nations have come into being. Empires like Great Britain and France have been shorn of most of their colonies. Once powerful Germany is divided into two parts. The map is dotted with countries which have been transformed from democracies to dictatorships and from free enterprise to communist societies. It should be clear to our generation that both the shape and the life of the state in God's plan is transitory. It serves men's present needs. It stands in contrast to the church, which abides beyond all the changing conditions of men and serves not only for this life but also for that which is to come.

Loyalty to the Lord Jesus is of course the overriding loyalty for Christians. They have to live in two realms, that of Caesar and that of God's Son. They are in this world but may never be identified with it. The time can come for all of us when we must learn to obey God rather than men.

The third theological presupposition is this: There is a constant danger that the functions of the church and the state will be confused. Serious consequences result when the two spheres exchange their roles.

Jesus reprimanded Peter, for example, when that impulsive disciple drew a sword in the Garden of Gethsemane. The mission of the church is not to be carried out with force. If the church employs the means of the state, it becomes something different from what God intended it to be. We see the results in such historic episodes as the Spanish Inquisition and the Puritan theocracy in New England.

Similarly the state departs from its assigned task when it concerns itself with the affairs of the church. The Book of Revelation warns of this development.[10] Luther was very critical of the lords temporal in his day for intervening in ecclesiastical matters to the detriment of the church. The Russian Orthodox Church under the czars exemplifies the plight of the church when it becomes a kind of branch office of the state.

It is not easy to keep the boundary between the jurisdictions of the church and the state clearly defined. American experience underscores the predicament. Despite the provisions of the Constitution, church and state activities in 18th-century America were often intermingled. It was taken for granted that all men acknowledged the existence of God and most Americans were thought to be Christians. Public life reflected these assumptions. Today the tide is running so strong toward absolute separation of church and state that the rights of the church over against secularism and irreligion are in danger of being ignored. The functions of church and state may become blurred as much by unreal divorcement as by intermingling.

The conflict today is centered in total claims. For the Christian, every aspect of life bears the impact of faith. He therefore finds it hard to accept social activity which leaves religion out. For the state almost everything in modern life may properly be brought within the purview of government. The secular power of the welfare state is capable of reducing the church to the level of a "kept" institution subservient to its desires. Alert Christian men and women cannot help being reminded of the Biblical warnings against the demonic potentialities of the state. Our era with its society of aggregates, its mechanical means for popular control, its emphasis on the mass mind and the need for conformity is especially difficult for those who would draw the line on governmental power.

The three theological presuppositions keep coming to the fore in contemporary evaluations of church-state issues. In studying the place of government we are forced back to the source of its authority in the creative providence of God. If God tells us anything about the relations of government and the church, it is that the two have separate purposes and functions and we have obligations to each. Trouble arises when the responsibilities of the two institutions are misunderstood. The value of these presuppositions derived from the Scriptures for the solution of present-day problems in church-state relations is becoming increasingly clear.

EMERGING CONSENSUS AMONG THE CHURCHES

As a practical matter we need to speak of the attitudes of the American church bodies in church-state relations. When the state deals with the church in our country, it confronts a bewildering variety of church organizations. In its relation to the state the church as a whole in America is a conglomerate of many organized churches.

It is easy enough to point out the disagreements among the denominations on specific church-state issues. As might be expected, Protestants and Roman Catholics do not see eye to eye on these problems. Official claims of the popes to secular powers were among the factors which precipitated the Protestant Reformation. History in succeeding centuries therefore saw Protestants and Catholics on opposing sides in many church-state controversies. Sometimes Protestants lost their challenge to Catholic political pretensions, as in the Huguenot persecutions of the 16th century. At other times Catholics have had great difficulty in even securing toleration from Protestants, as in American colonial experience. Contemporary debates on issues like public aid to church schools usually see Catholics on one side and Protestants on the other.

But Protestants themselves have not always shared common points of view on church-state relations. Again, history must be taken into account along with basic doctrinal disagreements. If we begin with the doctrines of John Calvin on predestination, for example, and the Geneva experiments in community living, we can understand why Calvinist churches are prone to make the state far more responsive to the needs of the church than is the case in Lutheran theology. In another instance the Anabaptists, who sought to separate themselves from the concerns of the state, provided a pattern in church-state relations which is still discernible in contemporary Baptist attitudes. Any attempt of Protestant churches to arrive at a mutually satisfactory position on specific church-state issues is likely to be frustrated at the very outset by disagreements along denominational lines.

A change, however, seems to be coming about in this situation. Roman Catholics and Protestants are carrying on "dialogs," Protestants are holding "conversations" with other Protestants, and Catholics, Protestants, and Jews are engaging in "discussions." The several church groups are beginning to discover the views they have in common on church-state matters. It is probably much too soon to say that we are arriving at any kind of consensus, but we can at least discern a sort of central tendency in ecclesiastical thinking on certain aspects that are important in the relationships of church and state.

The churches, whatever their denomination, believe in order. They agree on teaching respect for government and for those who are in authority. They support obedience to the law and the payment of taxes by all citizens. They encourage the offering of prayers for public officials. Although they may differ as to the use of the right to resist, they also show signs of willingness to take another look at this right in the expanding state of contemporary society. The approach of Berggrav, for instance,[11] in advocating a much firmer resistance to governmental abuses than most other Lutheran theologians is being evaluated along with that of Johannes Hamel of communist East Germany, who is trying to find a new option for the church's existence under a hostile government without compromising Christ for the benefit of Caesar.[12]

Churches of all kinds recognize the importance of the moral and spiritual foundations of the state. In a very broad sense they accept the validity of Justice Douglas' contention that "we are a religious people." Without a set of rules no society could exist for very long. In a democratic order, honor and justice and truth must be concepts taken for granted. There are never enough policemen to enforce the law among an apathetic people. The state must rely on the conscience of the people. The very processes of government itself would be paralyzed without self-discipline and integrity among citizens and officials alike.

Unfortunately the growing disruption of the American home, the increasing delinquency of the young, and the relaxation of standards in business and government are all symptomatic of the decay of our moral fiber as a people. The churches have with unanimous voice deplored these social trends in their concern for the spiritual foundations which are the strength of our nation. The preservation of moral and spiritual values in an unstable social order has been the subject of serious discussions across the whole spectrum of denominational affiliation.

Because the churches are devoted to the welfare of the human soul, they have a natural interest in the dignity and worth of the individual citizen. In Christian theology each person is not only uniquely made but called by name in the Lord Jesus Christ. When individuals are oppressed, therefore, the voice of God's people is often heard in protest. Sometimes this concern for the individual has meant a speaking up for the downtrodden, like a latter-day Amos. Sometimes it has meant carrying on works of mercy at great cost and self-sacrifice. For several denominations it has meant maintaining a large and expensive system of church schools for the complete education of the child. Whatever the claims of the state to the life of its citizens, the churches have always shown that the individual person is supremely important.

Agreement can also be discerned among the churches in support of the principle of voluntarism. Disestablishment of religion occurred in our country over a century and a half ago. The idea that each group may worship God as it pleases is firmly fixed among us. No church body would countenance the compulsion of any person in religious matters. And the churches pay the price for this sort of privilege. Voluntarism includes the understanding that the churches must raise their own funds and not depend on the government. This arrangement is generally acceptable to most people because they believe the independence of the churches and the freedom of religion are worth whatever the cost. Even the Roman Catholics, to whom such a church-state pattern is a relatively novel idea, give evidence of accommodating themselves to the American environment.[13]

Respect for governmental authority, concern for the moral and spiritual foundations of society, interest in the individual, and support of voluntarism — in these areas of church-state relations the churches have much in common. There are probably other common points of view which could be explored. One important step toward arriving at a reasonable, workable, and defensible position in church-state relations will be achieved when the Christian churches — and other religious groups as well — can broaden the scope of agreement as to what contacts with government the churches will find acceptable and what not.

The basis for consensus should be found in the Scriptures. From that point on ecclesiastical mutual understanding should be gained in increasing measure.

STATE ADJUSTMENTS IN WORKING RELATIONS WITH THE CHURCH

We have seen that the Christians of the Roman Empire in Paul's day had one pattern of relationship with the state. They could do little except obey it and pay their taxes to it. The power of Rome became so all-encompassing that only a minority of the people like the Christians dared to resist its complete embrace for the sake of religious conviction.

By the 11th century a different pattern of church-state relations had emerged. Under Pope Gregory VII the church became all-powerful. The papacy, and through it the church, was asserted to be supreme over all temporal kingdoms. The picture of Emperor Henry IV waiting three days in the castle courtyard at Canossa for papal forgiveness illustrates the relationship.

A still different pattern prevailed in the principalities affected by the Religious Peace of Augsburg in 1555. Each ruler was to decide whether Lutheranism or Catholicism should be the religion of his state. Exponents of the rejected religion would have only the right to emigrate.

The counterpart to these patterns could be found in one European country or another when the American colonies declared their independence. The predominant practice was the endorsement and support of an official state religion. However, some degree of toleration for minority religions had been achieved in a few countries.

Today, of course, in countries like England, which supports a state church, freedom of religion is assured.[14] Separation of church and state is almost as complete in France as in the United States. The established church continues to exercise great influence in Spain and the Scandinavian countries. Holland and Switzerland represent interesting variants to usual patterns, while in Russia something approximating the old Roman pattern of state domination prevails.[15]

In the United States, social and political conditions have provided a framework within which a unique pattern of church-state relations could be worked out. This pattern is built on three fundamental principles: religious liberty, pluralism, and cooperation.

Religious liberty was especially cherished by the early Americans because it had been denied many of them in the countries from which they came. For this reason the First Amendment was added to the Constitution. No matter what else might be read into the amendment, it is at least clear in this sense, that government cannot establish a denomination as a state religion, nor interfere with the worship life of the people.[16]

An essential ingredient of religious liberty is toleration. During the early years of our national history the right to worship freely was well established. Later the emphasis in religious liberty shifted toward the drawing of lines of demarcation to separate church and state. It is this aspect which has received increasing attention in recent decades. Separation of church and state has indeed become such a popular shibboleth that it is often mistakenly thought to be an expression found in the Constitution. Actually, of course, it is a formulation of the intention of the First Amendment. Separation of church and state is one means by which religious liberty is assured in this country. Not all nations which enjoy religious liberty have separated church and state. The United States has found it advisable to do so, even though there is no complete agreement among us as to how far such separation should go. The recently emphasized assumption, that the more completely church and state are separated, the more surely religious liberty will be secured, may be misleading. In the process of separation, political liberty may remain, but religion will have little significance for life under freedom. The scope of activity of religious groups will be so restricted that their contribution to the moral life of the nation will be marginal, to say the least.

As we have seen, the principle of pluralism is firmly fixed in our church-state pattern.[17] It is a consequence of religious liberty. Freedom of worship has provided the environment in which more than 250 religious bodies have come into being. The state thus deals with many churches in church-state relations. For church bodies which regard themselves as the true church of Jesus Christ, this situation presents special complications. For the state it means bewilderment as to what the numerous churches stand for in their relations with the state.

Pluralism requires that government shall be impartial in its treatment of religious bodies. It cannot favor one without doing an injustice to the rest. But the meaning of governmental impartiality is hotly contested. To some it signifies that government must not only be neutral but dissociated from religion. The effect of such a position, they say, is the secularization of society. To others the impartiality of government means that any favors dispensed by the state to one denomination must be given to the others as well. This outlook, some think, could lead to the outright support of religious groups. The midground involves a benevolent attitude by government over against all religions without direct governmental involvement in any of them. This has been the traditional understanding of pluralism throughout most of our history.

The state has not always been consistent in observing the implications of a policy of pluralism. A benevolent neutrality is difficult to maintain in practice. Government officials find it hard to deal with a host of Christian denominations and with organized non-Christians as well. Nevertheless pluralism remains a mainstay in the American system.

A third major element in our pattern of church-state relations is the principle of cooperation. The Supreme Court indicated the prevailing opinion in this respect by stating:

> When the state encourages religious instruction or cooperates with religious authorities . . . it follows the best of our traditions. To hold that it may not would be to find in the Constitution a requirement that the government show a callous indifference to religious groups.[18]

The assumption that religion is important in our society goes back to the very beginnings of our national history. It is not surprising therefore that religion and American public life and policy have continued to be intermingled at many points down to the present time. Important public occasions are almost invariably opened with prayer. National symbols like the Great Seal of the United States, the inscription on coins, and the pledge of allegiance to the flag reflect a belief in the existence of God. Church holidays are legally observed. Religious customs and practices have become a part of the warp and woof of our public life.

Governmental cooperation with religion becomes very tangible in some instances. Salaried chaplains in the military and in legislative chambers are commonplace. Clergymen are exempt from Selective Service requirements and jury duty. Church properties are not taxed. Contributions to churches constitute substantial federal income tax deductions. But cooperation is also a two-way street. The churches are expected to work with the government. They are regarded as corporate entities in the eyes of the law. They own and dispose of property in legal ways. They work with government in social welfare and educational undertakings. Ministers render legal services by performing marriages.

Cooperation between churches and the government may be taking some new turns in contemporary America. As Peter Berger points out in *The Noise of Solemn Assemblies,* religion itself is becoming so well "established" that it is being coupled with Americanism and democracy as sacred and almost indistinguishable concepts.[19] The churches are more and more expected to support and ratify the prevalent values. Their impact on important social problems is thereby diminished. They pay a price for the friendliness of government.

At the same time, government is faced with new complications in its policy of cooperation. The friendly attitude of the state toward religion has in the past been largely in a Protestant setting. Two developments are prompting a reappraisal. One is the increasingly vocal objection of secularists and strict separationists. Organizations like Protestants and Other Americans United for the Separation of Church and State are seeking to eliminate one area of cooperative activity of church and state after another. The other development is the expanding role and greater influence of the Roman Catholic Church. With the election of a Catholic President in 1960 the United States reached a turning point and probably entered a new era in church-state relations.[20] No longer can Protestantism be taken for granted as the framework within which Americans generally operate. And, as has been shown in previous chapters, the Catholic concept of church-state relations carries historical overtones different from those of Protestantism. If cooperation is to continue as a principle, its forms therefore are bound to change.

New dimensions are in the offing for all three of the principles on which the American pattern of church-state relations is built. Nevertheless religious liberty, pluralism, and cooperation may be expected to serve as accepted fundamental premises in any debates on the issues which arise along the borders separating church and state in our country.

ACCEPTANCE OF TENSION IN CHURCH-STATE RELATIONS

If there were no tensions between church and state in the United States, we might well have cause for concern. Without tensions we would have to assume that one of several alternative situations has come to pass. Our society might be static, with no changes being made at any time in the future — a most unlikely development. Or the church may have lost its voice or have little to say, and the state has assumed complete dominance. This eventuality can take place when people no longer maintain a vigilance over their liberties. Or the state somehow has been overwhelmed by the forces of the church, and the church — some church body — has everything its own way. This has happened in some Latin American countries, and it could happen here. All of these situations are deplorable, and it is only in the continuing tension between the church and the state that we can be reasonably sure they are performing their designated functions over against each other.

It is inevitable that church and state should occasionally be at odds. They have numerous points of contact which can easily produce friction. They have jurisdiction over many of the same people. Churchmen are also members of the body politic, and many public officials are devout members of religious bodies. They have obligations to both God and Caesar, and sometimes these obligations are in conflict. Furthermore, church and state have numerous overlapping interests. They are alike concerned with the education of children, the care of the ill, and the welfare of the aged. There is a constant tug of war between church and state for the time, attention, and support of the individual who recognizes he has obligations to them both.

The American process for the adjustment of tensions between church and state is twofold. The formal structure of constitutions, laws, and court decisions provides the official machinery by which tensions may be resolved. But these mechanisms are not usually employed except as a last resort. Most frictions are accommodated by the customs and usages of the people.

The pattern of American church-state relations has developed as much out of the folkways as out of the legally constituted processes. We have Thanksgiving Day proclamations because this is a long-standing custom. We are used to having chaplains in Congress. Christmas decorations in the public schools are part of our tradition. Popular acceptance is more significant in many instances of this kind than legal authorization.

Wherever communities are close-knit and generally of one mind in church-state matters, customary practices are seldom challenged. It is when social change occurs that the issue is raised. As minorities become more vocal and threaten to take a case to court, accommodation in the customary practices must be made. The past decade has seen an increasing need for this kind of adjustment. The mobility of the American population has disrupted the homogeneity of our communities. Growing numbers of Roman Catholics make their disagreement with folkways adopted in a Protestant culture more significant. The increasing sensitivity to the claims of minority groups in American society has brought quick response to protests. The multiplication of court cases on church-state issues has accentuated readiness to adapt the local customs to changing conditions.

Thus the variety in the pattern of a former day, which permitted stress on cooperation in one locality and stress on religious liberty in another, is giving way to a uniformity which leaves little room for local options by custom. It is doubtful that many of the practices long prevalent in the social order would be tolerated if they were starting today. We may therefore anticipate that future changes will be defined, either by the courts or by social adjustment.

The techniques for the accommodation of tension need to be worked out — and with patience. It would be far better that the adjustment be made within the scope of social custom than by legal prescription. The nature of the American pattern is essentially a delicate balance of forces in tension. When either the church or the state pulls too hard, the relationship becomes lopsided. Those groups which would have us suppose they are acting in the best interests of the church or the state but in fact seek to tip the balance in their favor contribute nothing to the common good. At any specific time the weight may be heavier on one side or the other, but sooner or later the balance must be struck again in a workable accommodation. This is the spirit of the American system. If it is to be forfeited, a new and different pattern of adjustment in American church-state relations will have to be sought. A healthy tension between church and state is one way of making sure that our system is in working order.

INCREASING AWARENESS OF CHURCH-STATE ISSUES

Two decades ago problems of church-state relations were hardly ever discussed. Today these issues have become one of the leading topics for group evaluation and for publication. Increasing awareness of the problems is all to the good, for an understanding of the issues is a necessary first step toward their solution.

A number of developments have brought the relations of church and state into the public spotlight. The problems are much closer to home than they used to be — as close as the local public or parochial school and the changing mores of changing communities. More and more people today sense they have a stake in the outcome of debates centering on baccalaureate services for public school graduations or the use of tax funds for a local church-related hospital.

Lately, too, decisions of the courts have focused popular attention on the varied aspects of church-state issues. Since 1947 a half dozen cases before the United States Supreme Court have resulted in major decisions affecting the course of church-state relations. Sunday closing laws, for example, were upheld, with significant ramifications for some parts of the economy.[21] However, the greatest impact of judicial opinion has made itself felt in the field of education.[22] Cases involving bus transportation for parochial school children, released-time classes, and Bible reading in the public schools are reaching into the lives of great numbers of people. Religious education is so intimately associated with the primary mission of the church that decisions affecting it quickly activate the popular reflexes. Meanwhile the state courts have been busy with similar cases and decisions of their own. Although less well publicized than the opinions of the federal courts, they nevertheless are often of vital importance to the legal environment in which church-state relations occur.

The debates in legislative halls run a close second to the opinions of court justices in stirring up public discussion of church-state matters. The outstanding example has been the controversy over federal aid to education and its inclusion or omission of benefits to parochial education. In recent sessions of Congress almost any proposal to provide federal funds for elementary and secondary schools has been vigorously resisted if church schools were to share in the aid, on the grounds that separation of church and state would be violated. At the same time the suggestion that church schools not share in such benefits has been strenuously opposed by the Roman Catholic hierarchy. Even federal grants and loans for college academic facilities involved the discussion of the church-state issue. It is not surprising therefore that the situation at the level of the state legislatures is comparable. Birth control legislation in Illinois for mothers receiving public aid has aroused a storm of controversy among the churchmen of that state.

The most dramatic way in which the church-state issues have been brought to popular attention in recent years was the setting of the presidential election of 1960. That one of the candidates was a Roman Catholic produced widespread discussion of Catholic and Protestant views on church-state relations. During the campaign many voters who had previously ignored the whole issue became well acquainted with the distinctions between religious beliefs and political rights. The American pattern of separation of church and state received careful public scrutiny.

A significant barometer of interest in church-state matters is the increasing number of pertinent books and articles. Popular magazines as well as learned journals devote much space to the issues. Bibliographies in this field show a rising proportion of books written within the past 15 years. Moreover, religious groups are engaging in formal studies of the subject. Among them are the Methodists, the Baptists, the Lutherans, the National Council of the Churches of Christ, and the National Conference of Christians and Jews. Even great foundations have undertaken to subsidize meetings on church-state problems.

What does this new awareness and widespread discussion mean for the future of church-state relations in America? It cannot but produce some good results if it does no more than make the citizenry intelligent participants in the formulation of public opinion. Our legislation and folkways in church-state relations will therefore have the advantage of public thought reasonably well informed. We can look forward with confidence to the clearing of a path to a consensus which recognizes the meaning of our constitutional guarantees of religious liberty and the values of our traditional usages. Alterations in the American pattern can then be made with deliberation and a due sense of proportion.

Two aspects of the discussion will need to have special attention. One is that the American pattern must be reexamined in the light of new conditions. Constitutions and court decisions have been pretty thoroughly studied. It is the interpretations and applications which must now be objectively reviewed. What may have been applicable a hundred or even 25 years ago could by now be obviously obsolete. Some of the features of that pattern are fixed; others are flexible. Which should be retained and which modified will require a collective wisdom of the highest order to determine.

The solutions arrived at by other countries may be useful in the search for our adjustment to contemporary conditions. The British and the Dutch, for example, have accumulated substantial experience in the relations of government with the churches, and we might well draw on them for our own predicaments. It would also be valuable to study the patterns of church-state relations which newly created free nations are adopting. They have often had the opportunity to assess the best and the worst features of previous experiments and could start anew without the entanglements of outmoded traditions.

The second important aspect of the continuing dialog on American church-state relations must be an understanding of the position of the churches. The American Christian church as a whole must keep in mind that for its success it is not dependent on any particular social or political order. While it enjoys the privileges constitutionally guaranteed in our democracy, its strength, it dares not forget, comes from principles ultimately theological, not governmental. The church therefore turns to the guidance of the divine Word for instruction in its attitudes toward any social institution.

Sometimes the church finds that God leaves the practical problems for human ingenuity to solve. This may be the case, for example, in deciding whether public funds should be accepted for a church-sponsored activity. Sometimes the problem is whether in a given instance Caesar is invading the domain of God. This may be the situation when a political act interferes with or assumes an ecclesiastical function. The church must learn to distinguish one from the other and avoid surrendering principles for the sake of an immediate advantage. Fortunately in the American social order the members of the church can, wherever the situation demands it, make their beliefs clear through the legal processes available to them. By continually leading its people back to basic fundamentals the church can meet its teaching responsibility in the issues of church-state relations.

THE SHAPE OF OUR TASK

The problems in the relationships of church and state are as old as man. In our country the times and conditions are bringing them into sharp focus. We are now beginning to discern some new dimensions in church-state issues. A renewed study of the Scriptures is providing fresh insights into approaches to contemporary problems. Although the churches in America are a long way from speaking with one voice on these matters, they are at least speaking with one another about them. Governmental authority is reevaluating the constitutional fundations of past practices in church-state relations, and social groups are adjusting their accustomed positions to changing pressures. At this time probably more people are involved in the discussions than ever before. There is some hope that sound reasoning and good sense will prevail from time to time as changes in the pattern will inevitably be made.

We have always had tensions in church-state relations. There is no reason to believe that they ever could or should be completely resolved, for only under a dictatorship by the church or the state could this be accomplished. Our problem is to reduce these tensions to a minimum consistent with the appropriate interests of both church and state and then to make the tensions serve the best interests of both institutions. This is one of the most important and difficult tasks we face as members of the modern state and citizens of the city of God.

NOTES TO CHAPTER 1

1. All quotations from the English Bible, unless otherwise indicated, are from the Revised Standard Version (New York: Thomas Nelson and Sons, 1946 and 1952).

2. Cf. *The Apostolic Fathers: An American Translation*, trans. Edgar J. Goodspeed (New York: Harper & Bros., 1950), p. 278.

3. John Milton, *Paradise Lost*, IV, 109—111.

4. J. Armitage Robinson, St. *Paul's Epistle to the Ephesians* (London: Macmillan and Co., 1909), p. 21.

5. Milton, IV, 51—55.

6. Denis de Rougemont, *The Devil's Share* (New York: Pantheon Books, 1944), p. 17.

7. Oscar Cullmann, *The State in the New Testament* (New York: Charles Scribner's Sons, 1956), p. 65.

8. See pp. 41—46.

9. Nikolai Berdyaev, *The Realm of the Spirit and the Realm of Caesar* (New York: Harper & Bros., 1953), p. 78.

10. We have quoted the marginal reading in the RSV as more accurately reflecting the original language of the apostle.

11. Emil Brunner, *The Divine Imperative* (Philadelphia: Westminster Press, 1947), p. 460.

12. Thomas Paine, *Common Sense* (New York: Willey Book Co., 1942), p. 1.

13. Article II of the Augsburg Confession, *Triglot Concordia* (St. Louis: Concordia Publishing House, 1921), p. 43; *The Book of Concord*, trans. and ed. Theodore G. Tappert (Philadelphia: Muhlenberg [Fortress] Press, 1959), p. 29.

14. J. E. Lesslie Newbigin, *The Household of God* (New York: Friendship Press, 1954), p. 18.

15. As quoted in Leo Pfeffer, *Church, State, and Freedom* (Boston: Beacon Press, 1953), p. 119.

16. See Ethelbert Stauffer, *New Testament Theology* (New York: The Macmillan Company, 1955), pp. 81—86.

17. John Bouvier, *Law Dictionary and Concise Encyclopedia*, 3rd rev. (8th ed.), ed. Francis Rawle (St. Paul, Minn.: West Publishing Co., 1914), III, 3120.

18. Eivind Berggrav, "State and Church Today," in *The Proceedings of the Second Assembly of the Lutheran World Federation*, Hannover, Germany (Gunzenhausen, Bavaria: Buchdruckerei Riedel, 1952), pp. 81, 83.

19. Cullmann, p. 76.

20. See Joseph C. Ayer, *A Source Book for Ancient Church History* (New York: Charles Scribner's Sons, 1924), pp. 19—22.

21. In Titus 3:1 ἐξουσίαι and ἀρχαί are linked together. Both refer to earthly authorities in this passage; yet both terms also mean angelic beings. An excellent excursus on the meaning of ἐξουσίαι, as used in

Rom. 13, is found in Cullmann, pp. 95—114. The term ἐξουσίαι is understood in the same way by Walter Kuenneth, *Politik zwischen Dämon und Gott* (Berlin: Lutherisches Verlagshaus, 1954), p. 34. In fact, the only notable individual that takes exception to this interpretation is Hans von Campenhausen, "Church and State in the Light of the New Testament," in *Biblical Authority for Today,* eds. Alan Richardson and Wolfgang Schweitzer (Philadelphia: Westminster Press, 1951), pp. 293—309. The most recent attempt to overthrow Cullmann's position is that of August Strobel in his article "Zum Verständnis von Römer 13" in *Zeitschrift für neutestamentliche Wissenschaft,* XLVII (1956), 67—93. However, Strobel begins by arbitrarily excluding Colossians and Ephesians from his consideration. Moreover, he works with the assumption that the apostle wrote only from a Hellenistic Greek background.

22. See George B. Caird, *Principalities and Powers: A Study in Pauline Theology* (New York: Oxford University Press, 1956), p. 12. Cf. Herbert U. Gale, "Paul's View of the State," in *Interpretation,* VI (Oct. 1952), 413.

23. The Greek verb κρίνειν ("to judge") can, and here no doubt does, include the thought of "rule," as in the case of O. T. judges. Cf. Walter Bauer, *A Greek-English Lexicon of the New Testament and Other Early Christian Literature,* trans. and adapt. William F. Arndt and F. Wilbur Gingrich (Chicago: Chicago University Press, 1957), p. 453.

24. *The Lutheran Liturgy* (St. Louis: Concordia Publishing House, [1958], p. 8.

25. Ibid., p. 18. An alternate wording is offered for use in the British Commonwealth of Nations.

26. See, for example, Phil. 2:3 and Rom. 12:10.

27. Stanley L. Greenslade, *The Church and the Social Order: A Historical Sketch* (London: SCM Press, 1948), p. 22. Eivind Berggrav, *Man and the State* (Philadelphia: Muhlenberg [Fortress] Press, 1951), p. 228, cites the oldest property law of Norway as an example of this kind of direct influence on legislation. This law began with the words: "The source of our laws is in the fact that we bow . . . before Christ."

28. Robert M. MacIver, *The Web of Government* (New York: The Macmillan Company, 1947), p. 198.

29. Martin Luther, "Secular Authority," in *Works of Martin Luther* (Philadelphia: Muhlenberg [Fortress] Press, 1930), III, 241. WA 11, 254, 255.

30. See Albert G. Huegli, "Our Church in the Area of Political Activity," in *The Lutheran Scholar,* XII (Oct. 1955), 423.

31. See Section IV, E, par. 66, in *Christ Frees and Unites,* Study Document, Third Assembly of the Lutheran World Federation (Geneva, 1956), p. 28.

32. See Berggrav, *Man and the State,* p. 298.

33. Article IV (II), Apology of the Augsburg Confession, *Triglot Concordia,* p. 127; *The Book of Concord,* p. 110.

NOTES TO CHAPTER 2

1. Kenneth M. Setton, *Christian Attitude Towards the Emperor in the Fourth Century: Especially as Shown in Addresses to the Emperor* (New York: Columbia University Press, 1941), pp. 11–39, 212–218, describes the patristic reaction to the emperors of the critical fourth century.

   Otto Seeck, *Geschichte des Untergangs der antiken Welt*, I, 2nd ed. (Berlin: Siemenroth & Troschel, 1897), 111. The text of Constantine's renowned Edict of Toleration was a document of Licinius citing the edict of Galerius. Cf. "Edict of Toleration, 311," in *Documents of the Christian Church*, ed. Henry Bettenson (New York: Oxford University Press, 1947), p. 22.

   Stanley L. Greenslade, *Church and State from Constantine to Theodosius* (London: SCM Press, 1954), emphasizes that the problems and many of the theories for their solution emerged during the course of the fourth century.

2. Walter Hobhouse, Bampton lecture III, "The Church Secularized by the World — Constantine to Justinian," in *The Church and the World in Idea and in History* (London: Macmillan and Co., 1910), pp. 83 to 125, is emphatic on this point.

3. In contrast to Ernst Bernheim and others, Henri Arquilliere, *L'Augustinisme politique*, 2nd rev. ed. (Paris: J. Vrin, 1955), sees the support of *justitia* rather than the preservation of *pax* as the positive function of the state in Augustine. The polar concepts kingdom of God and kingdom of this world are of course New Testament in origin. F. W. Buckler, "Regnum et Ecclesia," in *Church History*, III (March 1934), 16–40, argues that the idea of kingship in a Christian context was metaphysicalized into an eschatological otherworldly kingship, whereas the organic, corporate, concrete concept of kingship as the rule of the kingdom of God on earth was finally realized in the rule of Mohammed and the glorious Caliphate. Though not without errors, Alois Dempf, *Sacrum Imperium* (Munich: R. Oldenbourg, 1929), is a stimulating discussion of medieval ideas of history. Though in the Old Testament the covenant people were identified with Israel, Philo's interpretation of Sarah, the Sojourners, and Hagar as the heavenly city, an intermediate city, and the city of the rejected, had an obvious influence through Ambrose on Augustine's *City of God*, which was significant not only for the medieval theology of history but also for political thought in a secularized context.

4. See John T. McNeill, "The Feudalization of the Church," in *Environmental Factors in Christian History*, eds. John T. McNeill et al. (Chicago: University of Chicago Press, 1939), pp. 187–205. The best brief introduction to the *Eigenkirche* is still the inaugural lecture at Basel University of Ulrich Stutz, *Die Eigenkirche als Element des mittelalterlich-germanischen Kirchenrechts* (Berlin: H. W. Müller Verlag, 1895), depicting this institution as part of the Germanic concept of *Grundherrlichkeit*. It has been translated as "The Proprietary Church as an Element of Mediaeval Germanic Ecclesiastical Law" in *Mediaeval Germany 911–1250: Essays by German Historians*, trans. Geoffrey Barraclough, II (Oxford: Basil Blackwell, 1948), 35–70. Heinrich Boehmer, "Das Eigenkirchenwesen in England," in *Festgabe für Felix Liebermann* (Halle: M. Niemeyer, 1921) shows that the

institution was not limited to the continent. Indeed, to this day it is customary in parts of England for local nobility to submit names and indicate preferences for clerical appointments. Cf. Samuel Dill, *Roman Society in Gaul in the Merovingian Age* (London: Macmillan and Co., 1926), and Ferdinand Lot, *La fin du monde antique,* rev. ed. (Paris: A. Michel, 1951), for a discussion of the religious mentality of the Merovingian Franks. Basic documents for the imperial regulation of the church are to be found in *Capitularia regum Francorum* in *Monumenta Germaniae historica,* ed. Alfredus Boretius, Leges, Sectio II, 1–2$^{1-3}$ (Hannover: Hahn Verlag, 1883–1897), evaluated by Carlo De Clerq, *La législation religieuse franque de Clovis à Charlemagne,* Recueil de travaux, 2e série, fasc. 38 (Louvain: Univ. de Louvain).

5. Among the many works on the Investiture Controversy particularly to be recommended are Augustin Fliche, *Études sur la polémique religieuse a l'époque de Grégoire VII — Les Prégrégoriens* (Paris: Société Francaise d'Imprimerie et de Librairie, 1916); A. Fliche, *La réforme grégorienne et la reconquête chrétienne (1057–1125)* (Paris: Bloud et Gay, 1940); James P. Whitney, *Hildebrandine Essays* (Cambridge: The University Press, 1932); Zachary N. Brooke, *Lay Investiture and Its Relation to the Conflict of Empire and Papacy* (London: British Academy Proceedings, 1939); Gerd Tellenbach, *Church, State, and Christian Society* (Oxford: Basil Blackwell, 1940); Walter Ullmann, *The Growth of Papal Government in the Middle Ages: A Study in the Ideological Relation of Clerical to Lay Power* (London: Methuen & Co. Ltd., 1955). On the devastating effects of the controversy on the empire in preventing any possibility of unification under a strong monarchy, cf. Geoffrey Barraclough, *The Origins of Modern Germany,* 2nd ed. (Oxford: Basil Blackwell, 1949), pp. 101–134, the investiture contest and the German constitution. Walter Ullmann, *Medieval Papalism* (London: Methuen & Co. Ltd., 1949), assesses the contribution of the canonists to papal theory.

6. Though Walter Ullmann, *The Origins of the Great Schism* (London: Burns Oates and Washbourne Ltd., 1948), holds that the nationalistic rivalries in the College of Cardinals have been traditionally overemphasized in explaining the origins of the schism, the rise of national feeling is evident in the alignment of the powers behind pope and antipope in its further development. Cf. George J. Jordan, *The Inner History of the Great Schism of the West* (London: Williams & Norgate Ltd., 1930). Although slanted and dated, the essay of John N. Figgis, "The Conciliar Movement and the Papalist Reaction," lecture II in his *Studies of Political Thought from Gerson to Grotius, 1414 to 1625* (Cambridge: The University Press, 1907) is a stimulating discussion of the political thought resulting from the movement. Carl von Hefele's monumental *Conciliengeschichte,* trans. as *Histoire des conciles d'après les documents originaux,* 11 vols. (Paris: Letouzey et Ané, 1907–1952), discusses this period in Vols. VI, Part 2, to VIII, Part 1. Hubert Jedin, *Geschichte des Conzils von Trient,* I (Freiburg i. B.: Herder Verlag, 1949), presents the conciliar background to Trent. Brian Tierney, *Foundations of the Conciliar Theory* (Cambridge: The University Press, 1955), evaluates the contribution of the canonists from Gratian to the Great Schism.

7. Albert Werminghoff, *Verfassungsgeschichte der deutschen Kirche im Mittelalter* (Leipzig: B. G. Teubner, 1907), pp. 87 ff. Kurt Kaser, "Die landeskirchlichen Reichsfürsten," "Der deutsche Territorialstaat um 1500," in *Deutsche Geschichte im Ausgange des Mittelalters*, II (Stuttgart: J. G. Cottasche Buchhandlung Nachfolger, 1912), 259 ff. For examples of princely intervention in monastic life, cf. Willy Andreas, *Deutschland vor der Reformation*, 5th ed. (Stuttgart: Deutsche Verlags-Anstalt, 1948), pp. 121, 129; on the *Landesherrliches Kirchenregiment*, pp. 41–43. Heinrich Boehmer, *Luther im Lichte der neueren Forschung*, 5th ed. (Leipzig: B. G. Teubner Verlag, 1918), p. 253, observed: "Das landesherrliche Kirchenregiment steht, sofern es wirklich ein Regiment ist, wie sein Name besagt, zu Luthers principieller Auffassung der Religion in geradem Widerspruche. . . . Es ist kein Erzeugnis des reformatorischen Denkens, sondern . . . ein Produkt des von den Ideen des Eigenkirchentums befruchteten spätmittelalterlichen Staatsrechts . . ." See also Karl Müller, "Die Anfänge der Konsistorialverfassung im lutherischen Deutschland," in *Historische Zeitschrift*, CII (1908), 1–30.

8. Willy Andreas, pp. 43–46; Alfred Schultze, "Stadgemeinde und Kirche im Mittelalter," in *Festgabe für Rudolph Sohm* (Munich: Duncker & Humblot, 1914), p. 141. Though this development had not progressed equally everywhere, it helps to explain the action of cities like Nuremberg, Augsburg, and others during the Reformation. Cf. Alfred Schultze, *Stadtgemeinde und Reformation* (Tübingen: Mohr, 1918), pp. 12, 32, 48; Anton Stormann, *Die städtischen Gravamina gegen den Klerus am Ausgange des Mittelalters und in der Reformationszeit* (Münster: Aschendorffscher Verlag, 1916).

9. WA 11, 246.

10. Georg Jellinek, *Allgemeine Staatslehre* (Berlin: O. Häring, 1900), pp. 121 ff.

11. WA 8, 656. In WA 51, 238, 239, Luther explained that Peter and Paul did not have a foot of ground or a straw of their own, much less were they rulers or lords, yet at that time there were two kingdoms at Rome: Nero's against Christ, and Christ ruling through Peter and Paul against the devil.

12. WA 57, 108.

13. *Smalcald Articles* III, 12: De Ecclesia, *Triglot Concordia* (St. Louis: Concordia Publishing House, 1921), p. 498; cf. *The Book of Concord*, trans. and ed. Theodore G. Tappert (Philadelphia: Muhlenberg [Fortress] Press, 1959), p. 315.

14. For Luther the faith of the believer did not mean an autonomous subjective individualism, for he stressed the realization of the *heilige Gemeine* as the final purpose of God in time and in eternity. Cf. Ferdinand Kattenbusch, "Die Doppelschichtigkeit in Luthers Kirchenbegriff," in *Lutherana*, V, C. Heft 2/3 (1928), 237. Paul Althaus, *Communio sanctorum*, I, *Die Gemeinde im lutherischen Kirchengedanken* (Munich: Ch. Kaiser Verlag, 1929), compares Luther's picture of the church as *Gemeinde* with that of the New Testament and of Catholicism. See also Paul Althaus, *Kirche und Staat nach lutherischer Lehre* (Leipzig: Deichert Verlag, 1935), pp. 6, 7, and Herman Preus, *The Communion of Saints: A Study of the Origin and Development of*

Luther's Doctrine of the Church (Minneapolis: Augsburg Publishing House, 1948).

15. *Von den Konziliis und Kirchen, 1539, WA* 50, 624. In 1520, *Vom Papsttum zu Rom,* Luther leveled devastating criticism at the pretenses of Rome, *WA* 6, 285, 300, 301.

16. *WA* 7, 219, cited from *Works of Martin Luther* (6 vols., Philadelphia: A. J. Holman Company, 1915–1932), II, 373, hereafter cited as *WML.* See also *WA* 30 III, 89: "Let there be no doubt that the holy Christian church will remain on earth till the end of the world."

17. *WA* 50, 629. *WA* 8, 491: "The church does not make the Word, but rather it comes into existence through the Word." *WA* 3, 259: "For the Word of God preserves the church of God." *WA* 51, 507: "Oh, it [the church] is a lofty, deep, hidden thing which nobody can perceive or behold, but can only grasp and believe in Baptism, Sacrament [of the Eucharist], and Word."

18. *WA* 6, 301. *WA* 4, 189: "For the church, which is called the new heaven and the new earth, is invisible but is intelligible through faith." *WA* 3, 124: "For He [Christ] is concealed in the church, which is hidden from the world but known to God." *WA* 4, 81: "For the acts and works of the church will not show themselves openly, for her whole structure is invisible within, in the presence of God *(coram deo),* and so they are known not to carnal eyes but to spiritual understanding and faith." *WA* 7, 710: "Therefore as that Rock [Christ] is without sin, invisible and spiritual, perceptible by faith alone, the church also in its sinless nature must necessarily be invisible and spiritual, comprehensible by faith alone." *WA* 18, 652: "The church is abscondite, the saints lie hidden."

19. *WA* 3, 507, 508.

20. *WA* 4, 324.

21. *WA* 7, 683, in Luther's *Auf das überchristlich . . . Buch Bocks Emsers zu Leipzig Antwort."* Cf. Werner Elert, *Morphologie des Luthertums,* I (Munich: C. H. Beck'sche Verlagsbuchhandlung, 1931), 227–237, 437, 438, on the *sichtbar/unsichtbar* problem.

22. Luther to Amsdorf, 1542, in E. L. Enders and G. Kawerau, eds., *Luthers Briefwechsel* (Leipzig: Rudolf Haupt Verlag, 1884–1932), XIV, 175, hereafter referred to as Enders, with volume and number following.

23. *WA* 7, 720: "Therefore without place and body there is no church." *WA* 4, 169: "Because the church is always born and changes in the succession of the faithful . . ." *WA* 40 II, 103, 560, exegesis of Galatians and of Ps. 45.

24. *WA* 50, 631. *WA* 50, 629: "God's Word cannot exist without God's people." *WA* 42, 423: "God has always preserved unto Himself a people who retained the Word." Cf. Otto Scheel, *Evangelium, Kirche und Volk bei Luther* (Leipzig: Heinsius Verlag, 1934), p. 18. In his treatise *Von den Konziliis und Kirchen,* 1539, Luther has a lengthy discussion of the signs that mark the church, *WA* 50, 629–633.

25. Ernst Rietschel, *Das Problem der unsichtbar-sichtbaren Kirche bei Luther* (Leipzig: Heinsius Verlag, 1932), pp. 33, 34. Günter Jacob, "Luthers Kirchenbegriff," in *Zeitschrift für Theologie und Kirche,* N. F. XV, Heft 1 (1934), 16–32, emphasizes the close dependence

in Luther's understanding of the essence of the church on the actual dynamic of the Word.

26. *WA* 11, 408–416. John O. Evjen, "Luther's Ideas Concerning Church Polity," in *The Lutheran Church Review*, XLV (1926), 207–237, 339–373, reviews the early literature agreeing for the most part that the local congregation is the basic unit in Luther's system of church polity, the microcosmic church. Kattenbusch, p. 292: "What Luther demanded positively for the worship congregation is in principle only the 'preaching of the Word.'" Luther preferred the word *Gemeine* to the more abstract *Gemeinschaft* or the more foreign and ambiguous *Kirche*.

27. *WA* 6, 564.

28. *WA* 11, 408–416. The *ius vocandi* and the *potestas clavium* belong to the Christian congregation. Cf. Wilhelm Pauck, *The Heritage of the Reformation* (Boston: Beacon Press, 1950), p. 43: ". . . according to his innermost conviction, the task of establishing a true church order in the world belonged to the 'Christian people' themselves, not the men and women who happened to be members of historical christendom and its organizations but the Christian believers among them who had been apprehended by the Word of God."

29. *WA* 53, 231–260, *Exempel, einen rechten christlichen Bischof zu weihen*, 1542. The installation of the bishop in Naumburg shows the way in which Luther wished to go.

30. *WA* 26, 195, 196.

31. *WA* 10 III, 215, 216.

32. *WA* 10 II, 140–145; *WA* 12, 169–196.

33. *WA Br*, 3, 373, 374, Luther to Nicolaus Hausmann, Nov. 17, 1524; cf. *WA* 26, 175.

34. *WA* 19, 625. Gordon Rupp, *The Righteousness of God* (London: Hodder and Stoughton Ltd., 1953), p. 288, n. 4, lists seven of Luther's treatises especially concerned with *Obrigkeit*. Gunnar Hillerdal, *Gehorsam gegen Gott und Menschen* (Göttingen: Vandenhoeck & Ruprecht, 1955), p. 18, n. 2, lists the *sedes doctrinae* for Luther's distinction of the spiritual and secular rules.

35. Hillerdal, op. cit., pp. 53, 58. In his exegesis of Genesis Luther theorized on the origin and nature of the state, asserting that when a magistrate acts and speaks it is not *in sua persona, sed Dei* and God's judgment is *iudicia per homines* according to Scripture, *WA* 42, 129.

36. Rom. 13:1.

37. Cf. Julius Binder, *Luthers Staatsauffassung* (Erfurt: K. Stenger, 1924), p. 7. Gustaf Törnvall, *Geistliches und weltliches Regiment bei Luther* (Munich: Kaiser Verlag, 1947), p. 9: "Mit der Lehre von den beiden Regimenten will Luther das für das Weltbild des Glaubens grundlegende Faktum klarstellen, dasz Gott die Welt auf zwei verschiedene Weisen regiert — mit zwei verschiedenen Mitteln: nämlich einesteils dem Regiment mit dem Wort und andernteils der weltlichen Macht oder Obrigkeit." Törnvall's major contribution is his suggestion that Luther's understanding of church and state be approached from the twofold aspect of God's own rule rather than from the human institutional level.

38. *WA* 30 I, 152. Authority is the hand, the channel, and the means by which God transmits to us all good things, *Large Catechism,* 1529, *WA* 30 I, 136. Cf. *WA* 30 II, 554, 555.

39. Heinrich Bornkamm, *Luthers geistige Welt,* 2nd ed. (Gütersloh: Bertelsmann Verlag, 1953), p. 267. Törnvall, pp. 44, 94, 95, lists the terms which Luther used for the two regimes. God established three governances against Satan: the church, the government, and the family. Luther usually comprehended under secular rule both *politia* and *oeconomia.*

40. *WA* 36, 385: "This is what law *(lex)* means. It is also truly the kingdom of our Lord God, but it is a temporal law and government, but He wishes that one support it all the same and it is the kingdom of the left hand. But the kingdom of the right hand is where He reigns Himself, since He does not appoint parents, magistrates, judges, but He Himself preaches the Gospel to the poor." Franz Lau, *"Äuszerliche Ordnung" und "Weltlich Ding" in Luthers Theologie* (Göttingen: Vandenhoeck & Ruprecht, 1933), p. 18: God does not operate immediately or from heaven with angels, but *per ordinariam potestatem. WA* 31 I, 234: "He himself created and ordained it and divided the world up under it for it to rule, as St. Paul testifies, Acts 17." *WA* 52, 26: "Secular government may also be called God's kingdom. For He wants it to remain and desires that we should remain obedient to it. But it is only the kingdom of the left hand. His proper kingdom, where He Himself rules and where He appoints neither father nor mother, emperor nor king nor policeman but where He is Lord Himself, is this — where the Gospel is preached to the poor."

41. Werner Elert, *Die Morphologie des Luthertums,* II (Munich: C. H. Beck'sche Verlagsbuchhandlung, 1953), 46.

42. *WA* 19, 629, 630.

43. *WA* 30 II, 554—556. See also *WA* 6, 410; *WA* 26, 584. Cf. Erich Brandenburg, *Martin Luthers Anschauung vom Staate und der Gesellschaft* (Halle: Verein für Reformationsgeschichte, 1901), pp. 2—8, describes the view of the state for the suppression of evil as part of Luther's medieval inheritance.

44. Törnvall, pp. 166, 193; Hillerdal, p. 41, adds the reminder that Luther saw political misfortunes occasionally as punitive or chastening acts of God, just as sickness, plagues, or other evils. On man and the *regna dei et diaboli,* cf. Gustaf Wingren, *Luthers Lehre vom Beruf* (Munich: Chr. Kaiser Verlag, 1952), p. 11.

45. In his *Von weltlicher Oberkeit, wie weit man ihr Gehorsam schuldig sei,* 1523 (*WA* 11, 229—281), Luther observes that who wants to act like a Samson must first become a Samson; to act without a call is to become "the devil's monkey." *WA* 11, 261: "Such a wonder is not impossible, but it is rare and perilous." On Samson see Rudolf Hermann, *Die Gestalt Simsons bei Luther* (Berlin: Töpelmann Verlag, 1952). Cf. Paul Bard, "Luthers Lehre von der Obrigkeit in ihren Grundzügen," in *Evangelische Theologie,* X (1950—51), 126—144. See also Hillerdal, pp. 64—66, 94, 95, 118, 119. On resistance to the emperor, cf. Karl Müller, *Luthers Äusserungen über das Recht des bewaffneten Widerstands gegen den Kaiser* (Munich: G. Franzscher Verlag, 1915).

46. *WA* 10 III, 19. Cf. Rupp's sprightly discussion of the problem, pp. 301–309.
47. *WA* 28, 286. Ibid., 359, Luther gives the example of Jesus before Pilate.
48. *WA* 31 I, 196. Cf. *WA* 22, 264, an oral protest against the emperor.
49. *WA* 7, 583. Luther, for example, urged the princes to prevent men from becoming beggars, which is as good a work as helping a man who is one. Cf. Hillerdal, p. 75.
50. *WA* 8, 151.
51. *WA* 11, 251. *WA* 10 I, 454: "For the same reason God did not wish to eliminate the sword in the New Testament; in fact, He confirms it, although He does not want His people to use it, and for them it is also unnecessary . . ."
52. *WA* 11, 249, 250, cited from *WML*, III, 234, 235.
53. *WA* 11, 251, 252; *WA* 22, 69. Rupp, pp. 290, 291, collates a number of striking passages on this point. Cf. also Bornkamm, pp. 268, 269.
54. *WA* 11, 253. *WA* 16, 353: "The secular sword must necessarily be established, for there must be peace on earth or one cannot preach." Cf. also *WA* 31 I, 192.
55. *WA* 6, 408, 409.
56. *WA* 31 I, 436.
57. *WA* 30 II, 115, *Vom Kriege wider die Türken*, 1529, on Julius, Clement, etc. Cf. also *Von weltlicher Oberkeit*, 1523; *Ob Kriegsleute auch in seligem Stande sein können*, 1526 (*WA* 19, 623–662). See Hillerdal, pp. 104–106; Bornkamm, p. 270.
58. *WA* 43, 507. Cf. *WA* 11, 263: "Beloved, we are not baptized unto kings, princes, or crowds but unto Christ and God Himself."
59. *WA* 11, 260, 261.
60. *WA* 51, 238.
61. *WA* 51, 242. A Turk could be an excellent ruler, and a Turk or Jew could expect obedience from his subjects, *WA* 18, 398. Otto Hintze, *Die Epochen des evangelischen Kirchenregiments in Preussen*, in *Gesammelte Abhandlungen*, III (Leipzig: Koehler und Amelang, 1943), 67, errs in speaking of the princes as a "Christian authority." They were, as Luther thought in 1520, Christians in authority.
62. *WA* 30 II, 112.
63. *WA* 11, 273. In this connection Karl Barth's call for a Christological basis for state and law, *Rechtfertigung und Recht* (Zollikon: Verlag der Evangelischen Buchhandlung, 1938), is of interest in spite of his inadequate understanding of the positive role of the state for the reformers.
64. *WA* 10 III, 380.
65. Harold Diem, *Luthers Lehre von den zwei Reichen* (Munich: Evangelischer Verlag A. Lempp, 1938), pp. 73–80. Luther was fond of quoting Cicero's maxim *Summum ius, summa iniuria.*
66. *WA* 31 I, 191–194, cited from *WML*, IV, 290–293, as slightly revised in *Luther's Works*, 13 (St. Louis: Concordia Publishing House, 1956), 44–46.

Church and State Under God

67. Cf. John T. McNeill, "Natural Law in the Thought of Luther," in *Church History*, X (Sept. 1941), 211—227, an excellent study.
68. *WA* 51, 242. Luther here cites many classic authors, jurists, historians, and poets who can serve as the source of such wisdom.
69. *WA* 11, 279. Cf. Bornkamm, p. 273; Lau, pp. 32, 115. Wingren, p. 41, argues convincingly in opposition to Karl Holl's distinction between the *lex naturae* and the law of love that for Luther the two were identical and that the line of distinction for Luther ran rather between the law of love which makes demands on all men and the Christian's spontaneous love resulting from his new life in Christ. The "neighbor" is in the center of Luther's ethic, and love born of faith awakens a spontaneous joy in the Christian and delight in the neighbor. George W. Forell, *Faith Active in Love* (New York: American Press, 1954), p. 187, makes clear the difference between love as law and love flowing from faith: "Regardless of the world's attitude to the saving Gospel of Christ, it must for its own temporal preservation abide by God's natural law. Such obedience does not save man, but is conducive to the welfare of the commonwealth."
70. *WA* 18, 80.
71. Ibid. Cf. *WA* 6, 60: "Therefore when you seek an advantage over your neighbor which you are not willing for him to have over you, there love is done for and natural law torn up."
72. *WA* 51, 211: "People are now beginning to praise natural law and natural reason to the effect that all written law comes from and flows out of them, and this is quite true enough."
73. *WA* 18, 81: "Now where the law of Moses and natural law are one and the same thing, there the commandments remain . . ." Cf. Lau, p. 41.
74. *WA* 43, 355: "Times change laws and customs . . ."
75. *WA* 19, 440; *WA* 28, 527: "Everything runs smoother with wisdom than with force." In the realm of *politia* and *oeconomia, ratio* is supreme, *WA* 42, 138. In the *De servo arbitrio* Luther speaks of man's cooperation with God in the area of life below him, although he concedes free will vis-à-vis God Himself only in an evil sense. Luther elsewhere included human governance by reason as part of the command to subdue the earth. *WA* 30 II, 562: "All temporal government and bodily existence are subjected by God to man's reason."
76. *WA* 51, 212.
77. *WA* 51, 252. Cf. *WA* 42, 523: "Princes are never content with their own things and always desire that of others, if they are better."
78. *WA* 19, 648, 649. *WA* 42, 346, the inclination to tyranny and pride is "an evil figment of the human heart." In *Von weltlicher Oberkeit* Luther attacks the princes who think they can command their subjects to do whatever they wish, *WA* 11, 246.
79. *WA* 15, 278.
80. *WA* 51, 203, 204, cited in Rupp, p. 297; cf. also pp. 304—306 for a sampling of Luther's many criticisms of the prince. He was anything but a sycophant or Erastian.
81. *WA* 1, 638—643. Cf. the excellent article by Edgar M. Carlson, "Luther's Conception of Government," in *Church History*, XV (Dec.

1946), 257–270. Heinrich Bornkamm, *Luthers Lehre von den zwei Reichen im Zuzammenhang seiner Theologie,* 2nd ed. (Gütersloh: Gütersloher Verlagshaus, 1960), in a brilliant study describes Luther's two-kingdom theory *(Zwei-Reiche-Lehre)* as three-dimensional, embracing the relationship of church and state as developed in the Middle Ages, the relationship of the spiritual and secular kingdoms of Christ and of the world respectively, and the Christian's activity for himself and for others. Bornkamm's comparison and contrast of Luther and Augustine's views is very illuminating.

82. *WA* 11, 261, 262, 266.

83. *WA* 28, 281. Cf. the commendable work by Ernst Kinder, *Geistliches und weltliches Regiment Gottes nach Luther* (Weimar: Böhlau Verlag, 1940).

84. Wingren, p. 30. Cf. *WA* 40 I, 469.

85. Cf. S. C. Tornay, "Occam's Political Philosophy," in *Church History,* IV (Sept. 1935), 214–223. Occam was concerned in his antipapal writings to define precisely and delimit papal prerogatives.

86. *WA* 51, 239, 240. *WA* 49, 224, Sermon of 1541: "I have often written the past twenty years that the secular and spiritual rules must be carefully distinguished . . ." Cf. *WA* 11, 252, 262.

87. *WA* 45, 253. The English canonist Alanus, who laid the foundations for the later universally accepted doctrine of church and state, held that the pope's *plenitudo potestatis* embraced both the spiritual and temporal realms, but that he merely did not exercise it in the temporal sphere, directly.

88. *WA* 32, 300, 301. Cf. Diem, pp. 113 ff. Diem analyzes the confusion of the two kingdoms in connection with the interpretation of the Sermon on the Mount.

89. *WA* 19, 642, 643; *WA* 51, 240, 246.

90. Rudolph Sohm, the dean of the *corpus christianum* school, gave the classic formulation to this hypothesis, *Kirchenrecht,* I (Leipzig, 1892), 548 ff. This theory received wide currency through the work of Karl Rieker and especially of Ernst Troeltsch, *Die Soziallehren der christlichen Kirchen und Gruppen* (Tübingen: J. C. B. Mohr, 1912), pp. 466 ff., who accepted it uncritically, misinterpreted Luther's natural-law theory, and saw a "double morality" for the two kingdoms. The lasting impact of Troeltsch's misunderstanding is still evident in contemporary scholarship. See, for example, Charles Trinkaus, "The Religious Foundation of Luther's Social Views," in *Essays in Medieval Life and Thought,* ed. John Hine Mundy (New York: Columbia University Press, 1955), pp. 71–87. Richard Wolff, *Studien zu Luthers Weltanschauung* (Munich: R. Oldenbourg, 1920), pp. 45, 47, 54 — in a work dedicated to Troeltsch — stated flatly that "Luther remained within the limits of the two sword theory." Friedrich Löscher, *Schule, Kirche, und Obrigkeit im Reformations-Jahrhundert* (Leipzig: M. Heinsius Nachfolger, 1925), p. 20, suggested that Luther kept but changed the concept by referring to an inner and outer Christendom. Thus also Karl Müller, *Kirche, Gemeinde, und Obrigkeit nach Luther* (Tübingen: J. C. B. Mohr, 1910), pp. 4–7, wrote of Luther's concept of Christendom with its two sides, the inner and the outer. Friedrich Meinecke, "Luther über christliches Gemeinwesen und christlichen Staat," in

Historische Zeitschrift, CXXI (1920), 1—22, conceded that Luther tried to free himself from the "medieval" idea, but always remained in some way involved in it. The monograph by Kurt Matthes, *Das Corpus Christianum bei Luther im Lichte seiner Erforschung* (Berlin: K. Curtius, 1929), attempted to get beyond the schematic presentation of the idea to an assessment of its substantive content.

91. *WA* 6, 408, 410.

92. *WA* 6, 295.

93. Paul Drews, *Entsprach das Staatskirchentum dem Ideal Luthers?* (Tübingen: J. C. B. Mohr, 1908), p. 9, denies the presence of the *corpus christianum* in the *Address* and emphasizes the action of the nobility as part of the priesthood of all believers. Luther freely interchanged the terms which he uses for the spiritual community, the church, a few of which were: *Christenheit* (Christendom), *heilige Christenheit, Volk Gottes, Volk Christi, Gemeinde der Heiligen, Kirche Christi, Gottes Reich, Himmelreich, Reich Christi, Reich des Evangelii, Gemeinschaft der Heiligen, christliches heiliges Volk,* etc. Karl Holl even argued that Luther lacked a descriptive general phrase as *corpus christianum* or *societas christiana* and that such terms could not have had the modern connotation of a Christian society before the 17th century, *Gesammelte Aufsätze zur Kirchengeschichte,* I (Tübingen: J. C. B. Mohr, 1921), 292, 293. The following is an example of Luther's use of *Christenheit* for the church, *WA* 30 II, 130: "Denn der keiser ist nicht das heubt der christenheit, noch beschirmer des Evangelion odder des glaubens. Die kirche und der glaube müssen einen andern schutzherrn haben, denn der Keiser und Könige sind." Johannes Heckel, *Lex charitatis* (Munich: C. H. Beck'sche Verlagsbuchhandlung, 1953), pp. 167—179, on the basis of a close juridical examination of *An den christlichen Adel, Drei Mauern,* and later writings criticizes the attempt to read the *corpus christianum* concept into Luther. He believes that the idea of the *res publica christiana* as a diarchy of the spiritual and temporal rule over the *universitas baptizorum* was foreign to Luther but was renewed in the age of orthodoxy. Johann Gerhard, e. g., distinguished between the *potestas ecclesiastica interna et externa.* Cf. Johannes Heckel, "Luthers Lehre von zwei Regimenten," in *Zeitschrift für evangelisches Kirchenrecht,* IV (1955), 252—265.

94. *WA* 56, 123. Cf. Törnvall, pp. 70—104, on the difference between the spiritual and the secular rule. Karl Holl's reference (I, 104) to the temporal and spiritual rules according to Luther as *opus alienum* and *opus proprium* may be rightly understood but does not appear to do full justice to the positive idea of God's direct activity in the temporal realm.

95. *WA* 6, 411—413.

96. Enders, III, 347, 348.

97. *WML* VI, 173. See *WA* 10 II, 26; 12, 693. Similarly Luther's reaction to the *Reformatio ecclesiarum Hassiae* in cautioning Philipp against too sudden changes, because in matters of ecclesiastical government the people were in their infancy, reflected this problem, Letter to Philipp, Jan. 7, 1527. Cf. Evjen, pp. 218—226.

98. *Erlanger Ausgabe* LIII, 331.

99. Cf. Aemilius L. Richter, *Die evangelischen Kirchenordnungen des 16. Jahrhunderts. Urkunden und Regesten*, I (Weimar: Landes-Industrie-Comptoir, 1846): "Instruction und Befehch dorauff die Visitatores abgefertiget sein," 1527, pp. 77–82; "Unterricht der Visitatorn an die Pfarhern ym Kurfürstenthum zu Sachsen," 1528, pp. 82–101. The "Unterricht" also in *WA 26, 195–240.*

100. *WA 26, 200.*

101. For some of Luther's later references to the *Notbischöfe* problem, cf. *WA 28, 295,* Sermon, Jan. 23, 1529; *WA 46, 737, 738,* Sermons 1537 to 1538; *Erlanger Ausgabe LV, 223,* March 25, 1539; *WA 53, 255,* 1542; *WA Briefwechsel 10, 436,* Letter to Daniel Greiser, Oct. 22, 1543; *WA Tischreden 6, 329,* 1544. Cf. Diem, pp. 126, 127; Holl, p. 376. Holl concludes that "later the force of circumstances proved to be stronger than his own theory," p. 379. Erich Foerster, "Fragen nach Kirchenbegriff aus der Gedankenwelt seines Alters," *Festgabe für Julius Kaften* (Tübingen: J. C. B. Mohr, 1920), argued that the Saxon territorial church could not have been the antithesis of Luther's ideal in view of his expressions in his last years. Cf. Rupp, p. 324. The evangelical church indeed was the true church of Word and sacrament, but this did not mean that Luther approved of its outward order or viewed it as his ideal.

102. Cf. the inaugural lecture of Alfred Schultze, *Stadtgemeinde und Reformation* (Tübingen: J. C. B. Mohr, 1918), and Adolph Frantz, *Die Evangelische Kirchenverfassung in den deutschen Städten des 16. Jahrhunderts,* 2nd ed. (Leipzig: Opetz Verlag, 1878).

103. Cf. Franz Hildebrandt, *Melanchthon: Alien or Ally?* (Cambridge: The University Press, 1946), pp. 55–77, on Melanchthon's concessions to power, suggesting some interesting parallels to contemporary church problems. Clyde Manschreck, *Melanchthon: The Quiet Reformer* (New York: Abingdon Press, 1958), p. 251, cheerily puts Melanchthon on the side of the angels in "keeping church polity independent of the state." On the basic importance of natural law for Melanchthon's political theory, see A. Lang, "The Reformation and Natural Law," in *Princeton Theological Review,* VII (April 1909), 180–184. Cf. Werner Elert, "*Societas* bei Melanchthon," in Robert Jelke, *Das Erbe Martin Luthers und die gegenwärtige theologische Forschung* (Leipzig: Dörffling & Franke, 1928), pp. 101–115. Wilhelm Maurer, "*Lex spiritualis* bei Melanchthon," *Gedenkschrift für D. Werner Elert,* ed. Friedrich Hübner (Berlin: Lutherisches Verlagshaus, 1955), pp. 171 to 198, argues that Melanchthon agreed formally with Luther's conception of natural law, but that because of his different conception of spirit he in reality subverted it.

104. Cf. the excellent chapters in Harold J. Grimm, *The Reformation Era* (New York: Macmillan Company, 1954), pp. 143–264, on the growth and consolidation of Lutheranism.

105. The literature on the Lutheran Symbols is enormous. The most scholarly edition is *Die Bekenntnisschriften der evangelisch-lutherischen Kirche herausgegeben im Gedenkjahr der Augsburgischen Konfession 1930,* 4th rev. ed. (Göttingen: Vandenhoeck & Ruprecht, 1958) *(BS).* The latest edition in English is *The Book of Concord,* trans. and ed. Theodore G. Tappert (Philadelphia: Muhlenberg [Fortress] Press, 1959) *(BC).* The references hereunder are also

made to the still widely accessible *Concordia Triglotta* (St. Louis: Concordia Publishing House, 1921) *(CT)*. Of special interest is the treatment of church and state in the Lutheran Symbols by Edmund Schlink, *Theologie der lutherischen Bekenntnisschriften,* 3rd ed. (Munich, 1948), pp. 306—363.

106. E. g., Apology, XVI, 13 *(BS,* 310, line 19; *BC,* 224; *CT,* 332, 333, sec. 65); Augsburg Confession, XVI, 2 *(BS,* 70, line 12; *BC,* 37; *CT,* 50, 51).

107. *Status civilis (BS,* 309, lines 26, 27; *BC,* 223; *CT,* 330, 331, sec. 60).

108. Augsburg Confession, XVI *(BS,* 70, 71; *BC,* 37, 38; *CT,* 50, 51); Apology, XVI, especially 13 *(BS,* 307—310; *BC,* 222—224; *CT,* 328 to 333, especially sec. 63).

109. Large Catechism, Fourth Commandment, 141, 142, 150 *(BS,* 596 to 599; *BC,* 384—386; *CT,* 620—625).

110. Apology, XIII, 15 *(BS,* 294; *BC,* 213; *CT,* 310, 311); Large Catechism, Baptism, 19—21 *(BS,* 694, 695; *BC,* 438, 439; *CT,* 736, 737).

111. Large Catechism, Fourth Commandment, 167—169 *(BS,* 603; *BC,* 388; *CT,* 628, 629).

112. Apology, XVI, 3, 5 *(BS,* 308; *BC,* 222, 223; *CT,* 330, 331, secs. 55, 57).

113. Large Catechism, Eighth Commandment, 280 *(BS,* 631; *BC,* 403; *CT,* 660, 661).

114. Augsburg Confession, XXVIII *(BS,* 120—133; *BC,* 81—94; *CT,* 82—95).

115. Apology, XVI, 3 *(BS,* 308; *BC,* 222, 223; *CT,* 330, 331, sec. 55).

116. *Zwingli and Bullinger,* trans. and ed. Geoffrey W. Bromiley (Philadelphia: Westminster Press, 1953), p. 25. Cf. Alfred Farner, *Die Lehre von Kirche und Staat bei Zwingli* (Tübingen: J. C. B. Mohr, 1930), passim. In his *Schlussreden* of 1523 (arts. 34—43) Zwingli defended theses which seemed to reinforce the civil power to the detriment of the old church. In his *Exposition of the Faith* (1531), addressed to Francis I, Zwingli urged state intervention to establish the integrity of the visible church.

117. An excellent study in church-state relations in the Swiss reformation is contained in the splendid new biography, Werner Näf, *Vadian und seine Stadt St. Gallen,* II, *Bürgermeister und Reformator von St. Gallen* (St. Gallen: Fehrsche Buchhandlung, 1957). Pp. 392, 393 relate Vadian's fears in 1544 of reawakening the old hostilities of Zwingli's days.

118. Cf. J. W. Allen, *A History of Political Thought in the Sixteenth Century* (London: L. MacVeagh, The Dial Press, Inc., 1928), pp. 35 ff. Cf. Heinold Fast, "The Dependence of the First Anabaptists on Luther, Erasmus and Zwingli," in *Mennonite Quarterly Review,* XXX (April 1956), 104—119. Joseph Lecler, *Histoire de la tolérance au siècle de la Réforme,* 2 vols. (Paris: Aubier, 1955), I, 201, 202, 226, 227, speaks of "the ambiguity of the Anabaptists" on this question.

119. *Calvin: Theological Treatises,* trans. and ed. John K. S. Reid (Philadelphia: Westminster Press, 1954), p. 232. William A. Mueller, *Church and State in Luther and Calvin* (Nashville: Broadman Press, 1954), pp. 77—88, on the whole a very commendable study, except for occasional obiter dicta on pedobaptism. Cf. the excellent recent

survey E. de Moreau, "Calvin et le Calvinisme," in *La crise religieuse du XVIᵉ siècle* (Paris: Bloud et Gay, 1950), pp. 165 ff.

120. Josef Bohatec, *Calvins Lehre vom Staat und Kirche* (Breslau: Verlag G. Märtin, 1937), p. 171, cited in W. Mueller, p. 128.

121. *Institutes,* Book IV, chapter XX, § 1. Cf. *The Institutes of the Christian Religion,* trans. John Allen, 2 vols. (Philadelphia: Presbyterian Board of Christian Education, 1902), II, 633.

122. *Institutes,* Bk. IV, chap. XX, § 16. Allen ed., II, 649.

123. *Institutes,* Bk. IV, chap. XX, § 8; ibid., 640.

124. *Institutes,* Bk. IV, chap. XX, §§ 23–32; ibid., 655 ff.

125. *Institutes,* Bk. IV; ibid., 219. Cf. Henry Strohl, *La pensée de la Réforme* (Neuchâtel/Paris: Delachaux et Niestlé, 1951), p. 239.

126. *CR* XXXIX, 363, cited in Karlfried Fröhlich, *Gottesreich, Welt und Kirche bei Calvin* (Munich: E. Reinhardt, 1930), p. 75. Cf. also M. E. Chenevière, *La pensée politique de Calvin* (Geneva: Éditions Labor, 1937), pp. 245 ff.; B. Lecerf, *Études Calvinistes* (Neuchâtel: Delachaux et Niestlé S. A., 1949), pp. 55 ff.

127. *Institutes,* Bk. IV, chap. XX, § 2; Allen, ed., II, 634. Cf. W. Mueller, op. cit., pp. 138–147.

128. *Institutes,* Bk. IV, chap. XX, § 9; Allen, ed., II, 641.

129. The term "Genevan theocracy" enshrined in the older literature is used with proper reservations today. Cf. Adolphe Bossert, *Calvin* (Paris: Hachette et Co., 1906), pp. 180–199; Eugène Choisy, *La théocratie à Genève au temps de Calvin* (Geneva, 1897). The best recent work by a truly great Reformation scholar is John T. McNeill, *The History and Character of Calvinism* (New York: Oxford University Press, 1954), pp. 91–234, Calvin and the Reformation in Geneva. The texts of the *Articles* of 1537 and the *Ordinances* of 1541 are translated in *Calvin: Theological Treatises,* pp. 48–55, 58–72.

130. Cf. the fascinating study of Robert Kingdon, *Geneva and the Coming of the Wars of Religion in France* (Geneva: M. Droz, 1956). McNeill, *The History and Character of Calvinism,* pp. 237–350, describes the spread of Reformed Protestantism. Heinrich Berger, *Calvins Geschichtsauffassung* (Zürich: Zwingli Verlag, 1955), pp. 152–167, finds the *militia christiana* rooted in the Calvinist philosophy of history. The rectoral address of Carl Hundeshagen, *Calvinismus und Staatsbürgerliche Freiheit* (originally 1841; Zollikon: Evangelischer Verlag, 1946), pp. 22 ff., discusses the impact of the political realities in Franco on Calvinist political thought.

131. *Calvin: Theological Treatises,* p. 72.

132. Cf. William G. Zeeveld, *The Foundations of Tudor Policy* (Cambridge, Mass.: Harvard University Press, 1948), on Starkey, Morison, and other humanist Tudor theorists. Leonard J. Trinterud, "A Reappraisal of William Tyndale's Debt to Martin Luther," in *Church History,* XXXI (March 1962), 24–45, is representative of a number of recent studies emphasizing the importance of Zürich and Basel for the Anglican Reformation.

133. Cf. Allen, pp. 135 ff.; Grimm, pp. 289–306, 464–479, 577–581; Franklin Le Van Baumer, "The Church of England and the Common Corps of Christendom," in *The Journal of Modern History,* XVI

(March 1944), 1–21. "The Conception of Christendom in Renaissance England," in *Journal of the History of Ideas*, VI (April 1945), 131–156, demonstrates the continuity of ideas in 16th-century England. An excellent work on the Anglican establishment, fully aware of the continental precedents and influences, is Carl S. Meyer, *Elizabeth I and the Religious Settlement of 1559* (St. Louis: Concordia Publishing House, 1960).

134. See the interesting account of Luther's inspiration to resistance leaders during the Nazi occupation, Arne Fjellbu, "Luther as a Resource of Arms in the Fight for Democracy," in *World Lutheranism of Today: A Tribute to Anders Nygren 15 November 1950* (Lund: Diakonistyr., 1950), pp. 81–97. Relevant to this point was Gordon Rupp, *Martin Luther: Hitler's Cause or Cure?* (London: Lutterworth Press, 1945), an answer to the attacks of Peter F. Wiener and other Vansittartists.

135. Hans Baron, *Calvins Staatsanschauung und das Konfessionelle Zeitalter* (Munich: R. Oldenbourg, 1924), p. 37, argues that Calvin's natural-law concept, though designated as *ius divinum*, had the chief characteristics of the so-called modern concept. See also his article "Calvinist Republicanism and Its Historical Roots," in *Church History*, VIII (March 1939), 30–42, in which he argues that the vigorous antimonarchic spirit of political Calvinism was absorbed into the natural-law thinking of the 17th and 18th centuries, preparing the way for contract and constitutionalist thought.

136. "Commentary on Psalm 2," *Luther's Works*, 12 (St. Louis: Concordia Publishing House, 1955), 12.

NOTES TO CHAPTER 3

1. Heinrich A. Rommen, *The State in Catholic Thought* (St. Louis and London: B. Herder Book Co., 1945), passim.

2. *Apostolica sedes* of May 13, 1300, and *Unam sanctam* of Nov. 18, 1302.

3. Roberto Bellarmino, *Disputationes de controversiis christianae fidei adversus huius temporis haereticos*, V, i (Venice: Apud Societatem Minimam, 1599); I, 875.

4. Ibid., V, vii; I, 890.

5. The Latin text of the *Syllabus*, with an English translation, is in Philip Schaff, *The Creeds of Christendom* (New York: Harper & Bros., 1877, reprint 1896), II, 213–233.

6. Frederic Nielsen, *The History of the Papacy in the XIXth Century*, trans. A. J. Mason (London: John Murray, 1906), II, 433–444, passim.

7. *De moribus eccl.*, I, 30.

8. *The Great Encyclical Letters of Pope Leo XIII*, ed. John J. Wynne, 3rd ed. (New York: Benziger Brothers, 1903), p. 196.

9. *Singulari quadam*, encyclical of Sept. 24, 1912.

10. *Quadragesimo anno*, encyclical of May 15, 1931.

11. Robert A. Graham, *Vatican Diplomacy: A Study of Church and State on the International Plane* (Princeton: Princeton University Press 1959), passim.

12. Jacques Maritain, *Man and the State* (Chicago: University of Chicago Press, 1951), p. 163.
13. Ibid., pp. 154–157.
14. Ibid., pp. 148–154.
15. Ibid., p. 162.
16. Ibid., p. 178.
17. Edward E. Y. Hales, *The Catholic Church in the Modern World: A Survey from the French Revolution to the Present* (Garden City, N. Y.: Doubleday & Co., 1958).
18. Father Ong, for example, in a group of essays dealing with the issue, stresses the person-to-person aspect of church-state issues as Roman Catholicism confronts the secularism of the present era. Walter J. Ong, *American Catholic Crossroads* (New York: The Macmillan Co., 1959), passim.
19. Francois Charriere, "The Catholic Church and Religious Tolerance," in *Catholic Mind*, LVI (July–Aug. 1958), 293–304. Even when in a dominant political position, Roman Catholics are not required by doctrinal principles to interfere with the religious freedom of dissenters. However, this is not a renunciation of the axiom that "error has no rights."
20. For example, Gustave Weigel, "Inside American Roman Catholicism"; Thomas F. O'Dea, "The Ideologists and the Missing Dialogue"; William Clancy, "A Roman Catholic View of American Protestantism"; all from "Protestant-Roman Catholic Dialogue," in *Christianity and Crisis*, XIX (June 8, 1959), 77—88.
21. Robert D. Cross, *The Emergence of Liberal Catholicism in America* (Cambridge: Harvard University Press, 1958). Robert J. Alexander, "New Social and Political Trends in the Roman Catholic Church," in *Journal of International Affairs*, XII (Nov. 2, 1958), 144–149, argues that there have been shifts in the policy of the Roman Church on political and social matters in Europe and Latin America since World War II in the direction of a more general acceptance of political democracy and a greater concern with the application of Christian principles to the solution of social problems. By way of disagreement, Henry P. Van Dusen writes in *Christianity and Crisis*, XIX (Aug. 3, 1959), 115–117, that the trend in official Roman Catholic circles is retrogressive and reactionary, very little influenced by "liberal" Roman Catholics.
22. Thomas F. O'Dea, *American Catholic Dilemma: An Inquiry into the Intellectual Life* (New York: Sheed and Ward, 1958); John Courtney Murray, *We Hold These Truths: Catholic Reflections on the American Proposition* (New York: Sheed and Ward, 1960); *Religion in America: Original Essays on Religion in a Free Society*, ed. John Cogley (New York: Meridian Books, Inc., 1958).
23. Andre De Bovis, "L'Église dans la société temporelle," in *Nouvelle Revue Théologique*, LXXIX (March 1957), 225–247.
24. For example: Albert Hartmann, *Toleranz und christlicher Glaube* (Frankfurt a/M: Josef Knecht Carolusdruckerei, 1955), has a concluding chapter on "Freedom of Conscience and the State" which obviously argues quite differently about the issue than Pius IX presented it. The explanation is not that the Roman position has changed

essentially but that the emerging historical necessities require a different stance.

25. Thomas G. Sanders, "A Comparison of Two Current American Roman Catholic Theories of the American Political System with Particular Reference to the Problem of Religious Liberty," unpubl. Ph. D. diss., Columbia University, 1958.

26. Johannes Baptist Hirschmann, "Church, State and Society — A Roman Catholic View," in *Lutheran World*, V (June 1958), 16—27. Interesting, but rather diffuse in their emphases, are the excellent selections from the annual Lutheran Social Ethics Seminar at Valparaiso University, Valparaiso, Ind.: *God and Caesar: A Christian Approach to Social Ethics*, ed. Warren A. Quanbeck (Minneapolis: Augsburg Publishing House, 1959).

27. For sources see John Winthrop, "A Model of Christian Charity" and "Speech to the General Assembly"; John Cotton, "Limitation of Government"; John Wise, "Vindication of the Government of New England Churches"; Jonathan Mayhew, "A Discourse Concerning Unlimited Submission." Selections from the documents may be found in Perry Miller, *The American Puritans* (New York: Doubleday & Co., 1960).

28. "Christian Community and Civil Community," in Karl Barth, *Community, State and Church* (Garden City, N. Y.: Doubleday & Co., 1960), p. 169.

29. "*Rechtfertigung* and *Recht*," ibid., p. 118.

30. Ibid., p. 171.

31. Emil Brunner, *The Divine Imperative: A Study in Christian Ethics*, trans. Olive Wyon (New York: The Macmillan Co., 1937), p. 552.

32. Ibid., p. 553.

33. Ibid., p. 554.

34. Ibid., pp. 554, 560.

35. Ibid., pp. 438, 535.

36. Johann Gerhard, *Loci theologici*, ed. J. F. Cotta (Tübingen: J. G. Cotta, 1762—1789), IV, 292.

37. Ibid., V, 381.

38. Ibid., V, 140.

39. Ibid., V, 141: ". . . for we concede that unregenerate man has some capacity to do the outward things of the law."

40. Ibid., XIV, 125: "Positive law must be tailored to the condition of the people for which it is intended and the sort of government they have." XIV, 127: "Positive laws can be modified and eliminated when circumstances change."

41. Ibid., XIV, 126: "Positive law is a rivulet drawn from the spring of the law of nature."

42. Ibid., XIV, 74, 75.

43. Ibid., XIV, 76.

44. Ibid., XIV, 80: "The power has divinely been given to the Christian magistrate [to make] new laws other than the Mosaic, for use in administering public affairs, but they must be honorable, just, and in agreement with natural right and suited to the public good."

45. Karl Holl, *Gesammelte Aufsätze zur Kirchengeschichte* (Tübingen: J. C. B. Mohr [Paul Siebeck]), I (7th rev. ed., 1948), 155–287; 326–380.

46. *Loci theologici*, XIII, 288, 289.

47. Ibid., XIV, 9, 10. It is indeed remarkable that Gerhard's locus on the "political magistrate," comprising about 470 pages, offers us only 53 pages of discussion concerning the citizen or subject; and of these, almost 30 pages are used to argue the question whether the clergy are subject to the civil magistrate. Gerhard decides against Bellarmine that this is so. XIV, 315 ff.

48. Ibid., XIV, 355: "We concede that in these matters which concern religion and conscience, subjects are free from obeying the orders of the unfaithful or heretical magistrates."

49. Ibid., XIV, 359, 360: "But if flight is impossible, whatever happens must be endured rather than doing anything against the Word of God and conscience, and give up life rather than God."

50. However, care must be exercised in saying that "Luther allowed the magistrate special rights." Actually, Luther did not assign varying rights to subjects according to differences in status. See *WA*, 19, 643.

51. However, this point must not be pressed too far. The Lutheran doctrine of sin, original and actual, so long as it was taken seriously, avoided the Utopian dreams of a later age. Also, by way of contrast, with Gerhard, consideration should be given to the various complaints concerning territorial church administration voiced by Veit Ludwig von Seckendorff, *Der Christenstaat* (Leipzig: J. F. Gleditsch, 1686), III, 689, 690.

52. The history and structure of the territorial church government has had many modern students, such as Günther Holstein, *Die Grundlagen des evangelischen Kirchenrechts* (Tübingen: Mohr, 1928); Karl Mueller, *"Zur Geschichte des Episkopalsystems,"* in *Zeitschrift der Savigny-Stiftung für Rechtsgeschichte*, XXXIX (1918, Kan. Abt. 8), 15. Also Holl, "Luther und das landesherrliche Kirchenregiment," in *Gesammelte Aufsätze*, I, 326–380.

53. *Loci theologici*, XIV, 39 and 2.

54. Ibid., XIV, 47.

55. Ibid., XIV, 17.

56. Ibid., XIII, 225.

57. Ibid., XIV, 185–238.

58. Carl S. Mundinger, *Government in the Missouri Synod* (St. Louis: Concordia Publishing House, 1947), pp. 187, 203.

59. Joh. Guilielmi Baieri, *Compendium theologiae positivae*, ed. Carol. Ferd. Guil. Walther (St. Louis: Concordia Publishing House, 1879), III, 724–745.

60. Ibid., p. 744.

61. C. F. W. Walther, *Americanisch-Lutherische Evangelien Postille*, 8th ed. (St. Louis: Concordia Publishing House, 1882), pp. 339–344.

62. *Lehre und Wehre*, IX (Jan. 1863), 1–8. Abdel R. Wentz, *A Basic History of Lutheranism in America* (Philadelphia: Muhlenberg Press, 1955), pp. 170, 171.

63. Eivind Berggrav, *The Norwegian Church in Its International Setting* (pamphlet published by London University, 1946), p. 7.
64. Bjorne Höye and Trygve M. Agar, *The Fight of the Norwegian Church Against Nazism* (New York: The Macmillan Co., 1943), p. 118.
65. Berggrav, p. 9.
66. Ibid., p. 17.

NOTES TO CHAPTER 4

1. *Europe in Review: Reading and Sources Since 1500*, eds. George L. Mosse et al. (Chicago: Rand McNally, 1957), p. 73.
2. *Readings in Western Civilization*, eds. George H. Knoles and Rixford K. Snyder (New York: Lippincott, 1951), p. 409.
3. John David Hughey, *Religious Freedom in Spain* (London: Carey Kingsgate Press, 1955), p. 3.
4. Ibid., p. 3.
5. E. Allison Peers, *Spain: The Church and the Orders* (London: Eyre and Spottiswoode, 1939), p. 21.
6. Charles E. Chapman, *A History of Spain* (New York: Macmillan, 1958), p. 445.
7. Hughey, pp. 17, 18.
8. Ibid., p. 23.
9. Ibid., p. 34.
10. Ibid., p. 36.
11. Ibid., p. 74.
12. Ibid., p. 112.
13. Ibid., p. 132.
14. Ibid., p. 148.
15. Arthur Galton, *Church and State in France, 1300–1907* (London: Edward Arnold, 1907), p. 36.
16. Charles S. Phillips, *The Church in France, 1789–1848: A Study in Revival* (London: A. R. Mowbray Ltd., 1929), p. 58.
17. Ibid., p. 62.
18. Ibid., p. 93.
19. Ibid., p. 102.
20. Ibid., pp. 173–179.
21. Galton, p. 168.
22. Ibid., p. 170.
23. Ibid., p. 202.
24. Ibid., p. 204.
25. Ibid., p. 234.
26. Ibid., p. 241.
27. James Hastings Nichols, *History of Christianity, 1650–1950: The Secularization of the West* (New York: Ronald Press, 1956), p. 231.
28. M. Searle Bates, *Religious Liberty: An Inquiry* (New York: Harper & Brothers, 1945), p. 103.
29. Ibid., p. 104.

30. Leo Pfeffer, *Church, State, and Freedom* (Boston: Beacon Press, 1953), p. 50.
31. Ibid., p. 50.
32. William E. Gladstone, *Church and State* (London: John Murray, 1841), I, 89.
33. Ibid., p. 134.
34. Ibid., p. 190.
35. Ibid., p. 11.
36. Ibid., pp. 171, 172.
37. Ibid., p. 199.
38. Ibid., p. 273.
39. Ibid., p. 189.
40. Ibid., p. 230.
41. Karen Larsen, *A History of Norway* (Princeton: Princeton University Press, 1948), p. 246.
42. Knut Gjerset, *History of the Norwegian People* (New York: Macmillan, 1915), II, 135.
43. Ibid., pp. 135, 136, quoting Peder Clausson Friis.
44. Ibid., p. 194.
45. Larsen, p. 272.
46. Ibid., p. 317.
47. Ibid., pp. 337, 338.
48. Gjerset, II, 405.
49. Larsen, p. 360.
50. Gjerset, II, 425.
51. *Introduction to Contemporary Civilization in the West: Source Book,* eds. Justus Buchler et al. (New York: Columbia University Press, 1946), I, 536.
52. Henry Sacheverell, *A Discourse Shewing the Dependance of Government on Religion* . . . (London, 1710), p. 5.
53. Philip Skelton, *Some Proposals for the Revival of Christianity* (London, 1736), p. 35.
54. William Warburton, *The Alliance between Church and State; or the Necessity and Equity of an established Religion, and a Test Law demonstrated, from the Essence and End of civil Society upon the fundamental Principles of the Laws of Nature and Nations* (London, 1736), pp. 72, 73.
55. Joseph Priestley, *Essay on First Principles of Government* (London, 1768).
56. In Simon Backus, *A Dissertation on the Right and Obligation of the Civil Magistrate to Support Religion* (Middletown: T. and J. B. Dunning, 1804), p. 2.
57. Francis Warre Cornish, *The English Church in the 19th Century* (London: Macmillan, 1910), I, 56.
58. Ibid., I, 108.
59. Ibid., II, 266.

60. Ibid., II, 267.
61. Ibid., II, 270.
62. Pfeffer, p. 46.
63. Ibid., p. 46.
64. Erik von Kuehnelt-Leddihn, "Church-State Relations," in *Commonweal,* LXXI (Nov. 27, 1959), pp. 255–258.
65. Ibid., p. 257.

NOTES TO CHAPTER 5

1. Robert Harrison, "A Little Treatise vppon the first Verse of the 122 Psalm," in *The Writings of Robert Harrison and Robert Browne,* eds. Albert Peel and Leland H. Carlson (London: George Allen and Unwin Ltd. for the Sir Halley Stewart Trust, 1953), p. 118.
2. Daniel Jenkins, *The Strangeness of the Church,* Christian Faith Series (Garden City, N. Y.: Doubleday & Co., Inc., 1955), p. 130.
3. See Marshall M. Knappen, *Tudor Puritanism: A Chapter in the History of Idealism* (Chicago: University of Chicago Press, 1939), p. 424.
4. John Winthrop, quoted by Perry Miller, *Errand into the Wilderness* (Cambridge, Mass.: The Belknap Press of Harvard University Press, 1956), p. 5.
5. Ibid., p. 12.
6. William and Mary, cap. 18, No. CXXIII in *Documents Illustrative of English Church History,* eds. Henry Gee and William J. Hardy (London: Macmillan and Co. Ltd., 1896), pp. 654–664.
7. George N. Clark, *The Later Stuarts: 1660–1714,* in *Oxford History of England,* 2nd ed. (Oxford: At the Clarendon Press, 1955), p. 155.
8. Bernard Lord Manning, *The Protestant Dissenting Deputies,* ed. Ormerod Greenwood (New York: Cambridge University Press, 1952), passim.
9. *Church and State Through the Centuries: A Collection of Historic Documents with Commentaries,* trans. and ed. Sidney Z. Ehler and John B. Morrall (London: Burns, Oates & Washbourne Ltd., 1954), pp. 164–173.
10. Ibid., pp. 189–193.
11. Ibid., pp. 208–213.
12. Shelby T. McCloy, "Persecution of the Huguenots in the 18th Century," in *Church History,* XX (Sept. 1951), 56–79.
13. Shelby T. McCloy, "The Literary Campaign for Toleration of the Huguenots," in *Church History,* XX (Dec. 1951), 38–54.
14. *Readings in European History,* ed. James Harvey Robinson (Boston: Ginn & Co., 1906), II, 411.
15. McCloy, "The Literary Campaign for Toleration of the Huguenots," in *Church History,* XX (Dec. 1951), 51.
16. *American State Papers and Related Documents on Freedom in Religion,* 4th rev. ed., ed. William A. Blakely (Washington, D. C.: The Religious Liberty Association, 1949), p. 96. Hereafter cited as *American State Papers.*
17. Ibid.

18. *Church and State Through the Centuries,* p. 222; *American State Papers,* p. 97.
19. *American State Papers,* pp. 103–120, has the "Memorial of the Presbytery of Hanover to the General Assembly of Virginia of 1776," "Memorial of the Presbytery of Hanover to the General Assembly of Virginia Presented to the House June 3, 1777," "Memorial of the Presbytery of Hanover to the General Assembly of Virginia Presented to the House Nov. 12, 1784," "Memorial of the Presbytery of Hanover to the General Assembly of Virginia Presented to the House Nov. 3, 1785," and "Madison's Memorial, 1785."
20. *Church and State Through the Centuries,* p. 225; *American State Papers,* p. 121.
21. Frequently cited. The text used was from *American State Papers,* p. 150 for Article VI, p. 149 for Article I of the Amendments. See also *Church and State Through the Centuries,* p. 225, for the First Amendment.
    "The fear that the federal government would impose a national religion on the whole country was widespread. The desire to have the new Constitution explicitly state that the federal government could not do this was expressed in a number of state resolutions." James M. O'Neill, *Catholicism and American Freedom* (New York: Harper & Bros., 1952), p. 26.
22. *American State Papers,* pp. 162, 163 (editorial note).
23. Ibid., p. 151, and frequently elsewhere for the Tenth Amendment: "The powers not delegated to the United States by the Constitution, nor prohibited by it to the States, are reserved to the States respectively, or to the people."
24. Anson Phelps Stokes, *Church and State in the United States: Historical Development and Contemporary Problems of Religious Freedom Under the Constitution* (New York: Harper & Bros., 1950), I, 550, quoting from A. N. Holcombe, *State Government in the United States,* pp. 17, 18: "Many writers on religious freedom in the United States do not give adequate attention to this amendment, practically overlooking the fact that such statutes as may be adopted with reference to the Churches are primarily within the jurisdiction of the several states. These have — subject to the general provisions of the Federal Constitution — 'hitherto unfathomed powers to deal with vast subjects of religion, education, and the supply of public utilities.'" See also Stokes, *Church and State,* I, 358–364.
25. Ibid., I, 135.
26. Ibid., I, 395, 396.
27. Ibid., I, 402–404.
28. Ibid., I, 402.
29. Ibid., 403; *Quellen zur Geschichte der Trennung von Staat und Kirche,* ed. Zaccaria Giacometti (Tübingen: Verlag von J. C. B. Mohr [Paul Siebeck], 1926), p. 287.
30. Stokes, *Church and State,* I, 428, points out that "state constitutions preceded the Federal Constitution, and that consequently the fundamental battles for religious freedom were fought out in the state conventions prior to the Constitutional Convention in Philadelphia in 1787."

31. *Quellen*, pp. 678, 679, No. 196; Stokes, *Church and State*, I, 436, 437.

32. *Quellen*, p. 679, No. 197; Stokes, *Church and State*, I, 437.

33. *Quellen*, p. 696, Nos. 231, 232; Stokes, *Church and State*, I, 437.

34. *Quellen*, p. 274, No. 296; see also ibid., Nos. 294, 295 for articles from the constitutions of 1790 and 1838; the charter for the Province of Pennsylvania is given ibid., pp. 685—687, No. 209; the constitution of 1776, ibid., p. 687, No. 210; Stokes, *Church and State*, I, 438, 439.

35. *Quellen*, p. 688, No. 211, for the Charter of Rhode Island and Providence Plantation, 1663; ibid., p. 725, No. 297, for Article I of the constitution of 1842; Stokes, *Church and State*, I, 442—444.

36. South Carolina's constitution had the most detailed article (adopted in 1778) to insure Protestantism in its public officials. By 1790 significant changes had been made. Stokes, *Church and State*, I, 432 to 434.
    New Jersey also favored Protestantism, since Roman Catholics were not permitted to hold office there until 1844. The constitution of 1776 stated: "That there shall be no establishment of any one religious sect in this Province, in preference to another." Stokes, *Church and State*, I, 435, 436. See also *Quellen*, pp. 684, 685, No. 207; ibid., p. 719, No. 282 gives the pertinent sections of Article I of the constitution of 1844.

37. The charter of 1732 spoke of the "free exercise of religion"; *Quellen*, pp. 679, 680, No. 198; and so did the constitution of 1777, ibid., p. 680, No. 199. The phrase was repeated in the constitutions of 1789, 1798, 1865, 1868, and 1877; ibid., pp. 698, 699, Nos. 237, 238, 239, 240, 241. See Stokes, *Church and State*, I, 439, 440.

38. By 1793. See Stokes, *Church and State*, I, 440—442. *Quellen* has the pertinent paragraphs from the constitutions of 1777, 1786, and 1913, pp. 688, 689, 729, Nos. 212, 213, 306.

39. *Quellen*, pp. 680, 681, No. 201.

40. Ibid., p. 681, No. 201. No prior consent was required for a gift of less than two acres.

41. Ibid., p. 708, No. 261. The amount of land allowed as a gift to a clergyman or a church was raised to five acres.

42. Ibid., p. 709, Nos. 262, 263.

43. Ibid., p. 685, No. 208; Stokes, *Church and State*, I, 405.

44. *Quellen*, p. 720, Nos. 284, 285.

45. Ibid., p. 684, No. 206.

46. Ibid., pp. 718, 719, Nos. 280, 281.

47. Stokes, *Church and State*, I, 432.

48. *Quellen*, pp. 659, 660, No. 230; Stokes, *Church and State*, I, 408—420.

49. *Quellen*, pp. 682, 683, No. 204 (but he does distinguish between the constitutions of 1780 and 1833); Stokes, *Church and State*, I, 423 to 427.

50. *Quellen*, p. 705, No. 253.

51. Ibid., p. 716, No. 274.

52. The articles or paragraphs that are pertinent are given from most of the constitutions and their revisions ibid., pp. 678—733, Nos. 195 to 314.

53. Ibid., p. 692, Nos. 220, 221, 222.
54. Ibid., pp. 719, 720, No. 283.
55. Winthrop S. Hudson, *The Great Tradition of the American Churches* (New York: Harper & Brothers, 1953), p. 64.
56. Lyman Beecher, *Autobiography and Correspondence,* in *Collected Works,* ed. Charles Beecher (New York, 1863), I, 344.

    John Mitchell, pastor of the Edwards Church in Northampton, was not reconciled. In his *A Guide to the Principles of the Congregational Churches of New Endland* (Northampton: J. H. Butler, 1838), pp. 192–194, he still justified the taxation of citizens for the support of religion. He found it strictly equitable. "It is right that each member of the community, enjoying a common benefit, should bear his part of the common burthen according to his means" (p. 193). He cited the tithes of the Old Testament and justified civil taxes for ecclesiastical purposes. "This was the mode originally established by God himself for the support of religion" (p. 193). He laments (p. 194): "For a century and a half there was no objection to this mode in New England, the people being all of one denomination, and sensible enough of the importance of religion to be willing to support it. But as the state of society has changed, taxation for the support of the gospel has met with many obstacles from unreasonable and disaffected men, and has been laid aside, to a greater or less extent, for other modes."
57. Hudson, p. 65.
58. The Burial Hill Declaration of 1865 is the nearest approach to such a formulation.

    Gaius G. Atkins and Frederick L. Fagley, *History of American Congregationalism* (Boston and Chicago: The Pilgrim Press, 1942), p. 401. Philip Schaff, *Creeds of Christendom,* 4th and rev. ed. (New York: Harper & Bros., 1905), III, 735.
59. Hudson, p. 101.
60. William White, *The Case of the Episcopal Churches in the United States Considered,* ed. Richard G. Salomon (Church Historical Society Publications, No. 39, 1954), p. 20 (p. 6 of 1782 ed., publ. David C. Claypoole, Philadelphia).
61. William S. Perry, *The History of the American Episcopal Church, 1587–1883* (Boston: James R. Osgood and Co., 1885), II, 106.
62. Ibid., II, 107.
63. Schaff, III, 486; see also p. 826.
64. Ibid., III, 812.
65. Alexander Campbell, *The Christian System, In Reference to the Union of Christians, and A Restoration of Primitive Christianity, As Plead in the Current Reformation,* 2nd ed. (Cincinnati and Chicago: Central Book Concern, [1839]), pp. 159, 160.
66. Stokes, *Church and State,* I, 309.
67. *American State Papers,* p. 158; Stokes, *Church and State,* I, 310.
68. In his *The Bloudy Tenent of Persecution for the Cause of Conscience.* A convenient excerpt from this work can be found in *Great Voices of the Reformation: An Anthology,* ed. Harry Emerson Fosdick (New York: Random House, Inc., 1952), pp. 435–449.

69. George E. Horr, "The Baptists," in *The Religious History of New England* (Cambridge: Harvard University Press, 1917), pp. 137–163.

70. *American State Papers,* p. 104; *The Presbyterian Enterprise: Sources of American Presbyterian History,* eds. Maurice W. Armstrong, Lefferts A. Loetscher, and Charles A. Anderson (Philadelphia: Westminster Press, 1956), pp. 91, 92.

71. William Warren Sweet, *The Story of Religion in America,* 2nd rev. ed. (New York: Harper & Bros., 1950), ch. xiii.

72. *The Confession of Faith of the Presbyterian Church in the United States of America,* adopted by the General Synod in 1729, amended and ratified in 1788, and amended in 1887 and 1903 (Philadelphia: Board of Christian Education of the Presbyterian Church in the U. S. A., 1924), pp. 107–110; cf. also pp. 132, 133.

73. Abdel Ross Wentz, *A Basic History of Lutheranism in America* (Philadelphia: Muhlenberg Press, 1955), p. 32.
   Henry Eyster Jacobs, *A History of the Evangelical Lutheran Church in the United States,* Vol. IV of the American Church History Series, 5th ed. (New York: Charles Scribner's Sons, 1907 [1st ed. c. 1893]), ch. xvi; Lars P. Qualben, *The Lutheran Church in Colonial America* (New York: Thomas Nelson & Sons, 1940), pp. 209–216; A. L. Graebner, *Geschichte der Lutherischen Kirche in America* (Saint Louis: Concordia Publishing House, 1892), p. 360.

74. Qualben, Appendix V, pp. 304–314; Chr. Otto Kraushaar, *Verfassungsformen der Lutherischen Kirche Amerikas* (Gütersloh: Druck und Verlag von G. Bertelsmann, 1911), pp. 233–245.

75. Wentz, p. 55.

76. Peter Guilday, *The Life and Times of John Carroll, Archbishop of Baltimore, 1735–1815* (Westminster, Md.: The Newman Press, 1954 [1922]), p. 106.

77. Quoted from a letter to Father Powers, 28 Feb. 1779, ibid., p. 110. See also Carroll's "Relation of the State of Religion in the United States," quoted in full in the original Latin, ibid., pp. 223–225, with a variant translation, pp. 225–227. Annabelle M. Melville, *John Carroll of Baltimore: Founder of the American Hierarchy* (New York: Charles Scribner's Sons, 1955), pp. 73–75, summarizes and discusses the document.

78. Guilday, p. 113; Melville, pp. 85–99.

79. Guilday, p. 392, put it this way: "Independent at last of all ties with the Old World, except the one bond which has ever been jealously guarded – spiritual union with the Holy See – the Catholic Church of the United States inaugurated its organized life with an American as its chief shepherd."

80. Guilday, p. 726; Melville, p. 211. Both quote this section with references.

81. Horr, p. 157.

82. Sweet, p. 204.

83. Stokes, *Church and State,* I, 761.

84. See in part Stokes's "Summary of the Effects of Independence on the Protestant Churches," in *Church and State,* I, 778–783.

85. Sherwood Eddy, *The Kingdom of God and the American Dream: The Religious and Secular Ideals of American History* (New York and London: Harper & Bros., 1941), p. 116.

86. Michel-Guillaume de Crevecoeur, "What Is an American?" in *America in Perspective: The United States Through Foreign Eyes*, abridged, ed. Henry Steele Commager ([A Mentor Book] New York: New American Library of World Literature, c. 1947), p. 24: "If you recede still farther from the sea . . . Religion seems to have still less influence, and their manners are less improved."

Harriet Martineau, "Eccentricity and Originality in the American Character," ibid., p. 65: "The commonest of these causes in a society like that of the United States is, perhaps, the absence of influences to which almost all other persons are subject."

Alexander Mackay, "Every American Is an Apostle of the Democratic Creed," ibid., p. 94, spoke of "the faith which Americans cherish in the destiny of their country."

87. "The Autobiography of Flavel Bascom, 1833–1840," in *The Congregationalists [1783–1850]: A Collection of Source Materials*, ed. William W. Sweet, in *Religion on the American Frontier*, III (Chicago: University of Chicago Press, 1939), 252.

88. Luther Shaw to Rev. Absalom Peters, Romeo, Macomb Co., Mich., 15 Nov. 1835, ibid., p. 316.

89. Quoted from Bela Bates Edwards by John R. Bodo, *The Protestant Clergy and Public Issues, 1812–1848* (Princeton: Princeton University Press, 1954), p. 35.

90. Eddy, p. 137.

91. Gettysburg, Pa., 1846.

92. William Leggett, "Thanksgiving Day" (editorial), in *Plaindealer*, Dec. 3, 1836, in *Social Theories of Jacksonian Democracy: Representative Writings of the Period 1825–1850*, ed. Joseph L. Blau (New York: Liberal Arts Press, 1955 [1st ed., 1947]), p. 79.

93. *Cornerstones of Religious Freedom in America*, ed. Joseph L. Blau (Boston: The Beacon Press, 1949), p. 121; Bodo, pp. 46, 47.

94. Zelotes Fuller, "The Tree of Liberty, An Address in Celebration of the Birth of Washington, 1830," in *Cornerstones*, pp. 131, 133, 134.

95. Leggett, pp. 79, 80.

96. Quoted by Bodo, p. 36.

American State Papers, p. 192, reprints the letter written to Edward Livingston by James Madison, Montpelier, 10 July, 1822, in which he says: ". . . it was not with my approbation that the deviation from it took place in Congress, when they appointed chaplains, to be paid from the National Treasury."

On the question of legislative chaplaincies see also the Moulton-Myers report to the legislature of New York (1832), on which no action was taken. It is, however, an able argument against such chaplaincies. The report can be found in *Cornerstones*, pp. 141–156.

97. *American State Papers*, pp. 207, 208, gives the act.

98. Stokes, *Church and State*, II, 12–20; Bodo, pp. 39–43; *Cornerstones*, pp. 106–109.

99. The complete text of the committee report is given in *Social Theories of Jacksonian Democracy*, pp. 274–281. The first quotation is from p. 277; the second from p. 278.

A summary of the report with excerpts may be found in Stokes, *Church and State*, II, 15–17; see also *American State Papers*, pp. 210 to 216.

100. This report may be found in *Cornerstones*, pp. 110–118; *American State Papers*, pp. 216–225.

101. *American State Papers*, p. 226; Stokes, *Church and State*, II, 18, 19.

102. *American State Papers*, pp. 228–236. The quotation is from p. 235, from a speech by Garrison on resolutions adopted by the Anti-Sabbath Convention in 1848. The resolutions, too, are given, pp. 232, 233.

Bodo, pp. 40–43; Stokes, *Church and State*, I, 683.

103. Bodo, pp. 44, 45.

104. *The Methodists [1783–1840]: A Collection of Source Materials*, ed. William W. Sweet, in *Religion on the American Frontier*, IV (Chicago: University of Chicago Press, 1946), 222n.

105. *The Baptists, 1783–1830: A Collection of Source Material*, ed. William W. Sweet, in *Religion on the American Frontier*, I (Chicago: University of Chicago Press, 1931), 419.

106. *Autobiography of Peter Cartwright*, ed. Charles L. Wallis (New York and Nashville: Abingdon Press, 1956), p. 176.

107. Ibid., p. 177.

108. Stokes, *Church and State*, II, 260; *American State Papers*, p. 249.

109. *American State Papers*, pp. 250, 251; Stokes, *Church and State*, II, 260, has a part of this constitution.

110. Ibid., 1 c.; *American State Papers*, pp. 251–254, for excerpts from *The Christian Statesman*.

111. *American Social History as Recorded by British Travellers*, ed. Allen Nevins (New York: Henry Holt & Co., 1931), pp. 117, 118, 121, 122.

112. The indexes of the four volumes edited by Sweet, *Religion on the American Frontier*, may be consulted.

113. *Autobiography of Peter Cartwright*, pp. 128, 129.

114. Stokes, *Church and State*, I, 682, 683; Bodo, pp. 184, 185; John Allen Krout, *The Origins of Prohibition* (New York: Alfred A. Knopf, 1925), has the most complete account of the movement and the part played by the Protestant preachers in the movement.

115. Stokes, *Church and State*, II, 41, 42.

116. Bodo, pp. 185–190.

117. Quoted ibid., pp. 61, 62, from an address by the Rev. Charles B. Baynton, 5 July 1847, in Cincinnati.

118. T. Valentine Parker, *American Protestantism: An Appraisal* (New York: Philosophical Library, 1956), p. 27.

119. *The Presbyterians, 1783–1840: A Collection of Source Materials*, ed., William W. Sweet, in *Religion on the American Frontier*, II (Chicago: University of Chicago Press, 1936), 698, C. Washburn to the Rev. Messrs. Badger & Hall, Secs. A. H. M. S., Benton Co., Arks. 8th Sept. 1846. See also Stokes, *Church and State*, I, 826.

120. From a letter in 1830 of the American Home Missionary Society signed by Knowles Taylor, Treasurer. Sweet, *The Presbyterians*, p. 669. Bodo, p. 66, quoted a "Correspondence" in *The Home Missionary*, II (1829), 11, from Missouri: "The Jesuits are making rapid strides here in their usual way, building chapels, schoolhouses, and establishing nunneries. . . . Large contributions, by protestant people, or those who have been educated as such, are made to erect these buildings, and many are sending their children to these schools . . ."

121. Sweet, *The Presbyterians*, p. 81; an excerpt from the speech is in Armstrong, Loetscher, and Anderson, *The Presbyterian Enterprise*, pp. 140–143.

122. The best and most comprehensive study of this movement is by Ray Allen Billington, *The Protestant Crusade, 1800–1860*, reissue of 1938 ed. (New York: Rinehart & Co., Inc., 1952).

123. "The Pastoral Letter of 1833," in *The National Pastorals of the American Hierarchy (1792–1919)*, ed. Peter Guilday (Westminster, Md.: The Newman Press, 1954, [1923]), p. 76.

124. Stokes, *Church and State*, I, 800, 801; Bodo, pp. 69–73; Billington, pp. 122–125.

125. *National Pastorals*, pp. 81, 82.

126. Ibid., pp. 90, 91.

127. A rather complete and comprehensive presentation of the case is given by Stokes, *Church and State*, I, 838–850. The quotation is from p. 847. Other writers have failed to recognize the importance of this case.

128. *National Pastorals*, pp. 26, 57, 58, 74, 115, 124.

129. "The Pastoral Letter of 1843," ibid., pp. 152, 153.

130. "The Pastoral Letter of 1852," ibid., p. 191. See also "The Pastoral Letter of 1866," ibid., pp. 215, 216. In 1866 the plenary council decreed: "Teachers belonging to religious congregations should be employed, as far as possible, in parochial schools, which should be erected in every parish. Catechism classes should be instituted in the churches for public school children."

   At the first plenary council of Baltimore "bishops were exhorted to have a [Roman] Catholic school in every parish with teachers paid from the parochial funds." Stokes, *Church and State*, I, 803.

131. Ibid., I, 832.

132. "The Pastoral Letter of 1866," *National Pastorals*, p. 205.

133. Ibid., p. 206.

134. R. Freeman Butts, *The American Tradition in Religion and Education* (Boston: The Beacon Press, 1950), pp. 110, 111.

135. Sweet, *The Congregationalists*, p. 95.

136. Various histories of education will reflect this interpretation. Richard J. Gabel, *Public Funds for Church and Private Schools* (Washington, D. C.: The Catholic University of America, 1937), has two long sections dealing with "The Colonial Period" and "Private and Church Schools in the Early National Period, 1775–1820," pp. 35–262.

137. Newton Edwards and Herman G. Richey, *The School in the American Social Order: The Dynamics of American Education* (Boston: Houghton Mifflin Co., 1947), pp. 237–240.

138. Ibid., pp. 244–250. See also Butts, pp. 119–130, for the attitudes of Jefferson and Madison on the separation of public education from religion.

"Education as recently as 1830 was not a major public function. . . . The public school system was regarded by many as merely a supplement to private education." Dawson Hales, *Federal Control of Public Education: A Critical Appraisal* (New York: Bureau of Publications, Teachers College, Columbia University, 1954), p. 21. The entire chapter, "Early-Nineteenth-Century America and the Principle of Local Control," pp. 12–23, is valuable.

139. Edwards and Richey, pp. 257–263. They said, p. 263: "The work of these societies in New York, Philadelphia, and other cities provided some schooling for a large number of children who otherwise would have been neglected. The societies did good work in a way that was acceptable to the socially and politically dominant group of the period. They no doubt stimulated interest in education but one might well argue the case that they had the immediate effect of delaying the development of public school systems."

140. Ibid., pp. 222–256.

141. Horace Mann, "From the Twelfth Annual Report for 1848," in *Cornerstones*, p. 167.

142. Ibid., pp. 180, 181, 200, 201.

143. Gabel, pp. 267–271, n. 4, takes great pains to establish this.

144. Ellwood P. Cubberley, *Readings in the History of Education* (Boston: Houghton Mifflin Co., 1948), p. 576.

145. Edwards and Richey, pp. 376–379.

146. Gabel, pp. 271–275.

147. Ibid., p. 271, n. 6, quoted this sentence from the report of a committee in New York in 1841.

148. Edwards and Richey, p. 380.

149. Gabel, pp. 348–351; Edwards and Richey, pp. 380, 381.

Source Book and Bibliographical Guide for American Church History, ed. Peter G. Mode (Menasha, Wis.: George Banta Publishing Co., 1921), pp. 460–466, has the petitions of the Roman Catholics and the remonstrance of the Methodists.

150. Gabel, pp. 322, 323, 493–495; Stokes, *Church and State*, II, 649–652.

151. Edwards and Richey, pp. 381, 382; Gabel, pp. 311–318.

Gabel, in his exhaustive study, lists public aid given to various schools in different states. See especially pp. 323–326, 331, 332, 335, 337, 363–367, 382, 383, 387, 388, 414, 415, 417, 418, 422, 444–446.

152. Ibid., pp. 326–330, 334–346, 367–370, 383–385, 390–392, 415, 416, 420–423, 443, 444. See also Edwards and Richey, p. 403.

153. Reinhold Neibuhr, *The Irony of American History* (New York: Charles Scribner's Sons, 1952), p. 69.

154. *The Pocket Book of Robert Frost's Poems*, ed. Louis Untermeyer (New York: Pocket Books, Inc., 1946), p. 94, and again p. 95. The quotation is from "Mending Wall."

155. Claude G. Bowers, *The Tragic Era: The Revolution After Lincoln* (New York: Blue Ribbon Books, 1929), p. 86.

Bishop Ames had served on a commission appointed by the War Department in 1862 to visit Union prisoners in Richmond. William Warren Sweet, *Methodism in American History*, rev. ed. (New York and Nashville: Abingdon Press, 1953), p. 294.

Robert D. Clark, *The Life of Matthew Simpson* (New York: The Macmillan Co., 1956), p. 249.

156. Ira V. Brown, *Lyman Abbott: Christian Evolutionist, A Study in Religious Liberalism* (Cambridge, Mass.: Harvard University Press, 1953), pp. 41, 42.

157. Ibid., p. 45; italics in the original. Quoted from the Oliver O. Howard Papers in the Bowdoin College Library.

158. R. D. Clark, pp. 260, 261; Bowers, p. 193; Sweet, *Methodism in American History*, pp. 315, 316.

"Chief Justice Chase, who was presiding over the trial, was indignant. 'Think of legislatures, political conventions, *even religious bodies*, undertaking to instruct Senators how to vote, guilty or not guilty.' " R. D. Clark, p. 261; italics added.

159. Stokes, *Church and State*, I, 575–593.

160. *Autobiography of Peter Cartwright*, p. 227.

161. Ibid., p. 228; Stokes, *Church and State*, II, 42–47; Thomas F. O'Dea, *The Mormons* (Chicago: University of Chicago Press, 1957), pp. 61 to 69.

162. Ibid., p. 100.

163. Ibid., pp. 101–104; Stokes, *Church and State*, II, 275.

164. On the entire question see ibid., II, 275–285; O'Dea, pp. 107–110. Everett Webber, *Escape to Utopia* (New York: Hastings House, 1959), pp. 244, 245, 265, tells about polygamy among the followers of Stang.

165. *American State Papers*, pp. 544–552, the decision in *Reynolds* v. *United States*, 98 U. S., 145–169. See also Stokes, *Church and State*, II, 276–278.

166. Ibid., II, 280, 282. See ibid., III, 526, for the *Articles of Faith*, which support the position of the government. *Source Book and Bibliographical Guide*, pp. 487–507; see especially p. 506 for the Woodruff Manifesto.

167. Oklahoma and other Western states follow this pattern. Stokes, *Church and State*, I, 619. Half of the states expressly refer to forms of conduct dangerous to recognized society. Ibid., I, 621; II, 409.

168. O'Dea, p. 165.

169. Ibid., p. 166.

170. Ibid., p. 169.

171. Ibid., p. 171; Stokes, *Church and State*, III, 524–529. See also F. E. Mayer, *The Religious Bodies of America*, 4th ed., rev. Arthur Carl Piepkorn (St. Louis: Concordia Publishing House, 1961), pp. 454 to 464.

172. Stokes, *Church and State*, III, 535.

173. Ibid., II, 322–326; III, 535–539; Mayer, pp. 532–544; Mode, pp. 653 to 655.

174. Stokes, *Church and State,* III, 523, 524, 539, 540, 220–230, 541–546. Mayer, pp. 399–422, 439–450, 464–476.

175. Elmer T. Clark, *The Small Sects in America,* rev. and enlarged ed. (Nashville, Tenn.: Abingdon-Cokesbury Press, 1949), p. 223.

176. Ibid., pp. 154–156; Mayer, p. 452.

177. Vernon Louis Parrington, *Main Currents in American Thought* (New York: Harcourt, Brace and Co., 1930), III, 402, 403: "The cure for the evils of democracy was held to be more democracy, and when industrialism had been brought under its sway — when America had become an economic democracy — a just and humane civilization would be on the threshold of possibility." On p. 412 he added: "Accepting the principle of economic determinism, liberalism still clung to its older democratic teleology, convinced that somehow economic determinism would turn out to be a fairy godmother to the proletariat and that from the imperious drift of industrial expansion must eventually issue social justice."

178. *Edward Bellamy: Selected Writings on Religion and Society,* ed. Joseph Schiefman, American Heritage Series, No. 11 (New York: Liberal Arts Press, 1955), p. 135: "It is a religion most emphatically, but it is not a new religion. It is the religion Christ taught. It is applied Christianity. It is Christ's doctrine of the duty of loving one's neighbor as one's self, applied to the reorganization of industry."

179. Parrington, III, 302–315.

180. Charles H. Hopkins, *The Rise of the Social Gospel in American Protestantism, 1865–1915* (New Haven: Yale University Press, 1940), pp. 14–23; Stokes, *Church and State,* II, 255–271.

181. Washington Gladden, *The Christian Pastor and the Working Church* (New York: Charles Scribner's Sons, 1906), pp. 461, 463, 464.

By way of contrast a statement by Peabody may be noted. "The relief of destitution by the provision of food and shelter still remains a duty of any well-ordered State. . . . It is simply a political and social necessity, insuring public peace and decency." Francis G. Peabody, *Jesus Christ and the Social Question: An Examination of the Teaching of Jesus in Its Relation to Some of the Problems of Modern Social Life* (New York: The Macmillan Co., 1915, c. 1900), pp. 260, 261.

182. Ibid., p. 473.

183. Henry Churchill King, *The Ethics of Jesus* (New York: The Macmillan Co., 1912), p. 62 n: "Even the future kingdom, however brought in, is in any case conceived by Jesus as finally ethical and spiritual, so that the eschatological cannot be the dominating conception." See pp. 62–64.

184. Ibid., p. 141.

See also, e. g., David J. Hill, *The Social Influence of Christianity with Special Reference to Contemporary Problems* (Boston: Silver Burdett & Co., 1888), pp. 207, 208: "While Christianity does not demand incorporation in the State as an established religion, and does not claim to dictate the specific laws that shall govern men, it does create the spirit out of which better laws proceed. . . . Our representative republic of self-governed persons is the wonder of the world and the paradox of prophecy. Its vital secret is the Christian conception of man that is assumed in its Constitution and legislation. If ever that should change and cease to be the controlling idea of our national life, we should realize what it is so easy even for statesmen to forget, that the power of our Constitution is a moral power. The chief source of that power is the religion of Jesus Christ, the ideals of which are creating a nation whose outer form shall be a republic of free men and whose inner life shall be the presence in the soul of God's coming kingdom."

185. Richard T. Ely, *Social Aspects of Christianity and Other Essays,* new and enlarged ed. (New York: Thomas Y. Crowell & Co., 1889), pp. 158, 159. In another essay he said, p. 80: "Our prayer-books tell us that those in authority are ministers of God, but to most of us this seems an idle phrase, and in our view of the State we have fallen below an old heathen philosopher like Socrates."

186. Charles S. Gardner, *The Ethics of Jesus and Social Progress* (New York: George H. Doran Co., 1914), pp. 333–356. The first quotation, p. 336; the second, p. 338; the third, p. 339.

187. Hopkins, pp. 113–117; Ira V. Brown, pp. 113–115.

188. Hopkins, pp. 183–204. Hopkins remarks, p. 189: ". . . Herron's 'system' was, in brief, a challenge to the church not to reform but to reconstruct society in accordance with the standards of Jesus. . . . The goal was outlined as a 'Christian state' to be based upon the principles of social sacrifice."

189. Ibid., pp. 194–198.

190. Washington Gladden, *Tools and the Man: Property and Industry Under the Christian Law* (Boston and New York: Houghton, Mifflin and Co., 1893), pp. 16, 17.

191. Walter Rauschenbusch, *Christianity and the Social Crisis* (New York: The Macmillan Co., 1912), p. 380.

192. *A Rauschenbusch Reader: The Kingdom of God and the Social Gospel,* ed. Benson Y. Landis (New York: Harper & Bros., 1957), p. 144.

193. *Cornerstones,* pp. 205, 206.

194. Ibid., pp. 213–216.

195. *A Compilation of the Messages and Papers of the Presidents, 1789 to 1902,* ed. James D. Richardson (Bureau of National Literature and Art), VII, 334, 335.

196. Ibid., VII, 356. See also Stokes, *Church and State,* II, 722–728.

197. Theodore Roemer, *The Catholic Church in the United States* (Saint Louis: B. Herder Book Co., 1950), p. 286.

198. *American State Papers,* pp. 237, 255.

199. Butts, pp. 142, 143; the quotation, p. 143.
The Democrats affirmed their belief in "the total separation of church and state, for the sake alike of civil and religious freedom." *American State Papers,* p. 255.

200. Ibid.: "The [Roman] Catholic Church opposed federal aid to the states if it were to be confined to public schools, but on occasion favored federal aid if it were to be divided 'fairly' among public and parochial schools."
Readings in American Educational History, eds. Edgard W. Knight and Clifton L. Hall (New York: Appleton-Century-Crofts, Inc., 1951),

in a footnote, p. 728, lists among the reasons for the rejection of the Hoar Bill the argument that it "would tend to break down the principle of the separation of church and state."

201. Butts, pp. 144, 145. *American State Papers*, p. 265 (S. Res. 86; S. Res. 17).

202. Butts, p. 145.

203. Albert Bushnell Hart, *National Ideals Historically Traced, 1607—1907*, Vol. 26 of *The American Nation: A History* (New York and London: Harper & Bros., 1907), p. 215.

204. *American State Papers*, pp. 264, 265. The acts here given are all in the period after 1914, many of them, however, modifications of previous laws or restatements of those laws. See also Stokes, *Church and State*, III, 153—179.

205. *American State Papers*, p. 475.

206. Ibid., p. 669; cf. pp. 665—669 for the decision 20 Missouri, 216—220, *The State, Respondent*, v. *Ambs, Appellant*.

207. Ibid., p. 564; cf. pp. 552—565 for 143 U. S., 457—472, *The Church of the Holy Trinity* v. *The United States*.

208. Sweet, *The Story of Religion in America*, pp. 410—413. The literature on the prohibition movement is voluminous; Stokes, *Church and State*, II, 328—344.

209. Guilday, *National Pastorals*, pp. 246, 247.

210. Gabel, p. 493; Roemer, p. 291; Edwin H. Rian, *Christianity and American Education* (San Antonio, Texas: The Naylor Co., 1949), p. 136. Rian and Roemer gave translations of the decree.

211. Hales, pp. 45—47.

212. John Tracy Ellis, *American Catholicism* (Chicago: University of Chicago Press, 1956), p. 108: "It was — and it remains — a fundamental axiom of Catholic teaching that the child should be instructed in religion from his earliest years. It was true, as the Church's enemies declared, that [Roman] Catholics felt entitled to financial aid from the state for their schools since they looked upon the double taxation for their own and the public schools as unjust."

Roemer, p. 292: "Some of them could not understand why the state should not help defray the expenses of parochial schools, since [Roman] Catholics were paying school taxes like the other citizens and were at the same time saving the state much additional expense through their own schools."

213. Ibid., pp. 292, 293; Ellis, pp. 108, 109; Thomas T. McAvoy, *The Great Crisis in American Catholic History* (Chicago: Henry Regnery Co., 1957), pp. 71, 72. The "nominal rental" amounted to $1.00 per year. Stokes, *Church and State*, II, 361, 649—654.

214. Ellis, p. 109.

215. McAvoy, p. 72; see also Roemer, pp. 293—295.

216. McAvoy, pp. 89, 90.

217. Roemer, p. 295; see also McAvoy, p. 111.

218. Roemer, p. 294.

219. McAvoy, p. 110; Stokes, *Church and State*, II, 652, 653.

220. McAvoy, pp. 275—280, for a summary of the pope's letter; see pp. 379

to 391 for the entire letter. Roemer, p. 310, also quoted this same excerpt; Stokes, *Church and State,* II, 360, also has part of this quotation.

221. *National Pastorals,* p. 308; italics added.

222. Isaac J. Lansing, *National Danger in Romanism or Religion and the Nation* (Boston: Arnold Publishing Association, n. d.), p. 276.

223. Leo Joseph McCormick, *Church-State Relationships in Education in Maryland* (Washington, D. C.: The Catholic University of America Press, 1942), pp. 236, 237.

224. Gabel, p. 548.

225. McCormick, p. 246.

226. Luther L. Gobbel, *Church-State Relationships in Education in North Carolina Since 1776* (Durham, N. C.: Duke University Press, 1938), p. 197; cf. pp. 197–200 for the opposition of the Baptists.

227. Gabel, pp. 570–587, 601.

228. Ibid., p. 614; cf. pp. 614–659, 660–702.

229. Rian, pp. 52–56.

230. *Board of Education* v. *Minor et al,* Supreme Court of Ohio, 1872, 23 Oh. St. 211, in *Cases on Church and State in the United States,* ed. Mark De Wolfe Howe (Cambridge, Mass.: Harvard University Press, 1952), p. 329.

231. Francis X. Curran, *The Churches and the Schools: American Protestantism and Popular Elementary Education* (Jesuit Studies; Chicago: Loyola University Press, 1954), pp. 124–130.

232. See ibid.; Clark Spurlock, *Education and the Supreme Court* (Urbana, Ill.: University of Illinois Press, 1955), passim. James O'Neill, *The Catholic in Secular Education* (New York, London, Toronto: Longmans, Green and Co., 1956), discussed some of these problems; see especially ch. 6 on "Released Time in Public Schools," pp. 107–138. For the Presbyterian Church in the United States see Henry H. Sweets, *The Church and Education* (Richmond, Va.: Presbyterian Committee of Publication, 1939), passim. The literature here is voluminous, and only an indication is given by the citation of the above titles. Stokes remains the most valuable summarizer.

233. Henry Steele Commager, *The American Mind: An Interpretation of American Thought and Character Since the 1880's* (New Haven: Yale University Press, 1950), pp. 164, 167.

234. Merle Curti, *The Growth of American Thought,* 2nd ed. (New York: Harper & Bros., 1951), pp. 408–410. See also pp. 423, 492, 493.

235. Ralph Henry Gabriel, *The Course of American Democratic Thought: An Intellectual History Since 1815* (New York: The Ronald Press Co., 1940), p. 173; cf. pp. 173–216.

236. Sherwood Eddy, *The Kingdom of God and the American Dream: The Religious and Secular Ideals of American History* (New York and London: Harper & Bros., 1941).

237. Merrimon Cuninggim, *Freedom's Holy Light* (New York: Harper & Bros., 1955), p. 163.

238. Gerald Kennedy, *The Christian and His America* (New York: Harper & Bros., 1956), p. ix.

239. Hudson, p. 245.

240. Stokes, *Church and State*, III, 694.

241. Jacques Maritain, *Man and the State*, 4th impression, Phoenix Books (Chicago: University of Chicago Press, 1956), p. 177.

242. Stokes, *Church and State*, III, 92.

243. Pius XII, "The Church and History," in *Pope Pius XII and Catholic Education*, ed. Vincent A. Yzermans (St. Meinrad, Ind.: Grail Publications, 1957), p. 149.

244. Ibid., p. 151.

245. Pius XI, "On the Christian Education of Youth," in *The Church and the Reconstruction of the Modern World: The Social Encyclicals of Pope Pius XI*, ed. Terence P. McLaughlin, Image Books D54 (Garden City, N. Y.: Doubleday and Co., Inc., 1957), p. 89.

See William Gorman, "A Case of Distributive Justice," in *Religion and the Schools* (New York: The Fund for the Republic, 1959), pp. 34–63.

246. The documentation for this statement can be extremely lengthy. A convenient summary can be found in Stokes, *Church and State*, II, 716–721.

247. Ibid., II, 662–670.

248. *Pierce* v. *Society of Sisters*, Supreme Court of the United States, 1925, 268 U. S. 510, in *Cases on Church and State in the United States*, ed. Mark De Wolfe Howe (Cambridge, Mass.: Harvard University Press, 1952), p. 340.

249. *Ramon* v. *Ramon*, Domestic Relations Court of New York City, 1942, 34 N. Y. Supp. 2nd 100, *Cases on Church and State*, p. 235.

250. Paul Blanshard, *American Freedom and Catholic Power*, 2nd ed. (Boston: Beacon Press, 1958), p. 200.

251. *Nicholls, Jr.* v. *Mayor and School Committee of Lynn*, Supreme Judicial Court of Massachusetts, 1937, 297 Mass. 65, *Cases on Church and State*, pp. 342–346.

Minersville School District v. *Gobitis*, Supreme Court of the United States, 1940, 310 U. S. 586, *Cases on Church and State*, pp. 346–354.

Board of Education v. *Barnette*, Supreme Court of the United States, 1943, 319 U. S. 624, *Cases on Church and State*, pp. 354–360.

Alvin W. Johnson and Frank H. Yost, *Separation of Church and State in the United States* (Minneapolis: University of Minnesota Press, 1948), pp. 175–186.

252. *Everson* v. *Board of Education*, Supreme Court of the United States, 1947, 330 U. S. 1, *Cases on Church and State*, pp. 360–364. Johnson and Yost, pp. 146–164.

253. *McCollum* v. *Board of Education*, Supreme Court of the United States, 1948, 333 U. S. 203, *Cases on Church and State*, pp. 364–375. Johnson and Yost, pp. 125–131.

254. Blanshard, *American Freedom and Catholic Power* (Boston: The Beacon Press, 1949), p. 95.

255. *Zorach et al.* v. *Clauson et al.*, Court of Appeals of New York, 1951, 100 N. E. 2d 463, *Cases on Church and State*, pp. 375–393. Note p. 379: "It is thus clear beyond cavil that the Constitution does not demand that every friendly gesture between church and State shall

be discountenanced. The so-called 'wall of separation' may be built so high and so broad as to impair both State and church, as we have come to know them."

256. Johnson and Yost, pp. 74—99.

257. See my article, "Religion in the Public Schools," *Concordia Theological Monthly*, XXVIII (Feb. 1957), 81—109.

258. Quoted ibid., p. 83.

259. Quoted ibid., p. 85.

260. Quoted ibid., p. 93.

261. Quoted ibid., pp. 93, 94.

262. Wilbur G. Katz, "The Case for Religious Liberty," in *Religion in America: Original Essays on Religion in a Free Society,* ed. John Cogley (New York: Meridian Books, Inc., 1958), pp. 100, 115. See also the summary in M. Searle Bates, *Religious Liberty: An Inquiry* (New York: Harper & Bros., 1945), pp. 538, 539.

263. Quoted ibid., p. 201. See Tim J. Campbell, *Central Themes of American Life* (Grand Rapids, Mich.: Wm. B. Eerdmans Publishing Co., 1959), pp. 125—134.

264. *Cantwell* v. *Connecticut,* Supreme Court of the United States, 1940, 310 U. S. 296, *Cases on Church and State,* pp. 267—273.
   Murdock v. *Pennsylvania,* Supreme Court of the United States, 1943, 319 U. S. 105, *Cases on Church and State,* pp. 273—283.
   Martin v. *Struthers,* Supreme Court of the United States, 1943, 319 U. S. 141, *Cases on Church and State,* pp. 283—287.
   Douglas v. *Jeannette,* Supreme Court of the United States, 1943, 319 U. S. 157, *Cases on Church and State,* pp. 287—299.
   Stokes, *Church and State,* III, 220—230.

265. Ibid., III, 243.

266. Quoted ibid., III, 245.

267. Blanshard, *American Freedom and Catholic Power* (1958), pp. 232, 233; see the entire chapter on "Censorship and Boycott," pp. 212—243, especially pp. 231—238 on motion pictures. Stokes, *Church and State,* III, 230—239.

268. *Church and State,* XIII (Jan. 1960), 2.

269. *The Pope Speaks,* ed. Michael Chinigo (New York: Pantheon Books, Inc., 1957), p. 119.

270. Blanshard, *American Freedom and Catholic Power,* pp. 134, 135. See the entire chapter, "Sex, Birth Control and Eugenics," in the 1949 ed., pp. 132—155, and in the 1958 edition, pp. 160—184.

271. As quoted by Stokes, *Church and State,* III, 50.

272. *The Pope Speaks,* pp. 152, 153.

273. Stokes, *Church and State,* III, 42—67; Blanshard, *American Freedom and Catholic Power,* pp. 156—179.

274. "The State in Welfare Work" (editorial), in *Christianity Today,* IV (18 Jan. 1960), 23; see pp. 20—23 for the entire editorial.

275. See my article "Friction Points in Church-State Relations," *Concordia Theological Monthly,* XXVIII (July 1957), 499; pp. 481—503 for the entire article.

276. Stokes, *Church and State,* III, 102—109.

277. Ibid., III, 109.
278. Ibid., III, 126–129; see also pp. 307–335.
279. Ibid., III, 293–307.
280. Ibid., III, 642–644.
281. Martin E. Marty, *The New Shape of American Religion* (New York: Harper & Bros., 1959), p. 87: "Thus an intuitive quasi-religious American way of life with a sort of state Shinto has developed."
282. Stanley J. Rowland, Jr., *Land in Search of God* (New York: Random House, 1958), p. 71.
283. Ibid., p. 6; italics added.
284. Joseph M. Dawson, *America's Way in Church, State, and Society* (New York: The Macmillan Co., 1953), pp. 157–170.
285. Leo Pfeffer, *Creeds in Competition: A Creative Force in American Culture* (New York: Harper & Bros., 1958), p. 56.
286. A. Mervyn Davies, *Foundations of American Freedom* (New York and Nashville: Abingdon Press, 1955), p. 236.
287. See the multi-authored *Religion and the Free Society*, published by the Fund for the Republic in 1958.

NOTES TO CHAPTER 6

1. *Cline* v. *State* (Okla.), 130 Pac. 510, at p. 512 (1913).
2. *The Complete Jefferson*, ed. Saul K. Padover (New York: Duell, Sloan & Pearce, Inc., 1943), p. 958.
3. ". . . but no religious Test shall ever be required as a Qualification to any Office or public Trust under the United States."
4. "Congress shall make no law respecting an establishment of religion, or prohibiting the free exercise thereof, or abridging the freedom of speech, or of the press; or of the right of the people peaceably to assemble, and to petition the Government for a redress of grievances."
5. "Section 1. All persons born or naturalized in the United States, and subject to the jurisdiction thereof, are citizens of the United States and of the States wherein they reside. No State shall make or enforce any law which shall abridge the privileges or immunities of citizens of the United States; nor shall any State deprive any person of life, liberty, or property without due process of law; nor deny to any person within its jurisdiction the equal protection of the law."
6. *The Records of the Federal Convention of 1787*, ed. Max Farrand, II (New Haven: Yale University Press, 1911), 342.
7. Jonathan Elliot, *The Debates in the Several State Conventions on the Adoption of the Federal Constitution* . . . 2nd ed. (Philadelphia: J. B. Lippincott Co., 1941), I, 277.
8. Joseph Story, *Commentaries on the Constitution of the United States*, 5th ed. (Boston: Little, Brown, and Company, 1891), II, Sec. 1879. See also *Torcasco* v. *Watkins*, 367 U. S. 488 (1961).
9. *The Complete Jefferson*, p. 120.
10. *Reynolds* v. *United States*, 98 U. S. 145, at p. 164 (1878).
11. Elliot, III, 659.
12. Elliot, I, 328.

13. Elliot, I, 326.
14. Elliot, III, 357.
15. *The Writings of James Madison,* ed. Gaillard Hunt (New York: G. P. Putnam's Sons, 1900–1910), V, 271.
16. *Annals of Congress,* ed. Joseph Gales (Washington, D. C., 1834), I, 434.
17. *Annals,* I, 450.
18. *Annals,* I, 664, 665.
19. *Annals,* I, 729.
20. *Annals,* I, 729.
21. *Annals,* I, 766.
22. *Journal of the First Session of the Senate,* ed. Joseph Gales (Washington, D. C., 1820), p. 70.
23. *Journal,* p. 84.
24. *Journal,* pp. 87, 88.
25. *Everson* v. *Board of Education,* 330 U. S. 1, at p. 8 (1947).
26. *McCollum* v. *Board of Education,* 333 U. S. 203, at p. 212 (1947).
27. *Zorach* v. *Clauson,* 343 U. S. 306, at p. 319 (1952), dissenting opinion of Justice Black.
28. *Barron* v. *City of Baltimore,* 32 U. S. 243, at p. 249 (1833).
29. 44 U. S. 589 (1843).
30. 44 U. S., at p. 609.
31. *Twitchell* v. *Pennsylvania,* 74 U. S. 321, at p. 325 (1868).
32. "Section 1. . . . Neither slavery nor involuntary servitude, except as a punishment for a crime whereof the party shall have been duly convicted, shall exist within the United States or any place subject to their jurisdiction."
33. 14 *Statutes at Large,* 173 (1866).
34. 14 *Statutes at Large,* 37 (1866).
35. *Dred Scott* v. *Sandford,* 60 U. S. 393 (1857).
36. *Arver* v. *United States,* 245 U. S. 366 (1918).
37. *The Slaughterhouse Cases,* 83 U. S. 36 (1873).
38. 83 U. S. 36.
39. 310 U. S. 296.
40. Henry Sandwith Drinker, *Some Observations on the Four Freedoms of the First Amendment* . . . (Boston: Boston University Press, 1957), pp. 19–26. This work has been the source of much of the material in this chapter tracing the evolution of the word *liberty.*
41. *Hebert* v. *Louisiana,* 372 U. S. 312, at p. 316 (1926).
42. *Palko* v. *Connecticut,* 302 U. S. 319, at p. 325 (1937).
43. *Adamson* v. *California,* 332 U. S. 46, at p. 52 (1947).
44. *Adamson* v. *California,* at p. 53.
45. 88 U. S. 532.
46. *Palko* v. *Connecticut,* supra, at p. 323.
47. *Wolf* v. *Colorado,* 338 U. S. 25 (1949).

48. 83 U. S., at p. 102.
49. *Butchers' Union Co.* v. *Crescent City Co.,* 111 U. S. 746 (1884).
50. 127 U. S. 678 (1888).
51. 12 *Federal Cases* No. 6,546, 252, at p. 256 (1891).
52. *Meyer* v. *Nebraska,* 262 U. S. 390, at p. 399 (1923).
53. 262 U. S. 390.
54. *Meyer* v. *Nebraska,* supra, at p. 399.
55. *Pierce* v. *Society of Sisters,* 268 U. S. 510, at pp. 534, 535 (1925).
56. *Prudential Insurance Co.* v. *Cheek,* 259 U. S. 530 (1922).
57. 205 U. S. 454.
58. *Gitlow* v. *New York,* 268 U. S. 652, at p. 666 (1925).
59. *Fiske* v. *Kansas,* 274 U. S. 380 (1927).
60. *Near* v. *Minnesota,* 283 U. S. 697 (1931).
61. 293 U. S. 245 (1934).
62. 293 U. S., at p. 262.
63. 293 U. S., at p. 265.
64. *Everson* v. *Board of Education,* supra; *McCollum* v. *Board of Education,* supra.
65. Thomas Cooley, *Principles of Constitutional Law,* 3rd ed. (Boston, 1898), pp. 224, 225.
66. *Commentaries,* II, Sec. 1877.
67. McCormick Professor of Jurisprudence (emeritus), Princeton University.
68. Edward S. Corwin, "The Supreme Court as National School Board," in *Religion and the State,* Vol. XIV, No. 1, of *Law and Contempory Problems,* ed. Robert Kramer (Durham, N. C.: Duke University School of Law, 1949), p. 10.
69. *The Writings of James Madison,* II, 183–191.
70. *Statutes at Large of Virginia, 1619–1792,* ed. William W. Hening, XII (Richmond, 1823), 84.
71. *The Complete Jefferson,* pp. 518, 519.
72. *Everson* v. *Board of Education,* supra, at p. 15.
73. *Zorach* v. *Clauson,* supra.
74. *Reynolds* v. *United States,* supra.
75. 133 U. S. 333.
76. 133 U. S., at p. 342.
77. 175 U. S. 291 (1899).
78. 245 U. S., at p. 390.
79. 281 U. S. 370 (1930).
80. 330 U. S. 1.
81. See concurring opinion of Justice Douglas in *Engel* v. *Vitale,* 370 U. S. 421, at p. 437 et seq. (1962).
82. 330 U. S., at p. 13.
83. 330 U. S., at p. 18.
84. 330 U. S., at p. 20, dissenting opinion of Justice Jackson.

85. 365 U. S. 299.
86. 365 U. S. 299.
87. 333 U. S. 203.
88. 333 U. S., at p. 209.
89. 333 U. S., at pp. 209, 210.
90. 333 U. S., at pp. 235, 236.
91. *The Writings of Thomas Jefferson,* memorial ed., XIX (Washington, D. C., 1904), 414.
92. 343 U. S. 306.
93. 343 U. S., at p. 312.
94. 343 U. S., at p. 312.
95. 343 U. S., at pp. 313, 314.
96. 343 U. S., at p. 325.
97. 345 U. S. 395 (1953); see also *Fowler* v. *Rhode Island,* 345 U. S. 67 (1953), and *Niemotke* v. *Maryland,* 340 U. S. 268 (1950).
98. 330 U. S., at pp. 39, 40.
99. *The Writings of James Madison,* II, 186.
100. Elliot, III, 659.
101. *Annals,* I, 729, 730.
102. *Annals,* I, 730, 731.
103. *Annals,* I, 731.
104. *Everson* v. *Board of Education,* supra, at p. 39.
105. Elizabeth Fleet, "Madison's 'Detached Memoranda,'" in *William and Mary Quarterly,* 3rd series, III (Oct. 1946), 534–568.
106. Ibid., pp. 551–562.
107. Elliot, III, 93.
108. Hening, XII, 84.
109. 330 U. S., at p. 13.
110. *Annals* (1849), III, 30.
111. *Journal of the Virginia Senate,* 1789 (Richmond, 1928), pp. 61–64.
112. *The Complete Jefferson,* p. 518.
113. Ibid., p. 519.
114. Ibid., p. 412.
115. *The Writings of Thomas Jefferson,* XIX, 414–416.
116. Ibid., XIX, 410.
117. *Annals,* I, 932.
118. 1 *Statutes at Large,* 223 (1791).
119. See "The State and Sectarian Education," *N. E. A. Research Bulletin* XXIV, 1 (Feb. 1946), 4; and Table I, p. 36.
120. *United States Naval Academy Regulations,* Reg. C. 9, Sec. 0901, (1) (a); *Regulations of the United States Corps of Cadets,* Reg. C. 21, Sec. 2101; *Regulations of the United States Air Force Academy,* Catalogue, 1962–1963, p. 110.
121. *The National School Lunch Act,* 60 *Statutes at Large,* 42 U. S. C. A., Sec. 1751, et seq.

122. *The Servicemen's Readjustment Act,* 58 *Statutes at Large,* 38 U. S. C. A., Sec. 693, et seq.

123. *The Hospital Survey and Construction Act of 1946,* 60 *Statutes at Large,* 42 *U. S. C. A.,* Sec. 291, et seq.

124. *Engel* v. *Vitale,* supra, at p. 437, fn. 1.

125. 366 U. S. 420 (1961).

126. 366 U. S., at pp. 444, 445.

127. 370 U. S., at p. 422.

128. 370 U. S., at p. 425.

129. 370 U. S., at p. 437.

130. See Gerald Kirven, "Freedom of Religion or Freedom from Religion?" in *American Bar Association Journal,* XLVIII (Sept. 1962), 816, for a discussion of this thesis.

131. 83 S. Ct. 1560 (1963).

132. 83 S. Ct., at p. 1574.

133. 83 S. Ct., at p. 1571.

134. 83 S. Ct., at p. 1610.

135. 83 S. Ct., at p. 1615.

136. 83 S. Ct., at p. 1611.

137. 83 S. Ct., at p. 1612.

138. 83 S. Ct., at p. 1613.

139. 83 S. Ct., at p. 1575.

140. 83 S. Ct., at p. 1572.

141. 322 U. S. 78 (1944).

142. 322 U. S., at p. 86.

143. 319 U. S. 624, at p. 642 (1943).

144. *Minersville School District* v. *Gobitis,* 310 U. S. 586 (1940).

145. *Cantwell* v. *Connecticut,* supra, at p. 304.

146. 319 U. S., at pp. 644, 645.

147. 319 U. S. 583, at p. 589 (1943).

148. 293 U. S. 245.

149. 321 U. S. 158 (1944).

150. 321 U. S., at pp. 165, 168, 169.

151. *Reynolds* v. *United States,* supra.

152. *Davis* v. *Beason,* supra.

153. *Chaplinsky* v. *New Hampshire,* 315 U. S. 368 (1942).

154. 18 *U. S. C. A.,* Sec. 398.

155. *Cleveland* v. *United States,* 329 U. S. 14 (1946).

156. 310 U. S., at p. 307.

157. 318 U. S. 418 (1943).

158. 318 U. S., at p. 422.

159. 312 U. S. 569 (1941).

160. 312 U. S., at p. 574.

161. 318 U. S. 413 (1943).

162. 319 U. S. 105 (1943).

163. 319 U. S., at p. 108.
164. 319 U. S., at p. 111.
165. 319 U. S., at p. 112.
166. 321 U. S. 573 (1944).
167. 319 U. S. 141 (1943).
168. 319 U. S., at pp. 150, 151.
169. 326 U. S. 501 (1946).
170. 326 U. S., at p. 509.
171. *Martin* v. *Struthers,* supra, at p. 152.

NOTES TO CHAPTER 7

1. Samuel Tenenbaum, *William Heard Kilpatrick: Trail Blazer in Education* (New York: Harper & Brothers, 1951), pp. 169, 170.
2. *The Cresset,* XXIV (May 1961), 3.
3. For a survey of practices see Richard B. Dierenfield, *Religion in American Public Schools* (Washington, D. C.: Public Affairs Press, 1962).
4. *School District of Abington Township, Pennsylvania, et al., Appellants* v. *Edward Lewis Schempp et al. and William J. Murray III, etc., et al., Petitioners* v. *John N. Curlett, President, et al., Individually, and Constituting the Board of School Commissioners of Baltimore City,* June 17, 1963.
5. Walter Lippmann, "Sees Growing Disenchantment with Secularized Education," in South Bend *Tribune,* June 19, 1963.
6. *The Regents' Recommendations for School Programs on America's Moral and Spiritual Heritage,* University of the State of New York (Albany: The State Education Department, 1955).
7. Ibid., p. 13.
8. *Relation of Religion to Public Education: A Study Document* (New York: Office of Publication and Distribution, N. C. C. C. U. S. A., 1959).
9. Ibid., I, 7, a, b.
10. Ibid., II, 3, d.
11. *The Study of Religion in the Public Schools,* American Council on Education, 1948 report, p. 6.
12. *Moral and Spiritual Values in the Public Schools* (Washington: Educational Policies Commission, National Education Association, 1951), pp. 78, 79.
13. *Relation of Religion to Public Education: A Study Document,* Part II, 3e, (2).
14. *Illinois ex rel. McCollum* v. *Board of Education,* 333 U. S. 203 (1948).
15. *Zorach* v. *Clauson et al.,* 343 U. S. 306 (April 28, 1952).
16. Edwin Shaver, "How Fares the Weekday Program," in *Bethany Guide,* XXXII (Nov. 1957), 6, 7. For an extensive report see his "A Look at Weekday Church Schools," in *Religious Education,* LI (Jan.–Feb. 1956), 18–39; also *The Weekday Church School . . .* (Boston: The Pilgrim Press, 1956).

17. *Reports and Memorials* (1947), The Lutheran Church — Missouri Synod, p. 218; *Proceedings,* 1947, 1950, 1953, 1956, 1959.

18. *Pierce* v. *Society of Sisters,* 268 U. S. 532.

19. *People* v. *American Socialist Society,* 195 NYS 801, 202 App. Div. 640.

20. *People ex rel. Everson* v. *Board of Education,* 330 U. S. 1.

21. 29 A. L. R. 1448; Nebraka Ls. 1919, Chap. 249.

22. 262 U. S. 390, 43 S. Ct. 625, 29 A. D. R. 1446.

23. Fred F. Beach and Robert F. Will, *The State and Nonpublic Schools* (Washington: U. S. Department of Health, Education, and Welfare, 1958), p. 129.

24. Ibid., p. 79.

25. Ibid., p. 90.

26. Elizabeth Fleet, "Madison's 'Detached Memoranda,' " in *William and Mary Quarterly,* 3rd series, III (Oct. 1946), 555.

27. *Congressional Record,* IV (1875), 175.

28. Unpublished data collected by the U. S. Office of Education, cited in Shirley Cooper and Charles O. Fitzwater, *County School Administration* (New York: Harper & Brothers, 1954), p. 503.

29. Beach and Will, p. 54.

30. *School Bus Transportation Laws in the United States* (Washington: Legal Department, National Catholic Welfare Conference, 1946), pp. 164, 165.

31. *The Supreme Court on Church and State,* ed. Joseph Tussman (New York: Oxford University Press, 1962), pp. 210, 211.

32. Ibid., p. 211.

33. Beach and Will, p. 27.

34. Ibid., p. 68.

35. "The State and Sectarian Education," National Education Association Research Bulletin, XXXIV (Dec. 1956), 187.

36. Ibid., p. 187.

37. Ibid., p. 187.

38. Ibid., p. 186.

39. *The State and Nonpublic Schools,* pp. 27, 28.

40. *Summaries of Rulings of State Attorneys General with Respect to Church-State Questions as They Affect Public and Parochial Schools,* compiled by the American Jewish Committee and the Anti-Defamation League of B'nai B'rith (Feb. 1958), p. 13.

41. Ibid., p. 13.

42. *Packer Collegiate Institute* v. *University of State of New York.* 91 N. E. 2d 80, 298 N. W. 184.

43. *West* v. *Lee,* 29 S. E. 2d 31, 244 N. C. 79.

44. Sister Raymond McLaughlin, *A History of State Legislation Affecting Private Elementary and Secondary Schools in the United States, 1870–1945* (Washington: Catholic University of America Press, 1946), pp. 188–190.

45. *Education Digest,* XXII (Sept. 1956), 3.

46. *Public Education and the Future of America* (Washington: Educa-

tional Policies Commission, National Education Association, 1955), p. 98.

47. *Proceedings of the Forty-fourth Regular Convention of The Lutheran Church – Missouri Synod,* June 17–26, 1959, p. 328.

48. *Time,* LXXX (Feb. 26, 1962), 46; (March 2, 1962), 58 fn.

49. "Federal Aid: Second Round" (editorial), in *Commonweal,* LXXV (Feb. 23, 1962), 554.

50. *The Christian Century,* LXXVIII (March 8, 1961), 292.

51. Reprinted in *Reports and Memorials, Forty-fifth Regular Convention, The Lutheran Church – Missouri Synod,* 1962, p. 202.

52. Marion Snapper, "The State and the Christian Schools," in *The Reformed Journal,* XI (April 1961), 5–8.

53. *The Cresset,* XXIV (May 1961), 3, 4.

54. John D. Eusden, "Public Aid to What Schools?" in *The Christian Century,* LXXVIII (July 19, 1961), 872, 873, passim.

NOTES TO CHAPTER 8

1. For a detailed description of the military chaplain's duties and office see: Department of the Army, *The Chaplain,* Field Manual 16-5 (Washington: U. S. Government Printing Office, April 1952), chap. 1, pp. 3–5; Bureau of Naval Personnel, *Chaplains' Manual,* Manual 15664-B (Washington: U. S. Government Printing Office, 1952), chap. 2, sec. 2100, 2220, pp. 7, 8; Department of the Air Force, *The Air Force Chaplain,* AFM 165-3 (Washington: U. S. Government Printing Office, 1956), chaps. 3 and 4.

2. Department of the Army, *Army Regulations,* AR 165-5 (Religious Activities), (Washington: U. S. Government Printing Office, 7 Nov. 1960), sec. III, 13, speaks to this point: "Commanders will not detail or assign chaplains to duties unrelated to their profession as clergymen except on a temporary basis in cases of military emergency."

3. *The Writings of George Washington,* ed. Jared Sparks (Boston, 1834 to 1837), II, 188.

4. Ibid., II, 278.

5. Anson P. Stokes, *Church and State in the United States: Historical Development and Contemporary Problems of Religious Freedom Under the Constitution* (New York: Harper & Brothers, 1950), I, 268.

6. *The Literary Diary of Ezra Stiles,* ed. Franklin B. Dexter (New York: Charles Scribner's Sons, 1901), I, 484 (ed. under authority of Corporation of Yale University).

7. Roy J. Honeywell, *Chaplains of the United States Army* (Washington: U. S. Government Printing Office, 1958), p. 37.

8. Honeywell, p. 43.

9. *The Writings of George Washington,* III, 220.

10. Ibid., III, 456 fn.

11. Ibid., IV, 28 fn.

12. Clifford M. Drury, *The History of the Chaplain Corps, United States Navy,* I, Navpers 15807 (Washington: U. S. Government Printing Office, 1949), p. 3.

13. Department of the Army, *American Army Chaplaincy — A Brief History,* PAM 165-1 (Washington: U. S. Government Printing Office, Oct. 1955), p. 2.

14. A Catholic chaplain, Father Lotbiniere, was appointed chaplain of a Canadian regiment in the U. S. Army, Jan. 26, 1776; cf. Honeywell, p. 45.

15. Drury, I, 43.

16. *The Military Laws of the United States,* 4th ed. (Washington: U. S. War Dept.), p. 477, quoted in Honeywell, p. 105.

17. An arrangement still in force at the Academy, much to the displeasure of some Army chaplains, who feel that it reflects adversely on their corps. Cf. *The Military Chaplaincy: A Report to the President by the President's Committee on Religion and Welfare in the Armed Forces* (Washington: U. S. Government Printing Office, Oct. 1, 1950), p. 35.

18. *The Air Force Chaplain,* p. 2.

19. *The Military Chaplaincy: A Report . . . ,* p. 6.

20. Madison proved a poor prophet. Rev. Chas. C. Pise, a Roman Catholic, was appointed chaplain to Congress in 1833; cf. Stokes, III, 130.

21. Elizabeth Fleet, "Madison's 'Detached Memoranda,'" in *William and Mary Quarterly,* 3rd series, III (Oct. 1946), 558.

22. *Reports of Committees of the Senate,* 32nd Congress, 2nd session, No. 376, pp. 1, 2; cf. Stokes, III, 131, 132.

23. *Report No. 124,* House of Representatives, 33rd Congress, 1st session, March 27, 1854; cf. Stokes, III, 132.

24. Drury, I, 64, 65 (*Report No. 171,* House of Representatives, 31st Congress, 1st session, Vol. I, No. 583).

25. Drury, I, 65 (*Report No. 124,* House of Representatives, 32nd Congress, 1st session, Vol. II, No. 743).

26. Lorenzo Dow Johnson, *An Address to the Pastors and People of These United States on the Chaplaincy of the General Government* (Washington, D. C., 1857), p. 29; cf. by the same author *Chaplains of the General Government with Objections to Their Employment Considered* (New York: Sheldon, Blakeman and Co., 1856).

27. About 2,300 in Union forces; cf. *American Army Chaplaincy,* p. 8.

28. *The Military Chaplaincy: A Report . . . ,* p. 6.

29. Ibid., p. 6.

30. It was a term of wide latitude. Some Civil War chaplains held appointments from the governors of their respective states and accompanied the volunteer regiments. Others were designated by their denominations to hold camp services. Still others were self-appointed, itinerant camp followers. *American Army Chaplaincy,* p. 9.

31. Honeywell, p. 112; also *American Army Chaplaincy,* p. 9.

32. *American Army Chaplaincy,* p. 34.

33. Drury, I, 144.

34. *The Military Chaplaincy: A Report . . . ,* p. 7.

35. Drury, I, 166.

36. *The Military Chaplaincy: A Report . . . ,* p. 7. A few Jewish chaplains had been appointed during the Civil War (cf. Stokes, III, 13).

37. *The Military Chaplaincy: A Report* . . . , p. 7.
38. Drury, I, 172.
39. *American Army Chaplaincy*, p. 12.
40. Catholics, Episcopalians, and Lutherans were largely free of pacifist concern.
41. Dr. Samuel McCrea Cavert, in an address before the annual meeting of the General Commission on Chaplains in 1957, as quoted in Marion J. Creeger, *The Military Chaplaincy* (Washington: National Council of the Churches of Christ in the U. S. A., 1959), p. 6.
42. Between 1913 and 1917 the Navy experimented unsuccessfully with such an arrangement. Cf. Drury, I, 218.
43. "The Chaplaincy Question" (editorial), in *The Christian Century*, LII (Chicago: Christian Century Foundation, Jan. 16, 1935), 70–72.
44. Dr. Cavert's address (see note 41 above), in Creeger, p. 7; cf. also Drury, I, 221.
45. *The Military Chaplaincy: A Report* . . . , p. 9.
46. See note 17 above.
47. The General Commission on Chaplains acts for the more than 25 Protestant denominations which are members of the National Council of the Churches of Christ in the U. S. A. Protestant groups which are not members of the NCCCUSA have their own boards which endorse prospective chaplains, like the Armed Services Commission of The Lutheran Church — Missouri Synod or the Chaplains Commission of the Home Mission Board of the Southern Baptist Convention. The Roman Catholics screen their chaplain applicants through the Military Ordinariate, one of the oldest of the commissioning bodies. The Jewish Welfare Board acts through its Commission on Jewish Chaplaincy.
48. Department of the Army Field Manual, *The Chaplain*, FM 16-5 (April 1958), par. 15, p. 9; cf. *Army Regulations*, AR 165-15, Sec. II, 2e (Nov. 7, 1960).
49. Bureau of Naval Personnel, *Chaplains' Manual* (March 1959), par. 1204 and 1205, pp. 2, 3; Department of the Air Force, *The Air Force Chaplain*, AFM 165-3 (June 1956), pp. 13, 19.
50. Cf. *Army Regulations*, AR 135-173, par. 50, and AR 140-175, paras. 6b (6) and 7d (2).
51. Cf. *Army Regulations*, AR 165-15, Sec. III (Nov. 7, 1960), on "Responsibilities of Commanders" with regard to religious life and services in their commands.
52. *Chaplains' Manual* (Navy), par. 1101, p. 1; par. 3501, p. 22; *The Chaplain* (Army), par. 2, p. 3; *The Air Force Chaplain*, pp. 16, 17.
53. *Chaplains' Manual* (Navy), par. 3101b, p. 16; cf. *The Chaplain* (Army), par. 21, p. 12; and *Air Force Chaplain*, p. 19.
54. Stokes, III, 121 (italics added).
55. *Chaplains' Manual* (Navy), par. 4102, p. 24.
56. *The Chaplain* (Army), par. 23a, p. 13; *The Air Force Chaplain*, p. 42.
57. *The Chaplain* (Army), par. 21b, p. 12.
58. *The Chaplain* (Army), par. 28c, p. 16.

59. *Chaplains' Manual* (Navy), par. 5502a, p. 29; *Air Force Chaplain*, p. 19.

60. Creeger, p. 8. According to this there were about 300 VA chaplains at the time.

61. Chaplaincies in public institutions are often traced back to the pioneer work of Anton Boisen, himself once a mental patient, at Worcester State Hospital in Massachusetts, 1925.

62. "Navy to Educate Chaplains" (editorial), in *The Christian Century*, LX (March 10, 1943), 284, 285.

63. "The Chaplaincy Question" (editorial), in *Christianity and Crisis*, III (June 14, 1943), 1.

64. Department of the Army, *The Challenge of the Chaplaincy in the US Army*, DA PAM 16-2 (Washington: U. S. Government Printing Office, July 1960); Bureau of Naval Personnel, *No Greater Service*, NRAF 19501 (Washington: U. S. Government Printing Office, 1958).

65. Cf. discussion earlier in this chapter.

66. Drury, I, 65.

67. *Religious News Service*, Domestic Service, Dec. 21, 1955.

68. Carl Zollmann, *American Church Law* (St. Paul, Minn.: West Publishing Co., 1933), p. 33, quoting Thomas Cooley, *A Treatise on the Constitutional Limitations . . .* , 6th ed., p. 578.

69. Heinrich Emil Brunner, *The Divine Imperative*, trans. Olive Wyon (Philadelphia: The Westminster Press, 1947), p. 460.

70. Zollmann, p. 35.

71. Martin Luther, *Secular Authority: To What Extent It Should Be Obeyed*, in *Works of Martin Luther*, III (Philadelphia: A. J. Holman Company, 1930), 258.

72. Matt. 22:21.

73. Rom. 13.

74. 1 Cor. 9:22.

75. Luther, p. 255.

76. For a thorough analysis see Stokes, III, 403–418; Zollmann, pp. 102 to 194.

77. Ibid., pp. 102–194.

78. 80 U. S. (13 Wall.), 697.

79. Stokes, I, 445, 446; II, 680, 681; III, 418–428; Zollmann, pp. 325 to 367; also Leo Pfeffer, *Church, State, and Freedom* (Boston: Beacon Press, Inc., 1953), pp. 183–190; Joseph M. Dawson, *America's Way in Church, State, and Society* (New York: The Macmillan Co., 1953), pp. 33, 34; *Lundberg* v. *County of Alameda*, 298 P. 2d 1, at p. 7; "Constitutionality of Tax Benefits Accorded Religion," in *Columbia Law Review*, XLIX (Nov. 1949), 968; Monrad G. Paulsen, "Preferment of Religious Institutions in Tax and Labor Legislation," in *Law and Contemporary Problems*, XIV (Winter 1949), 144; Claude W. Stimson, "The Exemption of Property from Taxation in the United States," in *Minnesota Law Review*, XVIII (March 1934), 411; Arvo Van Alstyne, "Tax Exemption of Church Property," in *Ohio State Law Journal*, XX (Summer 1959), 461.

80. Gen. 47:26; Ezra 7:24.

81. Stokes, III, 422.
82. *Internal Revenue Code* 501 (c) (3); 511 (a) (2) (A); 3121 (b) (8) (B); 170; 2055 (a) (d); 2522 (a); 642 (c); Tariff Act of 1930.
83. Stokes, III, 418–428; "Constitutionality of Tax Benefits Accorded Religion," in *Columbia Law Review*, XLIX (Nov. 1949), 968; *Regulations Governing Tax Exemptions in Non-Public Schools in the Forty-Eight States*, compiled by Citizens United Against Taxing Schools, 681 Market St., San Francisco, Calif.
84. Claude W. Stimson, "The Exemption of Property from Taxation in the United States," in *Minnesota Law Review*, XVIII (March 1934), 422; Conrad Henry Moehlman, "The Wall of Separation: The Law and the Facts," in *Liberty*, XLVIII (First Quarter 1953), 20.
85. Paulsen, p. 150; Pfeffer, pp. 185, 186; Herbert H. Brown and Joseph J. Mahon, Jr., *Tax Benefits Granted to Religious Organizations*, Research Consultation on Church and State sponsored by N. Y. East Conf., Methodist Church, and Inst. of Church and State, sponsored by Villanova School of Law.
86. *Everson* v. *Board of Education*, 330 U. S. 1; *Illinois ex rel. McCollum* v. *Board of Education*, 333 U. S. 203; *Zorach* v. *Clauson*, 343 U. S. 306.
87. Pfeffer, p. 169.
88. 17 U. S. (4 Wheat.), 159, at p. 210.
89. California Constitution, Art. XIII, No. 1c; California Revenue and Tax Code No. 214 (West, 1956).
90. *Lundberg* v. *County of Alameda*, 298 P. 2d 1; *Heisey* v. *County of Alameda*, 352 U. S. 921
91. *Lundberg* v. *County of Alameda*, 298 P. 2d 1, at p. 8.
92. Ibid., p. 8.
93. *Heisey* v. *County of Alameda*, 352 U. S. 921.
94. *Christianity Today*, IV (Aug. 3, 1959), 6.
95. Ibid., V (Jan. 4, 1960), 20.
96. *The Law of Zoning*, ed. James Metzenbaum, 2nd ed. (New York: Baker, Voorhis & Co., Inc., 1955), I, 7.
97. *Village of Euclid* v. *Ambler Realty Co.*, 272 U. S. 365.
98. "Churches and Zoning," in *Harvard Law Review*, LXX (June 1957), 1428–1438; cf. also *Congregation Temple Israel* v. *City of Creve Coeur*, 320 S. W. 2d 451; commented on by John G. Hall, "Zoning — Municipal Government — Exclusion of Churches from Area Zoned Residential," in *Villanova Law Review*, IV (Summer 1959), 605.
99. For example, *State ex rel. Synod of United Lutheran Church* v. *Joseph*, 39 N. E. 2d 515 (Ohio).
100. For example, *Ellsworth* v. *Gercke*, 156 P. 2d 242 (Arizona).
101. *Corporation of the Presiding Bishop* v. *Porterville*, 203 P. 2d 823 (California); *West Hartford Methodist Church* v. *Zoning Bd. of Appeals*, 121 A 2d 640 (Conn.); *Miami Beach United Lutheran Church* v. *Miami Beach*, 82 So. 2d 880 (Fla.); *Galfas* v. *Ailor*, 57 S. E. 2d 834 (Ga.).
102. *Roman Catholic Welfare Corp.* v. *City of Piedmont*, 289 P. 2d 438 (Calif.); *Catholic Bishop* v. *Kingery*, 20 N. E. 2d 823 (Ill.).

103. *State ex rel. Wisconsin Lutheran High School Conference* v. *Sinar,* 65 N. W. 2d 43 (Wis.).
104. 338 U. S. 805; 349 U. S. 913.
105. The court then cited the Porterville case. *American Communications Assoc. C10* v. *Douds,* 339 U. S. 382, at p. 397.
106. 70 *Harvard Law Review* 1428, at p. 1436.
107. Alvin W. Johnson and Frank H. Yost, *Separation of Church and State in the United States* (University of Minneota Press, 1948), p. 219. The authors have an excellent summary of the issues and debates concerned in this question in chaps. xix and xx.
108. Ibid., p. 224.
109. *State ex. rel. Temple* v. *Barnes,* 22 N. D. 18, 132 N. W. 215, Am. Cas. 1913 E. 930 (1911).
110. *Soon Hing* v. *Crowley,* 113 U. S. 703 (1885).
111. *Petit* v. *Minn.,* 74 Minn. 376, 77 N. W. 225, 177 U. S. 164 (1900).
112. *Ex parte Jentzsch,* 112 Calif. 468, 44 Pac. 803, 32 L. R. A. 664 (1896).
113. *McGowan* v. *Maryland,* 366 U. S. 420; *Two Guys from Harrison-Allentown, Inc.* v. *McGinley,* 366 U. S. 582 (1961).
114. *Braunfeld* v. *Brown,* 366 U. S. 599; *Gallagher* v. *Crown Kosher Market,* 366 U. S. 617 (1961).

NOTES TO CHAPTER 9

1. Leo Pfeffer, *Creeds in Competition* (New York: Harper & Brothers, 1958), p. 35.
2. Will Herberg, *Protestant — Catholic — Jew* (Garden City, N. Y.: Doubleday & Company, Inc., 1955), p. 254.
3. Pfeffer, p. 150.
4. See Will Herberg's contribution, "Religion, Democracy and Public Education," in *Religion in America,* ed. John Cogley (New York: Meridian Books, Inc., 1958), pp. 118–147.
5. Will Herberg, "The Making of a Pluralistic Society — A Jewish View," in *Religion and the State University,* ed. Erich A. Walter (Ann Arbor: University of Michigan Press, 1958), p. 37.
6. John Herman Randall, Jr., "Naturalistic Humanism," in *Patterns of Faith in America Today,* ed. F. Ernest Johnson (New York: Harper & Brothers, 1957), p. 153.
7. Paul Blanshard, *American Freedom and Catholic Power,* 2nd ed. (Boston: Beacon Press, Inc., 1958), pp. 65–73.
8. Jacques Maritain, *Man and the State* (Chicago: University of Chicago Phoenix Books, 1956), p. 182.
9. John Bennett, *Christians and the State* (New York: Charles Scribner's Sons, 1958), p. 264.
10. Cited in Bennett, p. 264.
11. Ibid., p. 265.
12. See chap. xiv in J. Paul Williams, *What Americans Believe and How They Worship* (New York: Harper & Brothers, 1952).

13. Ralph Henry Gabriel, *The Course of American Democratic Thought,* 2nd ed. (New York: The Ronald Press Company, 1956), pp. 26–89.
14. Loren P. Beth, *The American Theory of Church and State* (Gainesville: University of Florida Press, 1958), pp. 136, 157.
15. Winthrop S. Hudson, *The Great Tradition of the American Churches* (New York: Harper & Brothers, 1953), passim.
16. Robert McAfee Brown, "Classical Protestantism," in *Patterns of Faith in America Today,* p. 47.

NOTES TO CHAPTER 10

1. Jean Anouilh, *Becket, or The Honor of God* (New York: Coward-McCann Inc., 1960), p. 113.
2. Anne Fremantle, *The Papal Encyclicals in Their Historical Context* (New York: G. P. Putnam's Sons, 1956), pp. 72–74.
3. Paul B. Anderson, *People, Church and State in Modern Russia* (New York: Macmillan, 1944), pp. 18, 19.
4. See chapter 4 for the experience of Spain, France, Great Britain, and Norway.
5. See chapter 5 for the experience of the United States.
6. Chapter 2, pp. 72, 73.
7. Chapter 3, pp. 124–127.
8. Chapter 3, pp. 131–136.
9. Chapter 3, pp. 143–147.
10. Chapter 1, pp. 37–40.
11. Chapter 3, pp. 143–147.
12. Johannes Hamel, *A Christian in East Germany,* trans. Ruth and Charles C. West (New York: Association Press, 1960).
13. Chapter 3, pp. 124–127.
14. Chapter 4, pp. 181–192.
15. William W. Brickman and Stanley Lehrer, *Religion, Government, and Education* (New York: Society for Advancement of Education, 1961), pp. 144–250.
16. Chapter 6, pp. 260–263.
17. Chapter 9, pp. 412–416.
18. *Zorach* v. *Clauson,* 343 (U. S. 306).
19. Peter Berger, *The Noise of Solemn Assemblies* (New York: Doubleday, 1961), pp. 34, 57–72.
20. Martin E. Marty, "Protestantism Enters Third Phase," in *Christian Century,* LXXVIII (Jan. 18, 1961), 72–75.
21. Chapter 8, 404–407.
22. Chapter 7, pp. 306–318.

INDEX

INDEX

Agnosticism 302, 361, 392
Alabama
  education 330
  religious liberty 205
Amendments
  Christian Amendment
    movement 216, 429
  Eighteenth Amendment
    237, 242; *see also* Temperance
    movement in America
  First Amendment 28, 152, 194, 200,
    257—259, 260—265, 269—273,
    276, 278, 281—283, 285, 287, 292,
    294—296, 315, 319, 321, 327, 331,
    352, 354, 362, 363, 365, 372, 384,
    388, 397—402, 404, 405
  Fourteenth Amendment 227, 257 to
    259, 262—271, 273, 275, 290, 325,
    402, 403, 419
  Thirteenth Amendment 263
Anabaptists 91, 96—99, 102, 108, 109,
  174, 442
Antiochus Epiphanes 40
Apocalypse 37, 39
Arminianism 183, 184, 260
Atheism 4, 161, 181, 202, 302, 307,
  361, 385, 388, 392, 426
Augsburg, Religious Peace of 198
Augustine 24, 36, 61, 68, 117, 121
Austria 62, 120

Baptists 99, 207, 209, 210, 253, 302,
  413, 415, 428, 442, 453
Barth, Karl 113, 115, 131—134, 136
Bellarmine, Cardinal Robert 113, 115,
  117—119
Berggrav, Bishop Eivind 34, 54, 113,
  116, 143—145, 442
Beza, Theodore 105, 106
Birth control 4, 251, 421, 453
Bismarck, Otto von 120, 122
Boniface VIII 61, 162

Bradfield v. *Roberts* 272
Brunner, Emil 23, 113, 115, 134—136
Bugenhagen, Johann 89, 177
Bullinger, Heinrich 96—98
Burke, Edmund 185

Caesaropapism 47
California
  education 330, 400
  Sunday laws 237
Calvin, John 47, 59, 90, 99, 100, 108 to
  112, 115, 127, 131, 255, 260, 414,
  416, 438, 442
Canossa 47, 121, 153, 445
Cantwell v. *Connecticut* 292
Capital punishment 92, 97, 138, 140
Censorship 195, 250
Chaplaincy
  institutional 253, 384, 385
  legislative 226, 254, 280, 283, 371,
    372, 448, 450
  military 213, 253, 254, 283, 363, 365
    to 393, 416, 448
Christian Scientists 229
Christian vocation, doctrine of 109, 111
Church
  authority 35, 48
  limits 42, 43
  origin 26, 27
  source of power 17
  tasks 31, 32, 35, 50—52, 53—58
Cochran v. *Louisiana State Board of*
  Education 272, 284
Colleges, church related 357—360
Colorado, Sunday laws 237
Communism 34, 55, 125, 143, 231, 440
Confessions, Lutheran 6, 24, 58, 59, 91
  to 93, 145, 318, 363, 383, 384
Congregationalism 204, 206, 301, 369,
  415
Connecticut
  birth control 251

disestablishment 206
education 221
religious tolerance 204
Constantine 30, 53, 184, 397, 404
Corporation and Test Acts (England)
    182, 184, 186
Corporation of the Presiding Bishop v.
    Porterville 403, 404
Corpus christianum 82—84, 101, 109,
    124, 136
Counter-Reformation 105, 156, 178
Cox v. *New Hampshire* 293
Cromwell, Oliver 115, 127

Davis v. *Beason* 272, 281
Declaration of Independence 141, 198,
    211, 310
Delaware
    disestablishment 202
    religious tests 202
Democracy 8, 49, 55, 102, 111, 142,
    211, 212, 230, 231, 242, 243, 247,
    255, 291, 300, 302, 310, 342, 343,
    345, 356, 384, 398, 414, 418, 419,
    425—427, 435, 436, 439, 443, 448,
    454
Denmark 90
Disestablishment 174, 181, 183—185,
    188, 192, 193, 198, 199, 201—208,
    397, 444
Divine-right monarchies 75, 76, 82, 153
    to 155, 163
Divorce 54, 189, 251, 252
Dreyfus case 171
Dutch Reformed 209

Eastern Orthodoxy 301
Edict of Milan 53
Edict of Nantes 163, 164, 199
Education 364, 450, 452
    schools, church 3, 7, 8, 93, 173, 187,
        190, 191, 217, 219, 220, 238, 241
        to 243, 264, 267, 268, 273, 275,
        284, 299, 317, 321, 322, 339, 340,
        403, 415, 416, 420, 421, 443, 452
    federal aid 346, 437, 452
    government controls 323—327
    health services 332
    public aid 221—223, 226, 234,
        235, 238, 240, 241, 327, 337,
        362, 420, 421, 442
    public bus transportation 329 to
        332, 435, 452

school lunches 335
    text books 273, 333—335
schools, public 219, 220, 224, 233,
    235, 237, 238, 246—249, 252, 267,
    268, 273—275, 277, 299—323,
    326, 329, 330, 336, 338, 342 to
    349, 353, 354, 357, 361, 403, 427,
    450, 452
    Bible reading 216, 219, 221, 234,
        244, 248, 286, 300, 302, 306 to
        310, 321, 452
    prayers 285, 286, 310
    released time for religious educa-
        tion 247, 274—276, 314—318,
        321, 452
    study of religion 312—314
    teaching moral and spiritual values
        247, 305, 309—312, 354, 360,
        361
Edwards v. *Elliott* 267
Engel v. *Vitale* 284—286
England 3, 105, 115, 127, 151—153,
    174—176, 181—192, 198, 199,
    404, 439, 445, 454
    Anglicanism 107, 109, 151, 174, 176,
        182, 189, 190, 192, 203, 206, 367
    Episcopalianism 54, 66, 85—90, 95,
        201, 203, 206, 209, 226, 370, 374,
        375
Erastianism 91, 93, 99
Everson v. *Board of Education* 273 to
    274, 276, 278, 284, 331, 420
Excommunication 92, 104, 153, 167

Farrington v. *Tokushige* 338
Fascism 123
First Amendment; *see* Amendments
Follet v. *Town of McCormick* 295
Fourteenth Amendment; *see* Amend-
    ments
Fourth Commandment 24, 68, 91
France 3, 105, 118, 120, 151—157, 161
    to 174, 186, 188, 193, 198, 199,
    439, 445
Francis I (France) 163—166
French Revolution 116, 118, 164, 165,
    185, 186, 199, 424

Gambling 8
Genevan catechism of 1545 100; *see
    also* Calvin, John
Georgia
    disestablishment 203
    religious liberty 203

religious tests 234
Gerhard, Johann 113, 116, 136—140
Germany 62—94, 105, 123, 124, 131,
    142—144, 174, 235, 438, 439, 443
Government, forms of
    anarchy 33, 50, 102, 186, 201
    aristocracy 102
    monarchy 55, 84, 88, 102, 106, 153
        to 155, 159, 160, 163, 165
    theocracy 25, 45, 89, 95, 98, 105,
        127, 130—132, 195, 197, 227 to
        231, 417, 419, 420, 429, 440
    totalitarianism 15, 20, 37—39, 49, 50,
        55, 57, 113, 116, 145, 362, 425
Gregory VII 61, 153, 445

Hamilton, Alexander 213
Hamilton v. *Regents of the University
    of California* 269, 291
Henry VIII 162, 174, 186
Herodians 28, 29
Holy Roman Empire 62, 121, 199
Hooker, Richard 107, 181
Hospitals 8, 195, 253, 284, 352, 452
Huguenots 105, 155, 163, 442
Humanism 94, 101, 177
Hutterites 97

Independents 99, 107
India 54, 185
Innocent III 61, 117, 162
Ireland 188
Ireland, John 238
Israel 3, 25, 45, 102
Italy 3, 62, 90, 123, 169

Jamison v. *Texas* 294
Jefferson, Thomas
    Declaration of Independence 141
    political philosophy 427
    on religion 275
    religious liberty 258, 260
    religious tolerance 200
    "wall of separation" 28, 58, 272 to
        274, 278—283, 413
Jehovah's witnesses 4, 249, 270, 290,
    429
Jesuits 117, 120, 156—158, 178, 180
Jews
    chaplaincy 376
    church and state, practical relation-
        ship of 180, 417—421, 428

education 301, 302, 304, 307, 308,
    312, 316, 345, 355
religious liberty 145, 158, 173, 180,
    201, 260, 405
Jury duty 387

Kennedy, John F. 245, 349, 350, 355,
    417, 449
Kentucky
    disestablishment 205
    education 330
    tax exemption 328

Largent v. *Texas* 293
Latitudinarianism 119, 181, 183, 189
Law 57, 58, 364, 365, 394, 448, 450
    civil law 77, 78, 102, 110, 118, 121,
        127, 137, 140, 394
    divine law 118, 129, 136, 137
    law of love 73—76, 102
    Mosaic laws 77, 92, 102
    natural law 23, 45, 61, 75—78, 102,
        111, 117, 118, 121—123, 127, 136,
        137, 140
Legal status of church organizations
    394, 395, 406, 448
Leo XIII 115, 121—123, 239, 244, 425
Locke, John 175, 182, 185, 197
Louisiana, education 330, 333
Lutheran Church — Missouri Synod 5,
    50, 141—143, 317, 321, 322, 329,
    345, 346, 383
    Board of Parish Education 5, 299,
        317, 350
Luther, Martin 6, 24, 27, 43, 56, 59, 60,
    62—96, 100—103, 108—112, 113,
    116, 131, 137—139, 142, 177, 391,
    414, 416, 438, 440

McCollum v. *Board of Education* 274
    to 277, 315, 420, 426
Madison, James 214, 260, 261, 271,
    278—281, 283, 328, 371, 372
Maine
    Bible reading in public schools 219
    temperance 216
Mann, Horace 221, 300
March v. *Alabama* 295
Maritain, Jacques 113, 115, 124—126,
    244, 422
Martin v. *City of Struthers* 295
Maryland

education 241, 330
religious liberty 203
Massachusetts
birth control 251
disestablishment 199, 204
education 199, 222, 223, 246, 330
Melanchthon 84, 89, 93, 139
Mennonites 97, 229
Methodism 182, 184, 186, 207, 208, 301, 453
Meyer v. *Nebraska* 267, 268, 291, 325, 337
Michigan, education 326, 330
Military draft 386, 387
Military service 72, 97, 99
Minnesota
education 238
religious tolerance 205
Mississippi, education 333, 334
Missouri, Sunday laws 237
Mormons 195, 227—229, 403
Murdoch v. *Pennsylvania* 294
Murray v. *Curlett* 286
Murray, John Courtney 424, 425

Napoleon I (France) 151, 165—168
Naziism 123, 124, 131, 143, 438
Nebraska, education 324, 326
Netherlands 97, 105, 156, 445, 454
New Hampshire
disestablishment 203
education 330
New Mexico
education 330
religious toleration 205
New York
disestablishment 199, 203
education 221, 238, 308, 310, 324, 330, 334
religious liberty 218
Niebuhr, Reinhold 224, 429
North Carolina
disestablishment 202, 260
education 241
religious liberty 203
religious tests 234
Norway 54, 90, 143, 144, 151—153, 177—180, 192

Oaths, taking of 97, 99
Obedience, civil 29, 30, 32, 39—43, 51, 52, 63, 69—73, 91, 95, 99, 103, 107, 110, 129, 130, 132—137, 139, 141, 207, 319, 321, 437—440, 445
Ong, Walter 424
Oregon, education 268, 330

Pacifism 97, 99, 254, 377, 385
Packer Collegiate Case 338
Paine, Thomas 24, 186
Papacy, powers of 61, 74, 81, 107, 108, 110, 115, 117, 119—125, 146, 151, 153—158, 162—166, 168—174, 185, 192, 210, 217, 218, 239, 244 to 246, 417, 423, 442, 445
Paul 16, 18, 21, 24, 30, 32, 33, 36, 41—46, 49, 58, 65, 68, 77, 108, 111, 138, 311, 366, 437
Pennsylvania
education 307
religious tests 202
Permoli v. *First Municipality of New Orleans* 263
Pierce v. *Society of Sisters* 275, 291, 323, 324, 337, 338
Pietism 179
Pius XII 123, 245, 252
Plato 65, 102, 136
Pledge of allegiance 448
Pluralism 242, 301, 304, 305, 313, 318, 342, 345, 354, 360, 412, 414, 418, 421, 424, 425, 429, 430, 446, 447, 449
Polygamy 98, 228, 272, 292
Poulos v. *New Hampshire* 277, 294
Pragmatism 299, 302
Presbyterianism 208, 241, 302, 414
Priesthood of all believers 66, 67, 84, 85, 96, 111
Prince v. *Massachusetts* 291
Protestantism
censorship 251
church and state, practical relationship of 255, 416, 418, 420, 428 to 431, 448
education 241, 242, 301—303, 307, 309, 310, 313—315, 322, 323, 343, 345, 346, 349—355, 416, 442
religious liberty 260
Puritanism 47, 107, 113, 115, 127—132, 134—136, 146, 174, 182, 197, 216, 225, 243, 255, 440

Quakers 99, 229, 241, 372

Reformation, impact of 13, 60—112, 113, 114, 153, 157, 163, 174, 176 to 179, 392, 414, 438, 442

Religious liberty 119, 124, 125, 159, 173, 179—181, 191, 200—206, 208, 210—215, 217—219, 229, 235, 244, 245, 248, 249, 256—296, 310, 336, 372, 385—393, 400, 404, 405

Freedom of the press 119, 168, 200, 269, 295

Freedom of speech 119, 200, 249 to 251, 269, 295

Religious tests for public offices 202, 207, 208, 260, 372

Reynolds v. *United States* 281

Rhode Island
education 325, 326, 330
religious liberty 203

Roman Catholicism
birth control 251, 421
censorship 250
chaplaincy 371, 375
church and state, practical relationship of 153—174, 178, 179, 181, 182, 192, 213, 217—220, 223, 244 to 246, 417—428, 430, 431, 438, 448
church and state, theological relationship of 23, 114, 116—127, 136, 146, 147, 438
divorce 251, 252
education 189, 219, 222, 223, 225, 237—241, 246, 251, 252, 273, 301, 302, 306, 308, 312—314, 322, 328, 329, 342—346, 348—355, 399, 421, 452
religious liberty 184, 186—188, 201, 203, 210, 218, 260, 423, 444

Russian 3, 46, 47, 164, 165, 434, 440, 445

Ryan, John A. 423, 424

School District of Abington Township v. *Shempp* 286

Scotland 105, 106

Secularism 316, 321, 353, 399, 405, 411—413, 415—423, 425—429, 441, 447, 448

Selective Draft Law Cases 272

Seventh-day Adventists 4, 229, 428

Slaughterhouse Cases 266, 267

Slavery 54, 142, 185, 186, 215

Snyder v. *Town of Newton* 274

Social Gospel 195, 224, 231—233, 243, 253

Socialism 122, 160, 230, 231, 255, 324

Social Security 397

South Carolina, religious tests 234

Spain 3, 90, 151, 152, 155—161, 173, 174, 180, 192, 245, 423, 445

State
authority 24, 30, 32, 40, 41
limits 31, 36, 37, 39, 40, 43, 45
origin 22, 23, 42
source of power 24, 31, 33, 39, 41, 42
tasks 31—35, 42

State churches 94—96, 100, 108, 136, 199, 204, 270, 434, 445

State ex rel. Wisconsin Lutheran High School Conference v. *Sinar* 403

Stoics 76, 102

Sunday laws 7, 195, 213, 216, 234, 236, 244, 254, 299, 363, 404—407, 428, 452

Sunday mail controversy 214, 215

Sweden 90, 179

Switzerland 94—97, 99—105, 115, 131, 174, 445

Taxation, power of 28—30, 41, 43, 204, 208, 220, 234, 241, 274, 275, 277, 282—284, 292, 294, 318, 321, 334, 351, 352, 362, 379, 387, 388, 392 to 394, 443, 445, 448, 452

Tax exemption of church property 234, 254, 280, 328, 363, 364, 387, 393, 396—402, 406, 416, 448

Taylor v. *Mississippi* 290

Teachers, church 8, 187, 203, 238, 322, 323, 326—329, 343, 350, 357

Temperance movement in America 195, 216, 237

Tennessee, Sunday laws 236

Tolerance, religious 198, 199, 201, 204, 211, 212, 225, 228, 446

Unitarians 181, 184

United States v. *Ballard* 289

Utah, religious tolerance 228

Virginia
disestablishment 201, 260
religious liberty 202, 278—281
religious tolerance 199

Voluntarism 225, 242, 243, 308, 314, 444

"Wall of separation" 168—176, 179 to 183, 319, 328, 357, 399; *see also* Jefferson, Thomas
Walther, C. F. W. 113, 116, 141—143
Watson v. *Jones* 395
Weigel, Gustave 424
Welfare state 34, 441
Wesley, John 182—185, 414

West Virginia State Board of Education v. *Virginia* 290, 291
Williams, Roger 208, 428
Wisconsin, education 330, 403
Wycliffe, John 91

Zealots 28, 39
Zoning laws 363, 394, 396, 402—404, 406, 438
Zorach v. *Clauson* 275—277
Zwingli 59, 82, 94—96, 100, 108, 109